THE

LEAST

LIKELY

The Memoirs of Judge Michael J. Ryan:

From the Housing Projects to the Courthouse

Library of Congress Cataloging-in-Publication Data

The Least Likely/Michael Ryan

ISBN 978-0-9892560-6-3

Front and Back Cover Design by The Intelligent Consulting Design Team

Edited By : Johnnie Dent Jr

WWW.ICANDP.COM

Table of Contents

DEDICATION

This book is dedicated to my mom Marguerite Ryan, my biological father Richard Solomon, my dad Allen Douglas, my Grandmothers Lula Belcher and Edna Petty who all had a hand, either negatively or positively, in shaping me to be the man I am today. To Bae (Robin Ryan), Lauren and Michael for their unwavering love and support. Lastly, it's also dedicated to those who have encountered seemingly insurmountable odds; this book is a roadmap to hope.

ACKNOWLEDGEMENTS

Many people have played instrumental roles in my life and I'm grateful for the impact they've had be it advantageous or disadvantageous because my character was molded by them. I start off by thanking and praising my Lord and savior Jesus Christ for protecting me while I was in my mother's womb and then of course while I've been out! If it hadn't been for the Lord on my side I don't know where I would be. I'm grateful to the two people who are biologically responsible for me being here- "Peggy" and Richard. Their chance meeting was no fluke it was orchestrated for a divine purpose. I'm appreciative of the sacrifice that Allen Douglas, "Daddy", made in deciding to raise another man's child and to incorporate me into his family as though I was a blood relative. I'm forever indebted to the four women who stood in the gap for me and my sister when our parents were unable to provide the care and supervision they were legally and morally obligated to do. Thus there are special places in my heart for Grandma Lula, Grandma Edna, Aunt Joann Douglas and Aunt Mary Douglas. I doubt that I would have been able to handle the entire trauma alone and so I'm grateful to have had a sister that loves me, watches out for me and is loyal; Thank you Ressie. This book... my story... would probably not have been told had I not met the love of my life, my wife Robin. In her efforts to find out if I was the ONE probed and encouraged me to open up. I love her with all my heart and soul and my heart beats to the rhythm of her name. I would be remiss if I left out three very special people in my life. Two of them have been the driving force behind a lot of my success. I knew I would have a family and that is what provided the impetus for me to work so assiduously so that I could create a life for them that was markedly different from mine; Lauren and Mike I will always love you. My mother-in-law Doris Nelson, who I affectionately call Ma, has been a model of hope, perseverance, faith and love for me. She is adored by many and reciprocates that adoration to others unconditionally. Also, Aimee Morris was a Godsend because she put my voice recordings to paper and made this process much easier and for that I'm truly grateful. Lastly, I want to thank my good friend and supporter Mr. Johnnie T. Dent Jr. His unwavering support and encouragement was the last piece of the puzzle for this awesome project. Thank you Johnnie.

PROLOGUE

I am naturally a very quiet and soft spoken person, unlike my wife, Robin, who is very gregarious and can light up a room with her smile and wit. She has had a profound impact on me and made me less uncomfortable in evolving into an extrovert. Our relationship blossomed after I began to trust her with the circumstances of my life, which contributed to my shyness. She and I would both return to our respective jobs from our lunch dates with eyes so red that even Visine had little effect in clearing them. She let me be open and transparent without fear that she would use the information to hurt me. Instead of her repelling she actually gravitated towards me. I revealed things to her that I never said to anyone else. She is the reason why I began to speak openly and publicly about who is Michael John Ryan. I assure you that without Robin Ryan's encouragement then the things you will read would have remained sealed in my mind, heart and soul forever.

I was born August 1, 1971 at 10:35 a.m. in Cleveland, Ohio at the St. Luke's Hospital. While this is the date of my birth, my story began on a fall day in September of 1970 at the East Technical High School Talent Show. East Tech was the local high school in one of the poorest areas of the City of Cleveland. It's a three story massive structure on the city's near east side. It was the educational institution that serviced children from the some of the toughest housing projects in the city: Longwood, Outwaithe, King Kennedy and Case Court. It's brick exterior with an elegant interior of posh floors, spacious classrooms, reliable furniture was synonymous of that of the individuals who live in the surrounding neighborhoods. They possessed a tough exterior to ward off attempts at physical assault or manipulation while maintaining an interior perspective of congeniality, strength and integrity. The surrounding neighborhood also produced some famous nationally and internationally known athletes and politicians like Jesse Owens the 1936 Olympic Gold Medalist and Carl 1 Stokes, the first African American elected Mayor of a major city (In fact Mayor Stokes was nearing the end of his second two year term, he was elected in 1967 and then 1969). The neighborhood's other famous alumnus included Carl's brother 26 year United States Congressman Louis Stokes.

According to my biological dad, Richard Solomon, people were sardined into the talent show and yet in the sea of those people my mom, told him that she saw his dark chocolate, six foot three inch slender twenty-two year old frame stroll in her direction. He looked like a skyscraper to my mother, Marguerite Arlene Ryan, a 14 year old ninth grader at John Adams High School. Peggy, as most people called her, locked her intoxicating big brown eyes on "Fatman," my dad's nickname, even though he was just the opposite of being fat. Her light caramel skin and bright beautiful smile were like blaring police sirens and oscillating lights. They made Richard respond in his deep and confident voice "You like what you see?" Peggy, using her four foot eleven inched 90 pound body, responded in a diminutive but strong voice, "What do you think?"

They began to date shortly after that meeting at the talent show. Neither one of their families knew much about them dating each other. Peggy did bring Richard over to her home on Alvin Avenue, Thanksgiving Day in 1970. She was living with her mom and step-father John Tomlinson. The house was filled with pictures of family members. They lived in a modest home in an upscale area in the Southeast part of Garfield Heights on the border of Cleveland. While Richard was a hearty eater he was also quiet and polite. He never said anything without first being spoken too. He answered Peggy's mom with "yes ma'am" and "no ma'am" responses. His quietness was deceptive, there was a side to Richard that no one knew and would not discover until a few months after Thanksgiving.

Christmas is the season of giving and receiving. The 1970 Christmas season was turning out to be a great season for Peggy. As my Grandmother Edna told me Richard was my mother's personal Santa Claus. He bought Peggy a brass bed frame and a fur coat. When my mom questioned her about the extravagant gifts she simply responded "Richard gave them to me." No one inquired about Richard's job status and he never revealed where, if any place, he worked or how much money he made. In fact no one knew what high school, if any he graduated from. His quietness was an integral part of his character, it assisted him in his livelihood- stealth. Richard's gifts were unlimited and tangible property. He'd also given her a gift that would mature in about nine months.

Richard had a history of taking things from other people without permission. He told me he was expelled from East Tech High School after he stole fundraiser money that was sitting in an unsupervised box. In fact, when he met Peggy he'd recently returned from Mansfield State Penitentiary for theft. Instead of using the two incidents as learning lessons to avoid future negative conduct, he used those events as later motivation to commit more serious crimes. While Peggy and her mom were oblivious to where Richard was getting his money to pay for the immaculate gifts, he knew full well that the money came from two banks in Lorain County. Richard did not have an account at any bank let alone one in Lorain. He didn't work for the Federal Reserve nor was he a teller or bank manager, so he lacked the authority to withdraw cash from any bank. Fortunately for Richard when the incidents initially occurred the authorities had very few leads about the culprit.

In January of 1971, my Grandma Edna noticed that my mother's breasts were getting bigger. They grew rapidly in a two to three month span. My grandmother initially believed that my mother's breast growth was due to an abnormality and took her to the doctor to assess whether the growth was benign or cancerous. My grandmother was very concerned since she had recently recovered from a bout of ovarian cancer a few years before my mom's unusual growth materialized. While cancer was not a new form of disease it was not something that was rampant amongst the youth and thus cause some fear and anxiety for my mom and grandmother. After the examination the doctor relayed some good news, my mother did not have cancer and instead informed my mother and grandmother that my mother, who was fourteen at the time, was approximately two months pregnant. My grandmother was relieved it was not cancer and also not angry or disappointed seeing that she had her first child at thirteen, she said "It looks like we're going to have a little stranger."

The little stranger's father was unaware of his pending parentage; Peggy hadn't spoken to Richard since early December of 1970. He vanished off the face of the earth. He hadn't evaporated into thin air, but instead he was arrested by the F.B.I, after a former friend told the authorities who robbed those banks. Richard refused to share the money with his friend and for that, Richard was arrested and then convicted, and shipped to Terry Haute Indiana Federal prison shortly after I was born.

Peggy didn't know where Richard went. He didn't write, or call, and because she didn't know his family, they were unable to communicate with her regarding his situation. Richard was simply like a passing season in her life; he was there for a short time, had an impact on her, brought her happiness and then disappeared. I presented my mother an opportunity to raise and love another human being. He gave her a chance to be responsible. Richard's illegal actions, however, relinquished him of his responsibility and thus produced a fatherless child.

Peggy was a very attractive young woman and did not let Richards's absence deter her from seeking affection from someone else. Her pregnancy didn't stop her from attracting Allen Douglas or Bruce; my mother dated Bruce shortly before she met Allen. Grandma Edna, said "Your mom never let the grass grow underneath her feet." Men were a constant in her life, especially older men; that may be due to my paternal grandfather's absence in her life.

As my Grandmother Edna told me, Donald Ryan, her first husband, was only able to provide a brief life of stability and love for my mom, her brothers and my grandmother. The latter was partly due to the brevity of his first marriage and his life. He was compelled to marry my grandmother when she was only twelve because he'd gotten her pregnant. He'd recently been released from the armed forces before he met and married my grandmother. She describes him as a Billy Dee Williams look alike. He was taller than the average man in the 1950's measuring in at over six feet tall. He had big brown beautiful eyes that his daughter inherited, with a persuasive smile and a silver tongue to match, that was inherited by his second son, Charles Ryan II. His light Carmel skin was like candy to the women who sought to take a bite out of the handsome country boy. He had a dangerous rebellious side that displayed an inability to respect authority. That trait was also inherited, but by his oldest son Michael Joseph Ryan.

He didn't know how old my grandmother was; ~ she didn't look like the average twelve year old from Western Pennsylvania in 1950. Her voluptuous body was more consistent with that of an eighteen year old. She was five foot six, had a Beyoncé type body shape, with fair skin color, along with unprocessed straight hair, her intelligence made her one of a kind. All of those qualities were sufficient, to attract and keep my grandfather, Donald Ryan for a short while. It kept him long enough to produce three children, but not until death. Granddaddy Donald divorced Grandma Edna when my mother was a toddler. He quickly turned to an absentee father, because he was spending most his time chasing skirts in Detroit, Michigan. He caught one of those skirts and got remarried and had three more children. I have family I've never met from my grandfather's other marriage.

He died when my mother was ten; she never established a relationship with him and couldn't recall the times he spent, if any, nurturing her, before he left my grandmother. Thus, it's not surprising that Peggy sought love, comfort and attention from older men. Richard was twenty-two years old when he met Peggy. Bruce was an adult as well; Allen was the only one under twenty years old but still three years her senior.

You may ask how does a fourteen year old acquire so much freedom and independence, well I believe that was primarily due to my grandmother's upbringing. Based on my conversations with Grandma Edna, who grew up in Midland, PA, which is fairly close to Beaver Falls, PA and New Castle, PA. As stated earlier she was a child herself when she got married and had to mature. rather quickly. The latter mentioned cities were by far the most rural areas of Western Pennsylvania. The cities probably had six to eight stop lights in each one. The homes are located on hills with wide open terrain in between. They are your atypical small USA towns where everyone knows your name, your parents and your grandparents. Notwithstanding the voluntary housing segregation there was less racial strife there than in the larger metropolitan cities. My grandmother once chimed after hearing about a racial incident that occurred on the news:" I never knew anything about racism until I got to Cleveland."

One day my grandmother was playing with baby dolls and going to school. A few years later she was lying about her age, drinking alcohol, and having sex with an adult. A few months later she's pregnant, married and then became responsible for an entire family. She went from being a toddler to an adult in light years without the benefit of instruction. Her beauty, intelligence and street savvy allowed her to manipulate situations for her own benefit. She convinced my grandfather, great-grandmother, and great aunts and uncles, that she was old enough to drink and date my grandfather. She obviously was not being closely supervised and that philosophy was passed to her children.

My grandmother's requirement to work during the night, due to raising her children in a single parent home, compelled my Uncle Michael, Uncle Chuck, and mom had to fend for themselves. My uncle Michael Joseph Ryan, my namesake aside from the middle name, was a juvenile delinquent, to say the least. He was always in trouble with the authorities and just did things in an unconventional manner. He was arrested several times in his life; he dated older women as well. I never got an opportunity to meet him because unfortunately he died when he was just sixteen years old. He was the spitting image of Donald Ryan, and possessed his strong chin, light caramel skin, broad shoulders and large owl like piercing eyes.

I believed that a significant reason behind my name being Michael Ryan was due to the relationship that existed between my mother and her big brother. He was the father figure for her that she lacked in an adult male.. Although he was only four years older than her, he provided the protection, care, guidance and love that she needed from an older adult male. While her middle brother also provided the care, love and protection it was not to the extent that Uncle Michael did. He was unable to realize how much of an impact that he had on his baby sister because of the choices he made when he was younger. The choice to be involved in nefarious criminal activities brought him before the Juvenile Court. He was summarily sentenced to be confined at a youth home as a way to rehabilitate him and turn him away from his wayward behavior. Uncle Michael became homesick and disenchanted with the efforts being made to correct his behavior and committed three final acts of defiance. He escaped from the home, stole a vehicle and then illegally drove that vehicle on a highway headed back to Cleveland. Uncle Michael never made it back to Cleveland because as he was driving, within the speed limit, another vehicle driven by an elderly couple, on the wrong side of the road, struck the vehicle he was traveling in head on. The elderly coupled died instantly while Uncle Michael was transported to the hospital. He would die at the tender age of sixteen (16) due to a genetic condition that prevented his blood from clotting.

Prior to but even more so after Uncle Michael's death my Uncle Chuck became the party animal of the house, as well as the playboy in the neighborhood. Many women called him little Billy Dee, because of his bronze skin color, six foot two inch muscular and athletic frame, megawatt smile and silver tongue, that was so effective and charming he could convince a bull to buy a red cape. He had several women throughout greater Cleveland. He was an excellent athlete and he met my cousin's mom while attending John F. Kennedy High School. Chuck was notorious for organizing parties at my grandmother's house when she was at work. My grandmother knew about their escapades but wasn't concerned about being a parent.   She was more concerned about whether she got along with her kids.   My grandmother's desire to ensure that her children had financial support. Her lack of supervision in her own childhood influenced her to do the same for her own children.

During my conversations with my dad, Richard Solomon, I learned that his family life was also filled with some drama. He was the sixth child out of ten. His mother, Grandma Gloria, had five children with her first husband and then subsequently met my grandfather, Richard English . She gave birth to five more children. All the children eventually took the last name

Solomon, for consistency purposes, and became notorious in the housing projects as the Solomon clan. My grandfather, Richard English, despite his strong personality was more concerned about maintaining family cohesiveness and accepted the decision for all of the children to have the surname of Solomon. Everybody knew the Solomon brothers for their athletic prowess.

My grandmother passed when Richard was only 15 years old, which caused him to go into foster care. He quickly became very close to the Bohanon family. In fact Ma Bohanon didn't call him her foster son but simply her son. So while Peggy came from a very small rarely supervised home life Richard was raised in a large controlled home environment. While they both had role models of family leaders who believed in a strong work ethic the latter was the only similarity that existed between the two and yet they met and were attracted to one another. Out of this dysfunction my teenage mother birthed me.

As I previously mentioned one of my personality traits is being very quiet; I use it as a way of gauging people and circumstances. I want to be assured that when I talk I'm aware of what I'm speaking about and who is in my audience. My biological father's quietness demonstrated his ability to mask who he truly was. His quiet demeanor was nothing more than, a ruse, a facade, someone who was manipulative and essentially a criminal. Why was he manipulative? Well, he manipulated a young, 14 year old that he met in the fall of 1970. He talked her into doing some things that she probably would not have done; at least, I don't think she would. The majority of teenagers in 1970's were graduating from high school and either entering the workforce or continuing their education at a college or university. I know there are some people who wished that she would have waited to be intimate with Richard everyone except me. This was not simply some chance meeting I truly believe it was orchestrated by God and they were destined to meet in order to form the basis of this story. All of the above factors clearly show that the odds were stacked against me even before I was born. I had the awesome task of overcoming these humungous hurdles that were placed before me even before I could crawl. Each challenge presented an impediment to me reaching the next rung on the ladder of success and accordingly being the least likely to reach my potential.

NOMADIC LIFE BEGINS

At the beginning despite being born to a teenaged, unwed, uneducated, unemployed, African American woman and having a biological father soon to be incarcerated for bank robbery before my birth I was surrounded by loving and caring people. Shortly after I was born my grandparents, Grandma Edna and Granddad John moved our family from Alvin Avenue in Garfield Heights, Ohio to Cleveland Heights, Ohio. Our family consisted of my grandparents, my mother, "my father" (Allen Douglas was the only man I knew to be my father) me, Uncle Chuck, his girlfriend, my Aunt Chris and their daughter my cousin Cherelle who, was six months older than I was. My Grandfather John's biological daughter and her daughter, who was the same age as me and my cousin Cherelle, all moved to a street called Lincoln Avenue in the spring of 1972, to a three story white with black trim home. We were the only African American family on the street. The street had rows of trees that were so full of large leaves and branches that it appeared to block out the sun. The home was a bright white outlined with black shutters and window panes. The inside of the home was vast and spacious and thus comfortably fit all of the people mentioned above. My grandparents both worked and owned their own successful consulting company. My grandmother allowed my mother to continue her education at Cleveland Heights High School while my grandmother took care of me and my cousin Cherelle. My grandmother was responsible for caring for us during the day, by bathing, changing, feeding and entertaining us. My Grandma Edna told me that my cousin and I were a handful and because we were so close in age caring for the two of us was like having twins. My grandmother managed fairly well and turned us over to our parents when they returned from school or work.

I was probably more problematic to care for than my cousins due to my hyperactivity. My grandmother, mom and other relatives were required to keep me bouncing at all times or else. Neighbors down the quarter of a mile long street could probably hear ": Waaa.aah.

Yaaaah. Waaaah Yaaah." as I tried to break every glass on the street. I needed someone to take my less than twenty pound, but chunky frame, and bounce me on their knee. The screams would then change to uncontrollable giggles. My family purchased a bouncer that is similar to a bungee jumping apparatus so that I would not wear out anyone's knee. The apparatus allowed me to jump until I was exhausted. I, however, jumped so often and hard that I had to be treated, because the seat caused an injury to my groin area. I was also the only baby in the house who had his own room. I was "fortunate" to have a single room, because I rocked my crib from one end of the room to another end in an effort to fall asleep. Visitors who were unfamiliar with my unusual behavior would run out of the home believing that the ceiling was about to collapse when I began to rock.

The latter hyperactivity caused my relatives some concern and I eventually, at the age of two, was prescribed Ritalin. After a few months of taking the medication my grandmother saw that the Ritalin slowed me to a virtual crawl. I would drag my tiny lower torso throughout the home. I avoided the bouncing machine, I did not cry when I was not the first to eat, I stop crying when I couldn't sit with my grandmother when she played the piano, and people were surprised by the quietness, which existed during the night when no rumbling was heard. After two months of my lack of energy, I told my grandmother, "I sick, I need to go back to the doca." The doctor took me off the Ritalin and I returned to the bouncy, screaming, rocking child, that everyone was accustomed to seeing.

My situation provided valid reasons for families to question the diagnosis of and subsequent treatment for Attention Deficit Hyperactivity Disorder (hereinafter ADHD). I hadn't even reached an age of substantial development and the medical community wanted to introduce a foreign substance into my physically challenged body. While I can't recall the discomfort or pain the medication may have caused I'm fortunate to have a family who sought a medical opinion as opposed to refusing to engage a medical expert. I'm also blessed to have a family that was receptive to the medical specialist's recommendation because if they hadn't accepted the opinion and acted accordingly then they wouldn't have discovered that I wasn't suffering from ADHD. However, if they failed to accept the recommendation and/or not even engage the doctor then we would have never known and if I truly suffered from the condition I would have never received the help to make me better. The lesson learned is for individuals to not be afraid or distrustful of the medical community when it comes to the mental or physical health of our children. It helped eliminate a concern my family possessed but could of helped expose a problem and provide relief if a problem did exist.

While my Grandma Edna and Granddad John were focusing on taking care of me during the day my mother was doing well at Cleveland Heights High School. She was in their Gifted and Talented classes due to her high intellectual abilities. She had been assessed in grade school and was selected to take classes that were more advanced than most of her classmates. She continued with those advanced classes at Cleveland Heights High School. While she changed neighborhoods, she did not change her behavior, when it came to men and soon she was pregnant again, only eight months after I was born. Again, my mother's baby's father (now Allen instead of Richard) was charged and convicted of some serious theft offenses–House breaking, Grand Petit Larceny and Auto Stealing. Also, my mother's baby's father (now Allen instead of Richard) would be incarcerated shortly after my mother gave birth; sentenced two months, in a state reformatory. Thank God my grandmother did not immediately abandon my mother and her two babies. She was upset, however, because my mother had allowed herself to get pregnant again, before I turned one.

As my Grandma Edna told me, she accepted me as a youthful mistake and agreed to assist my mother in raising me. She believed that my sister's conception was not a mistake, and that my mother and my father (Allen) would now have to learn how to be responsible parents. My grandmother felt that she had given my mom the benefit of the doubt with me. She, however, felt that fool me once shame on you, fool me twice shame on me. She was adamant about her decision to require my parents to raise us on their own. Thus, my parents shouldn't have been surprised shortly after my father's (I'm referring to Allen because I only knew him as my father until my pre-teen years) release from prison that my grandparents moved to

California and left the home in Cleveland Heights to them and my Aunt Chris and Uncle Chuck. The Lincoln Avenue inhabitants were required to simply pay the mortgage and the house would have been a family property. Their youth, immaturity, lack of a high school education, unstable employment and my father's conviction caused them to lose the home and it went into foreclosure.

My parents were forced to move to a rental property on the east side of Cleveland. This home was four times smaller than the home we had just vacated. We lived in a wood foundation two-family. It was there, that I first discovered that my family life was one far from what the normal child should experience. My father's decision to raise another man's child was admirable. He had no legal obligation to provide for me, but he took a responsibility that most men avoid with their own flesh and blood. If his actions were consistent with the latter perception then there would be no need to write this story. Allen's inability to control his anger however was one of the reasons why my childhood was a living hell.

Allen was very emotional, extremely volatile, deceptive, obsessive, and paranoid. He possessed a penchant for criminal activity just as Richard did. He would go off at the drop of a dime. He didn't know how to control his temper and would frequently take his anger out on my mother. She had a bad-boy complex that she never, ever got rid of and I think it was to her detriment. Her bad-boy complex was evidenced by the two men she attracted were both convicted felons. Allen was able to conceal his consistent violent acts from Grandma Lula and most of his siblings and relatives. His physical assaults were so frequent, usually once to twice a month. Most of them rarely stood out, as distinctive from the others.

I can still vividly recall the nights, and days that I was either awaken out of my sleep, or came running from my bedroom, or another portion of her house or apartment, when I heard my mother's screeches for help. Those memories have been ingrained in my mind from the time I was four years old.

MASQUERADE

It was 1975 and we were living on Easton, which is off of E.93rd,-one of the main arteries in Cleveland, Ohio. It was located on the east side of Cleveland in a community that was predominantly African American. Our home was located in an area that could be described as one for the working poor. My parents were renting the home and I was attending preschool at the time, my sister was two years old. My father was employed with Pepsi as a driver, and we appeared to be a well-adjusted family. One early spring morning I heard my parents argue, which was not unusual. This time, however, the screams were more intense and heightened. I first heard feet shuffling on the floor, like someone was trying to avoid being lifted off the ground. Then I heard, a thud against the wall which was my father slamming my mother's petite body against the thinly insulated wall. "Help, help, helppppp...Allen get off of me!" were the screeches of a female I heard emanating from my parents room. My mother's screech for help pierced through my body like needles through your skin, causing me to run to her bedroom door, only to see my father's massive hands around my mother's neck. I assumed it was her neck, because I couldn't see it due to the fact that his hands concealed any portion of her skin. His hands looked like a human hand scarf.

I saw her kicking and screaming to no avail, she was unable to remove his hands from her neck or push his torso off of hers. He then allowed her to get up only to sling her as she flew in the air like the female trapeze artist at the circus, but instead of landing on a safety net she landed on the bed with my father jumping on top of her again. I then watched his tightly clenched fist explode on her tiny face. I saw his arm swing back like a rubber band about to recoil, and then as his open hand with his fat fingers spread wide he slapped my mother in her face, and my tiny ears heard a sound that was similar to a gun shot. I remember my mother's body jerking violently as a result of the massive blows she received to her torso with his clenched fists.

I was in a state of shock this first time. I was confused, because most times I saw them being cordial to one another, and couldn't understand what would cause my father to be so violent. I hadn't seen them be overly affectionate towards one another; no holding hands, kisses, or playful teasing. Instead now I saw his punches, which seemed to not only rip through my mother physically, but ripped through me emotionally. The woman who was morally obligated to protect me now needed her own protection, but was unable to find some security to stop the onslaughts. My sister and I screamed in unison "Daddy no, Daddy stop", our eyes red as cherries and our cheeks were flushed with tears streaming like a water fountain, were insufficient to stop the beatings, instead our megaphone type voices simply intensified his fury.

It was as though our screams fueled my father's rage. He would punch my mother harder, when she would say" Allen you're going to do this in front of these kids" in between her attempts to catch her breath and her sobs. His acts were treacherous, relentless and frequent. We would witness those assaults nearly every month, and sometimes twice a month for the next six to seven years. I could almost set a watch and/or jot down on the calendar when a fight would ensue because they were so frequent.

What was even more heart wrenching, was watching my mother try to patch up the physical scars she received from my father's attacks. She would ask in her weakened exhausted state "Mike go get some ice from the refrigerator for me." I would take the ice and place it in a face towel, and wrap it to prevent the ice from escaping. My mother would gingerly place the ice on her swollen eyes, she would then transfer the ice to her nose. Eventually she would use tissue to clean up the blood that was streaming from her nose and lips, like water running down a mountain side, that hadn't fallen on the face towel. Her nose would at times swell, and when her eyes were simultaneously blackened she looked like a prize fighter. Sometimes she would be struck in her mouth causing her, already beautifully full lips to look more like balloons. Thus, I would have to return to the freezer part of the refrigerator to retrieve some more ice.

Ice was not the only mask my mother used to hide the abuse. Most women put on make-up to enhance their beauty my mother, however, used it to regain hers and cover the bruises and blackened eyes. I also recall white rimmed sun glasses, with the dark shaded lens that hid the black eyes. When she was out of make-up, she used them to shield the marks on her caramel face and small frame. I didn't understand why my mother stayed, despite the violence that was perpetrated upon her. She did not come from an environment that was rift with violence. My Grandfather Donald Ryan was definitely more of a lover than fighter. In fact, the men in my grandmother's life after Donald Ryan did not demonstrate any violent actions toward my mother, or grandmother in my mother's presence. My mother was raised in a household where violence was not the means, by which people solved conflicts with one another. I would later learn why it was so difficult for her to leave, while researching issues revolving around domestic violence as a part of my work as an attorney, and judicial officer dealing with those type of cases.

My father was a classic domestic violence abuser. He was the person who controlled the money in the home. He was the one working the better job and at one point the only person working. He had control over what was purchased and when it was bought. I saw him make several looks of disgust toward my mother. I saw him gesture with shoulders hunched and lunging at my mother. She reacted by flinching and putting her hands up in defense of attempts. He was also a great manipulator, and he made my mother feel that no one else would even be interested in her. He isolated her from her family, which was already small. I saw my grandmother Edna very infrequently, and my uncle Chuck may as well have lived on another planet, even though he also moved to California. My father stepped up to care for me, and included me in his family without any request for something in exchange, so my mom may have felt a sense of loyalty.

Not only did their relationship exhibit some of the classic signs of Domestic Violence but the acts themselves along with the things that proceeded them and occurred subsequently followed the Cycle of Violence format. I would witness the threats and arguments that would last for a few minutes and they would then disappear into a bedroom or outside in the hall to discuss their problems outside of me and my sister's presence. A day later or sometimes hours later the argument would recommence only this time they would not leave the area. Their verbal jabs at each other continued with voiced raised at a higher level. Eventually my father would get silent and the next thing I would hear would be the pounding of flesh. A few days later he would become more cooperative, cordial, and less menacing after the attacks. He was very apologetic saying things like "Peggy I'm sorry. You know I didn't mean it and I won't do it again." It was the same speech and same behavior after every episode. As a child, I was oblivious to why the volume was deafening, but realized after I got older it was done to drown out the noises that they were making as they were being intimate. The honeymoon stage did not last as long as the violent periods.

I did try, in vain several times to intervene but my dad simply tossed my frail body to the side and continued to pummel my mother. During some of the episodes I would simply close my bedroom door, and scream;" Ahhhhhhhhhhhhhhhhhhhhhhhh" and I would then scream Noooooooooooooooo" to the top of my lungs for about thirty seconds hoping that my misbehavior would distract my father, and maybe turn his attention from pulverizing my mother to correcting me. I would repeat the distraction three or four times. When that did not work I would simply cry and curl up in a corner in my room 'or in our living room and wait until the screaming and pounding of flesh stopped.

I internalized my feelings and began to build a hatred for my father. I detested him because of the frequent and vicious perpetration of violence upon my mother. I also vowed to never put my hands on a woman, because of the trauma I saw my mother experience on numerous occasions. I did not act upon the pent up anger and frustration I had against my father, at least not in a criminal manner. I learned how conversing, can at times ameliorate situations rather than using violence to resolve conflicts. I adopted this philosophy towards most people I had a conflict with not just in my intimate personal relationships. Talking in a civil manner rarely leads to a swollen lip, blackened eye, bruised ribs or trips to the emergency room.

The domestic violence was not the only source of dysfunction at our home. My parents were also a part of the 1960 drug culture. While marijuana use was common amongst young adults in the early 1970's, my parents use extended to my sister and me on one occasion. One particular night my sister and I were not complying with my parent's requests to fall asleep. While most parents' gave their children warm milk to aid in relaxing them and making them more susceptible to sleep my parents decided to use marijuana as a sleep aid. They both each rolled a marijuana cigarette and lit it with my sister, and I sitting on the couch.

They placed our cabbage doll size bodies, directly in front of them, I was four and my sister was two at the time. They then, unlike a former President of the United States of America, inhaled and exhaled the smoke generated, from the cigarette into our mouths, while holding our noses to ensure that we felt the effects of the mood altering chemicals in the marijuana. They performed this procedure several times before it had the desired effect, of putting my sister and me to sleep. I believe we slept so long that my parents were afraid to repeat that maneuver again.

INTRODUCTION TO MY INITIAL REFUGE

Physically, I wasn't growing too much, I was still small. I was starting to look like my mother; there was obviously a noticeable difference between me and Allen. I didn't recognize it, I just recognized him as being a father. I began Kindergarten in the fall of 1976 and enjoyed school immensely. The opportunity to interact with the kids was wonderful. I got an opportunity to just play and learn. Even from that time, I felt this addiction to learning; I couldn't get enough of it. I wanted to know and understand the world, understand people and comprehend concepts. I simply wanted to know how things worked. I was like a sponge that was thrown in an ocean of knowledge, soaking up everything I could contain.

Learning my ABC's, how to count, draw, tie my shoes, and how to be cooperative was exciting. Unlike most kids, those days I was exuberant about waking up to go to school. Learning how to read was intriguing to me, and my brain perked up when the teachers read to us. Listening to the stories generally took me to a different and better world, one that was not filled with anger and violence. Those stories allowed me to broaden my imagination and gave me the ability, to alter my family situation, even if only in my mind.

Our extracurricular school activities were invaluable learning experiences. We actually went to a pool once a month and were taught to swim. This is unique because most urban schools were not offering these type of opportunities.

Our diverse population may have given myself and others like me more chances to engage in activities, that other African American students did not enjoy. Our instructors only permitted us to swim from sideline to sideline in the shallow end of the pool of course. I learned how to square dance in my kindergarten class as well. The teachers assisted us in learning the basic maneuvers; we then practiced what we were taught with one another. Eventually, I participated in the annual evening, square dancing event the school sponsored.

My mother was my dance partner; I remember dressing in a straw hat with overalls and cowboys boots. I had a blast dancing with the other students and my mom. That was one of my fondest, mother and son memories and I cherish it to this day. She was patient with me, despite the fact that I kept stepping on her toes. She was gentle and understanding when I got tired, or simply wanted to go play with my friends. I still remember the glow in her eyes seeing me get the steps right and strike out on my own, without fear of failure. My early exposure to the above activities that were uncommon in my community made me more adventurous and willing to go beyond what was familiar and thereby allowed me the chance to take advantage of opportunities that others were never afforded. It help me feel like I belonged and would be the foundation for me to realize that I also belonged in places like college, law school or the legal community; I wasn't uncomfortable in those environments despite obvious cultural differences. Our children must be taken out of their environment and exposed to the world as opposed to being confined to one area, one view point, and one culture. We need to have a world-wide perspective not a village one.

THE ESCAPE

In the June of 1976, after my kindergarten year was completed, my mother decided to send me and my sister to California to visit my Grandma Edna and Granddad John. My mother said in a soft tone while my father glared at us, "Don't embarrass me by acting a fool when you go visit your grandmother." My father said "If you or your sister act a fool I'm whipping your ass when you come back home. "My mother also warned that if we were mischievous that grandma would probably not invite us to visit again.

My mother had to forewarn us when we went anywhere without her or my father for at least one night, because my sister and I had habit of aggravating one another, with me being the main culprit. I would pinch, hit or tickle my sister for no reason. I would get a charge out of hearing her cry for help or scream at me to stop. In fact when I tickled her, she would react so intensely that she would hold her breath, with a cemented smile with her petite body convulsing. If my sister and I would have eaten any candy we were like frogs in a pond full of lilies, jumping all over the home, apartment, store etc. Since neither one of them was traveling with us on the airplane we were required to travel with one of my grandmother's friends, Arlene and her son Ray.

I was afraid because this was my first time on a plane as well as my sister. My parents drove us to the airport and we took a picture, which was one of the few family portraits that I have preserved. The flight was smooth and they kept us very comfortable, it was not unusual at all. When we arrived, we ran into grandma and grandpa's arms.

My sister and I slept on the couch bed during the entire time of our visit. We did, on occasion jump onto grandma's bed that had the large soft pillows, whose sides looked more like arms. My grandma and grandpa lived in a modest apartment building in Los Angeles, California. I recall that most of the people in the apartment where my grandparents age.

There weren't many children, but my sister and I never really needed other kids to play with, we always found a way to entertain each other, even if it eventually resulted in us agitating one another. My grandma and grandpa kept us busy by taking us all over Los Angeles, California. We went to visit Universal Studios and had a ball. I got an opportunity to witness the special effects that go into; making a plane look liked it crashed on film. I rode in the boat that travels through Universal Studios and Jaws popped out of no where and caused me to scream with such a high pitch voice that some questioned whether my name was Michael or Michelle. I ate a lot of cotton candy, hot dogs and drank a lot pop. We also were able to visit Disneyland.

Eventually, my mother flew out to California alone and I thought she was coming out, to get us, but it turns out that she was coming out there to escape. My mom's true intention was not simply to have us visit for the summer but to provide the impetus for a thousand mile move away from my father and the violence.   We didn't leave California; we wound up moving to Inglewood.

The move to Inglewood brought something we hadn't experienced in years-peace and quiet. It was surreal, there was no fighting, yelling, or threats, and no face towels filled with ice, no tears streaming down nor bruises on her pretty face. We also experienced something that we hadn't since my sister was born, and that was just the three of us being together.

In first grade my love for learning grew even stronger. I began to recognize that, I could grasp concepts fairly quick and my recall was better than the average student in my class. I was frequently bored in the classroom, because unlike most of the students the teacher did not have to repeat concepts for me.   I had to wait until the teacher reiterated a theory before they moved onto to something new. I waited anxiously like a diabetic awaiting a shot of insulin, as the teacher was about to introduce a new subject area.

I couldn't wait to receive a worksheet so that I could complete it to show the teacher how well I understood her tutelage. I was highly disappointed when I did not receive homework; boy was I a strange kid or what? I did recall, receiving high marks through that first marking period.

My social skills were developing but not too well, because I was a transplant from a city and school district that was more than 3,000 miles away from Inglewood. I did not have friends when I started school, because we moved to our new home in Inglewood merely three or four weeks before school started. I was a quiet guy by nature, and thus it made it doubly difficult for me to make friends. I gained popularity, due to my intelligence because I would answer the questions posed by the teacher.

The kids got an opportunity to see, that I was smart so they invited me to play a game that involved less brain activity- marbles. The boys sat around a circle with a bag full of marbles. The object of the game is to take as many marbles from the other competitors as possible. I was permitted to play with the top marble players, because I was easy prey; ;due to my naivety. I loss many of my most treasured marbles. I discovered during this period of making friends, that I did not like the feeling that was associated with losing. I was usually one of the best when it came to the classroom and just couldn't stand the fact that I was losing when it came to a game involving some physical skill.

I learned how to play the game, by losing, observing other people and practicing. After a few weeks I was so deft at playing marbles, that I was able to retrieve the marbles that I loss and add more to my collection. It was here that I developed this competitive spirit that would serve me well in all my future endeavors.

That competitive spirit also compelled me to stay ahead of the other students in my class. Thus, when we were learning the basics of addition and subtraction, I was asking my grandmother Edna, who I thought was the one of the smartest persons I had ever met, "Can you teach me how to multiply?"

She would then say, "Michael why are you in such a rush?" I would not respond orally, but simply smile as wide as my face, with my pearly whites and one front tooth missing. That was enough to alter grandma's intentions, she would find a scrap sheet of paper and make several problems and then she would explain each component. She would solve the problem, and then explain the process she used to ascertain the answer. "Michael, honey, you need to get some flashcards to help you better memorize the multiplication table," is what she would say after each session. My mom took my grandmother's advice, and I began to slowly go through the multiplication table while I was learning first grade math.

My competitive spirit spilled over onto the athletic field when I began to recognize that I was faster than most of the kids on the street, and that my back yard was unable to contain the plastic baseball that I would strike with my plastic bat. I also realized that my dexterity was better than most of the kids' I encountered in school and in my neighborhood.

I could catch a baseball relatively easy when thrown in my direction. The same thing held true for a football. I enjoyed football more than anything else, because University of Southern California ("hereinafter USC)was down the street from our baby sister's house.

I saw the Rose Bowl when I was only six years old and decided that I would one day play football for USC. I wouldn't let my small frame preclude me from reaching that pinnacle of college sports. I never got an opportunity to see a game in person, but I watched enough USC games and Los Angles Rams games, to develop a passion for football. I was the star running back, quarterback and wide receiver on my street. We would play a game called "Down the

Man" in the front yard, of the homes on the street. Generally the first person to twenty-eight would win. You received four opportunities to score a touchdown, which was worth seven points. The object is to go from one end of the yard to the other end through a gauntlet of would be tacklers. If you are successful, you keep the ball and continue, until you are stopped from reaching the other end of the yard, or you score the required twenty-eight points.

Playing "Down the Man" was more of a metaphor for my life than I first realized. It symbolized me running through, over, and beyond the challenges that I faced that stood between me and my goal. My goal at that time was to merely score a touchdown. My goal in life was to become a high school graduate, college graduate and then a success in whatever profession I chose. Successfully navigating the field for "Down the Man" gave me the foundation, courage, and confidence to continue to run through, over and beyond the challenges that life would bring in an attempt to keep me from my goals.

I more often than not was the winner in down the man because most of the kids either couldn't catch me because I was too fast or I was so elusive that I would slip out of their grasps. I began to play down the man more than I played marbles. Sports and school became the outlets for me to relieve any pent up frustration and anger. I could legally tackle someone and reduce the anxiety or anger I was feeling for another situation and not be punished so long as I played within the rules. School impacted by self-esteem in a positive manner. I could control the results at school and therefore made every effort to ensure a positive outcome ensued for any type of assessment (i.e. tests, quizzes, and conduct reports) The more positive results I received the higher my self-esteem rose despite it being decreased by the events that were taking place outside of school. I would not allow the distractions, which were minimal now that we were in California, to keep me from gaining the knowledge and approbation I deserved from my educational pursuits.

A CHRISTMAS SURPRISE

My mother began dating other guys; nice guys, guys who didn't fight with her. I was enjoying everything: Living with my mother and sister, grandmother's frequent visits and First grade was wonderful. My mom was allowed to seek companionship because of our beautiful babysitter. She introduced us to the Hispanic culture even though she never taught us the language, but the food was great. We spent a significant amount of time with the babysitter so my mother could go to work and play. My mother worked as a switchboard operator holding held several of those positions in Cleveland after we left California.. She was responsible for routing the phone calls to the specific area, branches in department stores. She was able to acquire the necessary experience prior to leaving Cleveland despite the fact that she never received her high school diploma or G.E.D. She however, by not completing high school limited the expansive opportunities high school and college would have offered her especially based upon her inclusion in academically gifted classes when she did attend school.

My mother's relationship with the new guy lasted for three months. Then I witnessed the first and last physical altercation between them. He and my mother were about to go out on the town. An argument erupted between them and my mother picked up the keys to the car and sliced his face with the keys. The guy was approximately 145 pounds and maybe 5'3", clearly not as imposing as my father. Unlike my father, however, he did not react violently towards my mother. Actually the keys my mother used to scratch the man belonged to him. He politely grabbed his keys and left, we did not see him ever again after that day.

My mother, like a number of domestic violence victims, had taken on the abusive characteristics of their abuser. She had divorced herself from my father to avoid those physical confrontations, but she engaged in one and decided to strike out when she was not receiving the expected cooperation from her new boyfriend. She used the same philosophy that my father used to physically punish her. It was a complete role reversal and one I doubt my mother enjoyed. She had become the aggressive abuser but with a conscience.

Shortly after that event my mom sat me and my sister down. She said "Michael and Ressie, you are going to get a big surprise for Christmas. The best present ever!" She made the wonderful statement with wide eyes and face length grin. I assumed that it was a new amazing toy or maybe a puppy. My sister and I questioned my mother on a daily basis about the surprise present but she was mum about it. She would not even give us a hint about the overly anticipated gift.

It was a Friday of December 1977, the last day of school before winter break began, and I was both excited and surprised, because I couldn't wait to see what our special gift was. I was disappointed because we would be missing two weeks of school. I thoroughly enjoyed learning and a momentary gap in the process was not comforting to me. As I walked into our home on that day, I saw my mother sitting in the kitchen smiling. I heard a familiar deep voice say, "Hey Mike Mike!" it was my father Allen. He was chuckling as he reiterated my name again. I ironically was happy to see him, because I last saw him in June.

I ran and gave him a big hug and kiss on the cheek as the hairs on his beard pricked my lips. I had spoken to him, via the phone on several occasions, over the last six months but it was better seeing him in person. "Daddy, I missed you. Are you staying here for Christmas?" I said with my soft spoken voice. He assured me he was staying beyond Christmas.

In the midst of the fights and marijuana use, my father tried to act in a manner that was more consistent with the average parent. He provided for the family for a short period with a good paying job. He was a disciplinarian and made sure I followed the conditions he and my mom ordered, or suffered the appropriate consequences for not adhering to the rules. The appropriate consequences usually meant, either standing in corner of the home for several minutes with my face towards the corner and remaining quiet, during that time or a spanking.

While I was thrilled about my father being the surprise present, I was not satisfied with just him. We enjoyed a wonderful Christmas in California with no snow for the first time in my life!

This was a very long honeymoon period for my parents. Again, I didn't see the public or private display of affections that my wife and I constantly engage in, that completely horrifies my kids, but I didn't witness the huge arguments or my father pummeling my mother with a barrage of punches either. The peace we had without my father for six months continued with him. I was thinking maybe a change of scenery has changed my father's behaviors. I didn't see any bottles of Wild Irish Rose or Mad Dog 20/20 in the refrigerator either. My mom smiled more often we even purchased a dog and named him Blackey. He was a small mixed breed dog that was more of a playful pet, than a watch dog. The non-fighting and the dog weren't the only things that made us resemble a healthy, functional family my dad took my sister to teach her how to ride a bike, and to refine my knowledge about how to ride a bike. I already learned how to ride from my mom, and the other kids in the neighborhood where we lived before my father arrived. The method I used to learn how to ride was a pattern that I would adopt, and use for most of my life skill acquisitions.

I would get the basic foundation from an adult or other experienced people, and modify that information for a better understanding of how things work. I took the little mommy gave me, along with my friends and, then struck out on my own to learn how to ride. I rode well but my father was not aware, because the last time he saw me I still needed training wheels. He even escorted us to school and to softball games to watch Uncle Chuck. He eventually found a job with Avis Rental and everything appeared to be kosher.

My sister and I were spending time with our babysitter during the evening hours. My mom and father were actually going out on dates. In fact, the only picture I ever seen of the two of them out on a date, was taken during this period. My mother wore a black sequence dress, and my father had on a black suit with a white large collar shirt. They spent the evening drinking and socializing, on the Queen Mary boat. My mother was smiling, while my father showed no type of emotion. Times were good for almost a year 'and then things began to unravel.

The first negative omen was when I was struck by a car. I had been playing the age old game Hide and Go Seek with my friends with the wall of an apartment building located near the alley in back of our home functioning as home base. I had been designated the seeker and engaged in the customary practice of placing my crossed arms on the wall with my head leaning on my arms and my eyes closed. I actually didn't really need to cover my eyes or close them for that matter because the sun had just set and the street lights were providing most of the light in that area. I remember ending my count "27, 28, 29 30. Ready or not here I come" I then unfolded my arms, opened my eyes and turned towards the area that I knew my friends liked to hide. I, however, hadn't moved more than three steps into the alley when a car, clearly exceeding the posted speed limit, struck me in my midsection a few inches above the groin area. The force of the blow lifted me off the ground and threw me, about five to ten feet backwards. My buttocks, back and head all struck the ground in that order. My friends rushed to my house that was thankfully only a few yards away and summoned my parents to come to the alley. My father was livid, and initially his anger was surprisingly not directed towards the driver. Instead he yelled at me while carrying me in the house, "WHAT THE FUCK WERE YOU DOING IN THE STREET ANYWAY, DIDN'T I TELL YOUR ASS TO STAY OUT THE STREET?

My mother on the other hand, was trying to make sure I hadn't broken any bones, or that I wasn't bleeding anywhere. She then asked me "What happened?", and I told her what I told my father. My father went outside to get the information from the driver who was visibly shaken by what occurred; I think she thought she killed me. I was reluctant to go to the hospital and tried to develop my persuasion skills, by trying to convince my parents that a hospital trip was unnecessary. " I don't need to go to the hospital. I'll be fine just let me rest here on the couch, " is what I said as I was grimacing because of the pain. My parents were more concerned that I may have suffered a broken bone, and/or internal bleeding. Despite my claims, they did the responsible thing and took me to the hospital. It was my first time in a hospital since I was born. I was afraid but had no idea as to why I was so adverse to the hospital. The stench of sickness and disease had a vile smell similar vinegar.. Maybe it was all the brightness (i.e., white walls, white coats and the beds) that was surrounding the darkness (i.e., sickness and disease) I wound up, receiving a few tests, and was released after a few hours. I was lucky to not have suffered any serious injuries as a result of the accident. In fact I was outside, but not in the alley, a few days later playing and running again.

The next unfortunate event involved my father being the principal party in a horrific car accident around the corner from our house. I think he was actually intoxicated at the time, or maybe both intoxicated and high on drugs. I made that observation because when I saw him at home, and I had no idea how he got there, his nose was bloodied and he had cuts on his forehead and cheeks. I smelled an odor of alcohol and his eyes were blood shot and glazed. I didn't hear him say much to my mom so I wasn't sure if his words were slurred. I did make out my mother's statements as she was on the phone with an unidentified person "Yeah the car is around the corner and it's fucked up." I decided to venture around the corner and saw the tangled mess. The two vehicles front ends were mangled beyond repair. The windshields of both cars were shattered and the other driver was lying on a gurney waiting to be transported via ambulance to the nearest hospital.

After the car was totaled my father sought to rent a car from his employer. He, however, wound up losing his job and then received a criminal charge, because he kept the car and refused to return it. The arguments, between him and my mother recommenced, due to a lack of work. Then he again, started to become physical, beating my mother with his fists, slapping her with his massive hands, and me and my sister sitting there watching and crying again. The assaults were similar to the ones that he committed in Cleveland. The sunshine state was not sufficient to alter his actions permanently. My way of trying to mollify him since our voices, were unable to do so, was to write a letter saying that I was running away because I hated my father because he kept beating my mother.

My mother would read the notes and she would be so sad, because she felt that running away from my father also meant running away from her. We would talk on occasion, about why I wanted to leave but my mom simply provided excuses for my father's behavior. She would exclaim "he only behaved that way when he was drunk, or he was just having a bad day, and he really does love me, you and your sister. He's been having a hard time, since he lost his job." The notes did not have any impact on my father, because he never changed his behavior in terms of the way that he treated her. His physical attacks continued, her verbal attacks escalated and they just refused to engage in alternative ways of resolving conflicts short of violence.

The straw that broke the camel's back and caused us to return to Ohio was when my Grandmother Lula (Allen's mom) was involved in a terrible car accident in Cleveland. At one point her prognosis was dire. She eventually recovered, but her vision was impacted as well as her mobility; doctors stated that she was not going to be able to ever walk again. They also claimed she would have to wear corrective lenses, when prior to the accident she did not need any. Additionally, the accident also impacted her vision. My father was very concerned and we were soon on our way back to Cleveland.

It was March of 1979 and I was in the middle of my second grade year. I was not happy about returning to Cleveland, because I couldn't believe we were leaving the sunny confines of California, for the dreary winter doldrums of Northeast Ohio. When we left Los Angles, it was seventy degrees, and when we landed in Cleveland it was thirty degrees and snowing. I shook my head in disbelief, while my body shivered because of the shock of the cold weather that I hadn't felt for nearly two years. My parents escaped the financial complications, and the criminal inquiries, and landed without convenient shelter for our family. We went to live with my father's sister ,Aunt Joann. I hadn't seen Aunt Joann or my cousins Bonnie, Little Bit, Nikki, Kristie or Maya, for a long time. Kristee, Nikki and Maya were all around me and my sister's age. We had a new addition to the family, Brian my Aunt Joann's only son, who was a couple of weeks old.

I didn't realize it when we came back but we must have been a huge burden on my Aunt Joann and an inconvenience to my cousins. We all piled into this three bedroom, downstairs two family home on E. 105 off of Union Avenue on the eastside of Cleveland. I recalled that it only had one bathroom but due to the fact that my father's other sister Aunt Mary lived upstairs with her son Anthony and daughter Alesica it wasn't too crowded in the morning when we were getting ready for school. It was a very sturdy, all wood white home in the middle of the block. There was a huge backyard that had a gigantic tree that blocked out the moon and the sun with its massive branches and leaves. There was a small chain link fence no taller than four feet and it went the length of the backyard. It was our gateway to E. 106 from where most of my new friends would emanate. This was a family affair, going on here, on – East 105th, which was actually right around the corner from 93rd and Fullerton, where we were living before we moved to California.

So we basically had a family reunion every day. I wound up getting my own bed, but still shared a room with three other cousins. I received the bottom bunk and I forgot where my sister slept. I think she slept with one of my other cousins. My mother and father slept in this house as well. We stayed there until the end of the school year then we eventually moved over to Gorman Avenue, located in the Miles-Harvard area.

While we were living with my aunt, there was virtually no room, so, it was always crowded, and when you were eating, it was always going to be a big meal. I can't recall if my mother and father were working at the time, I think they were trying to find work. They were still getting into arguments, and fights. My aunt once observed my father beating my mother in a park near the home and intervened. She stopped her younger brother from continuing with the onslaught. That was kind of difficult, because my father did whatever he wanted to, and he rarely listened to his big sister, regarding how to deal with his woman.

I was trying to adjust to a new home, an old city, my parents continued turmoil and a new school. I enrolled in Mount Pleasant Elementary School in order to complete the final semester of my second grade year. I was inserted in a class with an elderly teacher who had very little control over the students, especially one named Carlan. He was at least twice the size of most of the students and it wasn't due to being held back he was just a naturally big kid. He looked like the Incredible Hulk's infant son with muscles at the tender age of eight. He was a bully wherein he made people do what he said based upon his intimidating stature. He, however, didn't say much to me since I was new and he had already established who his victims would be at the beginning of the year. I was the focus of the girls more than anyone else. They all giggled and whispered about how cute I was and who would be the first one to kiss me; we're talking about second graders. They were really advanced in their actions while I wasn't despite my knowledge about men and women interrelationships thanks to my mom who told me about the" Birds and Bees" when we were living in California. Thus, while I was armed with that info but decided not to engage in behavior that my mom told me about. I was more focused on sports, homework and schoolwork.

I was able to quickly grasp the concepts that I had missed and worked myself up the point in the year where all the other students happened to be. I was again able to distinguish myself in my grades by obtaining high marks in all areas: math, reading, science and social studies. I again wouldn't allow the overcrowding at home, transferring from one school to another midyear, being in an unfamiliar school with little to no friends in my class and still having to be concerned about my parents' abusive relationship deter me from excelling in school.

THE ENLIGHTENMENT (ESTABLISHMENT OF MY FAITH)

One of the most life changing experiences happened to me, while we were living with Aunt Joann. My aunt's, next door neighbor, Ms. Tanner and her daughter, attended bible study and Sunday church services. She was one of the most peaceful, and kindhearted individuals that I had ever met. Ms. Tanner was an elderly woman, who had to be in her early seventies whose grandchildren would visit her every weekend. She invited us into her yard to play with her grandchildren, and one day suggested that me, my sister, cousins Nikki, Kristee and Maya, go to church with her. It was my initial introduction into religion of any kind. I was overwhelmed by what I experienced when I went to St. Paul's Missionary Baptist Church, which was located on the corner of 79th and Kinsman in Cleveland, Ohio. The understanding of who God is and what God does in your life, and how if you're faithful even despite the fact that you have rough times in life, eventually things are going to pan out for you, was something that resonated with me.

We went to church every other Sunday, and I am forever grateful to those two women who decided to reach out to me, and become the conduit for me to find my Savior and Lord Jesus Christ; I love them. I walked into that small but electric palace of worship. A sense of calm, peace and joy fell upon me like the mist after a refreshing rain falls on your head. I was excited to go to church so much so that it was difficult to go to sleep on Saturday night. I went there each Sunday I had a chance expecting something great to happen. What I wasn't learning, about how to be a man at home, I was observing and learning from the men involved with the church. The pastor was married as well as the deacons of the church. I saw the affection they expressed to their wives: holding hands, speaking fondly about them. I saw the men helping the women- young and old- by escorting them to their seats, or holding out their hands or arms when the women were descending or ascending steps. I saw them opening the church doors and car doors for the women, letting them enter before the men did. I listened to the pastor as he preached and taught about how people ought to treat their neighbor like they would want to be treated. The pastor relayed messages of hope over despair, of love over hate, tolerance over prejudice, nonviolence over violence, cooperation over disagreement. He indicated that those were the virtues of Christians and I desperately wanted to become one.

I heard the Pastor say it was easy to become a Christian by being saved. He said to be saved, I only needed to believe in my heart and confess with my mouth that Jesus was Lord that he was crucified and rose on the third day. I was also told that I needed to be born again, by water and that meant being baptized. Unlike my cousins and my sister, who had also decided to become Christians and be baptized, I was excited about this significant event in my life. I would now have a standard by which I could respect and live up to. I wasn't nervous about being baptized, since I had taken swimming lessons as I stated earlier, and unlike my family members, I was not afraid of being dunked in the baptismal pool by the pastor. I wanted to become a Christian because I thought that my prayers would help protect me, help change the course of my life and make my home life more secure and stable.

I wanted to live right, I wanted God to bless me and I wanted to eventually go to heaven. On the day of the baptism, which occurred after the service, I waited patiently until I was called to the men's room to change. I stripped down to just my underwear and was given some oversized white sweat pants, sweat socks and a sweat shirt. I was lead to the front of the church were the baptism pool was underneath the pulpit. I was the last person to get baptized. I watched my sister and cousins, who had gone from giggling to a quiet nervousness; they were taken to the pool one by one. The remaining church members sang the song "Take me to the waters, take me to the waters, take me to the waters to be baptized, none but the righteous, none but the righteous, none but the righteous, shall see God."

After being baptized I became more disciplined. I prayed at each meal and every night before I went to bed. I read the Bible and took it to church so I could follow along with the pastor. When I got an opportunity to go to Sunday school, I read the lesson and asked questions to see how the message would apply to my life. I prayed for my parents' relationship to get better. I prayed for us to live in our own home so we could have more room. I prayed for safety for my mother, me and my sister. I showed more faithfulness than my sister and my cousins; being baptized for them was just something to do. It had an impact on me. I drew nearer to God and developed a trust in the religious leaders in my life who I believed were God's messengers. While I generally had a passion for things I could control, like school, this was one instance, where I had a deep passion for something for which I didn't know the outcome. Yet, I felt confident that prayer worked and would change my situation.

DIFFERENT LOCATIONS SAME BEHAVIORS

After that summer living with Aunt Joann, Aunt Mary, and my parents still fighting each other, we moved to Gorman Avenue. Finally, we had more room and didn't have to share one bathroom with a multitude of people; that was tough. Now, it was just me, my mother, sister and father on Gorman. Being away from the family, meant that my father didn't have anybody watching him, and could treat my mother any way that he wanted to, and he sure enough began doing so. The fights became even more brutal than they were before, despite my prayers.

I would see my father grab my mother around her waist, as she tried in vain to hold onto a chair, and drive her onto the cold tile kitchen floor. I could hear the air being pushed out of her lungs and through her mouth as she let out a grunt when she was slammed. My father used his entire body as opposed to just his hands to prevent my mother from rising off of the floor. She looked like a fish out of water as she squirmed on the floor in an effort to get up. My father kept her pinned down while simultaneously punching my mother in her head and face. His punches did not stop her from talking as she begged between sobs "Allen please stop. You're hurting me." His response would simply be another shot to her face or head and the comment "You should shut your mother fucking mouth sometimes." He would then grab her by her hair at times and extremities at times and drag her out of me and my sister's view to the living room. My mother would try, in vain, to grab the kitchen table or chairs in an effort to avoid being slung from room to room. He would then throw her against the wall, or onto the couch once they arrived in another part of the house. The punches would continue to fly as well as the knees continuing to suppress the breath in her tiny chest. This again would be a continuance cycle for the next few years.

Ironically, I discovered that we had moved next door to the bully in my second grade class at Mount Pleasant. Despite his initial teasing of me when we met at Mount Pleasant we became friends, especially after we became neighbors. Carlan's mother and father were very good parents and role models for their children. Carlan's mother was physically challenged, due to being confined to a wheelchair. That didn't stop her from being an excellent parent.

While she didn't work, from my knowledge, she did provide a clean home, cooked meals and she disciplined her children. She taught them responsibility, because many things she would normally do she delegated to them. She kept a watchful eye on the kids to ensure they completed their tasks and they helped her maneuver around the house and neighborhood. Carlan and his father would help escort his mom down the ramp of their house into their vehicle. I frequently saw Carlan, or his dad taking his mother on walks throughout the neighborhood. If they had knock down verbal or physical fights like my parents I would not have known because I never witnessed it or heard about it from Carlan. In fact, when my father began assaulting my mother, I would cross the bushes and go over to Carlan's. We would talk, his mom would cook, or we would get on our bikes and ride around the neighborhood. I avoided going home, until I knew that the fight had ended. I would walk into the house when my father disappeared. My mother would be sitting in the living room, with her lips a size bigger, or holding a face towel filled with ice on her eyes.

I believe one of the things that fueled the altercations between my parents, were both of their possible increased drug use. At that age I never saw the tools they used for drugs, but their behaviors drastically changed. My father did not have a steady job; in fact it was like he was moving from one job to another every other month. My mother was working for a while and then she would either quit or was terminated. We lived next door to my father's best friend from high school Todd. Todd actually was the one who was responsible for introducing my mother to my father. I believe that all three of them were using drugs at that time.

My father would return after being out with Todd and he would have this dazed looked on his face. Additionally, he would move his bottom jaw area from side to side and would be very animated. He was jittery and could not sit still, when he first came home and would be up either causing a ruckus with my mother or trying to fix something he should have fixed weeks ago. My parents on many occasions would return from upstairs after being in their room for at least a half an hour, and alight from the room and exhibit the same characteristics, as my father did after he returned from a drug binge, the night before. My parents engaged in this behavior notwithstanding the fact that my Grandmother Lula lived only three blocks over from our house on East 98th street, off of Miles Avenue, another main artery in Cleveland, Ohio.

I believe that my mother began receiving public assistance, because we were allowed to take advantage of the free breakfast and lunch programs at Miles Park Elementary. She received a cash stipend, as well as food stamps through the Federal program called Aid to Dependent Children.

The cupboards and refrigerator were generally full each month for the early months during our stay on Gorman. My father's infrequent paychecks supplemented the income we were receiving from the state via the federal government plan. We didn't want for any necessities, and if we had any desires we could go around the corner and ask Grandma Lula. It was the beginning of my third grade year at Miles Park Elementary and I was already attending my fourth school since kindergarten. I quickly adjusted, made new friends and again was one of the brightest students in my class. Notwithstanding my God given ability to rapidly comprehend, and retain information I still developed this hard work ethic by completing my class work in a timely manner. My homework was done after school before I went outside to play, and I assisted my sister when there was an area where she struggled. I was controlling my performance in class, but had no control over what was transpiring at home.

When we came home from school there wasn't much chaos, because usually my father wasn't home from work or hustling~ trying to make money legally or illegally outside of his normal job. Therefore, my sister and I, more so me, were able to do our homework, change our clothes and then go outside and play until it was time to eat. My father was usually home around dinner time and would come in and sit down very quietly, eat and really not engage me or my sister in any type of discussion. Eventually we would watch television or he would change his clothes and go back out with Todd or one of his other friends. The drama would begin when he returned. If he was high or drunk an argument would sometimes ensue with my mother. The yelling would wake me up, as it did on Fullerton as well as it did in Inglewood. My bedroom was next to my parent's room and we had paper thin walls. I could hear thumps against the wall, as my father hurled my mother through the air against the wall.

I could hear her screaming for my father to stop. I could also hear the slaps and punches that bruised my mother's body. There were many nights when this occurred we again found ourselves over Carlan's. Since my parents were so loud, Carlan's parents knew exactly why we asked to come over. I couldn't stand to hear and watch my mother continue to be treated like she was a rolling punching bag. I couldn't stand to hear her beg and cry for him to stop the onslaughts.

Eventually my father either quit or loss his job around the beginning of 1980 and we were forced, due to limited income provided by the public assistance checks my mother was receiving to move to the Longwood Housing Projects. I again was compelled to pick up my backpack and move to another neighborhood, and attend another school in the middle of the school year. I had not been privy to any conversations or stories about Longwood Projects reputation. The reputation was that it was a crime ridden, drug infested, depressed neighborhood that was ignored by the powers that be because there was a lack of concern, care and respect by the residents for their community. Since I was unaware of the reputation that preceded the community, I went in with a belief that it was just like the other predominantly African American residential areas I resided in for the last couple of years; not affluent but not completely downtrodden either. I was given a huge wakeup call on my first day in the neighborhood.

One of my mother's dearest friends lived in a townhouse that was near the place we called the Office. The Office was the building that housed the administration department for the Longwood public housing estate. Accordingly, security was also in that building, something most if not all the young men, even me, knew and had encounters with at least once during their stay in Longwood. My mom's friend had children whose ages paralleled my sister and I. After taking a break from moving a few things into our apartment which was parallel to the Office and separated by a parking lot that was approximately seventy-five yards long, I ventured over to my mom's friend's house and her son and I took a stroll through the projects; he was giving me a tour of the hood.

We walked to an area where a group of guys were playing "Down the Man." The guys recognized that I wasn't a familiar face and stop playing and approached me and my "tour guide".

They asked me, in a bold and confrontational manner, "Where you live cuz?" I told them I had just moved down here from Miles. They then said "Only punks and bitches come from Miles." I had a Napoleon complex, seeing that I was only about 4'10" tall at age nine so notwithstanding the obvious physical differences, I responded that "Only punks and bitches came from Longwood." Within seconds of my comment one of the kids swung his right arm with a tight fist towards my head. I however, was able to avert the punch by ducking, and was able to respond with an upper cut punch and strike him right underneath his chin. The guy stumbled backwards and then bull rushed me, by simply running at full speed with his head down and his arms making a u shape that wrapped around my tiny frame. Since he outweighed me by approximately twenty pounds, when he hit me it was like a Mack truck hitting a Pinto, and it caused me to fly through the air.

We landed on the ground with punches flying feverishly, by myself and this unknown assailant, and the two of us wrestling on the ground. The altercation was halted when his friends intervened by pulling him up and my friend grabbed me. I got up with a busted lip; my hair filled with grass and dirt; and my torn dirt stained shirt was hanging out of my pants. The guy and I continued to yell profanities at each other, but we never engaged in any more fisticuffs, and instead walked in different directions. I decided to head back to my apartment and cut the tour short. I would have a lot of time to find out about the hood in the next three years.

As I walked back to my apartment building I got a better view of Longwood. It is quite different from the Longwood Housing Projects that my mother knew as a child when she lived here with my grandmother Edna and her brothers. The brick buildings, either apartment high rises or small townhouses, look faded and were deteriorating with chunks missing from the corners. The areas that were painted looked like a puzzle because paint was chipping. There were maybe three or four trees throughout the entire complex which was more than six blocks long and more than three to four blocks wide, thus it was hard to find some shade or much grass. When the wind blew it was eerily similar to a Dust Storm in the Nevada Desert. My apartment building had three floors with four apartments on each floor. A large ominous tree with sturdy branches and a minute number of leaves was planted in front of our apartment. The dirt surrounded the tree like the ocean surrounds an island.

The only signs of vegetation appeared on the fringes of the dirt near the metal barriers that separated the concrete from the dirt that was supposed to function as a barrier to keep people off the grass. A foul horrendous stench of urine slapped you in the face at each entrance to the building. The stench was so powerful one would think that the hallways co-functioned as a men's urinal. The doors were made of steel, impenetrable from the outside and inside as well. Heat could not effectively escape the apartment in the summer, turning the non-air conditioned apartment into a sauna.

We had a two bedroom apartment that contained one bathroom, a kitchen and living room area. Our apartment was located on the second floor in the front of the building. The huge tree's thick branches would stretch towards our kitchen window. Me and my sister's room was on the south side of the building that had a view of other townhouses and a church, Triedstone Baptist Church, and a small grassy area below our second floor window.

Despite the fact that all the rooms aside from the bathroom had a large pain window only a small fraction of the large pain windows opened at both ends to allow fresh air inside or the heat to escape when the thermometer was malfunctioning. The floors were all linoleum tile that felt like I was walking on ice in the winter, especially when the gas had been shut off due to nonpayment. We had the basic furniture set, a coffee table, kitchen table, four chairs, couch, and used television, that was moved from my parent's room to the living room at their discretion. We had a small refrigerator and stove, and my sister and I functioned as the automatic dishwasher. Many people see their home as a place to escape, to relax ,to close out the stress of the world, a place people feel comfortable and safe; a place people seek to return. I had the complete opposite feeling towards my home. It was not a place of solace, and repose, instead it functioned as a den of hell, confusion, hatred, violence and despair.

A few days after we moved in I had to walk a few hundred yards through Longwood into an area that was unfamiliar territory. My mother directed me to go and pick my sister up from her friend's, because she was having a play date. My sister was seven years old and in the middle of first grade so she could not walk home by herself. I strolled through the area oblivious to anything other than making sure I picked up my sister. I saw other kids in the neighborhood, which didn't recognize me, and they gave me an unwelcoming look. I hurried my steps toward the apartment building, but I was stopped fifty feet short of the apartment building by a member of one of the notorious family gangs, The Mueller's. Deandre was probably the worst of the entire bunch because he was always fighting, and knew that he could count on his brothers and sister to assist him if he ever was on the losing end of an altercation.

He was a lot larger than most fifth graders. His skin complexion was much darker than most of the kids who lived in the neighborhood, but no one dared call him "midnight blue" like they would some other kid, since he was a Mueller. On this particular day he knew that I didn't live in the neighborhood, and interrupted his football game to run towards just like the guy the day before, asking me, "Where do you live?" because he knew I wasn't from this hood. I continued at a brisker pace without uttering a word, trying not to run and give him the belief that he scared me, while also trying to avoid another fight. My attempt to avoid the fight was futile. Deandre jumped in front of my path and unlike the guy on the previous date his clenched fist, struck me square on my forehead, and caused me to lose my balance but not fall.

I attempted to grab him but was unable to do so as he rushed towards me he grabbed me by my waist, lifted me in the air and drove me to the concrete. I began to punch and kick as hard as I could while he was doing the same. I was out of breath and it seemed like the fight lasted a half hour 'but it was actually over in three or four minutes. He finally stopped punching and got off of me, when I was able to say in an exasperated voice "I just moved over here." I gingerly got off the ground holding my back and ventured on to pick up my sister. The woman who was watching my sister asked, "Are you okay Mike?" "What happened to you?" I assured her I was okay even though my lip was busted, the area under my eye was slightly swollen and my clothes had dirt and grass stains. I assured her that my sister and I would be fine.

I walked home using the same path, that I did going to pick my sister up and while Deandre was there again playing catch with his friends and family, he did not confront me again, but only ran a few steps and shrugged his shoulders like he was going to attack. He simply smiled and went back towards the other group of kids. While I did not win the fight, I gained Deandre's respect and he and I never fought again; I guess it was his way of welcoming me to the neighborhood and him finding out if I was someone that could withstand growing up in Longwood. I did not enjoy the confrontation I had, but understood its significance. I knew that for me to survive in the neighborhood, I had to show the guys that I belonged. The only way for me to prove that was to not retreat when I was threatened. I had to show them that I was not someone who was prone to be taken advantage of by bullies.

I held my own and it helped me build my character, by planting a seed of being prepared and ready to meet challenges instead of walking around them, away from them, or underneath them, I instead met them head on.

THE MODERN DAY NAZARETH-LONGWOOD PROJECTS

After my paperwork approving my transfer from Miles Park to Longwood Elementary was completed, I entered the school with only two marking periods remaining in my third grade year. I made more lasting friendships in my Longwood third grade elementary class than I did in any other school. I still communicate with those friends and I only had four months to foster a relationship with them, during and after school. Longwood Elementary school was built well before I was born. It, like most of the other buildings in Longwood, were dilapidated. It housed kindergarten through the sixth grade. Most of the school aged children in, or around Longwood attended Longwood. It, however, was inferior to the other public schools located on the West side of Cleveland; which was filled predominantly with Caucasian students.

Despite the schools lack of exterior or interior aesthetic qualities, the students did possess a drive towards excellence. I noticed that right away, because of my inability to come and dominate the academic landscape, as I did previously in my old schools. There were two students that I found and immediate connection with- Mitchell Taller and Maralon Kerriweather. I had never met two students who were as passionate and talented as me, when it came to their academics. Maralon and Mitchell were the top two in the class, but I figured there was room for another student. I was eventually able to squeeze Mitchell out of the top tier, and I competed with Maralon from third grade until the initial part of my ninth grade year, when I transferred to another school. I enjoyed the friendly rivalry because I think it made us better students and ultimately helped us in the professions we eventually chose.

Maralon and Mitchell were two of the brightest individuals I have ever had the opportunity to attend school with, but it's also a tale of two people. Mitchell wound up spending some serious time incarcerated mainly, because of the associations he formed with people he believed were well intended individuals who would not lead him astray. Today, Maralon is a successful director of an agency in city government. All three of us grew up in an environment where those who lived outside possessed low expectations regarding our academic abilities, and our professional futures. Thank goodness a good number of us tied tube socks around our eyes as blind folds, and put cotton balls in our ears as ear plugs, ignoring the negative things we saw and heard.

I anticipated remaining at Longwood until a natural promotion from sixth grade to seventh grade, at Central Middle School that was located only a few streets away from our apartment. All the students in the fourth through sixth grade for the upcoming school year, however, were compelled to switch schools due to a federal law suit initiated in Cleveland, Ohio, that declared the Cleveland Public School system must be desegregated. Accordingly, Longwood was permanently closed and we transferred to Tremont elementary school in the fall of 1980.

The summer of 1980 was enlightening and difficult. I say that because I discovered one of the major reasons we were living in the Longwood Projects. While the projects were considered to be an area, where a majority of the residents were downtrodden, hopeless, lazy, shiftless, involved in criminal mischief, like gang activity, muggings, burglaries, rapes, murders, domestic violence my parents were lured there to the availability of drug.

During the summer after we arrived in Longwood my sister and I obviously had more time to spend at home and thus was either outside playing or in the apartment pestering my mother. I noticed something that I was not aware of because I was at school during the day, and it was that we had a lot of traffic in and out of our apartment. My parent's friends, our neighbor down the hall and our neighbor right below us would come into the house and head to my parents' bedroom and then the door would shut. A few minutes later this horrible stench would begin to permeate the tiny apartment. It smelled like someone was burning something but the oven was not on at the time. It was not a sweet savory smell like barbeque ribs, cooking on an open grill on July 4th either. It was distinctly different from the marijuana smell that we would also be subjected too shortly after, or before this other atrocious awful smell.

It was more reminiscent of the smell one encounters if they drive by a factory located in the inner city; burnt boiled eggs A few moments after the smell dissipated the people who were in the room alighted from it and seemed as though they were in a zombie like state. While they walked out they did so quite different from the way they walked into the bedroom. Their gates were much more unbalanced, their speech was slurred, their eyes were barely open and their jaws and lips combined to make that a strange twisting gesture, from one side of their mouth to the other side. My sister and I were oblivious to our parents until their high wore off. I was aware what the signs of drug use were, because of the education we received in school and in the streets. The kids in the neighborhood discussed those types of issues and talked about people who were strung out. I knew that there was definitely something unusual about the smell that was seeping from underneath my parent's bedroom, and their resulting behavior after the smell evaporated.

One day after they had a closed room session and came out in their familiar state, I went to their bedroom. My sister and I were repeatedly told that their bedroom was off limits, unless they were in the room or they had directed us to get something out of the room. I went in the room, which had a full size bed, with a used mattresses, an old black and white television with the rabbit ear antenna, a very small closet and a large dresser with a mirror attached to it.

While none of those items were that remarkable, what did stand out was the leather belt that was curled up on the dresser, next to a spoon, a lighter, and a package that had a small amount of brown residue left inside and a hypodermic needle. I began to understand what that horrific smell was, and why my mother and father's arms, and eventually their legs had all of these marks that looked like they had been attacked by cats or any wild animals with claws. The marks were from them trying to find areas to inject themselves with the heroin they were burning from the powder form, to the liquid form and then inserting the liquid heroin into the syringe and eventually repeatedly injecting the poison into their bodies.

Upon my confirmation of my worst fears I would try to find peace in other areas of the neighborhood, especially when I knew my parents were in the bedroom with the door closed. I would leave the apartment and venture to an all concrete playground, the Willy Walls. The Willy Walls was a symbolic place because it helped in the construction of the character of the kids that lived in the neighborhood. It was a very intimidating, unforgiving, it helped to increase one's agility and mobility, and it increased one's desire to engage in risk taking. Most adults would not attempt the jumps or playing tag in the Willy Walls let alone allow their children to play in the concrete playground. It was an imposing place that the faint of heart need not enter or watch kids play in for that matter. I was ignorant to where the Willy Walls name derived from, and none of the kids who I played with in the Willy Walls knew the origin either.

The Willy Walls was primarily used by the male kids who lived in Longwood. There were two games played in the Willy Walls. The first game was the challenge, which involved a group of individuals trying to match or better the current king of the Willy Walls in jumps from wall to wall. The second game was tag on the Willy Walls which got pretty exciting at times. It was simply the same type of tag that most kids played in neighborhoods across the country; however, this game was played on the walls themselves.

The surrounding walls were also a part of the playground. It was the shortest and most accessible wall to most participants. It was maybe two or three feet tall and eight to ten inches in width. It took balance of a gymnast on the balance beam and the speed of a sprinter to run on the wall and avoid being tagged by the person designated as "It" (The person required to tag the other players). In addition to the short gray concrete wall there was a fence that was in the corner of the Willy Walls, that connected the small wall to another gray, but a little larger wall. In order to navigate the fence one had to show extraordinary balance, because it had a metal top, that was surrounded by bushes and it was maybe two inches wide. Inside of the Willy Walls were several small, medium and large walls.

Additionally, the walls were four to five feet away from one another, and as I stated some were five to six feet high which made ones jump from one wall to the other more, or less difficult depending on where you alighted to where one landed. During the game of tag most people made the two feet together, flat footed jumps from one wall to the other or from a wall to the fence or a fence to a wall. The most dangerous and treacherous times in the Willy Walls occurred; when we played tag after it rained and the player who was it, chased a person towards the fence. The person would be compelled to either jump inside the Willy Walls landing on its concrete floor or traverse the slippery metal piece over the fence, and risk slipping and causing a severe injury. I've watched many unsuccessful people who tried to jump from one wall to another and miss the landing and fall backwards off the wall striking their head on the concrete. I've seen kids break bones when they jumped and their feet never made it to the top of the wall and their knees instead struck the unrelenting brick wall.

I was a victim of such an incident wherein, I was playing tag and was actually being chased and decided to avoid the tag, and take on the fence, after a torrential rain. One of my friends was "It", and had chased me from the small surrounding grey wall towards the fence. I jumped about two feet into the air on top of the fence and placed my six or seven foot shoe on the metal piece of the fence and began to run. I didn't even look back, when I felt my foot slip off the metal fence. My reflex was to reach for the fence; unfortunately there was a piece of metal that had become unhedged from the fence that sliced my left thumb down the middle as I hit the ground. Blood spewed everywhere. I jumped up, ran into the house and showed my mother. She called my father and they drove me to the hospital, I had four stitches placed into my thumb. As soon as I was released from the doctor I went back out to the Willy Walls determined to be the King.

In order to become King you had to beat the reigning champ, by executing certain jumps throughout the Willy Walls. It was similar to horse in basketball, wherein the King would complete a jump and if the challenger didn't make it then he would receive a strike. If the King could not complete a jump, he called before he jumped then the challenger would be given the chance to make a jump, and therefore give the King the chance of losing his title. The first person to accumulate three strikes lost the match.

I returned a few weeks later with the intent of claiming the title. I spent hours on the Willy Walls away from my apartment especially after the door was shut or soon after another round of vicious violence ensued. I practiced jumping with one foot to another wall and landing with one foot. I practiced jumping off of two feet and landing with two feet. I practiced jumping off one foot and landing with two feet, and jumping off two feet and landing with one. I practiced jumping from one part of the large wall to a small portion of a small wall. I then practiced jumping from a portion of a small wall to a large wall using all the above stated jumping and landing positions. I figured consistent preparation would lead to success. It would be a theme that I embodied throughout my educational, athletic and professional pursuits.

My dedication paid off when I faced an older more experienced King one day. I think he was initially taking it easy on me' because of my size and age. The King made his single leg jump from the red wall to the taller white wall on a one legged landing. I quickly followed and completed the same jump. He then jumped made a flat footed two leg jump from the white wall back to the red wall on a two legged flat footed landing. I followed that jump as well. He then attempted to make a single leg jump from the bottom of the white wall, to the top of the red wall with a one legged landing, but his foot slipped off the wall giving me the opportunity to make the jump and take a one strike lead.

I made sure my shoes were tied, I took a deep breath and I leaped with one leg and landed on the red wall with my right foot and my left leg dangling. I DID IT!! My confidence went through the roof. I made a number of easy jumps from the big walls to the smaller walls to set up my last two big jumps. I then, went back to the same jump the King had missed. I made it and then stood, and dared him to make it. After he missed it I understood why; he was taller than me and his center of gravity was not as low as mine, and therefore it caused his balance to be off. I decided to kill two birds with one stone on my next jump. I wanted to take the title and also conquer my fears about the fence. I marched over to one of the other medium level walls that were parallel to the fence; people use to access the fence by simply stepping a few feet in the air from the small surrounding wall.

The other medium level wall however, was rarely used especially during tag; it was only used in the case of last resort. Usually, people were making the jump from the fence to the wall not the opposite way. I, however, was always up for a challenge; it would define my life. I decided to do the most difficult jump- jumping from a lower location, with a single leg jump to a two footed landing on a metal ledge that was only three to four inches wide. I tied my shoes, took a deep breath, and said a little prayer before I leaped into the air, and my feet rose, I ascended and then landed on the metal part with a thud. I then looked like a novice skater trying to remain vertical with my arms falling a. The oohs and awws, by the crowd that gathered didn't shake me, and I was able to gain my balance. I grabbed the bushes, only after I was able to balance myself on the fence, which was legal. The King refused to do the jump and congratulated me. I don't think I ever smiled so hard or so wide.

The King gave me a high five and left while most of my friends my age said "YOU WON AND YOU JUST MOVED OVER HERE !!" I responded simply by saying "Whew!" I knew that taking the title, would gain respect with the older kids as well. Being respected was probably better than being feared in my neighborhood. Generally, those who were feared didn't have many friends, because most people didn't want to be around them that often. If, however, you were respected you had a number of friends and peers that didn't mind associating with you. You didn't have to be involved in criminal mischief, gang activity or assaulting people just for fun, to gain the respect needed to survive in the hood.

I wasn't satisfied by just winning; I wanted to maintain my crown. It would be difficult; in fact I lost it within a few weeks but then won it back. The title would move from one kid to another kid throughout the year, except for winter of course; we were strong and tough kids but not foolish. I also found peace in the Cleveland Public Mobile Library that was a converted massive recreational vehicle (Also known as a RV).

I could see the huge mobile home, with its white exterior, six huge wheels come around the corner each Wednesday during the summer, because we did not have a local library within reasonable walking distance. The RV was loaded with so many stories that took me away from the despondent atmosphere that permeated my home and my surroundings. I was more likely to have a conversation with a wino, prostitute, gang member or a drug addict than I would a high school graduate, college graduate or a professional. It was this thirst for knowledge that kept me from being distracted by the horrific events that were unfolding around me. I would have to employ the tactic of avoiding distractions throughout my life, just as I did in California and education was always the refuge for me. I was able to effectively use that tool even before I had the Willy Walls or the RV when I was in California.

My uncle, father, mother and my uncle's friend were all encamped in a room at my Aunt Gina Ryan's (Before she married my Uncle Chuck) shooting up Heroin. I was oblivious to their behavior and my Aunt Gina, an educator, sat with me and helped me read while we waited for them to finish. She said she knew that I would be something special because I was able to block out the negativity that surrounded me and focus on something that was nourishing and helpful for my future.

Despite the lack of exterior motivation I had an internal drive to make my life better. I bought into the things that my teachers were saying and what I heard sporadically in the media "A mind is a terrible thing to waste." "People can take everything away from you, but they could never take away your education." "Education is the key to opening doors for you in the future." I believed that reading more often in the summer would make me more prepared for the next school year. It also occupied my time and kept me from listening and watching my parents argue and/or my father assault my mother. I also got a reprieve from smelling the burning drugs. When I read, I was able to imagine worlds far from mine. Worlds that were serene, worlds where parents expressed love towards one another, worlds where parents weren't abusing drugs, and worlds full of elegance and beauty.

I read about science, math, fiction and non-fiction to broaden my mind. I spent every permissible minute inside the RV; it didn't hurt that they had air conditioning on the RV as well. I was upset when I was ordered to leave, but I didn't leave empty handed. I left with some armor in the form of the books, some armor to protect my mind and my sanity. I passed the time in between the RV library's weekly visits, by playing in the Willy Walls, reading the books I checked out from the RV, playing imaginary baseball or football games and playing football with the other boys in the neighborhood. I developed a passion for the game well before, I moved to Longwood.

Additionally, I was faster than most of the kids I played against, and more athletic. I would generally play the position of wide receiver, because most of the kids couldn't keep up with me, and I was usually open for a pass. I, however, was not the kid who always got open and the ball bounced off my stone hands. In fact, Deandre and I became better friends when he nicknamed me "Magic Hands", based upon my ability to make some of the most difficult, outrageous and acrobatic catches most of the kids had ever seen. I was also able to take some of the pent up frustration I had out in a legal way, against some of the kids I was tackling or blocking. I was not out of control, but instead probably was more aggressive than my counterpart's because of the anger I had for my parents actions.

I couldn't literally strike out against him, so I did it vicariously through the guys I was tackling. I made sure that I didn't do anything improper that would have resulted in an injury to any of the players. It was here on the football field that I realized I could control the outcome to a degree, and like in the classroom I began to dedicate myself to being one of the best. I recognized I had a certain talent level, but knew that I needed more development and thus I worked hard at improving my skills. Whenever I could get my hands on a football, I would try to coax any and everyone to play catch with me for hours. I was even successful in getting my mother, after she'd just gotten high to help me; that was only for a few minutes.

My father played with me a couple of times before he was summoned by my mother to come inside, and away they went back into their bedroom. I would spend a sufficient amount of time just throwing the football up in the air and bending my head backwards, which simulated a spinning spiral football coming towards me. I simply put my hands up and made a spade shade with my two thumbs and index fingers. I would repeat that action anywhere between twenty to thirty times.

A DIFFERENT WORLD

I waited with eager anticipation for the summer to end, so that I could begin the fourth grade at Tremont Elementary school. Tremont was located on the west side of Cleveland. Most of the kids had nervous energy about attending a new school. This would be my sixth school, despite the fact that I had only been attending school for five years. The nervous energy was due to the fact that I would be going to a school for the first time, where everyone did not look like me.

My school population went from being predominantly African American to forty-nine percent, with two percent Hispanic, and forty-nine percent Caucasian. Tremont was located in the area of town that was not predominantly African American. In fact a majority of the people in the Tremont neighborhood were not receptive to our arrival. Some of the people in the neighborhood believed that we were being forced on the school and neighborhoods based upon a ruling in the Federal District Court of the Northern District of Ohio, which required the Cleveland Public Schools to desegregate.

On the first day of school I waited at our bus stop which was approximately one hundred yards away from our apartment on Community College Avenue. I had new pants, new shoes and a new shirt and was anxious about my new school. I stood there with the other kids playing, laughing and talking until the bus arrived. This was my first time riding a school bus so I was excited.

Once we boarded the bus the anxiety and excitement turned into fear, especially after we got on the freeway. While we only traveled about ten miles it seemed like 100. When we descended from the exit ramp, I noticed the homes looked like those I read about in my books: beautiful, clean, maintained, rich; they didn't look like the homes in the neighborhoods where I lived. The streets, sidewalks, and the yards were devoid of litter and debris, something that was a constant site in some of the neighborhoods where I lived. The lawns were so green that one would think that the Cleveland Indians landscaping crews were responsible for the upkeep of those lawns. I felt uneasy, because it was like I was in a different world. My fear was heightened when it took us several minutes to actually enter the school, because we had to circle the school many times due to the protestors that were surrounding the school. I stepped off the bus with some trepidation but entered the school awaiting my new teacher and friends.

Mr. Sopko, my fourth grade teacher, was excellent. He was average height, but to me he looked like he could suit up for the Cleveland Cavaliers. He wore glasses with thick black frame which made him look very intelligent, and for the first time in my educational career my teacher's skin color would not be similar to mine. He was a great communicator and he didn't show any favoritism, discrimination, nor was he condescending or lenient. He did not set low academic expectations for his students of color; he expected all of his students irrespective of color to do well. We were all given the same material, same tests, and the same amount of time to complete assignments and tests. We received, the same overall opportunities to succeed.

I got hooked on the multiplication fact tests sheets. When I did the first one I didn't do well because I didn't realize the time was so limited. I, however, did progressively better after the first one and began to master the sheets as the year progressed. My improvement was a direct result of Mr. Sopko's passion for teaching. I believe he got a charge out of seeing us develop into better students and better citizens. I am not naive to believe that there was no racial animus among many of the students but Mr. Sopko made sure that it never manifested itself in the classroom.

In addition to my math skills being developed, my reading and comprehension were greatly improving; partly due to my summer reading and Mr. Sopko's passion for reading. He introduced me to Raymond Bradbury, a science fiction author whose books I read earnestly as a child, after Mr. Sopko's class. The book that had a lasting effect on me was "Fire Starter." It was intense, intriguing, and educational. I learned writing patterns and how to be descriptive in my own creative and academic writings. I was interested in reading because I enjoyed the subject of the book. I started Mr. Sopko's class as an average student, something I was not accustomed to doing and with hard work and dedication to understanding Mr. Sopko's teaching methods, and expectations, I concluded the year as one of the top students.

I was able to overcome the challenges that Tremont caused and the chaos at home, by staying focused on my education and praying at each meal and every night before I went to bed. I would not allow my transfer to a school in an unfamiliar hostile and uninviting area of town impact my ability to remain a high achiever. I worked hard and became more accustomed to how things worked academically. I was able to divert my attentions away from my parent's drug use towards my homework and studying. I avoided joining gangs, despite the requests to do so, because I only associated with those who belonged to gangs when I was playing football or playing in the Willy Walls. I didn't allow the lure of easy money, wanting to be accepted, wanting to belong to a group, wanting to avoid being deemed lame or wanting protection to convince me to join the number of gangs that existed throughout my neighborhood. I knew that jail, the hospital or the cemetery were the potential places I would more than likely find myself if I decided to join a gang.

My fourth grade year ended in the spring of 1981, and my summer was similar to the previous one. I again was present at home with both parents, because now neither parent was working and I was a witness to the constant violence and drug usage. I again sought the same sources of refuge that I used the previous summers to avoid the barrage of blows the stench of sulfur burning and the high degree of despair. So it was back to the Willy Walls, library on the RV, playing catch football and baseball by myself or with my friends. I also began swimming at the local pool that was about a block away from our apartment.

It was this summer, however, that my parents' drug abuse exacerbated, essentially growing out of control. The drugs became more readily available for them, because of the relationships they had forged with other addicts and dealers in the neighborhood. Instead of my parents shooting up drugs occasionally, it seemed like they were doing it every day. It wouldn't be just them but it would be a steady stream of derelicts coming in and out of our apartment and back to my parent's room. The individuals were all shapes and sizes, both male and female but they were all African American. I was puzzled as to how my parents were acquiring the funds to purchase the Heroin, because neither one had a job.

I noticed during the first month that we were out of school, June of 1981, that the third week we ran out of food. The lack of sufficient food in our home was attributable to my parents failure to use the food stamps, that were provided as part of the public assistance program my mother was a part of, in the proper manner; they essentially committed food stamp fraud. While they purchased some of the food during the first week of each month with food stamps, our cupboards and the refrigerator would literally be bare towards the middle to end of the month. I would go back to the refrigerator and cupboards maybe two times an hour just praying that food would magically appear. I, however, was thoroughly disappointed when I opened the fridge and cupboards and the only thing present was an echo. The lack of food was attributed to my parents conversion of food stamps into cash. They would take a particular amount of food stamps that was more than the amount they would receive in cash from the grocery store. The grocery store owner was lawfully permitted to receive a cash amount from the government for the amount they reported to the government. My parents would then take the cash and purchase more drugs and accordingly leave me and my sister foraging for food.

We were fortunate, during the summer, some of those days during the week that a free lunch was provided by the recreational centers, or the two churches in our neighborhood. They would provide a sandwich; a piece of fruit and either juice or milk. My small stomach would devour what amounted to a snack for most kids like it was a steak dinner. I would wake up in the morning knowing that there wasn't anything in the home to eat. I would be so hungry that it felt like my stomach was scratching my back. I would wait outside the church or recreational center shortly before noon, like a lion stalks a Gazelle right before it pounces. I would sometimes take the brown paper bag lunches and eat them away from the location because I didn't want any of my friends to see me begging for food. I would sometimes, if a couple of people I knew were getting a lunch as well, sit inside the recreational center or church and eat alongside the young people I knew, figuring they were as bad off as me.

There, however, were days on the weekends when school was not in session and throughout the week during the summer that times got extremely dicey, because the recreational center was closed and the church wasn't serving free dinners or lunches on Sundays. Therefore, we were forced to just bear it to next day. There were many nights I simply cried or rocked myself to sleep to avoid thinking about eating. My body was able to build a defense mechanism that allowed me to still be able to function despite the lack of nutrition. When one is deprived of a proper diet it can have negative effects on their mental and physical development. I was blessed not to have my intellect severely handicapped by the deprivation that my body was experiencing. My body and mind adapted and I was able to survive off a little or nothing and yet still be able to compete academically against those who had enough or an abundance.

There, however, was one particular incident that epitomized the dilemma my sister and I experienced were in when it came to our nutritional needs. One day during the summer I was extremely hungry and it was one of those days that was close to the end of the month. I opened the refrigerator and there wasn't anything edible inside unless mold is edible, but since we didn't have an infection, and penicillin had been discovered already I didn't need that mold. I opened the cupboards that I could reach, only to see the faded brown doors reveal a vast emptiness.

I then remembered that my mom had bought a box of crackers earlier in the month. The crackers were usually placed on the top shelf of the cupboard and I couldn't reach it without a boost. I then got a chair, stood my short skinny frame on top of the chair and then reached on the top shelf of the cupboard. I was able to grab the box of crackers. My mouth was watering like Niagara Falls I couldn't wait to bite into those crackers. I jumped off of the chair with the box of crackers in my right hand and landed with a bright smile and little giggle. I was disappointed when I looked inside the box, because there was only one wrapper remaining. I could not tell how many crackers were left because the wrapper was not transparent. I reopened the wrapper that contained a few crackers and before I could stick my hand inside to get the crackers I noticed that the crackers were moving by themselves.

I was initially startled and for good reason because I discovered that there were three or four brown adult cockroaches inside the wrapper eating the crackers. I threw the box in the trash since I did not want to fight the roaches for those crackers and sadly I went the rest of the day hungry again. Lack of proper nutrition can have an impact on a person's ability to learn to focus and to be motivated. I, however, was able to continue to thrive despite, not having a steady healthy diet. The lack of food at home increased during the next school year, but because we were eligible for the free breakfast and lunch meals that were provided by the government I ate well during the week for breakfast and lunch. I dreaded the weekends because I found it very difficult to find nourishment the latter weeks of the month. When we weren't missing complete meals we were only eating hot dogs without the bread. I would cut it up in pieces to stretch the meal. On other occasions I would eat a piece of bread and hope that it would tide me over until the next time I ate.

My father's increased substance abuse also lead to more serious violent maulings against my mother that extended beyond our apartment building. One day my father came home after being out with his friends, while my mother was visiting one of her friends at a town house. The townhouse was approximately one hundred yards from our apartment building. Apparently he and my mother had a disagreement either before he left or while he was gone, because he approached my mother as I was sitting outside with my friends and didn't even acknowledge me. He pulled my mother by her arms outside the townhouse and began to yell and scream at her. My mother exchanged unpleasant words with him as well. He then persuaded my mother to go over to the car as he got in the driver side. As they were still yelling and screaming at each other, they began to bring more attention to themselves and people started to watch them more closely, including me and my friends.

Then all of sudden, to my surprise (because there were so many people watching), my father hauled off and punched my mother square in the face. Her head and neck snapped back. He then grabbed her by her hair with his left hand and drove the car with his right hand down the parking lot towards our apartment. He drove slow enough that he could hold onto my mother and simultaneously keep the car moving. My mother tried valiantly to remove my father's super grip by scratching, clawing and pulling his hand, but could only eventually grip the door area and jog alongside of the car to preclude being dragged. He did this while stating to my mother "SO YOU WANT TO SHOW OUT IN FRONT OF THESE PEOPLE?" " I ran alongside the car and yelled for my father to turn my mother loose, but his eyes were filled with rage akin to that of a starving man, whose last morsel of food was snatched from his mouth as it was falling from his fingertips.

My father was able to park the vehicle, as well as could be expected, in a parking spot near our apartment. He then dragged my mother upstairs by her neck threw her in the apartment and began to punch, strike ,and kick her mercilessly from the kitchen, through the living room and into their bedroom. I heard the door slam and heard the pounding against the wall and bed. My knocks on the door were drowned out, by the sounds of my father's blows striking my mother's flesh and her screams of agony for him to stop.

THE BEGINNING OF THE END OF OUR FAMILY

I began my fifth grade year in the fall of 1981 with renewed confidence, because I wasn't nervous about Tremont having become acclimated to the educational expectations. I was going to the same school for a consecutive year; something I hadn't done in few years. I was excited to be back in school because I could quench my overriding thirst for more knowledge. I wasn't embarrassed about my clothing like I was for at least half the school year and the summer, because I had on new school clothes. My parents were kind enough to send us to school with new clothes for at least three days during the first week. I was then, resigned to wear those same clothes for the remainder of the year. I didn't receive any new clothes during the school year despite the fact that I was growing albeit, at a snail's pace compared to my friends but growing nonetheless.

Thus, my pants looked more like skinny jeans and Michael Jackson flood look-a-likes, by the time the middle of the school year and summer rolled around. Additionally I had three good pair of underwear each year that I was forced to consistently wash out. While I would usually have five pairs of underwear, the poor quality of the underwear made them susceptible to extensive damage. I had man made air conditioning in my underwear. My underwear had so many holes in them when I put them on I looked like I was wearing "brown" and white poke-a-dots underwear. I was also forced to use the same soap most kids bathed with to wash my clothes so as to remove the horrible odor and stench that permeated through the clothes over the weeks and months; I saw myself as the "Pig Pen" from Peanuts. I got more mileage out of a pair of sneakers than most children.

I was the consummate boy and wanted to play, run and jump as often as I could which meant that my shoes would take a beating. Unfortunately for me, I didn't receive the shoes with the best quality. Also, since my parents weren't focused on replacing most of our worn clothing items, due to other priorities, I was forced to wear the shoes beyond their general usefulness. I would wear shoes until my toes were bruised because they were crammed at the top of the shoe trying to burst out. I would seldom go out when it rained because the bottom of my shoes were filled with holes and thus my dirty dingy socks would be susceptible to getting wet. It should be self-evident that if my parents didn't find food to be a necessity for us, then clearly clothing and detergent would be even lower on their list of necessities.

Despite the latter circumstances, I seemed to really come into my own with respect, to my understanding and focus when it came to my education. My homework, class work, tests and quizzes, were supposed to be more difficult, but fifth grade seemed easier. I simply tuned out the violence that was perpetuated throughout my home and community as well as, the criminal behavior that was a constant.

I determined that I could not control my father's merciless assaults; I couldn't control my parents overwhelming desire to strap that belt around their arms to make their veins more pronounced, and then inserting a needle filled with heroin in liquid form into their veins. I couldn't control their neglect, and abuse that was exacerbated by the drug use. I could, however, control whether I studied for a test; I could control whether I completed my homework; I could control whether or not I did the work to obtain an A on a test ,or didn't do the work and earned a F. I could control whether or not I would ask questions, if I didn't know a particular area for a specific subject; I could control whether I would comply with the rules established by my teachers, the administrators, and those who had authority over me in the community.

Notwithstanding my parents lack of overview, I didn't manipulate the situation to act out of control but instead I did just the opposite and focused on what could help me rise above my current situation. It was in Fifth grade, when I truly realized that I could use my education as the tool to construct a better life for me in the future. I knew that it would require a great deal of sacrifice, but I looked around and decided that I didn't like where I was and knew I was destined for something better. I refused to let my circumstances be insurmountable obstacles to my success.

Accordingly, when our lights were cut off I used the light from the street corner to illuminate the pages on the books I was reading. When the gas was turned off I did my homework as soon as I got home instead of waiting until later in the evening, when it would be colder inside the apartment and uncomfortable to do homework. It was difficult to write when you're blowing on your fingers to keep them warm. I didn't let the fact that our water was shut off to stop me from studying for a test or a quiz. It was that focus that gave me a smile that was wider than Lake Erie when I received my grades for the first marking period, during my fifth grade year. When anyone read my report card instead of it sounding like they were stuttering (D,D,D,D,D,D) it actually sounded like they were trying to get someone's attention (A,A,A,A,A,A)!!

I saw the distractions that surrounded me like worrisome fruit flies, ones that annoy you but can't really disturb you to the point that you become frustrated and refuse to continue with your appointed tasks, and I simply shooed those fruit flies away. My mother's shift in apparel to long sleeve shirts with turtle necks and pants, to hide the track marks that were on her body due to her constant attempts to find new paths for the intravenous needles didn't distract me. My father's constant comatose state or his enraged violence didn't distract me. The horrific event on Christmas day in 1981 wasn't a distraction either.

My sister and I woke up on Christmas day like we had on other Christmas days in the past. This Christmas was unusual because we didn't have that many things underneath the tree. The tree looked more like a coat hanger with pine branches attached to it than a pine tree, because of the lack of funds my parents had to purchase a healthy one. There weren't many ornaments on it because too many would tip the poor tree over. Additionally, the things that we had were very inexpensive, since two of the toys broke that morning. In fact the only toy that survived longer than two weeks was the one I received from the Salvation Army that was giving toys away before Christmas for the underprivileged kids. It was also different because my mother and father had been having some intimacy issues. In fact my father had actually started sleeping with one of my mother's friends who just happened to live in the apartment on the floor beneath ours.

My father's presence that morning was shocking but nonetheless appreciated by my sister and I, and my mother as well because he alighted from the back bedroom with his hair matted, no shoes, no shirt and his beltless pants to watch my sister and I open and play with our gifts. After about an hour of playing with the toys, my mother, in her tattered robe and heavy eyes retired to the bedroom with my father, leaving me and my sister in the living room with our toys. Approximately thirty to forty-five minutes later, there was a knock at the door. My mother went to the door thinking that maybe it was one of her friends only to hear the deep voice on the other side say in response to my mother's inquiry "Who is it?', "We are Detectives Smith & Jones from the Cleveland Police Department we need to speak to you." My mother told them to wait because she was not dressed. I was perplexed, which was evident from my facial expression wherein my eyebrows were arched, my lips pinched tightly and my eyes slanted because my mother's robe was in no way revealing.

She then went closer to the bedroom and stated "You say you're the police", clearly in earshot of my father who was hurriedly trying to get dressed. He was contemplating jumping out the window which would of allowed him to land two stories down on a hill of grass, however, there were two detectives staged on the side of and in back of the apartment building. My mother moved towards the door because the detectives were threatening to knock the door down if she didn't open it immediately. She pulled the chain off the door and opened it since our lock was broken and we were only able to keep people out via the chain. The detectives entered and sat my mother down at the kitchen table and grilled her about my father's whereabouts. She initially denied knowing where he was or when she last spoke to him. I, however, heard them threaten to arrest and charge her for Obstruction of Official Business and thus requiring the Department of Children and Family Services to be awarded emergency temporary custody. My mother eventually relented and told them my father was in the back room.

The large robust detective, with his red cheeks that made him look like a Santa Claus clone, his tan trench coat and pure white hair stood, with his gun brandished, headed back towards my parents' bedroom and yelled for my father to put his hands up and stand away from the bedroom door. A few minutes afterward the detective emerged from the back area with my father in handcuffs and my sister and I watching and crying as he was led away to jail. My father had been identified as a suspect in an aggravated burglary, and the detectives had been looking for him for a while. They had been watching the apartment, but since my dad had been in between our apartment, his girlfriend's apartment and other places they couldn't catch him, until he let his guard down on Christmas.

Things got progressively worse after my father was in jail for a few weeks and we had very minimal contact, other than traveling to the Justice Center to see him. My sister and I became frequent visitors at the Justice Center. We were there so much, they should have given us permanent badges that we could carry home and bring back with us on visiting day to the tall imposing building housed the Cleveland Municipal and Cuyahoga County Courts, the Cleveland Police Headquarters and the Cuyahoga County Jail. My sister and I knew the routine for entering the jail: remove your shoes, empty your pockets take off your hat, raise your arms, and for my Grandmother Lula which was embarrassing for her she was forced to remove her wig. We would have to wait for my grandmother or mother to give the guard at the window money so that my father or uncle could pay for commissaries at the jail.

We then were moved to a waiting area, and told to be patient until they were able to locate the prisoner we came to see. Once the prisoner was located we were taken through a series of large steel cold doors that had one window to allow you to look through to the outside world. Once we made it through one door the door behind us would slam, making a jarring sound that scared me the first few times I visited relatives. We then were sent into a room that was similar to a cafeteria, with a table and sat across from my father at one time, then my uncle another time and even my cousin. We got a chance to talk, laugh, reminisce, and hold hands and hug. The hardest part was releasing their hands after only a half an hour which at times seemed like a few seconds. They were whisked back into their holding area to wait until they were escorted back to their cells.

I returned to school after the holiday season with the same focus and desire to learn that I left with on the last day before the break. It was reflective in my grades which continued with straight A's for the second marking period. I was able to transfer the anger and distress that my father's absence was taking on our family, to something positive in the form of continuing to excel at school. I vowed not to follow in my father's, uncle's or cousin's footsteps. I didn't want my children to experience the things I did, so I worked extremely hard to avoid placing myself in the position that my parents found themselves in. I didn't think that just doing the work to simply get by would be good enough to rise above the low expectations, that were being heaped on me by the media, community and those around me, who knew about our dysfunctional family situation.

I believed for me that the key to reaching heights that most kids in my neighborhood only saw on television or the movies was to never be satisfied with being average. I would be upset if I received a C on a paper, test, quiz, or any assignment for that matter and would work even harder in preparation for the next test, quiz, paper or assignment ,so that I could avoid that feeling again. I knew it didn't take much effort to be average or marginal but that a good deal of work and sacrifice was necessary for me reach the level, I knew I could attain if I stayed focused, faithful and worked harder than everyone else.

I was not attending church as regularly as I did a few years ago, yet I was occasionally able to receive some biblical instructions from the pastor at TriedStone Baptist Church which was a stones' throw away from our apartment. I also continued to pray before the few meals I ate as well as every night I went to sleep. I continued to believe that our family struggled, me and my sister particularly, because God destined something greater for us and he was simply building my character ,knowing I would have to recall and rely on the things I learned in these tough situations to help myself as wells as others in the future.

My mother began to rapidly deteriorate after my father's absence became more routine. He was dealing with his case and also trying to please two women. He eventually moved to an apartment which was a few blocks away from my Grandma Lula's house. My sister and I visited only a few times. My mother lost about ten pounds off her frame that could not afford to lose an ounce. Her desire for drugs outweighed her desire for food.

While their separation was good for my mother physically, she could not emotionally handle his decision to move and curtail the time he spent with all of us. I didn't let his absence or my mother's conduct derail me from doing everything in my power to keep the straight A's for all marking periods. Accordingly, when I received my report card for both the third and fourth marking periods I didn't have anything but A's. I was proud and excited. What made me even more elated was that, when we had our end of the year awards ceremony, my parents were the only parents who found their way over to Tremont for the acknowledgments. They both walked in with tattered wrinkled clothing that smelled like mildew. My mother was wearing an old and scruffy dress with worn flat shoes while my father was wearing his unkempt hair, thick beard, untrimmed mustache and his tight shirt and pants. Their eyes were blood shot red and their chins twitching, which was evidence that they had been shooting up before they arrived.

I was happy because they were the only parents present but somewhat embarrassed because of their attire and overall demeanor. Most of the kids didn't know they were my parents or if they did they didn't make me feel any worse because they didn't say many mean or insensitive remarks. I received several awards for my academic accomplishments and was able to share that one bright moment with my mother and father, not knowing that there wouldn't be many more after that point.

Approximately two weeks after our summer began my parents took me and my sister downtown on a sight-seeing adventure. It was June 28, 1982. My father came over and got us dressed in what was considered our best, which was like rags to most people, he had a nice shirt that he must have borrowed and my mom wore the same dress she wore to the awards ceremony. We visited places we had never gone before like the Mather ship that was docked on Lake Erie that was now a museum. We also visited Cleveland Municipal Stadium, although it wasn't open at that time.

My father snuck us all in and I got a chance to personally see the field that the Cleveland Browns and Cleveland Indians use, I had only seen it on television. I was excited because I loved all sports, but I knew about the history of those storied franchises and I loved anything and everything in Cleveland. I saw how small the field looked in comparison to the vastness of the stadium itself. I wanted to run on the field but my father restrained me and said "Michael if you do, then I am going to wear a hole in your ass." I believed that he would because despite his own inability to comply with established rules, he made sure my sister and I did. We both received whippings with belts and my parents hands when we did something wrong. They used the following philosophy to discipline us "Do as I say not as I do." After we left the stadium they bought us a hot dog, chips and something to drink from the hot dog stand near the Justice Center.

We then walked up the brick laden steps that lead to the Justice Center. I was not unfamiliar with the Justice Center because we had visited my father several times since he was arrested that past Christmas. The Justice Center was a scary building for me, because I was little and everything seemed so massive. The darkened windows didn't seem to allow much light to penetrate inside maybe because there was so much darkness inside. This place was built to determine the truthfulness of some of the most heinous allegations, committed by human beings against other human beings. The lighting inside was dull and drab. The sheriffs weren't friendly but instead were stern and rigid. The elevators squeaked and rocked when we entered them, which made the trip even more nerve wrecking for me. We traveled for approximately thirty seconds to the twenty second or twenty-third floor and alighted from the elevator, after it dinged for us to exit.

We then entered a courtroom and sat in the back with my mother while my father continued beyond the barriers that were reserved for attorneys, their clients and court personnel. Eventually, an elderly, Caucasian male, with gray hair, glasses and a black robe entered from around the corner and sat on the bench. The courtroom had an eerie feeling because it was quiet, callous feeling, the stripes that functioned as wall paper cause me to be dizzy, and I couldn't wait until we left. The Caucasian male that was assisting my father, his attorney, the other attorney who was sitting close to the box area with the twelve seats inside and Judge Fred Guzzo began to speak to one another. I was not paying attention to their conversation until Judge Guzzo asked my mother if she had anything to say on behalf of my father before he sentenced him. My mother said in between her sobs and while she had her arms draped around me and my sister "We don't want to see him go to jail, I brought his kids for you to see that he has a family and they need him."

I was initially upset because it felt like we were being used as pawns to either have my father's time reduced or avoid any retribution for his conduct. I also felt that his absence could accelerate my mother's demise without him being near to help guide her. The next thing I heard was Judge Guzzo say to my father "You shall serve a sentence of four to twenty-five years at the Mansfield State Penitentiary." My mother then began to sob uncontrollably, which then was simply a domino effect for me and my sister. We all cried so much we could fill a dried up portion of Lake Erie. The deputy sheriff put the handcuffs on my father and escorted him through the doors while me, my sister and mom left the courtroom and rode the bus back to our apartment in Longwood; what a way to start a summer vacation.

My heart and my mind reacted differently to that situation. I didn't want my father being escorted to jail. I loved him and didn't want him to be away from us for so long. Notwithstanding the situation, he placed us in, I didn't wish anything bad upon him and I believed that jail would be worse than living in the condition he left us in. I knew that my mother's physical pain would be diminished because he wouldn't have the opportunity to perpetrate any more violence on her for a significant period of time.

My mother's conduct became more outrageous and dangerous during that time. She rarely took my sister and I to see my father, we would only see him when my Grandma Lula would come and pick us and take us to Mansfield. My mother began dating some guy who had a Jerry Curl and was doing drugs. I knew the drug use continued because that burning stench persisted. Her boyfriend had a friend, who was a transvestite, who also began living with us; there were just more and more strangers in our apartment.

My sister started to spend more time with Grandma Lula, Aunt Joann and our cousins. It was getting really dangerous in our apartment. One day after my mother and another gentleman, I never met came out of the bedroom, the guy suffered a seizure as he fell to the floor and went into convulsions. I saw his eyes rolling back into his head, he began to shake uncontrollably, his tongue began to swell, a white foamy substance that looked more like cotton balls began to form around his mouth and he lost his ability to communicate. My mother, too high off the recent hit couldn't help, instead one of our neighbors entered and provided some assistance by grabbing a spoon and placing it inside this strangers mouth and stopped him from biting his tongue during this seizure. I just stood there in shock, after the man recovered; I quickly went outside because the RV had arrived.

This particular summer the Cleveland Public Library was sponsoring a contest where students would receive a prize for reading books and then completing a report on each book. I read more than fifty books and completed more than fifty reports and had the highest total of all the kids in my neighborhood which resulted in me being invited to the downtown branch to receive an award and a book. I was elated when I got that opportunity, another chance to visit downtown Cleveland but with a better ending. I entered the wonderful palace that others simply referred to as a library. The marble floors didn't impress me; the expensive and unique paintings didn't excite me, what made my eyes jump with joy or gave me more adrenaline was all the books I saw. I could understand my parents to a degree because I had an addiction to books and learning that was on par with the addiction they had for drugs. I was mesmerized by the sheer volume of the books that I saw; I could stay there forever if I were permitted too. My mother, me and my sister sat through the entire program. I received my certificate and a book that I could keep and didn't have to return after I read it. I also acquired a desire for academic awards because it was the prescription for the pain, agony, suffering and grief that I was feeling in other aspects of my life. Thus, the kid who had many reasons to give up continued to strive to do the unexpected.

GOD'S WORKING OVERTIME TO PROTECT ME

My sister was spending more time away from Longwood leaving me and my mom to fend for ourselves; or me fending for myself. I tried to stay safe by spending the night with friends instead of my mother. One reason was because there were several nights that I went to sleep with her in the apartment, only to wake up and find that she was gone and that the door was wide open, because she did not bother to tell me that she was leaving, and the apartment could only be locked from the inside. This was similar to the same type of behavior that both my parents exhibited when my sister and I were at the apartment together, but at least then they had the ability to lock the door from the outside.

Both of my parents left my sister and me alone on several occasions which resulted in some very frightening events. First, my Uncle Donnie was babysitting me and my sister one night. When we went to sleep he was in our front room watching television. My sister and I slept through the night and we didn't even realize that our door had been closed shut during the night. When I got up to enter the hallway I initially couldn't move the door, because there was something blocking it. Eventually, I was able to push the door open and was alarmed by the scene. Boxes, linen, an old broke ten speed bike, and blankets had been pushed against the door. The living room was in disarray wherein the couch and chair were on different sides from where they normally were positioned.

The pillows from the couch were a part of the debris that was in front of our door. The television was gone as well as some other economically exchangeable items. My uncle, nor my parents could be found. I calmed my sister down because she realized what I suspected, and that was the fact that we were burglarized. I directed my sister to help me put these things back together and we waited until my mother returned. My parents had disappeared due to their desire to feed their addiction.

One incident that illustrated how leaving us at home exposed us to danger occurred, when my sister, fortunately, was visiting one of our aunts. It was a particularly warm night because we kept a window open that was in the kitchen and near the large tree that sat in front of our apartment building. There was a sturdy branch that stretched directly towards our kitchen window. We were able to keep the animals and insects out via a screen, however, the screen was worn and old and eventually in order to get air into the apartment my mother agreed to forgo the screen. The need for convenience outweighed the concern that the open window allowed access to intruders. During the early morning hours, my mother had gone down the hallway to her friend's apartment with whom she routinely engaged in illegal drug usage. I woke up and realized that she was gone and decided to put the chain back on the door, turned the light on in the bathroom and kitchen and went back to sleep. While I slept and for a change had a very nice dream, all of a sudden a shadowy figure entered my dream. I saw a man who was peering through our apartment in a crouching position from side to side. An eerie feeling came over me and then a voice; I steadfastly believe it was God's voice, whispered "Wake up."

When I awoke, the dream I had, became reality because, there was actually a black male, medium size build, with a full beard and mustache, bending at his knees moving from side to side through the apartment. My heart began to race faster than Usain Bolt runs the hundred meter dash. I jumped out of my bed and asked due to my fear and anxiety and wanting him not to be an intruder or someone who would hurt me. "Hey, did Peggy let you in?" He stopped immediately stood up and said "Yeah, Peggy let me in." I walked briskly into the living room, while the guy stood up and walked towards the kitchen table. He asked me how old I was and did I like school. He sat there for about five or ten minutes and then asked me if it was okay to use the bathroom. Of course, I said, "That's fine".

While he went to go use the bathroom, I went and grabbed a wrench and sat it next to me on the couch because I had an uneasy feeling about this man. He went to the bathroom first, ran the water I believe to distract me, as he then opened my mother's bedroom door. He then re-entered the bathroom, flushed the toilet and then turned the water off. He must have been watching my mother, sister and our apartment for some time. After the toilet flushed, he came back out of the bathroom and sat down on the chair in front of me and he looked at me for what felt like thirty minutes but was actually ten minutes. My mind was still somewhat fuzzy because I had been awaken from a sound sleep, and so while the intruder claimed my mother had let him in I was still fearful. We sat across from one another and didn't say a word. He was sitting approximately thirty feet away at our kitchen table. He must have noticed the wrench that I had next to the chair because he didn't make any attempts to attack me.

Eventually, I heard my mother knock on the door because she could not get in without someone removing the chain. When I got out of the chair, mistakenly leaving the wrench because I felt secure that my mother was returning, I went towards the door and I didn't realize the guy was close behind me. I said to my mother as I unhooked the chain "Mommy do you know this man", and he then to reached over me, pushed me aside and grabbed my mother by the arm. My mother immediately sobered up and firmly placed her feet on both sides of the door and pulled as hard as she could to prevent him from pulling her through the door into the apartment. She was also scratching, screaming and punching. I was screaming and punching the intruder on the top of his head and back. Eventually, she was able to break a loose from this man and she ran back over to her friend's apartment, banged on the door yelling and screaming "let me in, let me in, let me in, please let me in!" She's crying, "LET ME IN, LET ME IN, LET ME IN," and they eventually opened the door and she entered and someone shut the door. I was standing outside in the hallway by myself.

This guy looked at me, turned , ran and jumped out of the window he had entered. I ran over to the apartment banging on the door and my mother realized that I was outside. She yells "MY BABY IS OUT THERE IN THE HALLWAY, OPEN THE DOOR !!" They opened the door and they pulled me in and they shut the door. Our apartment was wide open at this time and the rapist was gone. I was trembling and shaking because of the harrowing event. We would eventually come to find out that the man was a serial rapist and had raped three or four other women in the past month. They didn't initially want to call the police and especially not call the police over to Pat's apartment, but eventually someone called the police but all the adults left the apartment my mother included.

When the police came, I was peeking out of the window trying to see if the man was going to return and not necessarily whether the police would arrive. The police came and they made the assumption that, I did something wrong, because I was peering out the side of the curtain. Additionally, they were suspicious because I didn't initially let them into the apartment. I told them what happened but I indicated to them that this was not my apartment and that I was not given permission to let them inside; so they spoke to me from the hallway. Eventually, my mother returned prior to the police leaving the scene and she gave her statement in the hallway. I suspect that they did not want the police into the apartment because they were back there smoking drugs. My mom eventually persuaded them to conduct the remaining portion of the interview in our apartment.

The incident with the rapist was only one of several incidents which lead me to believe that I needed to get out of Longwood, before I got seriously injured.

My mother had met another man who she spent a lot of quality time with who was physically challenged due to a leg injury he suffered and he needed to be supported by a cane. I am not sure that he knew about my mother's addiction because he was a clean cut guy: His hair was always very well groomed, his mustache was pristine, his clothes were up to date for that era, and if he didn't have such a severe limp I would have thought he had a good steady job. He was a prime target for anyone but more particularly to people who knew my mother personally.

My mom, her friend and I were all sitting in the apartment when our neighbor's cousin came to the door and asked if my mother or her ei had any cigarettes, and my mother told her no she didn't have any. About five minutes later my mother's neighbor asked my mom to walk with her to the store to get some cigarettes. Approximately five minutes later my mom's friend's cousin returned and again asked "Ask your mother or her boyfriend if they have some cigarettes," and before I could say "...didn't you just ask that question a few minutes ago," a guy I had never seen before stuck a .45 caliber magnum gun in my face and told me to take the chain off, shut the fuck up and don't say another word, because I began to scream. He was at least six feet tall, over two hundred and fifty pounds, he had a mustache, with processed hair and was a shade darker than my mom but lighter than me. He stuck the barrel of the gun on my forehead.

What frightened me was that he and his partner did not have on masks. They were either confident that they would not be caught, or they weren't cold-blooded killers, and simply wanted a quick hit. I was scared to death , because I watched too many movies and had heard of other people in my neighborhood being pistol whipped or shot for any or no reason. I cowered into a semi fetal position and then as he continued into the living room I shrunk into the chair near the window where the rapist entered. The guy who initially entered the apartment told my mom's boyfriend "GET DOWN ON THE FLOOR, ON YOUR KNEES." He took my mother's boyfriend's wallet, rifled through it, took the money out, told him to take off his watch and any other jewelry that he had in his possession.

While the men were brandishing their guns and taking the small number of profit generating items from our apartment I kept my arms and hands up with my elbows firmly placed on the kitchen table. I was whispering prayers to God:" Please God provide protection for me tonight. Take away any anger or hatred from these men. Please place on their hearts the desire for property only and not blood. In Jesus name. Amen"

In addition to praying I was also looking outside the window measuring the distance and what objects if any were on the ground that would break my fall. My only fear about jumping out the window, was whether the first intruder would start shooting. Additionally his accomplice was running back and forth and I didn't know who else may have been assisting those two. My knees were banging against the table like drum sticks against the base drum. I also wanted to make sure that if they started shooting I could at least make a feeble attempt to escape and the window was my option. Thank God that I had been practicing jumping out my bedroom window in case of a fire. The kitchen window was a little more treacherous due to the huge tree, metal railing and the lack of soft grass landing that existed below my bedroom window.

My face looked like I put my entire head underneath a shower, due to all the sweat that was streaming down my head onto my face; I was scared to death. My emotions were mixed about my mother returning. Most kids feel that mothers have the ability to resolve anything and accordingly a part of me thought if my mother was there I would feel less frightened and more secure that I wouldn't be hurt. The other part of me felt that if my mother was here she may actually recognize these guys by name and face which would have placed us in a more precarious position. It probably took no more than five minutes for the entire ordeal from beginning to end; it however felt like an hour. The two men eventually left, all before my mother and her so-called friend returned.

When my mother returned I could hardly speak, because I was crying and yelling about what happened. After I calmed down and stop sniffling, my mother finally realized what I said. My mother confronted her friend and her friend's cousin when she went next door and banged on the door. My mother yelled, "BITCH YOU KNOW WHAT YOU DID WASN'T RIGHT!! IF YOU NEEDED SOMETHING, YOU COULD HAVE JUST ASKED, YOU DIDN'T HAVE TO LET THEM PLACE A GUN TO MY BABY'S HEAD." Her friend then exited the apartment, and as she towered over my mother her voice was so loud that everyone in their apartment building could hear the argument. My mother's friend says, "FUCK YOU PEGGY, I DIDN'T DO SHIT, AND YOU KNOW I WOULDN'T DO THAT TO YOU AND MIKE."

They went back and forth with one another, poking their fingers in each others face but they never struck each other. My mother walked back into our apartment and I put the chain back on the door and went to bed praying that I would make it through the night. I tried to escape from the fear, neglect, and depression, by going to Willy Walls and playing ball with some of the fellas. Going to the R.V library to past time and I was making rafts out of flats that were thrown out, by the grocery store and "sailing" in the back parking lot, after a heavy rain.

The sewers would back up and turn the parking lot into a lake. The "lake" was not as serene as some areas of Lake Erie that was only ten minutes away from where we lived, but could have been hundreds of miles away for most of us, because we didn't venture away from Longwood. I felt like Huck Finn on the river as me and friends circled on the dirty man made lake. It was a way for us to use the things we had at our disposal to bring some relief and peace. We used our imagination to make our situation appear less bleak. We made lemonade out of lemons. It only lasted for a day or so and then the rain would eventually dissipate and sometimes our hope as well.

MY EARTHLY SAVIOR-GRANDMA LULA

About a month before school began my sister decided to move in with my Grandma Lula, but I didn't follow her even though I had an overwhelming desire to get out of Longwood before I became a statistic. My concern for my mother also played a role in me staying. I wanted to continue to check on her but also move to an area where I would be safer. So I decided instead to go live in a two bedroom apartment in Euclid with my mother's friend Pat's sister, Pat and Pat's children. Since I moved with them I was able to continue to attend Tremont, because I never officially moved, and thus I was able to catch the bus and be dropped off in Longwood. Once I was in Longwood I could go and check on my mother before I rode the bus out to Euclid. Although the accommodations weren't ideal, since I was sleeping on the floor of the one bedroom apartment, I gladly accepted them in lieu of the emotional harm, abuse and neglect and exposure to danger I was encountering in Longwood.

After arriving back from school during the day I would get off the bus after school was over and try to find my mother. It was difficult at times because now with my sister, me and my father gone she had no distractions or responsibilities, so she was trying even harder to find a fix. I would wait until night fall at times to see if she would show up at the apartment. The door was always open because when she left the door had to remain open in order for her to gain access again. I don't know how she slept or if she slept. I did recall catching up to her one day in the Longwood Plaza and said with an excited voice "MA WHERE YOU BEEN, I HAVE BEEN LOOKING FOR YOU? She simply turned around, smiled and said in a faint and exhausted tone of voice "You just got out of school boy?" I said "Yea," "Why are you standing up here?" She looked at me with her mouthwatering, her hair matted and her bones protruding out of her skin and said "None ya", which means loosely translated none of your business!! I stayed much longer than I should have, because shortly afterwards a man I had never met before walked up to my mother whispered in her ear and then stuck his hand down the front of her shirt. I was confused regarding his actions initially and then he apparently made some hand transaction with my mother. I deduced what transpired and felt ashamed, embarrassed and heartbroken for my mother. Her addiction had taken her to a level that I knew was going to be difficult from which to elevate. The action did not seem to impact my mother it was as though it was routine. I left with my hands over my face to cover the tears, too bad I didn't have something to console my heart.

I kept in touch with my sister, by calling her and telling her not to reveal to my Grandma Lula that I wasn't living with my mother. Despite the apparent inconvenience of living in such small confines, and with non-family members, I felt safer than I had felt in years. I continued the academic excellence in the sixth grade that I ended the fifth grade with notwithstanding being in a different home, different city and different neighborhood. While none of the people I laid my head down next to were members of my family I knew that things were much better there than where I was months ago. I knew I could flourish because I had a little bit of peace. The peace I had, however, would be shaken one night when my Grandma Lula found out that I was not living with my mother. So she called out to Euclid and told Pat that if I didn't come and live with her that she was going to put me in foster care.

I had a decision to make, either live with my Grandma Lula and then maybe severely cut off hopes of keeping open some line of communication with my mother or stay with my mother's friend and her family and risk having the county place me into a foster home. I choose my grandma!

I choose continuing stability over unknown but potential family alienation. I did not believe that I had the wherewithal to make what amounted to an adult decision in a child's frame of mind. I understood that I had been living" independently" for a while, that did not constitute me being able to continue to make competent, effective, lawful, future developing decisions in my life. I had to stop thinking about what I could do to save my mom but instead start focusing on saving myself.

So I packed up my nap sack and moved with my Grandma Lula on E. 98th street which was off of Miles. Me and my sister were blessed to have my Grandma Lula open her home to us. She did not have any legal obligation to take care of us; that ended when she raised her youngest son Donald. My Grandmother Lula was a very strong woman. She was sort of robust, she had huge hips, and she was beautiful before the accident and sexy enough to court a man almost ten years her junior, after my grandpa William Belcher died.

Grandma Lula was the matriarch of the family which included six children and more than fifteen grandchildren at that time. She also knew how to have a good time, she liked to drink and party but never to excess. She was the quintessential matriarch of the black family that you see; Strong black woman that controlled her family, a trait that she passed down to her daughters. They were controlling in their relationships; it was also passed down to her granddaughters. I thought Grandma Lula was rich because whenever I went to her house it was always neat, had a fresh smell and there was always something on the stove and a full refrigerator.

She never refused to give us anything that we asked for; mainly because she knew the dilemma that my sister and I were enduring. She wore what I thought was designer clothing and drove an average car. I, however, overvalued everything about Grandma Lula's because I compared it to what I had, or for that matter didn't have. Thus her house was a mansion compared to our apartment, and her refrigerator looked like the cooler at the grocery store compared to ours, her car was a limousine when compared to ours. I quickly learned that grandma was not wealthy. In fact she only lived a few blocks away from where we stayed three years ago when we lived on Gorman and while the area was not as impoverished as Longwood, it couldn't be mistaken for a suburb of Cleveland.

There was also more vegetation and accordingly more life. The green grass brought out the worms, which attracted the birds, which then attracted the squirrels. There were huge trees in back of Grandma Lula's yard which looked like a mini forest because of all the trees and, the grass that covered the area. The front yard was extremely tiny, but I spent most of my time playing down the man on my neighbor's yard which was more spacious. My grandma didn't own the home but had rented the same house for a number of years. She had lived there since we had moved back from California. The house had two bedrooms, a dining room, living room, kitchen, basement and bathroom. The basement reminded you of the ones in horror movies. The basement steps would creek and crack when you put the slightest weight on them. It was dark and gloomy and the lone light would illuminate only a corner of the basement. It appeared to be smoky because of all the cement and rock that surrounded the basement.

The rooms above the basement were small and quaint. Grandma did not intend to have more than one child or dependent in the home when she rented it, besides Uncle Donnie. Thus, when my sister and I moved in accommodations had to be made in order for us to be comfortable. There were two beds in one bedroom where my uncle and I slept. The second bedroom was located off of the living room was the only room that gave you access to the bathroom. Thus the carpet looked like the path through a grassy area that people use to cut from one street on another, because everyone had to come in and out of this bedroom to use the bathroom for any purposes. I found it difficult to sleep at night because everyone was coming in and out of our room all night long. My bed was positioned directly in front of the door to the bathroom and when the door remained open I had a clear view of a bathroom that had a roaring twenties aura. There was a cast iron white tub, with no shower, that sat in the back of the narrow bathroom. There was only two feet between the wall, and the side of the tub that wasn't against the wall.

The tub was supposed to be white but looked more like it was gray due to its age. The tub and mirror were so close you could sit on the tub's side and check your face and hair. You could then move another foot or shorter distance and use the toilet. The room felt crowded with just one person in it; if you were claustrophobic you couldn't stand in that bathroom. There was also an eerily looking wooden cabinet that was over the tub. My grandmother kept clothes, linen, and other household items in the cabinet.

While I had a bed to sleep in, my sister, however, was forced to sleep on a cot that was in the dining room. Every night she would get the cot out of the closet or my grandmother's bedroom, get the linen and the blankets and then unfold the cot and put the linen and the blanket on the cot and lay down and fall asleep inches from the dining room table. In the morning she would simply take the linen and blanket off and then fold the cot and place it in either of the above mentioned places where she retrieved it. She would do that consistently for years until my uncle moved out.

The living room was one of the largest rooms in the house. It's the only place that I could watch television, of course only after my homework and chores were complete. There were two large chairs that sat across from one another that were separated by a large glass table. There was a large sofa that was placed against the wall with the large pane window in back of it and the glass table in front of it. We spent a lot of time in this room talking with Grandma about school, friends, family and life in general. The living room had the most light in the house which was ironic because it's where we learned. It was a far cry from the street light I used in Longwood to illuminate the pages when the lights had been turned out for nonpayment.

Grandma not only gave us what I refer to as agape, unconditional love, she gave us structure as well. We were forced to make sure our beds were made every morning, we had to wash the tub out before we used it as well as after we used it, we had weekly schedules for washing and drying dishes, we had a curfew and were required to be on the street headed towards the house when the street lights came on and we were required to adhere to any demands or commands made by older more mature neighbors. We had to clean the house on a routine basis in the form of vacuuming, washing woodwork, polishing furniture and other chores. This was a different experience for us because we weren't required to do those things when we lived with our parents.

Supervision was not one of my parent's fortes for a number of years, especially after we moved to Longwood. If we didn't adhere to Grandma Lula's rules then we were given whippings with anything she could get her hand on at the time; some days that would be a belt, a branch off a tree, wrapped up magazine, her hands and other readily available items. Grandma Lula was tough and she required us to learn and she taught us responsibility, which once we completed the tasks she compelled us to complete she developed some respect for us. Despite her tough exterior that she sometimes exhibited to some of my cousins, she was more consistent and reliable than any of the other previous adults who had charge over our lives. Instead of waking up either in the middle of the night or the next morning only to discover that neither one of your parents were present. I woke up with glee and not fright because I had confidence that my Grandma Lula would be present to give me a good morning kiss when I headed to school or hug and comfort when I awoke from a nightmare.

Grandma didn't hover over us when it came to our grades; she just wanted to make sure that we didn't fail. She had no problem with me and my sister because failure was not an option for either one of us. Since we moved with my Grandmother Lula we had to transfer schools again I had to make new friends and forge new relationships with new teachers and administrators. This wouldn't be as difficult as the transition to the other schools because I was going back to a school I attended in third grade- Miles Park Elementary. I didn't remember too many of the kids I met during my first stint at Miles Park because I was only there for two marking periods. It was here, however, that my entire academic path was altered for the better, because of a teacher that impacted me more than any other educator up to that time.

MY EDUCATIONAL COURSE ALTERED

Mr. Bruce Hill, Sr. was one of two sixth grade teachers at Miles Park. The sixth graders enjoyed a certain status in the school because they were the older more mature group of kids. Some of the sixth graders expected special treatment because of our status; well Mr. Hill was not one to provide special treatment. He was a Marine, whose arms looked like canons, because of the muscle that protruded out of his shirts, he was extremely fair skinned, handsome, with naturally curly hair. He was only approximately 5'7" but his well-built frame, made him appear to be 6 feet tall to the sixth graders in his class. Mr. Hill demanded respect from his students and their parents or guardians. His hard core external image made everyone respect and fear him. His years in the military were evident by the discipline he imposed on his students. He was one of the most demanding educators I ever experienced but one I was grateful to have in my life.

Mr. Hill also had a unique way of motivating students regarding their academics. My first day there after having spent more than two months of the school year at Tremont, I was again compelled to establish myself as a bright, reasonably articulate young student, who is interested in learning. I initially despised Mr. Hill's method of identifying and labeling the students in his class. Mr. Hill believed in hard work and did not believe in giving handouts to anyone. Thus, despite my academic success in my other schools I began where most new students started- at the bottom. Mr. Hill arranged his room so that there were five rows of desk going west to east, with four to five desks in each row. The row that was close to the chalk board was the F- row. There were four rows that followed the F -row and they were called D-row, C-row, B-row and A-row. The only way you progressed and moved backwards towards the A-row was to do well both in your school work and your conduct. Additionally someone on the ascending row needed to do worse than you in order for you to replace them.

A week after being in the F-row I took a test and received a B. I, however, was not afforded the opportunity to move to the next row because the other students did well. A few days later I received an A on a quiz and one of the other students in the D-row did poorly so I got an opportunity to replace that student. I was so excited; Mr. Hill did not announce the scores but simply told the students to exchange desks. Many did not agree with this method because they thought it demoralized, or demeaned students who didn't do well. While many others saw it as breeding competition and motivating students to do their best, I agreed with the latter proposition well at least until I got stuck in the C-row.

I had made a rapid ascension to the C-row but it was difficult to crack the B and A-row because those were the top students in the class. I believe I was trapped in the C-row for approximately two weeks, notwithstanding the fact that I received nothing lower than a B+ (With the majority of the grades being A+) on all of my homework, class work, quizzes or tests during that period.

The problem was that the other students were consistently as good. I was not accustomed to being a C student. I did not feel that I was average or that I was doing average work. This troubled me to the point that one day after school, while most of the other students walked home I waited outside to speak to Mr. Hill. I approached him as he left out the front doors, and asked" Mr. Hill why are you keeping me in the C row?" He explained that he has a process, and that provided I keep up my good work and, when someone else slips up I could replace the individual. I then asked him, the following questions while my eyes swelled with tears and in between deep breaths "What if they don't ever slip up? Will I be trapped in the C-row forever? Mr. Hill I am not a C student. I have never been a C student and I don't belong in that row", Mr. Hill responded while he was chuckling "Boy ole boy. Michael I have never had a student like you. The rules are the rules, and you just keep working and you'll be able to move I promise." I went home defeated but not completely discouraged. I still had the same zest in completing my homework that I did when I anticipated that the next grade would move me to at a minimum the B-row.

My words and emotions must have pierced Mr. Hill's heart that night because when we reported to school the next day, there was an extra empty desk in the A row. Mr. Hill did not reveal our conversation with the class and simply said "Michael that desks belongs to you and I don't think you'll let me down." I didn't let him down either, because I simply applied the same process that I did while I was in an unstable, constantly changing, distracting environment, here in this consistent stable atmosphere. I recognized that being assertive is beneficial, especially when you have the evidence to support your cause. If I had remained passive and quiet I still may of made it to the coveted A-row but it would have taken much longer. Essentially the old adage, "Closed mouths don't get fed" is something I learned to avoid. I blossomed beyond the expectations of most people who knew of my struggles. Mr. Hill was astonished when my grandmother revealed to him some of the challenges that me and my sister experienced. I completed my homework before I went outside. If I had questions I usually waited until I got to school, to ask Mr. Hill because my grandmother was not receptive to helping with our school work. I continued to do above and beyond what was considered normal for the kids in my class, by studying longer, reading ahead, doing extra math questions.

I indicated earlier that Mr. Hill altered my academic course and it was not primarily due to showing confidence in me, or designating me the top student in the school instead it was for challenging me. I was taking a test and received a score of 99 out of 100. I knew that when I took the test that I didn't get any of the problems wrong and was perplexed by the one answer that was marked incorrect. I recalculated the problem approximately three times, and came out with the same answer. I took the test to Mr. Hill and questioned him on why my answer was wrong. He then went to the book that contained the answer key and compared the answer key for that particular problem with my answer and they didn't match. He said with a slight annoyance in his voice, "Michael the answer key shows your answer was wrong. By the way you still received an A." I wasn't satisfied and I asked "Mr. Hill can I at least do the work on the chalk board?" He responded "Go right ahead."

I then completed the problem on the board, with Mr. Hill closely watching each step waiting anxiously to point out the mistake in the analysis to only find at the end, that there was no mistake in my analysis and to conclude that the book's answer key was incorrect. He then stated that" we aren't challenging you enough at this level you need to be placed in Major Work", or what is more commonly known as honors or gifted and talented, in other programs. Major Work entrance is normally not accepted at the end of the school year they like to identity students, well before the summer session begins. I, however, was fortunate to be accepted into the Major Work program. He stressed that I would be operating from a disadvantage because a number of the students had already been taking more advanced classes since third or fourth grade, but that he had confidence in my abilities to compete and excel amongst that group of children. I possessed the same confidence and agreed to accept the challenge no matter how daunting the it appeared. I believed that by taking on a tough task it would help me in the future when I would face similar or worse hurdles.

I celebrated this wonderful life changing year, by giving the student address for my sixth grade promotional ceremonies. Grandma Lula sat in the audience beaming with pride of seeing me standing, body shaking, but voice steady during my five minute speech, and first of many public oral presentations. Speaking at the sixth grade promotional ceremony wasn't the only reward that I received for my academic success. I was chosen as one of two of the top sixth graders at Miles Park, and given an invitation to attend a dinner honoring all of the top sixth graders across the Cleveland School District. I was given the opportunity to have a parent/guardian join me at the dinner. Most people would have assumed that my Grandma Lula was the logical choice; because of the stability she gave me and my sister. I, however, having not seen my mother in months, wanted her to see the progress I made in hopes that that would be, motivation for her to get better and go into rehab and to become the mom my sister and I always believed she was destined to be, so I invited her to attend the dinner. My Grandma Lula, never admitted it to me, but she was heartbroken when I chose my mom. I just wished I could have taken two people but I was trying to do something to save my mom's life.

I don't regret inviting my mom, who did show up, and ate dinner with me. She wrapped her small petite arms around me and gave me a huge kiss and hug. She sat down beside me and ate most of her meal, which didn't surprise me because it appeared that she hadn't eaten in a while. I missed her and I wanted her to be motivated and inspired to do her best to get better, and I believed that if she saw me receiving a prestigious award she would work harder to change her behavior. I received some beautiful awards and left the dinner smiling, with a naive belief that my mom was going to seek the necessary help.

I left Miles Park with a sense of accomplishment, a ton of confidence and not just in my academic abilities, but physical abilities as well. I had established myself in the neighborhood, as one of the best receivers, with respect in playing football. Along with my academic pursuits I surprisingly was crowned the fastest sixth grader, and then I had to race a kid who was deemed the fastest kid in the neighborhood even though he was only in the fifth grade.

The fifth grader's name was Aki Bradley , for those who are aware of track and field middle school, and high school, lore Aki was known as one of the fastest guys to lace up a pair of spikes. I was nervous because not only was Aki a part of this race, but so was the two other sixth graders I defeated, earlier along with two other fifth graders. We all began the race on a straight paved area in front of the school building. People were shouting for Aki, me and a few of the other students. The gym teacher yelled "ON YOUR MARK". I then bent my legs, put my right leg back to push off on, and left leg forward for balance. My left hand was up while my right hand was at the side of my right leg. He then said "GET SET s", and my body froze. He quickly said, "GO" and I exploded out of my stance like a swimmer making a turn on the wall in a pool.

I started off ahead of the other group of students, and eventually when we got to the finish line no one else crossed before me. I had beaten the fastest guy in the neighborhood. It was exhilarating because I enjoyed, when I won regarding those things I controlled. I loved competition because it only made me better, and I enjoyed the feeling of euphoria, because I could say this time "I'm not the loser." Despite the overwhelming odds that were against me and all the pundits, predicting a loss, I not only decided to race but I dismissed the fear of losing. This would be a theme for my life when I faced challenges. I didn't run away from the challenges, nor did I try to go around them, nor underneath them, nor over the top, but instead I met the challenges head on. I was able to again demonstrate how the least likely person can rise above and become the victor.

VIOLENCE FOLLOWS

I'm grateful that times with Grandma Lula weren't that similar to the things we experienced with our parents. There, however, were still some issues of poverty that we endured. My grandmother was not a healthy woman, due to the debilitating injuries she suffered during the car accident that brought us back to Cleveland. According, this meant she was unable to work on a consistent basis. She had to take several medications for the constant pain. Her eyesight was extremely poor and she was not being given that much in the form of public assistance, for me and my sister. We received the bare minimum, in the form of clothing, shoes, food, supplies and other necessities. I didn't mind the bare minimum because it was way better than what we had been getting- which was virtually nothing. An example of bare minimum was the fact that we were wearing clothes that would either tear and/or fade after the third or fourth wash. The only sneakers I wore had plastic on the bottom, instead of rubber so I would ice skate on the concrete when I played outside. After one incident where I nearly killed myself after sliding on the concrete, I decided to just to wear the shoes that had holes inside in lieu of the plastic bottoms.

As described earlier the house was in disrepair and we were non-paying tenants like roaches and rats living in the home. In fact one night as I was trying to fall asleep, the bathroom door was open with the one light over the medicine cabinet, providing a miniscule amount of light; I saw a rat jump out of the linen closet onto the bathroom floor and scurry from the bathroom floor to the carpet in my bedroom. Then it climbed up the bed and ran towards me. I screamed "Ahhhhhhhhhhhhh" as I simultaneously placed my right hand, which was outside the covers, onto the rat, that was underneath the covers, as his ran near my thigh. I then, with a vast amount of adrenaline, squeezed the rat with my right hand for approximately thirty seconds. My grandmother yelled at me and asked what was wrong with me. I told her a rat crawled in the bed with me. By the time she made it into the room I had jumped out of the bed and was standing against the wall, with the dead rat and its bloods and guts on my sheets and blankets. I had to throw the dead rat away while my grandmother gave me some new sheets and she took the old ones and threw them away.

There were other issues I would have to contend with as distractions even in Grandma Lula's home. First, my Uncle Donnie's intentions to try to negatively influence me to act in an abnormal criminal manner. He was irresponsible and very immature. He stole all the meat out of Grandma Lula's deep freezer, he stole the pit bull dog we used for protection and claimed someone else took the dog. We all knew better because the dog wouldn't let anyone get near him except for family.

A close unnamed relative also tried to pressure me to sell drugs. They were selling marijuana and their entrepreneurial acumen, made them believe that my school would be a great place to increase their profits, so they recruited me to sell. I had to evaluate the situation because we were not well off and there were things that I saw that my friends had that I wanted. The most up to date designer shoes, pants, shirts, hats etc. As I stated earlier we were living with the bare minimum.

I saw the little wad of money that made a small budge in this individual's back pocket that looked like a tumor on his posterior. I wouldn't have to ask Grandma for a few dollars, instead I would be giving her hundreds to thousands of dollars. I would be considered cool by all the students and my ability to attract women would not simply depend on my handsome looks anymore. I then thought about the negative consequences that could result from engaging in that business venture. If I got caught I would have been arrested and sent to juvenile detention, and heading down the same path as my father, cousins, and uncles. I would have placed my life at an even greater risk because guys in my neighborhood who served-sold drugs-, were more susceptible to being the victim of hungry greedy drug dealers or simply hungry desperate people looking for a quick infusion of cash.

Also, with this kind of decision I would lose respect from my friends and family, like my sister, who knew how drugs had harmfully impacted our lives, and the one place I felt comfortable, and free, the place where I excelled would have probably been foreclosed from me, school. I more than likely wouldn't even have to deal with those concerns if my grandmother found out I was dealing. She would have beaten me so bad that even Satan himself would have cringed. Thus, after weighing the pros and cons, I decided to stand up to my relative and tell them no; I wasn't going to mortgage my future on the temporary thrills of the present.

While we were enjoying tranquility there was an incident that dealt a slight blow to my peace of mind and hopes of continuing to reside in a secured stable environment. During a night while at one of my relative's house my sister had relayed to my Grandma Lula that my Uncle Donnie pushed her, for what reason I never discovered, but it sent my grandmother over the edge. She was disgusted with my Uncle's behavior and said enough was enough and she promised "Donnie I'm going to shoot you when we get home." As soon as we exited the vehicle my uncle ran into his room. I then asked him to open the door, so I could come in because I didn't take Grandma's words seriously. I heard people tell their children all the time when they're upset with them, "I brought you into this world and I will take you out." I thought he was being facetious and wouldn't act on her threat. He relented and let me and my cousin Alesica in the bedroom with him.

If you lit a lighter as Grandma Lula and Uncle Donnie spoke you could have melted steel because it would have caused a huge flame due to their alcohol content. My Uncle Donnie was more inebriated than my grandmother. He began this horrible exchange with grandma and he enticed her to shoot him. His words were dragging like a forty-five record being played on the thirty-three speed. Their argument, took place with grandma standing outside the bedroom and her words slurred with her wig slightly pulled back so that a part of her natural hair with hints of gray can be seen. She then waddled back to her room and said "I've had enough of your shit Donnie," and she went to her room and retrieved a twenty-two caliber gun. She waddled back towards the door as my uncle peered through the door. My uncle realized that grandma is not playing and decided to hold her off by putting his legs and arms against the door.

Unfortunately for him, grandma was older and knew her limit when it came to drinking, while Uncle Donnie did not know his limit and was unable to match Grandma's determination to teach him a lesson. Uncle Donnie directed me and my cousin to go into the bathroom, close the door and to get into the bathtub. I made my cousin get in the bathtub and decided to watch to see what grandma was going to do. Grandma was able to crack the door just enough, that I could see the barrel of the gun through the door. My Uncle Donnie was trying in vain to stop her from firing, but could not and grandma fired the gun three times " pop, pop, pop" and then I saw my uncle collapse on the bed and smoke floating to the ceiling from the area where the barrel was once positioned. My uncle's reaction did not look anything like you would see in a movie, so I initially thought he was faking his injuries.

Upon a closer examination I knew he was not faking because I saw the three bullet holes in his stomach and pelvic areas and I also saw the blood beginning to trickle from the bullet entrance areas. He asked me to run to get help. I didn't really need to because Grandma Lula had already called the police and ambulance for herself and Uncle Donnie respectively. She told the police with slurred speech, "I just shot my son come over here and pick him up!" I ran next door and told my Uncle's best friend that my grandma had just shot him. In a matter of minutes both the police and the EMS were on scene. They took grandma to jail and Uncle Donnie to the hospital. Uncle Donnie would survive his wounds but none of Grandma's kids or grandchildren ever got out of line again, at least not when it came to grandma. Grandma spent the night in jail and was released earlier the next day, she was never charged for the offense because the complaining witness, my Uncle Donnie, refused to cooperate.

Uncle Donnie recovered from his wounds but one bullet remained lodged in an area too sensitive to try to remove. This incident was a real life demonstration of the Bible scripture

Exodus 20:12 "Honor thy father and thy mother; that thy days may be long which the Lord thy God giveth thee." Uncle Donnie nearly shortened his days because he failed to honor Grandma Lula. The night grandma was in jail was the only time during the period I lived with her that she wasn't home when I woke up in the morning, due to her voluntary actions. My uncle wasn't the only person I saw shot on E. 98th. I also saw a young man, who had tried to bully our next door neighbor, meet his match. My next door neighbors sister's boyfriend was standing in the street, a few feet from our porch when the bully returned after threatening his girlfriends brother. The bully began to taunt the boyfriend by saying, "What yo old ass gone do. You can get your ass kicked too!" The boyfriend had a brown paper bag in his right hand, that I assumed had sometime of beverage. It, however, was something more powerful than Mad Dog 20/20 wine. The boyfriend pulled out the silver revolver from the bag and tried to grab the bully's hair, but his fingers slipped through his greasy curly hair. The bully ran only a few feet away before the boyfriend fired two shots striking the bully in his leg. The bully limped around the corner and the boyfriend bolted from the street only to return months later when things cooled down.

TAKING ADVANTAGE OF OPPORTUNITIES

Despite the fact that I moved from Longwood, my desire and thirst for knowledge was not quenched simply because I was in a more stable environment. In fact I was able to actually use the resources of a stationary library rather than the RV library. I also spent my time learning a little more about girls during that summer

My grandmother often believed that I was either asexual or homosexual, because I rarely spoke about girls or rarely displayed an overzealous attitude about girls, like I assumed she witnessed from her sons or my older cousins. I was very much interested in girls, but I was never exposed to anyone who could teach me from a male perspective how to attract girls. I was quiet due to some of the horrors I had seen, and was not a social butterfly. I was awkward around girls, unless they were my cousins and I didn't feel comfortable asking them for help. Girls didn't flock to me either, because I was so skinny. I didn't wear the designer clothes, I didn't have money I was not the neighborhood bully nor did I have any game (ability to speak to women, in such a way that I could manipulate them to do my beckoning).

The one thing I did offer was potential. I was athletic and most of the girls, generally said that I was cute. There was one teenage girl who lived down the street who thought I was cute but initially too young for her. Collette was an eighth grader, who attended a local junior high school but knew the caliber of students that I would associate with at Central Middle School in the fall. I guess you can call Collette a cougar because she was nearly two years older than me. She said I would have to be careful when I went to Central because the girls were very aggressive and they may simply take me, throw me against a wall or locker and kiss me. I told her I didn't know how to kiss and she offered to give me kissing lessons each night during the summer. Every night from mid-August until school started, she would meet me on my back porch and I would give her a kiss goodnight. First it was a peck and then the peck turned into longer durations. I can't reveal the feelings I started to have when I kissed Collette or even thought about her without keeping this memoir from being labeled x-rated. I was excited each night before the street lights came on, because kids were told to be in the house or on their porch after the street lights were on. My hands would sweat, my underarms would be a little tart, and my eyes were wide open. Eventually, Collette taught me how to "French Kiss." I became a good kisser because of the instruction I received from Collette. Collette started a trend that I consistently followed except on one occasion, of me being romantically involved with older women.

After the summer ended I arrived at Central with some trepidation. I still had the vision in my head that Collette described of an older female student grabbing me by my collar and slamming me against a locker, and having her lips smother me with saliva, and me both liking it and hating it simultaneously. That event never materialized, either at school or on the bus, which I rode traveling to and from Central Middle School. I walked approximately ten minutes, each school day to wait at a bus stop to take me to Central. It was generally dark and lonely, because none of the friends I went to Miles Park with were attending Central with me. Instead they were assigned to A.B. Hart which was the neighborhood middle/ junior high school. I was required to attend Central because it was the nearest middle school that provided a Major Work curriculum.

The bus ride was usually thirty minutes. We went from one extreme, with respect to neighborhoods, to another extreme. We began in a mixed neighborhood, poor and simply surviving, (Where I lived), to the more affluent area (Where most of the Caucasian students resided), and to Garden Valley (A housing project), then to Central, which was located on East 40th off of Quincy. It was only a few blocks away from a number of public housing project complexes, including Longwood. Central was a massive school, especially for a twelve year old seventh grader. Central Middle School seemed so vast because it was once a high school.

It had great history and legacy, most of the students was not aware of the standards that had been set. If they were informed, maybe that would have caused them to work harder in their classes and avoid misbehavior, in the school and community and vigorously participate in extracurricular activities. Central looked like a museum because of the dark halls, old architecture and the absence of any technological advances of the day. Its size was imposing and intimidating, only the seventh graders attended the first three days of the initial week of school, to give us an opportunity to get accustomed to the school without the distractions from the eighth and ninth graders.

I would return to a school that was multicultural because the students from the Westside and another predominantly Caucasian neighborhood were bused to Central. I was back in a multicultural class; as opposed to the one I had at Miles Park, where the vast majority of the students were African American. I saw a distinct difference between my Major Work classes and my regular classes. Firstly, the teachers were excited about the lessons. They appreciated the fact that we came to school with the desire to learn. They fostered and encouraged competition between all of us. They brought out the best in us and the best in them. I'm not necessarily sure that the same type of energy or level of expectation existed in the non-advanced classes, from either the students or the teachers.

If it did, then our ratings probably would have been higher and the test scores would have been much better, as well. There was an optimism regarding our abilities that was not present when the teachers taught other groups of students. We were labeled the cream of the crop, a part of the talented tenth W.E.B Dubois spoke about. Accordingly, they bombarded us with the work they knew we could complete, because they labeled us bright, confident and dedicated even though other children in the school were intelligent as well. While most seventh graders throughout the Cleveland Public School were going to learn the standard seventh grade math over the duration of the entire seventh grade year that was not the plan for our Major Work Class. We were given the seventh grade book and told that we would not need it come January 1984. We did not need the book because we finished it in three months.

The teacher did not wait for students who did not understand different theories or concepts. Most if not all the students were able to grasp the formulas and equations relatively easily, and moved along with the math teacher. We then completed the entire eighth grade book, along with some Pre-Algebra in three months, so that we would be prepared for Algebra I in eighth grade. I enjoyed my math class, because I had always been a student who thrived off of learning new and interesting academic concepts. I also liked the challenge of completing two huge subject books in a one academic year. I finished with one of the highest averages in the class and distinguished myself as one of the best students in the entire seventh grade, if not the entire school.

Unlike Math, English was more difficult for me to decipher. I was raised in a home and communal environment, where the King's English was not the primary means of communication. I had statements, concepts, sentences, and words that were ingrained in my mind that were inconsistent with what was deemed proper grammar. My mind was a battle ground, between what I knew and what I was being taught. It was so pervasive that many times, I assumed I was bilingual and the language other than English was Ebonics. Ms. Largent was the seventh grade Major Works teacher and she began correcting the problems, but it would be an enormous task.

She was patient, kind and knowledgeable but not lenient. She provided constructive criticism that helped me improve but did not allow me to slide, because I was otherwise a good student, and that was reflected in my average grades. My reading, reading comprehension and writing ability, at least with respect to substance were above average. However, I struggled on putting everything together in a grammatically correct way. Despite the struggles I had in English, I didn't slack off when it came to reading or writing assignments. I studied longer and harder for those tests because I just couldn't accept any dismal performances.

Math along with social studies and science were never that difficult to comprehend, because they required a great deal of memorization. I had the uncanny ability to read most things once and retain and recall the information for an extended period of time. Thus dates, places, times, events, formulas, elements, theories, etc, were easy to learn, research, and understand. While science was fun, interesting learning, about how the earth was formed, atoms, electrons, protons, and neutrons. Therein were the building blocks for all the elements that make up life.

The experiments were enlightening because I got an opportunity to see the information, we were digesting put in action, and thus it gave us more incentive to study and learn. Social studies peaked my interest more than anything else because I always enjoyed learning about the past and how it impacted the future.

I was enthusiastic about going to social studies class because I knew that each day I would learn something new about the world. I would learn about different cultures, governments, parts of the world, distant times, how and why certain cultures survived ,while others perished and why and how this country was formed and grew from what it was at that time until that day.

I learned about varied ways to govern, and how our country was different or similar to others. I was intrigued about a number of social issues that we discussed, especially when it came to anything involving economics, access to quality, educational resources and race. The fact that I was attending Central was related to race. The Cleveland School District was still in the infancy of the U.S. District Court's Desegregation which I believed led to the decision to place the Major Works program at Central. I lived miles away from Central and actually drove past the street that led to A.B. Hart, where most of my neighbors attended. A.B. Hart, however, I believe had more Caucasian students and there may have been some controversy if the Major Work Program was placed at that school. The location of Central, in one of the most impoverished areas of the city, in an old dilapidated building, with archaic desks, chalkboards, halls, gym equipment and learning tools, sent a message that the District could cultivate the best and brightest in the city, notwithstanding race, in one of the least likely areas.

Accordingly, the issues I mentioned earlier had a direct impact on me, as an adolescent. I wanted to know what precipitated the hatred, distrust, lack of cooperation, and lack of respect that existed between the races. I was determined to find a ways to bridge the gap that existed by mingling with the Caucasian students, talking with them, learning from them and sharing with them. I extended myself by explaining some misconceptions that the other students had about African Americans. We weren't lazy, we didn't have a negative attitude, we weren't disinterested in education, we weren't involved in criminal activity, we didn't disrespect our women, we were concerned about our future, we were very much interested in attending and graduating from college, we were respectful and tolerant of other cultures.

I understood that the economic struggles that were prevalent in the African American community, were the results of a number of factors that arose after slavery. There was discrimination in the following areas college admission, job placement, job promotion, housing, by loaning institutions and the criminal justice system. But we have our own level of accountability with our insistence of engaging in criminal activities, self-terminating our own educational opportunities, focusing on instant gratification for material things, and possessing a philosophy that one should live for today because there is no hope for the future. I wanted to avoid the above pitfalls that I saw so many people who were related to me and who lived in my community experience. I believed that each high score I received on a test, all the approbation I received for my academic efforts, the awards I received for my athletic abilities and the decisions I made to avoid confrontations with those in authority, be they teachers, administrators or law enforcement all functioned as scoops of dirt that I placed in the pitfalls and was able to walk over those pitfalls. While it did not necessarily guarantee me, the wealth that most people seek, it did put me in a better position than those who were my immediate role models.

Although education and adhering to the rules were my primary focus areas at Central, I also was very interested in sports. My first love, football, was not available to seventh graders and I would be required to wait and prepare for the next year. I, however, was permitted to participate in track and field and I tried out for the team. The head coach for the track team was ironically the coach for the football team the next year, his name was Mr. Voss. He was a physically fit, Caucasian, twenty something year old physical education teacher, who enjoyed developing young people's natural athletic skills. He, like most of the coaches I would come to respect and admire, tried to get the very best out of you, which may include the very tasty lunch you ate, prior to practice.

He believed in you using your talents and skills to help the team and would place people in events that he believed were proper for those students, even if the student thought otherwise. I believed that I should be one of the fastest kids in the school. I had just beaten one of the fastest kids in my neighborhood last year, so what would change? We had runoffs and the coach was able to see whether the person could help the team in sprints, distance or the field events.

I discovered that I wasn't as fast as a number of the older kids on the team, meaning the ninth graders. The coach did not want me to leave the program, since I was one of a very few number of seventh graders who even tried out. He saw the talent I had and he moved me to the distance races. I struggled through the thousand sit-ups we did, which resulted in me developing my oblique muscles which eventually formed into a six pack. My weak and frail arms and the bird chest I had before training began to leave, slowly but surely I developed a little muscle recognition. Instead of a mocking bird my chest began to resemble a pigeon, and my arms went from skin and bone to a mosquito size enlargement, because of the tons of push-ups. Lastly, we ran hundreds of laps around the school and each time around, I would see and hear some neighbors cheering us on. That gave us pride in knowing the neighborhood and people we represented were rooting for our success. We also saw some winos, drunks, prostitutes, drop-outs, and, drug dealers; it helped encourage me because that was something I was running away from becoming. Watching the deteriorating homes, businesses, the streets in disrepair and abandoned buildings motivated me to run towards a profession that would permit me to provide a cure for the neighborhood. My assiduous work ethic caught the attention of the coach, and he accordingly gave me the chance to compete with older students and develop a rapport with him.

Coach Voss eventually designated me to run the 880 yard race. It was twice around the track and was quickly becoming one of the more grueling races in track and field. He exclaimed that it required you to have some stamina and speed. I had natural speed and because of all of the new exercises, the laps around and inside the school, and the strength program, I was developing the stamina. I began the year behind two of our top 880 yard runners and they would push me to get better in practice and at the meets. I detested losing, so I did everything within my power to ensure that I would not finish last and that I would eventually finish ahead of the other runners.

I persevered; though my lungs felt like I could spit fire each time I took a breath. Despite the fact that my legs felt like cement was attached to them, and there was a two hundred pound sack of potatoes on my back I continued to push towards the finish line. While I finished most of my races ahead of the other older and stronger runners, I had no first place finishes. I did realize a marked achievement, each week,~my time got better and better each meet. It would become a rallying call for me, that despite the obstacles, challenges, losses, and inability to see the positive within reach, and disappointments, that as long as I continued to prepare myself for the race and stay in the race, eventually the rewards would come, I just needed to stay patient and humble.

My participation in track also assisted me in the classroom and the community. First, unlike many of my classmates and friends because of track I had very little time to goof off and still be prepared for my classes. The downtime that many of my classmates and friends had was a luxury for me when it did occur. I was usually coming home on the late bus because of practice or a meet. I only had time to do homework, study, eat and watch a little television before grandma said lights out, which was usually 9:00 p.m. during the week, sometimes 10:00 p.m. if a good show was on that day. I was forced to create and maintain a schedule, so that I would not fall behind. I would be able to continue to do well in my academic pursuits as well as my athletic career.

Secondly, I didn't have time to be involved in the risky activities that my friends were participating in. They were forming street gangs to fight, against rival streets who happen to walk on or near their street. I thought it was ludicrous because neither one of us owned any property. We couldn't lay claim to something that ultimately belonged to the City of Cleveland. They were fighting over immaterial juvenile issues. I wasn't going to be tempted, with the little free time I had, to engage in activities that put my physical well-being and my liberty at risk. I ended the year on the honor roll and established myself as an excellent student, athlete and citizen on behalf of my city, state and country. I just needed to make sure I continued to progress so that my eighth grade year would be memorable.

WHO'S MY DADDY?

The summer before my eighth grade year would be a life altering one for me, due to a shocking discovery that my mother revealed. My birth certificate is quite distinctive from most people. It lists my full name, the place, time and date of my birth; the medical specialist who performed the procedure; the individual who reported the birth and of course my mother's full name and age at time of my birth. What is distinctive, however, is the fact that the box designated for father was empty. That is significant because children generally take the last name of their father. The history, traditions, the reputation of that family name is heaped upon that child. It is supposed to provide the child with some identity and foundation.

The child feels an obligation to work towards making the name better and stronger. A male child feels even more attached to the name because he can then carry that last name and legacy to his children, while the female child generally will marry and substitute the family name with her husband's last name. I started out with an anomaly, by not even having a father listed on my birth certificate. I began life with some obstacles and this added to it. The fact that no father was listed was perplexing and troubling for me. Was my mother so promiscuous that she did not know who my father actually was, or was it her intention to avert any connection with a man she knew would not help shape me into a positive productive man? I had viewed my birth certificate, well before 1982 and noticed that no father was listed on it. I never questioned why because I undoubtedly believed, that Allen Douglas was my father. I didn't have any reason to doubt that he wasn't, I called him daddy.

The incident that led to my mother's great revelation started when my Grandmother Lula needed our birth certificates in order for us to participate in summer track. My sister reviewed both of them together and told me about the disparity (Allen Douglas was listed as father for my sister), which again awakened my curiosity. During one of the varied visits with my mother, my sister and I questioned her about why our birth certificates were different, regarding the space assigned for father. My mother was driving at the time, my sister in the front seat and me in the back and she stated "Michael, Allen is not your father," I was twelve years old at that time and was about to turn thirteen in a few months. My mother, however, asked that we not reveal our knowledge of the truth to daddy or anyone else in the family. She told my sister and me that my real father's name was Bruce and I cannot recall the last name she gave us that day. She never mentioned anything about Richard Solomon.

I was not emotionally traumatized as one would imagine if they received news that the person they believed was their parent actually wasn't. It, however, made perfect sense at that time that I was not his son biologically. He didn't show any favoritism towards my sister because she was his biological daughter nor was he harsher with me when he doled out punishment, nevertheless the differences were more illuminated once the great mystery was uncovered. I saw the major differences in our personalities wherein he was quick to anger I was very deliberate and calm. I noticed that I was darker and he was much lighter and that I lacked the facial hair he possessed at an early age. I was addicted to education and he was addicted to substances that numbed his body and mind. His actions made it difficult for us to forge an unbreakable bond that usually exist between father's and their son's and so without that bond it was easy to accept the news that someone else was the second actor responsible for my birth.

My sister and I eyes were opened at that time. It was here that we finally recognized that we looked different. I always thought that my sister was the odd one since her skin complexion was so much lighter than everyone else, and she was the only one in the house with hazel eyes. I would venture to say that our similarities drowned out the obvious and glaring differences. We were both intelligent, had thin frames, above average sized lips, and we were both athletic. My mother's deception, however, continued beyond that date about my true father. Her concealment extended to her criminal behavior as well. She had been indicted for a felony titled Grand Theft Poor Relief, during the summer before my seventh grade year. She, however, failed to appear for her arraignment that was scheduled on June 17, 1983 and, was avoiding answering those charges or even discussing them, with anyone let alone me and my sister. She was a fugitive from justice but continued to behave as though nothing was wrong. Her denial of her criminal issues was as clear as her denials that she needed help to kick her drug habit.

We continued on our visit with my mom. She would take us to the apartment she was sharing with her mom, Grandma Edna and my Great-Grandmother Ethel Burns, as mentioned earlier better known as Grammy. Grammy had moved to Cleveland from Pennsylvania, due to concerns about her ability to care for herself and to live autonomously. My grandmother was now required to care for her daughter and her mother, which became an herculean effort at times. She was generally happy to see us when we would come and visit, as I was happy to see her. Grammy would enjoy our visiting because she loved to hear and watch my sister and I fight. She would laugh uncontrollably when we yelled or screamed at one another, or if I grabbed my sister and played like I was going to squeeze and instead began to tickle her until she turned blue. Grammy didn't mind nor did mommy or Grandma Edna. They made sure we did our homework if we had any, fed us, gave us things so we could bathe and made sure we had plenty of sleep.

A majority of the time would be spent with Grammy because my Grandma Edna was working, and my mother would leave and return hours later; not much had changed. She didn't seem high when she picked us up or when she spent time with us. It was wonderful, however, to have a few days with my mother. I adored her no matter what issues and challenges, she voluntarily took us through. I knew deep down inside that she loved us and wanted the best for us, but knew that she couldn't provide that for us at that time. I didn't see much effort on her part to regain custody of me and my sister; even with the apartment that she shared with my grandmother's that was miles away from Longwood. She was essentially single without any responsibilities, and loving it. She would only have to monitor and care for us for a few days and deliver us back to Grandma Lula to fulfill her obligations. I was not mad at my mom but disappointed because she was missing out on seeing us mature from kids to adolescents and I simply missed her.

So other than that revelation and me participating in the summer track club, called the Cobras my summer was uneventful. I returned to Central with confidence because of my performance during seventh grade, and because of the new leadership role my classmates were forced to accept. Our school was a part of a new process wherein, the ninth graders would be sent to the high schools. Accordingly Central Junior High and A.B. Hart ,would only have seventh and eighth graders at the school. While it required us to mature faster than most of the other kids in the District's middle schools, it also put us in a competitive disadvantage when it came to sports and academic challenge. I took on the challenge with a pride and belief that despite the proposed disadvantage, we would be competitive and dominant in some areas.

I finally got an opportunity to participate in organized football, albeit flag football because Cleveland Public Schools had terminated full contact football for middle school students, well before I arrived at Central. I had the blood lines to play football. My father, Richard Solomon, according to my uncles was one of the best running backs to ever step foot on East Tech campus. He, however, showed his prowess on the neighborhood fields, because his grades and behavior kept him from staying in school long enough to suit up. My uncles described my father as being smooth and fast enough to avoid, any would be tackler. Simply put, he made people grab air when he played.

I had the uncanny ability of making moves and not knowing or being able to explain, how I was able to contort my body, apparently it was a talent that was inherited from my father. On my mother's side of the family, my Uncle Chuck was a star quarterback for Mr. Kidd at John F. Kennedy. He led the Eagles to a number of victories during his tenure. My Uncle Chuck, 6'3" 200 pounds was a great athlete, who also played basketball and had been offered a football scholarship to Michigan State University. According to my Grandma Edna Michigan State University withdrew their scholarship offer after my uncle injured his knee playing basketball. My Uncle Carlin Ryan played alongside the great Joe Namath at Beaver Falls High School. In fact my Uncle Carlin was slated to start at quarterback, until Joe decided to attend Beaver Falls and they put together one of the most prolific back fields in the history of Pennsylvania High School football. My uncle would go on to the University of Iowa and play a few years of college football.

It was no surprise when I made the team and was selected to start at tight end, not due simply to my blood lines, where the natural talent existed, but due to the hard work I put in during the tryouts. There were at least, thirty to forty guys who tried out for the team but only eight of us were selected. I enjoyed the camaraderie that we had among the team and the talent that we possessed. We, however, lacked the size and experience that other middle schools held, because we were all eighth graders while everyone else had ninth and eighth graders. The teams didn't show us any mercy nor did we request it, because of our special condition, we simply put on our uniforms and cleats, and played as best we could. Unfortunately we only won one or two games that year, but again the experience taught me how to persevere, despite the disadvantages you may face that are not necessarily caused by something you did or failed to do. I played well once the coaches figured out that I wasn't this slow distance runner they presumed because of my participation in track the previous year. Instead I demonstrated in tryouts, practice and games that I had the speed and soft hands to impact games and thus they began throwing me the ball in more opportune situations.

It was the beginning, of a very fruitful year for me. I was proud to begin taking Algebra I in the eighth grade. Algebra was a very fun and interesting class. I liked using Algebra to determine the unknown when figuring out a problem. I got a thrill out of using the formulas we were given and applying the data and determining the answer.

Our teacher was very strict, informative but helpful. His Asian accent did not impact our ability to comprehend, and a number of students, including me excelled in his class. My science teacher for eighth grade was phenomenal. Mr. Woda, a fixture at Central well before I arrived, loved teaching, especially those kids who had a thirst for knowledge like me. I arrived to his class, well aware of his reputation for being eccentric, tough but at the same time enjoyable. One of my friends from the track team, Steve, was in Mr. Woda's eighth grade major work science class the year before me. He said he was his favorite teacher. I came in with an exuberance to learn and learn we did. We were able to participate in experiments that other students were precluded from doing. We learned at a faster pace than the other students and were taught and grasped more complex scientific themes. We were given higher expectations than the other students in our building.

We were required to complete a science fair project. We, however, had the alternative to partner with another student. My lab partner for most of the year, as well as a guy who indicated his desire to run track this spring was Anthony Borowski. He and I developed a project, wherein we used solar panels and regular light bulbs to operate a mill that Anthony constructed. He and I did the research and graphics on the project. We received an A on the project and our project was then submitted to the Regional Science Fair that pitted us against students from other Cleveland Public Schools and other suburban schools as well.

We arrived on the sprawling John Carroll University campus, with an overzealous eagerness and pride. We were representing Central, the school in the hood. While this was not the first time, I had ventured onto a college campus it was the first four year college, I had an opportunity to tour. I was more accustomed to Cuyahoga Community College's Metro Campus. It was there that I won my first trophy after participating in the summer Jessie Owens program. The program emphasized physical fitness in the form of education and training, with regards to non-traditional sports like gymnastics and Judo. It also required students to attend and complete academic courses as well. I did not receive any acknowledgments for my athletic prowess in the aforementioned activities; instead I received the award for an essay I drafted.

I wouldn't be truthful if I claimed I knew the subject of that essay but I can recall the thrill I had when I won the trophy. I was living in Longwood at the time and I was experiencing more negative events, so this was refreshing. I also recognized that being successful or receiving awards did not always revolve around how well someone did in a particular sporting event. I saw that using my mind could be beneficial.

On John Carroll's campus we weren't expected to receive the praise, that the other suburban students were accustomed to getting. I was overwhelmed by the sheer volume of projects, which included but was not limited to erupting volcanoes, robotics, and test tubes filled with unknown substances, that crowded the over populated gymnasium.

Mr. Woda was not as excited as we were, since he had been requiring his honor students to participate in this science fair for years. Mr. Woda's traditional Jewish beard and mustache made him different from many of the teachers and males I knew. He, however, developed an appreciation within all of us for being proud of who we are, where we were from and the fact that we were smart and deserved to be at the competition. It was a memorable experience because we received the chance to compete against some of the best students in the region. We wore our Sunday's best and were prepared with note cards and hours of practice in Mr. Woda's class.

We watched as the other judges went to other areas and evaluated the other projects. When the judges finally made their way towards our project and began their analysis we were not nervous at all. We were articulate in our description of the graphics, the experiment, the items we used and the results. While we did not win in our category, we did receive an honorable mention ribbon for the Science Fair. You could have knocked me over with a feather; because of the elation I felt when we left the college. I have always been more energized by the awards I received from my academic pursuits, than I was for the athletic ability because I knew I wasn't always going to be the most gifted athlete; Notwithstanding how much energy I put forward to make my body stronger, faster and quicker. I could, however, build my mind to be one of the fastest, one of the most knowledgeable, one of the most used, one of the most logically thinking and one of the most innovative.

Mr. Woda, as well as my other teachers lauded my accomplishments and made me feel that being smart was not a badge of dishonor. A number of the kids in my community would sneer at other kids, who happen to be bright and would harass them to such a degree that they felt better if they did poorly, because then they avoided the ridicule. I, unlike, my other easily influenced friends, simply ignored the name calling i.e. Nerd, Professor, Geek, Bookworm and Teachers Pet, and simply kept working at getting smarter. I would be sick if I received a C on a quiz, test, homework or class work. I would experience a sense of euphoria, almost like a high, when I received a B or A on a quiz, class work, homework or a test. It was like a competition for me I had to do better than the students who were in class with me.

I was losing to them in every aspect of my life: most of them lived in a stable environment, they weren't witnesses to domestic violence, they weren't exposed to criminal behavior, they weren't neglected by their parents due to the latter's drug abuse nor were most of them fighting roaches for food. Education was the one place I could win and I did everything within my control to excel. Whether it was science with Mr. Woda, American History with Mr. Charney or English my teachers expected the best from me and my classmates.

It was in Mr. Charney's American History class that I felt the most comfortable and confident. Mr. Charney looked like the typical teacher during the Mid-Eighties because of his many plaid shirts, his baggy pants that were pulled up above his waist and his wire rimmed glasses looked similar to Mr. Woda's. He too, had the traditional Jewish beard like Mr. Woda, with hair balding in the middle and with accidental saliva showering during conversations with students. Just as the year before, I really enjoyed history and it was my best subject again. I hung on every word that Mr. Charney said about politics, race relations, history of this country and the different factions that existed and why. He even spoke about the history of politics in the City of Cleveland. He was the first person that informed me of the significant contributions made by Carl and Louis Stokes to the City of Cleveland and the surrounding communities.

He also introduced me to real life politics when he suggested that I run for Student Council President, which I did and won my first election. He asked some of his students if we were interested in working on a real campaign, ~ his wife C.J. Prentiss who was also an educator, was running for a position on the State Board of Education. On one crisp Autumn morning before November, Mr. Charney picked us up from our home and then took us to a large home on Euclid Avenue in East Cleveland, Ohio early in the morning. We were given a very short speech from C.J. Prentiss, thanking us for helping her during her first statewide political campaign. We then went walking door to door placing the literature inside the screen doors, or if people were available we would hand it to them personally and asked them to support Mrs. C.J. Prentiss. I didn't really know much about her only that she was Mr. Charney's wife and if she was good enough for him and she was a teacher, then she was good enough for me to provide some assistance. I really enjoyed the door to door canvassing and I got the political bug that was planted and would get larger as I grew older and more involved in politics.

While I enjoyed and performed at a high level in Social Studies English again was a tough subject for me. My teacher was as tough as Ms. Largent. Despite the fact that I was not one of the highest performing students in her class, she still selected me as one of the members of our Academic Challenge Team because of my high abilities in my other classes. We would use our study hall time and some class time to practice for the Academic Challenge Team, because I had after school responsibilities, football and track. She understood my obligations to those sports and respected that and gave me the option of missing a few practices. I really appreciated the opportunity to participate in academic competitions, as well as athletic competitions because it showed my ability to be diversified and not one dimensional. I encourage all our youth to do the same and thereby find the necessary balance so that you are not overextended and able to enjoy your adolescence and young adult life without an abundance of stress. .

The last subject I performed well in was German and it was an unusual ability to grasp the language and its proper usage. I was one of the top students in the class and was getting an unexpected excellent grade. I initially believed that my understanding of German was just due to my hard work, but my Grandmother Edna advised me that it may be hereditary. My Great, great,g reat great-grandfather was a slave who purchased his own freedom from his master and moved the family to New Castle, Pennsylvania. His name was John Gardner. He then worked and saved enough for his wife and his two sons' freedom. He enlisted in the Civil War to help the Union defeat the Confederate Army, and returned to New Castle after the war was over. In addition to being a general laborer, he was a minister and had two congregations~ an English speaking congregation and a German speaking congregation. He spoke and wrote German fluently. He met his demise quite tragically, when he died after his cloak got caught in the rails after he alighted from the train heading from one congregation to another. My Great-grandfather not only passed down his gene to readily understand German language but his perseverance gene as well. He survived slavery, freedom and war and left a legacy for his descendants to live up to.

MOTHER & FATHER ON DIFFERENT PATHS

My life couldn't have been going much better, when my mom began to experience some very unfortunate events. First, my Grandma Edna decided to leave Cleveland and accordingly the apartment she had was unavailable. My great-grandmother began to live with my great aunt and there was clearly no room for my mother. Second, my mother had to spend a few days with us at Grandma Lula's house because of a health condition. She was sick and neither Grandma Lula nor mommy revealed why she was so sick and why she was staying with us. I later learned after she left, but never questioned her about it, that she just had an abortion and needed some place to stay and be nursed back to health by my Grandma Lula. She laid on the couch most of the day and into the night. I didn't care that she didn't interact with me or my sister because I got a chance to see her when I woke up even if she didn't feel good. I got a chance to hug and kiss her before I said my prayers and went to sleep at night. I knew that at least for a few nights my prayers for her to be in a safe place would be answered.

As far as I could see she was in no shape to have a child in the first place; the child probably would have had a number of, health problems, because of my mother's addiction. She didn't have a job, and didn't have the health care that she would need to provide a healthy foundation the baby needed to survive and then thrive. Also, to make matters worse the alleged father was not involved with my mother at the time of her procedure.

Ironically, my sister and I were still going to Mansfield, to see my father and he looked healthy and scary. We would get prepared the night before, which was usually a Friday or Saturday, by choosing something to wear and making sure it was clean and pressed. I was excited because usually we only communicated with my father via letters, cards or pictures and very seldom, we got a chance to say hello to him over the phone.

We would write letters that were short but sweet generally, telling him how much we miss him and couldn't wait to see him again. He would send us letters indicating how much he missed us and couldn't wait to see us again, and he reminded us to behave or else be prepared for a good whipping when he was released. That threat was sufficient to keep us in line for the most part because he had several years to accumulate anger, for each incident of rebellion or misbehavior by me or my sister. We would wake up early in the morning, generally before or shortly after 8:00 a.m. Me, Grandma Lula and my sister would begin our trek down I-71 towards Mansfield, Ohio. It was always a very long and tedious trip for us.

We would make very few stops so that Grandma, usually the only driver, could make it back to Cleveland before it got dark. She would drive the speed limit, which was only 55 M.P. H. in a used but reliable vehicle, which accounted for the hour and a half drive. I would watch out the window for cows and horses that were in the pasture, for the many farms we passed. I would point out to my sister the interesting things I saw in this area of Ohio that seemed like a foreign country at times. I saw vibrant, colorful trees, gray squirrels, beautiful wild flowers and other animals that were not prevalent in my neighborhood, chickens, roosters, deer, beavers, etc. Everything on the drive depicted freedom, meanwhile my father was only able to enjoy what I witnessing when he was released.

I could always feel we were close to our destination because the huge fence that surrounds the facility would come into view, as well as the vast tangled pieces of barbwire, that was used to deter people from believing they could scale the fence and escape. There were also guards positioned at different points above the fence, which had access to firearms and wouldn't have hesitated to use them, if someone tried to cut their sentence short without judicial intervention. We went through the same procedures that we did at the Justice Center when we went to visit my father and other relatives. I didn't initially understand why we had to be searched, because the only thing I was bringing in was hugs and kisses. Each time we went to see my father; he looked like he put his mouth over one of those helium machines and inhaled because he had muscles everywhere.

I thought to myself when I saw him and hugged him, "there was no way I was doing anything bad when he did get out. "Before he was shipped to Mansfield he was about 5'11" and maybe 150 pounds at his heaviest but he looked like he was 180 to 190 pounds now, and all muscle. I got the opportunity to hug kiss and talk to him, I would tell him how I was doing in school, and how we were behaving at home, listening to Grandma and so forth. We couldn't bring him any food inside the visiting area; we were restricted to simply talking and physical contact. My sister and I often begged for money to put in the few vending machines they had in the visiting area.

Prison had a noticeable impact on my father because he seemed calm, less agitated, less anxious, and focused. He was finally focused on correcting his mistakes and forging a new path once he completed his sentence and was permitted to return home. His new philosophy was manifested in the physical form when he acquired his General Equivalency Diploma (G.E.D) while he was in Mansfield. He even completed two years' worth of college credit courses. He didn't look like the monster I was accustomed to seeing. The monster who would beat my mom, the monster whose eyes would be blood shot red and his veins would be enlarged so much, they looked like they were going to burst through his skin. His voice would sound worse than a lions roar. My father appeared to now be more conscientious, he wasn't high (at least not when we visited), he spoke rationally and he seemed genuinely concerned about my sister and my well-being. It was sad to admit, but prison had altered his course, he needed to be in a controlled environment in order to control his behavior. It was now hard to leave him because he was a different person I liked the person he had become and hoped Allen Douglas that entered Mansfield Correctional Facility was different from the one who would eventually leave.

We traveled back to Cleveland going North on I-71 and I felt a sense that things would be better when my father returned. I believed that he still had a huge influence over my mother. Maybe he could convince her to voluntarily enter a rehabilitation program, conquer her addiction, regain custody of me and my sister, and raise us like she was morally and legally obligated to do. We would need my father to come home sooner than later because my mom's condition began to worsen.

My mother was becoming desperate because her sources of income were drying up. My Grandma Edna was no longer in town, and my Uncle Chuck lived 3,000 miles away. She was not working and unable to obtain steady employment because the drug addiction, would not let her maintain any type of consistency needed to work. No stable home, no good diet, no strong support system, no criminal activity, no hope and no apparent potential.

My mother knew the way to recover some of the income she lost was to regain, custody of me and my sister . She called Grandma Lula one night and I overheard Grandma talking and responding to my mother. After about two minutes into their conversation I overheard my Grandma Lula say "Peggy I don't think you are ready to get these kids back yet. I am not going to give up custody until you can show me you are ready. I will keep these kids forever if I have too." My mother must have responded "Well I can just take Michael because he's not Allen's!" Grandma Lula "The hell you will, that boy is not leaving here." I then heard Grandma slam the phone down on her night stand and I saw her wiping the tears that were slowly dripping from her eyes, onto her chunky cheeks. She didn't even notice me standing outside her bedroom because she exclaimed "Ohh you scared me Michael what are you doing?" I responded by saying "Nothing, I'm just looking outside the door." She asked me, "Did you hear me on the phone with your mother?" I said "No.". I then asked, with the intent to change the subject from whether I overheard the conversation to something else, "Why didn't mommy want to talk to us?" "I don't know, but I think she is going to call back later," she said sniffling and wiping her eyes with some tissue. I asked her "Grandma are you okay?" She said "Yes baby I'm doing fine don't worry about Grandma." She then leaned down and kissed me on my cheek and I kissed her on her cheek. I could taste the salt that had been deposited from the tears she shed regarding the conversation with my mom. I believe she was worried that my mother had some legal grounds to remove me from Grandma Lula's care since I was not a blood relative. My mother was making a desperate attempt to regain custody but for the wrong reason.

MY WORST FEARS REALIZED

It seemed as if every time something good happened something worse would occur, and what seemed like progress to some, was me simply walking in place. When I moved ahead something knocked me back again. In March of 1985 my sister and I went to visit my mother who was now incapacitated at St. Alexis Hospital. My sister and I rode public transportation from a stop near our home to St. Alexis, since the hospital was only ten to fifteen minutes away from E. 98th street. We stood at the bus stop with a hand full of exact change to get us to the hospital and then back home. We watched patiently for the bus as it drove westbound on Miles Avenue towards us. The bus was loud, metallic and smoky.

We entered the bus via the large steps and placed our coins in the machine like it was a piggy bank, however we knew that was one piggy bank that we would not be able to break. We quickly sat down on the soft cushioned vinyl chairs and sat through the ride. We bounced approximately a half a foot in the air after we hit each bump on the road towards St. Alexis. It was a neighborhood hospital that serviced mostly European (Slavic) immigrant communities on the east side of Cleveland. This was an established hospital and very proud, popular and competent health organization. My sister and I hadn't been told why my mother was in the hospital. So she and I were laughing and joking on our way to the hospital.

The bus eventually stopped in front of St. Alexis and its massive building with more than eight floors. It was an old building but with a lot of character and strength, it was a reflection of the people who lived in the community. Nevertheless, the hospital was still an eerie place for me. I was still uncomfortable being at the hospital. I disliked the smell and the fact that it is always freezing inside the rooms and hallways. I know that germs can't survive at low temperatures but did they think about making sure people don't walk out with frost bite.

My sister and I eventually entered an elevator, went up a couple of floors and the doors parted open, and we walked down the hall. It was completely white, of course, with the enamel floor. We walked into mommy's room and saw her lying in the bed with the hospital gown draping her. She looked like she only weighed about 70 pounds at this time. Her once beautiful bold eyes were sagging baggie pants and she could barely keep her eyelids from shutting close as she talked to us. Her hair was matted and up in the air as though she were related to Don King; it didn't look like it was actually groomed. Her face was pale. She was always a fair-skinned person, but now she looked as though she was a shade lighter. She just didn't look good. We sat there and we talked to her for a few moments asking her how she was doing and why she was there in the first place. She wouldn't disclose to us why she was in the hospital. I believe that she was in a state of denial, especially based on the next exchange we had with her.

My mother asked my sister to escort her to the bathroom. My sister said sure and stood next to my mother's hospital bed while my mother took her right arm and put it around my sister's left shoulder. My mother gingerly rolled out of the bed onto my sister's back. While my mother put all of her weight on my sister's shoulders, she stepped across the floor as though she were trying to avoid a mine, similar to the ones military personnel are trained to avoid. I observed with a watchful eye and an aching heart. My mother was wincing in pain each time she took a step. My sister entered the restroom with my mother and helped her sit down to use it.

Afterwards, My sister then carried my mother back to her bed. Once my mother finally pulled the sheet and blanket up to her shoulders, my sister and I looked at each other and in unison began to cry out of concern for her. I had seen my mother after she was the victim of a number of brutal assaults. I saw my mother after not eating for several days or weeks and I saw my mother after she shot drugs through her veins. Through it all, she never appeared as vulnerable or as weak as I witnessed that day. My mother looked at us and said "Why are you guys looking at me like that? Why are you crying? It's not like I'm going to die." When she said that, I was somewhat reassured and the tears stopped pouring out like water flowing down a mighty river, because she had this confidence in her voice when she proclaimed, "I'm not going to die, I'm going to be okay." I'm sick right now, but I will be fine."

The emotional roller coaster was operating full-time, because soon after my mother's medical emergency in the hospital, we learned that my father was being released from Mansfield. He was not released directly to our house but instead was sent to a halfway house in Cleveland. He was only permitted to leave, at certain times of the day and he could not have visitors.

The halfway house on Euclid was sort of like a mansion. Big, beautiful exterior, I would describe it as maroon in color, and it looked like a castle on the outside, but inside, there was notorious people who had committed crimes like theft, strong arm and armed robbery with a gun, as well as some individuals who had committed murder, not aggravated murder, but they were being housed in this particular environment. Inside was rampant with those who were considered as society's derelicts. These individuals were supposed to be rehabilitated as well because they had gotten an opportunity to come to this halfway house. A halfway house is a halfway point to home. They may be home, but they aren't on their own. They aren't independent yet and that's the reason why they are required to stay in those particular locations.

We now had the opportunity to see my father on the outside of Mansfield, outside of those wires. We didn't have to take a long trip to Mansfield and back home. What was originally two hours, turned in to be, maybe 20 minutes. He also had the opportunity to leave and visit with us, as long as he returned by curfew time. His failure to comply with the rules of the halfway house meant that he was then placed in jeopardy of being sent back made him do so consistently.

While my father was putting his life back together my mother's was rapidly unraveling. She left the hospital, against doctor's orders and returned to her prior temporary residence that happen to be with a man who was old enough to be her father. I wasn't aware of any intimacy between them but ventured that something was amiss, when I was visiting and discovered some pictures in her drawer of her nude in his bed in a provocative position.

I knew that she was not working and that Mr. Leonard was employed at a Laundromat on Kinsman road. I could only imagine, what if anything my mother had to exchange for her roof over her head, food in her belly and a way to continue to get high. She had only put a few more pounds on, from the time when she was in the hospital. She weighed approximately 110 pounds at her heaviest weight, and that was probably when she was pregnant with me and my sister, but appeared not to have gained any weight since I saw her at the hospital. She was more concerned with finding the next fix than fixing her life or her relationships, especially the relationship she had with her children. I became overly concerned that she was going to get extremely sick and not be able to recover. I became concerned when I was at Grandma's Lula's house and the phone would ring, that someone on the other end was relaying to my grandma that my mother overdosed or that someone found my mother badly beaten or dead. I had all this anxiety, stress, nervousness and depression and I had to take that to school every morning and try to concentrate on my work.

I was flourishing when it came to my academic subjects, athletic performances, community and political participation and now even my social life would receive uplift because of the student council's requirement to organize and direct the talent program. As president of student council I, along with other participants including teachers, were required to choose the acts as well as their order for the talent show. We began working on this project around the time my mother was released from the hospital. I was also selling candy to get my track shoes and new jogging suit. I was also preparing for the Academic Challenge and training every other day for track. The little time I had left out of the hours remaining in the day were designated for studying, sleeping, eating and worrying about my parents. I was finding positive distractions to diminish the impact of the uncontrollable situation that was threatening our stability. My father's desire to re-interject himself into our daily lives and my mother's personal plan of destruction were heavy weights that felt like a two ton elephant sitting on my chest. Yet, I refused to allow anything to deter my course in school. Again, school became the refuge for me. I dove into reading ahead, I could concentrate on more Algebra problems instead of the other pressures I was experiencing. Track allowed me to run and cry out without anyone hearing me and questioning what was wrong. I cried and let the wind that blew on my face as I ran dry the tears. I didn't take my frustrations out on loved ones by being disrespectful or cold. I didn't engage in mischievous or abhorrent behavior and then blame the latter on my unfortunate circumstances. I just kept moving forward despite of the setbacks.

My father was eventually released from the halfway house and placed on parole without the other restrictions he had at the halfway house. He actually began to live with us at Grandma Lula's house and my Uncle Donnie moved out. He tried valiantly to get my mother to enter a rehabilitation facility but she refused to listen. He would argue and curse on the phone and he actually tried to talk to her in person. While his voice would be full of rage and discontent, my mother would ignore his rants by exclaiming her adulthood. They, however, to my delight never engaged in any physical confrontation. My mother was simply bull-headed and my father didn't want to return to prison so he kept his cool.

My father was keenly aware of the trouble my mother was in and decided that the only person that may be able to influence her was my Grandma Edna, who was currently residing in New York. She had actually received her G.E.D and had taken several courses at New York City College, which according to her is better known as "The Poor Man's Harvard." My father contacted my Grandma Edna and she hurried to Cleveland to find out how sick her only daughter was. Grandma Edna came directly to Grandma Lula's shortly after she arrived in Cleveland. She had rented a car at the airport and she, my father and I quickly drove over to Mr. Leonard's where my mother happen to be present at that time.

I had just received my new track shoes and my new track sweat suit. I only had the top on, I didn't wear the pants and I wanted to show my mother. I had the red hooded sweatshirt with the Central Middle School and the Trojan man in the middle. I also had my all white track spiked shoes with the candy red Swoosh on the sides of the shoes in a box. I didn't initially get an opportunity to say anything to my mother because my father and grandmother told me to stay in the car. My mother came out of the upstairs apartment with her sleeve rolled up with a white turtleneck sweater on. Her hair was still in disarray and matted in one area. Actually she looked worse than she did when I saw her in the hospital, but she was a little more defiant today than she was that day because she appeared to be more energized than she did when we saw her at the hospital that last time.

I could hear my mother and grandmother yelling at one another. Mommy didn't want Grandma there, but Grandma Edna had been involved in the medical field for an extensive amount of time and she knew that Mommy was not well and she wanted to get her to a hospital, but Mommy was not having any of it. Eventually my mother came outside on the porch with a thick white turtleneck sweater and began to yell obscenities toward my father as my grandma and father were descending the upstairs suite of this two family dwelling. My mother screamed "Why the FUCK did you bring her over here Allen?" My father for the first time in my life ignored my mother without a response and instead got in the car. My Grandma expressed her concern for my mother and begged her to return to New York with her immediately.

My mother, I think just to get rid of her, stated in a nonchalant manner, "I'll think about it Mama!" I shouted to my mother, in the midst of her relentless tongue lashing and half-baked agreement to consider going back to New York, "Look Ma, I got my new uniform, do you want to see it?" She half-heartedly acknowledged me and said "Yeah baby where is it?" I got out the car and modeled the sweatshirt top minus the pants;. I also was able to take my shoes out of the box and show her the track shoes. She simply said "They look nice Mike!!" Apparently, I was not her chief concern, neither was her mother, my father or anything that was not traveling through her veins and giving her that feeling of euphoria she received from the heroin.

My mother turned her head violently towards the door, stomped so hard that it sounded like the porch's wooden floor was cracking and she then grabbed the screen door and slammed it with so much force as she re-entered the house that the windows on the porch shook.

Grandma Edna took me and daddy back to Grandma Lula's house. I had an uneasy feeling the entire way back to the house. Grandma said, "Allen I'll go back tonight and try and convince her to listen and to get some help." Grandma knew that mommy had checked herself out of the hospital without the approval of any medical staff person. She wanted her to return because she was very concerned about her demeanor and the way she looked. Daddy then responded, "Mama, I think that's fine. But I don't think I should have any contact with her right now." I sat in the back seat quiet during the entire trip. I would wait until I arrived at the house to tell my sister what happened. I told my sister what occurred, but she was unaware of the possible consequences of our mother's behavior. I prayed longer and harder than I ever had, because of the uneasy feeling I possessed.

According to Grandma Edna, she returned to my mother's house on Saturday. She and my mother had a very long and honest conversation about my mother's health status. My mother, despite her stubbornness extended both hands to my Grandma Edna so that she could help her. Grandma sensed how weak mommy was but would wait until after Easter Sunday to take her back to New York. She ran the water in the tub for mommy and then helped her into the tub. She sat on the toilet that was near the tub and washed mommy's back and her hair while mommy sat in the tub and relaxed. It was like the hundreds of times that she bathed her as a child.

Grandma told me that she could see exhaustion in mommy's eyes but simply counted it towards mommy coming down off the high. After mommy sat in the tub and relaxed for approximately thirty minutes, Grandma Edna helped her out of the tub and wrapped the large bath towel around her petite frame. She helped her to her bedroom and put lotion on her legs that were covered with the needle marks. Her skin was so tight, because of her weight loss, that one could see the path of the veins and arteries in mommy's body without the assistance of a MRI machine. Mommy laid down and Grandma watched as mommy fell asleep not too confident that her baby girl would be better.

Although, Grandma was so uncertain about my mother's condition getting better she still got up on Easter Sunday morning to attend services at Cleveland Church of Christ. She wanted to make sure that my sister and I went to church with her so she called so we would be ready. She checked on my mother and while her breathing was slow, it wasn't at an emergency level; Grandma Edna wanted to give mommy more time to rest. I always enjoyed Easter Sunday, especially since we stopped going to church consistently, because I knew for at least one Sunday morning I could hear some words of encouragement. It wouldn't be a fire and brimstone message because the preachers were usually before a congregation that was at capacity. People who didn't regularly attend church would find their way to some place of worship and request forgiveness for a year's worth of sins. I also liked the fact that we would usually get a new outfit that I would wear that day and maybe other days when I went to church service by myself.

On this Sunday we waited patiently for Grandma Edna to arrive probably more so, than before because we thought mommy would be in the car with her. We were upset by not seeing mommy but grandma was a good substitute. I don't recall the message that Bishop James Haughton Sr. preached that Sunday mainly due to my inability to concentrate because of my concern for my mother's condition. Grandma must have sensed our concern because after service instead of taking us straight home, she decided to take us to mommy's house. I was ecstatic because I would have to a chance to talk to my mother, to get the uneasy feeling out of my system. When we arrived on mommy's street Grandma turned right into my Aunt Jessie's driveway instead of left into Mr. Leonard's driveway.

We hadn't seen my Aunt Jessie or our "Uncle" Freddie, and "Aunt" Stella for a while, primarily due to Grandma Edna's absence. We sat over there for a short time watching television while Grandma went across the street to see about my mother. She too must have had a bad feeling because she didn't even allow us to go over to see mommy. I grew even more anxious, as did my sister, when my Grandma failed to return for more than ten minutes. I heard some commotion coming from outside and so I went to the living room where a large pain window facing Mr. Leonard's house was placed. I took the curtain and moved it slowly so as to peek outside through the window without exposing myself to anyone. My sister was at the other end also watching.

I saw my grandma on the left side of my mother with my grandma's arm in a flexed position with my mother's right arm being cradled by Grandma Edna's arm. The unidentified person was on my mother's right side with his arm in the same position as Grandma's with mommy's other arm cradling his. Her legs were dragging across the pavement with her shoes barely on. She had a knitted hat and a long trench coat on to keep the cool air from making her sick. I tried to call out to my mom, through the thick glass pain window, but unbeknownst to me she was unconscious. We only saw the back of her head and her body; we never got a chance to see her face that day.

They eventually placed mommy into Grandma Edna's car and the car screeched out of the driveway. Aunt Jessie then took me and my sister back to Grandma Lula's. Grandma Lula must have known that something serious was wrong because she simply asked us how was service, gave us our Easter dinner and then made sure my sister and I went to the movies with an older relative. She didn't give us any details about what mommy's status was or where she was. We didn't even know that she was at the hospital.

We drove out to Randall Mall and watched one of the several popular movies that were out during that time. I don't recall the name because my focus was on why my mother was being dragged into a car with her knees bouncing off the pavement. I couldn't wait for the credits to roll. When we entered the movie theater it was light outside but when we exited the sky was dark and ominous. Grandma Lula didn't mind that we were coming home a little late because she knew we didn't have school the next week, due to the beginning of spring break. Grandma Lula was even more distant than she had been before we left. She didn't tell us anything about my mother and while I was still worried I believed that Grandma's reluctance to tell us anything meant nothing was wrong.

My father's absence also failed to alert me to any impending ill regarding my mother because. my dad would routinely be gone at night, especially since he knew Grandma Lula was caring for us. He recently was released from the Halfway house and was trying to catch up on the two years he lost when he was incarcerated. At about 10:00 p.m, Grandma made me and my sister, go to bed. My sister did her usual routine of getting her cot out and then getting in the bed. I put my pajamas on and knelt down beside the bed like I had done for most of the nights since I was eight, (8) but this time was different. I was scared because no one was giving us any information about mommy. Grandma Lula was quiet and kept wiping her eyes, daddy wasn't home and Grandma Edna hadn't called or came back over. I prayed for God to watch over my mother. I prayed that he would help her overcome her addiction and that he help her simply get better. I then rocked myself to sleep.

At about 11:00 p.m., while I was dreaming, I had a terrible feeling overcome me. It felt like a sense of sadness and grief that was unexplainable. It felt as though my body was experiencing this emptying feeling. It was similar to taking a deep breath and then exhaling for approximately thirty seconds. I then woke up and looked over in the bed next to me and daddy still wasn't home. I laid back down until about midnight when I heard the front door open.

Daddy came in to the house and stumbled over the chairs and I overheard him tell my sister to get up and put some clothes on, because we had to go for a ride. He then came into the room and he woke me up and said in a slurring fashion, "Mike get up and get dressed." I smelled a beer and wine mixture on his breath that almost singed my eyebrows. I was a little nervous to go anywhere with him, but he was pretty insistent on us getting dressed and not making too much noise. I came outside my room into the dining room and my sister was already dressed and looking confused and scared, because she was unsure why my father was behaving irrationally.

We all left the house and my father was able to lock the door but he had some trouble getting off the porch. He could barely stand up and instead was stumbling down the porch with his arms wrapped around me and my sister. His words were slurred but she and I both were able to follow his directions. He told me and my sister to both get in the front seat of the car. My father's eyes were bloodshot red, and I automatically assumed it was from the alcohol, especially since he also had trouble putting the keys in the ignition. He fumbled the keys several times and finally put the key in the ignition and started the car. He then put the car in reverse and hit the accelerator so hard that rocks flew in into the air and the car then moved backwards jarring us a little and then finally struck a bush less than ten feet away from the car's parked position.

He then placed the car back into drive and hit the accelerator again. More rocks flew up and he drove toward the house, to get out of the bushes, and stopped abruptly to avoid hitting the house. He eventually turned the car off, started crying and his voice started to tremble. I never saw him show this type of emotion and it was scary. I knew something was wrong and tried to brace myself for the news, but before I could he said through his sniffling, through the wiping away of tears, through his trembling voice, "Michael and Ressie your mother didn't make it. Mommy is dead" I just looked at him and said "No, no, no, no, no, no, no, no" with my voice high pitched and my eyes watering like a broken fire hydrant spewing water without restraint. I then responded, "That can't be right! Let's go to the hospital I want to see her. Can I see her?" My father said, "No. We aren't going to the hospital. I just came from the hospital. She is gone and she's not coming back!"

My sister and I held each other and then we hugged Daddy, and all three of us were crying, with me and my sister yelling "WHY?" We stayed in the car for what seemed like an eternity. As we got out of the car I was simply numb. I was in a state of denial and thought that when I woke up in the morning, someone would tell us that a mistake had been made and that she would be okay. I cried myself back to sleep and kept an unrealistic hope that this was a dream and that I would be able to see my mother alive again.

I would never see my mother alive again, despite my delusions of grandeur. Despite her valiant attempt to fight, her body was too small and to weakened by the disease she contracted from using hypodermic needles. The blood disease is what caused her initial hospitalization, when we saw her several weeks before her death. She must have had some inkling that she was not well and decided to check herself out of the hospital. She determined she was not going to spend the rest of her days on earth in a hospital.

Ironically she found herself back in the hospital nonetheless trying to fight for her life on a day when Christians celebrate Jesus' resurrection. As my Grandma Edna told me she delivered my mother to the hospital she was unconscious, with a negligible heartbeat, low blood pressure and barely breathing. My mother's heart was resuscitated more than eight times that day and into the night. My Grandma Edna knew how precarious my mother's situation was, prior to the final resuscitation, and decided to call Bishop James Haughton from Cleveland Church of Christ.

Cleveland Church of Christ was the primary place of worship for most of my family. My Grandma Edna was a member of the church prior to leaving for New York, my cousins were members, my Aunt Chris, my Uncle Bill her husband, and my Aunt Jessie. Although, my mother was not a member but had visited on a number of occasions, Pastor James Haughton Sr. was very receptive towards my Grandma Edna's request for him and his son Elder Lincoln Haughton, to come and provide last rites for my mother. That would be the last time any minister spoke over my mother while she was living.

COPING WITH AN UNBEARABLE LOSS

That next morning I was up early because I was accustomed to waking up early for school. Grandma woke up, drawing the shade, and bringing some natural light into the house to brighten up what was going to be a dreary day. It was sunny outside, but inside my heart and my mind, it was pretty dark. Grandma poked her head into the bedroom that I and Daddy shared, and told him, "Allen wake up so you can talk to these kids!" Daddy said in a groggy and melancholy voice "Mama, I already told them." At that point I didn't need any more clarification. I knew that if Grandma Lula was saying that mommy was dead then that was true.

The feelings I experienced earlier that morning in the driveway came rushing back and I sat on Grandma Lula's lap with my head on her shoulder, and cried uncontrollably for another five minutes, asking her "why, why?" She just rubbed my head, kissed and consoled me. Then, she told me everything was going to be fine. I didn't have school that day, or track to take my mind off of my mother because we were on vacation. That's all I thought about the whole day, good and bad times. I thought about the times I had with my mother, her beautiful caramel face, and the times where she would hug and kiss me.

I can recall the times when she would help me with homework if I needed it. I rarely needed it, but when I did, she helped. I remember times when she was cooking and just smiling. I remembered the holidays with her cooking and us opening presents. I remembered some of the birthdays and the presents. I remembered the bad times as well. The times when she was high, the times where she wasn't able to make it to my academic or athletic events, the times she exposed us to danger, the lack of food and stability. I remember the times she was beaten, and the times she tried to conceal the physical and drug abuse that was perpetrated upon her and what she did to herself respectively.

When I realized that my mother was dead I began to question God's love for me. I had prayed, behaved like I thought a Christian should behave, I didn't do or sale drugs, I wasn't in a gang, I wasn't mean, I was cooperative and disciplined. I thought I did everything right and didn't understand why my prayers to keep my mother safe and to help her get better weren't answered. Why would he take my mother at such a young age? I then blamed myself and thought I did something to anger God and that I was being punished somehow by my mother's death. I was wondering if God knew that my mother was suffering and that she was being disobedient, why didn't he give her just one more chance? Why wasn't mercy spared on her just one more day?

I couldn't reconcile what happened to my mother with my understanding of Jesus' compassion and his words about hope and redemption. It wasn't until I started to go back to church on a more consistent basis that I was finally able to understand. Nevertheless, the pain of losing your mother, the person who gave you life, the person who was morally responsible for ensuring that you make it to adulthood and that you thrive, therein would dissipate but never be completely extinguished.

The pain was intensified on the day of my mother's funeral service. Mommy was given a pauper's funeral because she didn't have any insurance, and she wasn't working. Grandma Edna didn't have any insurance and didn't have much money for an average celebration of life service. My Great Uncle James Gohanna assisted my Grandma Edna with the funds to pay for the small service at the Baldwin Funeral Home. My mother's body was displayed in a borrowed coffin and my Grandmother Edna chose to have my mother cremated because she could not afford a coffin, vault, or plot. We drove to the funeral in a car that was provided by Baldwin's Funeral Home. It took me a while to get dressed because I knew that would be the last time, I would see my mother's face aside from my dreams and pictures. I didn't want to rush to that event. The limousine drove down our street and parked in front of Grandma Lula's house. Limousines appeared in our neighborhood on two occasions, for a funeral and maybe prom. They were as uncommon as two parent households and thus just like when the latter occurred when a limo drove down the street everyone thought of it as a phenomenon. I used to dream about getting in my first limo, as a wide receiver in the National Football League. I didn't want this practice opportunity to be for my mother's funeral.

Me, daddy and my sister all entered the limo where my Grandma Edna was already sitting inside. It was so quiet on the ride there; you could hear an ant pissing on cotton. My eyes looked like I had been chopping onions all day. My father with his square jaw and stern eyes said nothing.

We drove approximately twenty to thirty minutes through the east side of Cleveland. People tried to peer through the tinted windows, not sure whether we were celebrities, going to the prom, or to a funeral service, since we were not trailing a hearse or a funeral director car. When we arrived at Baldwin's, I was the last person to get out of the car. I hesitated going into the funeral home because it was such a sense of finality between me and my mother that I didn't want to accept so soon.

My father who was usually pretty terse when he thought I was taking too much time, was more patient and understanding. He said with a very low voice "Michael it's okay I'll wait." When I did drag myself out of the limousine my chest began to heave up and down and my eyes began to water uncontrollably. My father simply placed his arms around my neck, in a loving, comforting manner, unlike what he did to my mother on many occasions, and pulled me away from the stairs that lead to the funeral door entrance. My father and I took a walk around the block and we didn't say a word to one another. I realized that it was difficult for him too, because of the sniffling and the constant wiping of his eyes with the tattered tissue he held in his hands.

Eventually we made it back around to the front of the funeral home and we made the long trek up the front stairs and into the funeral parlor. I walked down the aisle on my father's right side, while my sister was on his left side. I noticed my cousins, aunts, uncles and my mother friends in the seats closest to the exit. My grandmother and my great uncle were already sitting down in the front row, directly in front of the coffin. It seemed like every step I took towards the casket; more tears would build in my eyes as well as a sharp stabbing pain in my heart. We all ultimately made it to the inexpensive coffin.

My mother was wearing a light blue dress with a collar up to her neck and long sleeves. Her dress was reminiscent of the dresses that southern belles wore in the early 1800's. The long sleeves covered up the track marks that were left by the numerous times she injected herself with the needles, filled with heroin. Her face looked like someone had taken an air pump and put it in the back of her neck and pressed on the trigger. She looked like she weighed more than 120 pounds when I doubt she ever weighed more than a few pounds over 100. Her face was clear as a baby's bottom. She looked like she was asleep, like all I needed to do to wake her, was to whisper in her ear "It's okay to wake up now Mommy." I actually tried to whisper that in her ear but was alarmed at how cold and stiff her arms were when I touched them after reaching down towards her ear.

I was shocked because I didn't realize that when you died your body felt like a rock; I was accustomed to having my mother's soft hands and skinny arms around me. I leaned over and kissed her on her cold and hard cheek and then sat down next to my father as the service commenced. I cried throughout the service. I saw and heard my father and my sister crying as well. My Grandma Edna was devastated; my mother was the second child of her three children that died before she did. It simply was not natural for her to be burying her children. I cried so hard at times that I couldn't catch my breath. There were fluids coming from my eyes and nose. I would yell at times, like a person afflicted with the Turrets condition, "NO MOMMY NO." I was just a total wreck.

Eventually the service ended. It was one of the toughest days I've ever had in my entire life. I don't recall any other day being as tough as that day. It was emotionally traumatizing seeing them close the casket on my mother especially, as a teenager and knowing that I'll never be able to hold her again. I'll never be able to feel the warmth of her hugs or kisses, receive any advice from her or get the opportunity to see her turn her life around. It was unnatural for a teenager to be standing over the casket of their parent, especially when the parent and child were only separated by fifteen years. When they closed the casket, all hope of my mother seeing me become a man, all hope that she would celebrate my promotions from middle school, high school, college and law school, all the hope that she would meet my wife and help me raise her grandchildren were foreclosed by her death.

The days following the funeral were really excruciating, and emotionally painful because I just walked around in a daze, in a sense simply numb. I was a little more reactionary, short-fused, to say the least. I think most people didn't find it hard to excuse my behavior although it wasn't something that was just abnormal or erratic.

I went back to Central, a little depressed, but I was still able to focus, because this was my eighth grade year and I had other activities to keep my mind from reflecting on my mother's death. I was working hard in class, preparing for the upcoming track season, and I was president of student council. I was also being inducted into the National Junior Honor Society and I was the Co-Master of Ceremonies for the talent show. I had little if any time to grieve at school but was overwhelmed when I arrived at home, because I had constant nightmares and daydreams about my mother's death and funeral. Grandma Lula did the best she could to help me and my sister. She gave us our time and space to grieve but she didn't want us to be so consumed by what happened to the extent that we forgot how to live and how to do well so that my mother, if she were here, would be proud.

Grandma Lula was ecstatic about my grades, National Honor Society award, captain position on the track team, and participation as president of student council. She, however, was reluctant about me applying for the A Better Chance (ABC) program. The ABC program allowed intellectually gifted children from poor impoverished areas, to attend private schools at little to no cost. Philip Exeter, was the private school in Massachusetts, that was featured during the presentation at Central. I came home and told Grandma about the school and the program. My Grandma Lula didn't want me to leave and instead of saying that publicly, she instead claimed that she would not release her tax return because she didn't want anyone in her business.

One of my friends, Duane, did take advantage of the program and enrolled in a private college preparatory high school in Tennessee. Neither I nor my Grandma Lula knew there were schools in our area, that participated in the program-, University School and Hawken, she heard Philip Exeter in Massachusetts and that was the end; she didn't want to hear anything else about ABC. I would have missed my sister immensely, I would have missed my Grandma Lula very much as well but I needed to escape from Cleveland. I thought a change of scenery would change my fortunes. I was somewhat content with living with Grandma Lula, but my knowledge about my true lineage made me more inclined to not want to be a burden. I wouldn't leave until high school, so I had the remaining part of the school year and the summer. I decided not to object to Grandma's decision to restricting my growth and instead refocused on my Eighth grade year and my ensuing freshman year in high school.

BREAKING OUT OF A SHELL DESPITE HEARTACHE

As President of Student Council, I was also required to be the Master of Ceremonies for our talent show. I, however, had a dilemma because the talent show was scheduled the same day as my track meet, and since I was captain I had a greater responsibility to my track team. I decided that as president of Student Council, I could perform my Master of Ceremonies (MC) part of the talent show but I would need someone to co-host it with me. Thus, I enlisted one of my friends "Klondike" to Co-MC the talent show. I would introduce the acts in the first half and he would introduce the rest during the second half.

He and I had to create an opening to the talent show, but I was more of an introvert, without much rhythm. I worked harder on creating an opening performance, than I had done outside of school and athletics. I knew I had to do a good job because this could change the perception that some people had about me,- from nerd to cool. We decided that we would dance and rap as a way to open the talent show. We devised the lyrics for the original rap song, as well as the dance moves that went along with the song. We kept most of it a secret so that people in the school would be surprised.

I woke up on the morning of the show with butterflies in my stomach. I got dressed and put on my track jogging suit since we were allowed to wear it to school on days when we had a tack meet. I looked like a skinny black Santa Claus, minus the beard, with all my red hoodie and matching pants. I headed to the bus with my backpack and my costume for the talent show. When I arrived at school I snuck my costume into the auditorium, so that no one could discover what I was wearing for the performance. This was one of the few days that I couldn't concentrate in class; the time seemed to melt away like icicles on a cold winter day when the temperature is just above freezing. I was anxious about how the students would react to my performance. In the midst of a half-hearted attempt to listen to my teachers lessons, I was going over my lyrics and dance moves in my head in each class. When the bell rang for the second to last period of the day, I was able to report to the auditorium to get dressed.

I brought my book bag that was filled with homework and books. I also had my track bag that was filled with my spiked track shoes, uniform and replacement spikes. I found a place to disrobe from my track clothing and then placed them in a conspicuous area, so I could locate them relatively quickly. I needed to make sure that I could make an expeditious wardrobe change and get on the bus before it left for the track meet. I put on my burgundy shirt, white pants, rundown penny loafers and one white glove, Klondike had the same outfit. The other acts were also getting prepared and by the time the final bell rang for the last period we were all ready.

There was an excitement among the students, teachers and administrators, both behind the curtain and those in the audience. I was concerned that people would laugh, boo, yell obscenities at us or simply provide token applause, as a way of getting us off the stage and onto the real talent. My hands were so wet from nervousness, that I could have used my hands to seal a thousand envelopes. The audience was packed, I saw all of my friends from Major Work, friends I grew up with in Longwood, flag football and track teammates, my teachers Mr. Woda and of course Mr. Charney. Mr. Charney was the Student Council advisor. I also saw people who didn't know anything about me.

I could hear the crowd chatting and abuzz. The lights went out and it was time for the show to begin. Soon thereafter Klondike and I came out from behind the curtain together and the music started up with the song we selected. I started off with my rap and then began pop-locking starting with my fingers moving down, with my wrist following, and my elbow locking all the way up to my shoulder. Eventually, Klondike joined in but by the time he joined in I could hardly hear him, because of all the noise from the girls that were screaming. "Ahhhhhh", "Yeahhhhhh", and "Ooooooooo" were yelled by everyone with most of the sound being amplified in my ears, because of the adrenaline that course through my body. I could also hear the girls alternating my name and Klondike's by saying "Go Mike" "Go Klon" "Go Mike" "Go Klon" as their hands waved from

side to side.

At that moment I was able to hide behind all the tragedy, heartbreak, and the disappointment. I wasn't the nerd who carried the book bag that alternated as a small overnight luggage bag. I was wonder Mike and I was rocking the mic, like the rap stars of the day. It was rewarding because whenever I appeared on the stage to introduce the next act, I got more applause than the other acts. As the talent show neared the halfway mark, I had to change like Superman from my talent show gear to my track team gear. I jumped on the bus with a renewed pride and confidence because I was no longer just the nerdy kid. Instead I was multitalented, and that made me different, not strange but instead unique. I was so thrilled with the talent show reaction that I ran one of my best races that day in the mile relay.

The track we went to was similar to most of the city tracks, since it was all cinder with faded lane lines. The long jump pit had grass covering the sides of the pit as well as grass growing in the sand. I did my warm up laps at a slow pace, so as not to exert too much energy but enough to wake the muscles up, that hadn't been used in the talent show. I sat down on the ground with Anthony, who also ran the mile with me and we stretched before our event. Just like in other meets I had the chance to rest before my race began so I watched and cheered for my teammates. After my teammates were nearly finished with their events, I would walk to a grassy area, near the starting line and take off my heavy sweatshirt. It would reveal my ultra-thin frame, which was reminiscent of J.J. Walker from Good Times that was swallowed by the small red and white track tank top. I then pulled my sweatpants down over my spiked track shoes, trying to ensure that the small spikes on the bottom of my shoes don't rip my sweatpants.

When I finally did get them off, unlike my arms and chest, my ostrich legs do have some semblance of muscular development. Soon after the track clears, the starter calls our race.

I got on the track and try to get the lane closest to the grass knowing that those who run in the outside lanes actually run further than everyone else. After the loud pop and I took off.

I didn't shoot out like a bullet out a gun because the mile was a tactical race and I needed to pace myself. In this race I was not running against anyone who had a reputation around the city as a good distance runner. I was actually the best runner in that particular race. I ran my normal pace but never permitted anyone else to get ahead of me. If someone tried to run around me I would move to the outer part of lane one or I would attack the curves to make sure they would have to work harder to pass me. The strategy worked for that particular race because I won with relative ease. I ran the mile in the high four minute or low five minute mark. It was not my fastest race in the mile by any stretch. My ending to this mile race was different from the subsequent races because I stayed upright.

In one of my most grueling races I created a signature ending that followed me the rest of the season. The meet was a few days after the talent show. I wound up facing one of the best milers in the city. He was a ninth grader but I'd faced and beaten other ninth graders so I wasn't intimidated. I tried to run with him for most of the race, we exchanged first and second place several times. He would lead for two hundred feet yards; I would then take it back and lead for about one hundred feet. Eventually he took a fifty to seventy-five foot lead in the final lap. I was able to close the gap to forty feet as we were running the curve near the back stretch.

He lifted his extra-long legs and began pulling away while I used my sprinter speed to make it appear as though I was a fisher. I had my hook in him and was reeling him in like a fisherman does his prey. While I made up a lot of ground, I eventually lost the race and was so exhausted that I fell in the arms of a teammate that happened to be waiting at the finish line for the next race. I would look and be provided a personal catcher for each time I completed the mile for the remainder of the year. I used an extensive amount of energy and was rewarded with both victories and physical support after my races. I would have to cool off and then run a quarter of a mile, on the mile relay with three of my other teammates.

We had one of the fastest mile relay teams in the city due to Duane, myself and two other descent runners. While we won our race at districts, we were unable to continue at the City wide meet, because at that time only the top teams were permitted to go to the City meet. We had talented individuals and some relay teams but overall we were at a disadvantage, we still had ninth graders competing against us. I enjoyed the camaraderie since it help breed success on a team that was not expected to compete, because of the age differences.

While we did not have our best showing in the district and school history, we did finish higher than earlier predictions. The track team paralleled my life, wherein we were young and had many challenges but were talented. We didn't let our challenges suffocate our talents and we worked harder than most of the other track teams across the city because we recognized the disadvantages. We made no excuses either, we just competed and we were excited when we won and disappointed when we lost, but it was never to the extreme on either occasion. I made no excuses for the challenges I had in my life nor did I expect to be treated differently because of them. I met the challenges head on and notwithstanding the results, I neither boasted nor sulked. I wholeheartedly believed that I and my team's humility was a vital character, in all of our development. It allowed all of us to excel beyond anyone's wildest imagination. The Least Likely runners, competing against older more developed athletes, were able to win at times but also build our self-confidence and self-esteem even when we lost.

My hard work, perseverance and humility allowed me to collect more than track awards but academic awards as well. Since my grade point average was high I was selected and inducted into the National Junior Honor Society. It was a beautiful ceremony, with candles and a few of my other classmates dressed in their Sunday best. We received certificates and a pin to recognize our efforts in the classroom, school, and our community. I remember standing on stage and reflecting on how much more special this would have been if my mother could have at least had the opportunity to come and watch her oldest receive a prestigious academic award.

Mr. Charney, as an added surprise, also gave me an award that he believed best resembled my personality and talents. He gave me the Paul Robeson award. He stated that my intellect, (High grade in his class and Academic Challenge), activism, athletic ability (Flag Football and Track) and my ability to entertain (Talent Show performance), were similar to the gifts Paul Robeson shared with the world. My classmates would then bestow upon me an honor that I was unaware they even knew I was voted the male student who was "Most Likely to Succeed" and the smartest male student as well by the eighth grade students. Mr. Charney then conferred a wonderful opportunity for me, where he allowed me to provide the student address for our promotional ceremonies.

He assisted me in drafting the message I gave to students, administrators, parents and loved ones. It was the second time that I would be given the opportunity to address my classmates during a promotional ceremony, seeing that I did it in sixth grade as well. I was excited and nervous simultaneously and did a much better job than I did two years ago at Miles Park. There were more people present at this promotion ceremony than Miles Park since more than three elementary schools combined to make up the kids who attended Central Junior High School. I read my speech in what seemed to me like warped speed. In my mind I sounded like the person that conducts the auction where you can hear some of the numbers but wished they slowed down just a bit.

I didn't want to stand up there long since my knees were knocking so hard and I didn't want to embarrass myself or my Grandma Lula by fainting or tripping. Despite the beads of sweat that were dripping off my forehead like sweat drips off a basketball player, who has just finished an hour long practice, I completed the five minute speech and sat down in the audience. I thought it was good and effective, several people approached me afterwards and gave me a pat on my back, as their lips stretched in a sincere encouraging smile and they firmly stated "Great job Mike." All the gains I realized seemed so miniscule compared to my devastating loss and it wasn't until I decided to go back to church that I could overcome this languishing hurt and confused feeling.

ANOTHER UNBEARABLE UNEXPECTED LOSS

My summer was very uneventful unless you count the night that our house was surrounded by a few of my cousin's, Dude's, enemies who were yielding guns. It was about 10:00 p.m. and Grandma Lula, her boyfriend Calvin, my sister and I were sitting in the living room when we heard people yelling and running. We knew they were running because we heard feet trampling over the concrete and then we heard the gravel swishing as they ran through the front yard.

We ran outside and saw about four guys in the front yard, two in the back and three on the side. We all ran outside on the porch and my grandmother yelled "WHAT THE FUCK IS GOING ON?" One of the boys with his hands behind his back like he was concealing something said were looking for "Brim", which was my cousin's nickname. Another kid was bolder and took his gun and waived it in the air side to side and said "Where's the motherfucker at?" My grandmother said she did not know and asked "Why are you looking for him anyway?" They then said they were going to come into our house and search for him. My grandma said "Over my dead body. Calvin go get my gun." Calvin scurried inside the house and retrieved her gun and returned to the porch with it and handed it to Grandma Lula. We all stood there without saying much but eventually Grandma won the standoff because the boys heard that the police were called and they left. While I doubt that the police were ever called my cousin did appear from underneath the backyard porch shortly after the boys had left. Grandma Lula had some choice words for him but she was happy they did not hurt him. He stayed with us a few hours before he walked home without any problems.

I thought that since I was going to high school and since South High School had a good academic reputation I could stay in my neighborhood and attend the high school that was only ten minutes away. Instead I was required to attend East Technical High School because it was the closest school that offered Major Work, which meant that I would be with most of my friends again from Longwood, Tremont and Central.

The academic rigors of high school were not as difficult as the social environment. We were in school with people who were adults.-Most of the seniors and some of the juniors, were more mature with full mustaches and beards. Some of the older guys looked like they swallowed weights. The females weren't little girls but instead were beautiful voluptuous young women that made it difficult for young boys like me to concentrate when I was in the halls. I was fortunate that most of those women were not in my classes otherwise I may not have performed so well.

I was taking, Biology, Geometry, Ninth Grade Social Studies and Ninth Grade English and German along with other electives. I was generally enthusiastic about the classes because of the infectious attitudes of the teachers I had in my core classes. The teachers voices were raised but with an air of excitement about teaching, not one of disdain as they exhibited for students who were misbehaving. They had the day's lesson posted on the chalkboard even before we entered the classroom. In Biology we dissected frogs by using a scalpel and slicing their underbelly. We then were required to expose the inner organs of the frog and appropriately label them for our grades. The more I learned in Biology about the way the body worked, the more afraid I became of my own mortality. Biology just demonstrated to me the complexity and the frailty of the human body. I saw the class as a double edged sword because I loved to learn and was doing well but I was also scared to hear anything else about the body. The latter education coupled with my mother's recent death made me a little nervous.

In all of my core subjects, the teachers placed higher standards upon us than they did on the students who were not in Major Work. They knew we were the cream of the crop and expected us to perform at a high level. They required us to be responsible for knowing what was due for homework, and to be prepared for quizzes and tests. While the latter was expected for the students not in Major Work, I sincerely doubt that it was emphasized to the level it was with us. Unlike the other students, they were shocked and surprised when we did not do well. I enjoyed the academic environment at East Tech, my dilemma was with the social climate.

While there were at least seven grade levels in elementary school it wasn't as populated as high school which was a small cause for concern. The students were much larger, older and sophisticated. The hallways were crowded and at times difficult to navigate, especially when you are young and precocious like most of the freshman who were in my class. There were two experiences that lead me to believe it was going to be a long four years at East Tech. First, Caucasian students that lived near the Garfield Heights border and due to bussing were required to attend East Tech. Some of the students would stand outside East Tech waiting for the bus, when on random days, some young African-American male students, would punch those students in the face or other body parts and then run.

They would go down the line, like an assembly line and punch one kid in the stomach, they'd run down and do the same thing to the next, and the next, and the next and the next. Most of the kids, who were watching either laughed, cheered the predators on or was just in utter disbelief, I was part of the latter group. I did not move to intercede because I was unsure if their hate would then transfer to me, I was thinking about self-preservation. What perplexed me was that the victims were unwilling to fight back or to run. They could have escaped by going back into the building but declined to do so. I wished I had more courage at that time to at least utter something, about how hypocritical their behavior appeared because African Americans had been the brutal victims of the same type of violence, not less than the thirty years before that incident.

We couldn't erase years of frustration, discrimination and anger by exacting violence on young people, who did not cause or were not causing the angst they may have felt because of their perceptions of race relations in our country at that time. This culture of violence was not limited to just Caucasian students, but was pervasive throughout the school. I also witnessed a violent food fight. It started off just like the ones you see in the movies. First there was a French Fry thrown across one table and then a "Motherfucker" was uttered by the person who was hit in the face. That individual then threw a hotdog in the general vicinity of where the fry came but hit a person who was not involved. That individual then yelled "OH NO THE HELL YOU DIDNT", and then threw their entire tray in the area where the hot dog originated. That then led to food flying like asteroids in space.

Me and one of my classmates from Central, was sitting next to one another laughing and trying to avoid being hit with any of the Pizza, Applesauce, Hot Dogs, Hamburgers, French Fries and other unidentified food items, that were being tossed. Eventually the food fight evolved into a mini riot, because one of the participants got angry and decided to throw a chair. Someone else responded in kind with a chair and that's when I decided to move towards the exit. I was trying to locate my friend and figured he had made it out of the cafeteria. I, however, learned that he hadn't escaped after I witnessed one of the students try to pick up one of the tables, my friend was hiding underneath.

I didn't stay at East Tech for the whole year because my Grandma Lula realized the neighborhood where we lived was too dangerous and she didn't want to be a target for retaliation for what transpired with those kids from that night they surrounded the house. We eventually relocated to a home on the corner of E. 116th and Kinsman. When we moved it was to an area in the district where I could attend one of the best junior high schools in the city and state, Whitney Young. Every time I drove on Harvard Avenue near the intersection of Lee Road, I saw the white and blue sign that read Blue Ribbon School. Whitney Young generally had the highest standardized tests scores because all of the students were in Major Work, not just a select few in each grade.

It was a place where learning was accepted and highly recommended from each person that was a part of the student body. The school had a reputation of producing some of the brightest students in the district. The students were always winning academic awards and going on to shine in high schools throughout the district. I knew those students had been a part of the district's honor program since they were very young. I was required to transfer and did not initially want to back down from a challenge. I would essentially be digressing because I was going from high school to junior high school. I would only spend three marking periods there since I completed my first marking period at East Tech high school.

I entered Whitney Young with an expectation that I could succeed despite the fact that I would be slightly behind those students. I quickly caught up when it came to the class work and performed well. I had to again prove myself to another set of students, teachers and administrators. I think that my zest for knowledge was received better here because the competition was not centered upon who was the toughest, who had the best clothes, who was the best athlete, or the best looking but instead upon how one performed when it came to their academic performance. I had to establish friendships with people I had never met. It was not too awkward for me to adjust since I had done this before on prior occasions.

I found that helping people with their class work endeared me to some of my classmates. I also found that telling them stories about high school made me a little more interesting. I decided to participate on the track team which also helped me gain more friends. In fact, one of the friends that I met via track and several classes would become one of my college classmates-Stan Drayton. Stan was a good guy because he knew how uncomfortable I felt and he approached me and made the transition from East Tech to Whitney Young smoother. He gave me advice on the teachers and the girls who were in the school, to which I was very much appreciative.

While my time at Whitney Young was very short I did acquire a great sense of confidence because I competed with the best students, and did well despite their years of elementary preparation for middle school honor work. I didn't receive straight A's but I did receive the merit roll despite trying to play catch up. The only two subjects I had trouble, but didn't receive anything lower than a C in was English and Geometry. I was also able to demonstrate my abilities when it came to track. I helped the Whitney Young team win the district championship and qualify for the City Championship in the mile relay. I was again able to balance my academics with my athletics participation.

It was also here at Whitney Young that the young ladies started to notice me a little bit more than they did in the other schools. Overall the girls were a little more forward than what I had experienced. I kind of noticed that some of them were talking to me more than others and I didn't realize until afterwards that they were whispering about me, "He's cute. A little skinny but cute anyway." I was quiet, a recluse, I was a stranger, and I wasn't funny but I liked to laugh and so I didn't have any of the "qualities" that young ladies usually seek especially at that age. The girls generally wanted the more popular guy, the jock, the guy who has the funniest jokes, or the most money and that just wasn't me. I had a cute face and I was smart, but that's not what the young ladies were attracted to at that time.

The neighborhood that we moved to was nice, similar type of home compared to the one we just vacated, a tad larger and in much better condition. Oh my, was it in much better condition. I thought Grandma Lula actually had purchased the house. It turns out that she was just renting, but nonetheless, you could have fooled me. I thank God that we actually moved from the house off of Miles, because it was rat infested and it had some other roaches just like those in Longwood, but not as numerous. The only negative thing I associated with the move to 116th was that I never received a mattress and had to sleep on a sheet and blanket for a year in a half that covered just a box spring; it wasn't great for my back!

Grandma Lula's health was in a precarious state when we moved to the house at the intersection of 116th and Kinsman and I could tell she was declining with respect to her energy. She was still cooking but was directing me and my sister to do more chores around the house. She made more frequent visits to the doctor and she would return back home with more bottled filled medication. I would see her with a glass of water and swallowing two to three pills. She also increasingly made comments to me and my sister that "When she was gone that my sister and I would be taken care of and we wouldn't have to worry." I didn't pay much attention to that, I just assumed she meant when we were adults. I knew she wouldn't be alive forever; she was in her mid-Fifties when she secured custody of me and my sister. I, however, didn't have any inclination that she was severely sick. I actually was not contemplating that because I was still trying to deal with my mother's death. Grandma Lula was dealing with the new move, trying to raise a teenager and a pre- teen, her own health concerns and the depression that my sister and I were experiencing because of my mother's death.

A week after the one year anniversary of my mother's death, I found myself sitting in the living room having completed my homework and watching a little television. I had already eaten and Grandma Lula was in the kitchen. She came from the kitchen area and sat at the dining room table. Grandma indicated that she was not feeling well and first asked my father to retrieve her medication from her bedroom. My father was upstairs and may have been sleep because he did not immediately respond to grandma's request. A few minutes later she yelled upstairs again but this time she said "ALLEN COME TAKE ME TO THE HOSPITAL, I DON'T FEEL RIGHT. MAKE SURE YOU BRING MY MEDICINE DOWNSTAIRS." She went and retrieved her coat and hat and then sat at the table again with a glazed look and labored breathing.

I noticed something was amiss because I could hear her breathing, despite the fact that the television's volume was moderately loud. I decided to get up and see what was taking my father so long to come downstairs. Grandma soon got up from the table and headed towards the door in a hurried fashion with her cloth hat halfway cocked on her head and her coat semi-fastened. She yelled "ALLEN COME ON HURRY UP", as she fumbled for the knob. Grandma eventually was able to open the door and stepped outside, only to collapse after she got beyond the foyer onto the wooden porch. I saw her hit the porch and called "DADDY, DADDY HURRY GRANDMA FAINTED AND SHE'S ON THE PORCH." I ran outside and began to cry.

I tried to talk to grandma but she was incoherent. Her eyes were glazed and her breathing was very shallow. I could only detect a faint heartbeat. She was mumbling something but I couldn't understand it. She was barely moving and I didn't think that she would make it off the porch alive. My father called 911 but it seemed like forever before any medical professionals arrived to provide any assistance. I was tempted to run down the street to the fire station that was located a mere two hundred yards away from the house. I thought about trying to administer Cardio Pulmonary Resuscitation (CPR) because I believed that she had suffered a heart attack; I would later discover that it was a stroke instead. I was frightened for Grandma because I knew she was in serious trouble. I couldn't fathom life without her, since it had been the best I'd experienced since I was old enough to remember, and I didn't want her to die. Eventually, the ambulance arrived but Grandma Lula had experienced a major health crisis and was transported to the hospital and placed in the Intensive Care Unit (ICU).

My aunts made huge sacrifices to make sure me and my sister were cared for while Grandma Lula was in the hospital. My Aunt Mary, Aunt Joann or Aunt Marie would make sure me and my sister would get a chance to visit Grandma Lula. They would also ensure that we got off to school, and that we had something to eat as well. They took on an additional burden because we were family and they knew they had to help their brother assist with providing for his children. They never publicly complained to me or my sister regarding, their extra responsibilities despite dealing with their own grief because of their mom's serious medical condition. The visits to the hospital were heart wrenching. The doctor's expressed to us that grandma was in a coma and being kept alive by a ventilator.

I didn't understand the severity of her condition because I was convinced, all I needed to do was speak to her and she would summon the strength she needed to arise, from the coma and be on the road to recovery. When I came to the hospital, it looked eerily similar to the place I visited shortly before my mother died. The white walls and the indescribable hospital smell, the one you know when you smell it but can't compare it to anything else, was common for all medical facilities. I would pass each room every day and see other patients in the ICU, that were hooked to machines via large plastic tubes with the bells and whistles on, those machines blaring loudly.

A sense of hopelessness would consume me because those people were generally alone with little to no visitors. I didn't think that way with Grandma Lula because she had so many kids (6), grand kids (20+) and other relatives, family and friends. She had supportive children and qualified, competent doctors at St. Luke's hospital. I quickly learned that despite that support, prayers and time, grandma's body was weak and battered. Her exterior, depicted a very strong, courageous woman but even she was vulnerable to the issues of life. I wished her desire to raise us had more power and strength, than the natural causes that lead to her hospital stay. My aunts, uncles and my father realized that they had to make a very tough decision. They could leave my grandmother on a ventilator, the only thing keeping her alive, for virtually the rest of her life or simply turn it off and let her go.

The two women who had been instrumental in making me the man, that I was at age fourteen (14), suffered medical ailments that I had no control over. My aunts, uncles and my father would be losing the matriarch of the family. She was the leader, adviser, mediator, bank, etc. my sister and I saw her as a savior because without her we would have been in foster care or worse. She sacrificed for me and my sister when she was not legally bound to do it. Her desire and dedication to me was even more remarkable due to my lack of blood ties. She loved me unconditionally and for that I was grateful.

It was hard trying to maintain school work, focus, and go back and forth to the hospital and seeing grandma on the ventilator. I had a false sense of hope because her eyes would blink and she would squeeze our hands, but according to the doctor those were simply involuntary actions the body made. All of the kids were going to have to weigh in on this, in terms of whether or not to keep her lungs working on a ventilator, knowing full well that she would never be able to regain, the mental ability or capacity that she needed to function like she normally did. She essentially would be a vegetable for the remainder of her life. The doctors were saying that she was clinically brain dead.

My sister and I would not be consulted about the life or death decision concerning Grandma Lula, even though we would be impacted more than anyone else. It was a blessing that we didn't have to decide because doing would have been like an anchor to a cruise ship docked at a port. It was difficult to watch her struggle as opposed to feeling her kisses on my cheek, or her warm soft and jelly like arms surround my thin frame and squeeze until I felt safe or to smell the delicious aroma of pork chops, collard greens, sweet potatoes permeating the house. I couldn't imagine her not being present anymore, not having her be the protector that she had been for us for the last 2 ½ years. That was just an unnerving feeling for me again. I was in another emotionally troubling state because I didn't know what was going to happen next.

Approximately a week in half after Grandma Lula was admitted into the hospital my father and his siblings made a heart-wrenching decision, they decided to take Grandma Lula off of the ventilator. I, however, was able to say goodbye even though I doubt that she was able to understand me before they removed all of the tubes and detached the machine that was keeping her alive. I whispered in grandma's ear as the tears simultaneous poured into my mouth, "I love you grandma. I'm going to miss you. I will make sure that I do things that will make you proud of me. I'm so sorry that you have to go so soon. Thank you for saving me and I promise to take care of my sister. Please give my mommy a kiss for me when you see her in heaven!" I wiped away the tears and snot from my nose with my sleeve and left the hospital room. My sister and I were home when we got news that Grandma had died. While I was emotionally spent I didn't feel as cheated as I did just 373 days ago. I felt cheated when it came to my mother's situation because I didn't get a chance to say goodbye, while warm blood was still coursing through her veins. I was emotionless at times. I refused to cry publicly when I was told Grandma Lula died because I was secretly crying myself to sleep on the nights when I went to bed and Grandma Lula was in the bed at the hospital. I cried when I walked to the bus before I boarded it with a melancholy look. I couldn't manufacture any more tears because of the pain of my mother and then watching my grandma slip away from me from the porch to the hospital to the life support machine to the funeral.

My Aunt Mary came to the rescue after Grandma Lula died. She tried to fill the void that grandma left. She sacrificed her own family by accepting the responsibility of raising two more children. Her first order of business was to help organize Grandma Lula's home going service and take care of her own son, daughter, me and my sister simultaneously. I thought she did a magnificent job of keeping me and my sister emotionally intact during this trying time. Our relationship with Grandma was different than most of our cousins because of our daily interaction with Grandma Lula; we essentially were her kids and now we had lost our primary caregiver.

As I stated earlier I had tried to keep my pain, insecurity, misunderstanding and agony secret but the morning of the service brought reality to me, that she was not returning home. I sat at the living room table and was overcome by emotion and simply began to cry. I thought that God had given us a blessed substitute for my mother in the form of Grandma Lula. She was supposed to at least watch me graduate from high school, at minimum see me win my first race in high school, see me catch my first pass in high school, see me go to the prom, get married, hold, and kiss my children, etc. All those hopes were dashed when she took her last breath. My realization of the latter facts caused my body to find tears that I thought had dried up like the Sahara Desert.

My eyes continued to water profusely, such that wiping them did no good because the tears simply refused to subside. My sister and I soon had to ride in another funeral home limousine and drove to E. 105th street to the Strowder Funeral Home. The view was not much different from what we experienced last year around this time. People stopped to pay their respects, some even taking their hats off as we passed. My Grandma Lula's funeral service was much different than my Mommy's. My grandmother had so many relatives and just so many loved ones because she had a policy that took care of her burial, in fact she would be buried next to her late husband, William Belcher and he died, in 1982 or 83. So in the span of six years, I lost three people that I really loved and cared immensely about. Grandma Lula's kids ~ ~~~ grand kids and great ~grand kids, cousins, aunts and other relatives came to the funeral service.

My Aunt Joann was more impacted by Grandma Lula's death than anyone else, at least her public demonstration indicated as much, where she boisterously yelled "NO MAMA, No!" Tears were streaming down her face, while she leaned on another person who was helping carry her down the aisle towards Grandma Lula. After much melodrama, she reached Grandma's casket and threw herself onto Grandma Lula's casket as her wails grew louder and louder. I vaguely remember her daughters and other family members trying to pry her away from Grandma Lula, which was almost impossible because of Aunt Joann's monster grip.

She eventually made it to her seat but had to be consoled throughout the service. My cousin Andora had a beautiful voice and wanted to share it with the family and sing a song in grandma's memory. She started off well but the words of the song had such an impact on her and reminded her of Grandma Lula, that her tears and sobs began to drown out her voice. Her emotional breakdown was like a domino effect and caused most of the people at Strowders to start crying as well. Most people reflected about how the matriarch, the one who pretty much held the family together was now gone. She was the glue that bound the family and that glue sort of melted away, you could see the beginning stages of the deterioration of the strong family bond.

Grandma had on a beautiful black dress. I actually took some of my trophies that I won for track and I put them in the casket, they're still there to this day. I wanted her to know that she meant the world to me. I was able to excel in track, school, community and at home because her sacrifice gave me an opportunity. I figured that she surrendered so much for me, that giving up my trophy was the least sacrificial/unselfish act I could perform. I believed that the love Grandma Lula showed me was different from the love she gave my sister because she loved, treated, protected and provided for me with the same vigor, that she did for my sister notwithstanding the uncontested knowledge that I was not her biological grandson. She pulled me and my sister out of a dire situation and gave us the stability, which children normally receive in traditional families, that allowed us to blossom and not wither. I think it was something that impacted the course of my life and diverted me from becoming a negative statistic to a positive one. I am forever grateful for what Grandma Lula did on behalf of me and my sister.

While the latter thoughts were parading through my mind, I was still very fearful about life. I was taking Biology learning more about human anatomy, and dealing with the loss of two prominent people in my life, and thus I was keenly aware of the frailty of human life and was concerned that my Grandma Edna would be the next person to die unexpectedly. I expressed my concerns to her at Grandma Lula's service by pleading between my sobs and tears. I said, while I was holding her as tight as a new born holds onto the parent who swings them around during a game of Ring around the Rosie's, "Don't die on me too Grandma", She said. "Don't worry honey; I'm not going to go anywhere." That was comforting at the time, but I didn't really believe it because, the women caregiver's who were in my life, I just couldn't trust that they would be there for a significant amount of time. After the service at the funeral home we drove to Grandma Lula's final resting spot, which actually took me back to a familiar area. Grandma Lula was buried at Calvary Cemetery, which was two blocks away from our previous home on E. 98th. I visited infrequently because of my inability to drive and her plot was located well into the cemetery.

I was a nervous wreck by the time the fall approached for my tenth grade year at John Adams High School, actually that summer I couldn't sleep because I was afraid that I wasn't going to wake up. I had nightmares about dying. I had nightmares about my mommy's death, Grandma Lula's death, and my maternal great-grandmother's death that occurred during the summer after Grandma Lula died. I went to my Aunt Mary one night and told her about my restlessness and she said, "Pray to God and ask him to take away your dreams so that you could sleep." I followed her advice and subsequently bent down on my knees on the side of my bed and reiterated what Aunt Mary suggested. It was as though I took a sleeping pill and was completely unconscious from the time my head hit the pillow until I woke up. While I probably did dream, I had no recollection of my dreams and went to sleep.

My Aunt Mary, her son Anthony Douglas, and daughter Alesica, who we called Boo-Boo had all moved into Grandma's house. My cousin actually graduated from high school after being promoted from the tenth grade to the twelfth grade. He definitely was a smart guy and athletic as well. I think if he had been really passionate about football, he could have played college football. He was between 6' and 6'2" and weighed over 280, and was a mountain of a man. When he played football they would put about two or three guys on him because he was so big and strong. When it came to athletics he did just like an appetizer, he gave you enough to be teased, while you waited in anticipation of the full course meal. You'd, however, discover that you left your wallet and only have cash for the appetizer and can't eat the main course; that's how many felt about Anthony's potential.

He, however, rarely disappointed when it came to his success in the classroom which was evidenced by him skipping an entire year. He also obeyed his mom and stayed out of trouble. He was the perfect role model for me because he was cool, tough, smart and genuinely a nice guy. The girls loved him and he and my cousin Howard protected the younger generation of the family, especially me. Ant was my biggest fan; a big brother. I was glad that he was there, even when we were younger, he would take up for me. Ant would also teach me how to fight so I could take up for myself, he made sure I wasn't weak and didn't allow anybody else to bully me. We got into a lot of run-ins, but ultimately he loved me and I loved him, so it was really no issues about me doing anything to seriously harm him or him doing anything to seriously harm me.

Anthony was one of the few positive male role models in my life. To my knowledge, he hadn't been arrested, unlike my other male cousin who was only a few years older than

Anthony. We did not have to visit Anthony at the Ohio Department of Youth Services as I did with my other cousin. Also, I don't think he missed any of my football games when I played for John Adams Junior Varsity team. He was there when I caught a fifty yard bomb from Shannon Billings on the first play, from scrimmage against John F. Kennedy, our arch rival. I mention that game because it was pouring down raining and there weren't any seats in the stadium under cover from the torrid weather.

I could see Ant with his towel that he was using to cover his head waving it as I stretched and lifted the ball, as it was only a few inches from striking the ground. I caught the ball and ran it in for a touchdown my first of two for the game. I caught several more passes that day and we won the game. My uniform looked more like it was made out of mud as opposed to fabric. The rain did subside at halftime but then a steady drizzle returned for the remainder and yet Ant stayed for the entire game. He was the only family I had in the stands for support and I really appreciated his sacrifice.

He didn't have to give up his time, money or risk his health for me but he did; that's what a real cousin does. Anthony didn't miss any of my games that year. He saw me rack up approximately 7 touchdowns, more than 21 catches and an average of 25 yards per catch in eight games for the Junior Varsity.

COACH CLAUDE HOLLAND'S INFLUENCE

John Adams High School was a breeding ground for young people who would eventually become some of the most prominent business, political, religious, social and educational leaders in the greater Cleveland area. The school hadn't changed much since the time my mother traversed the halls, only fifteen years from the time I stepped into Adams; ironically this was my second time attending John Adams, wherein I was in my mother's womb the first time.

John Adams was built in the early 1900's, the community was once predominantly Hungarian descent until white flight, to the outer ring suburbs caused the school's population to drastically shift to virtually one hundred percent African-American, by the time I arrived. One thing that didn't change was the academic reputation of the school, at least with respect to the honors programs. I began tenth grade with a renew vigor because I was again physically in a high school building. John Adams was old but appeared sturdy. The ceiling was not caving in and although we had meager resources, I believed them to be sufficient. I was taking Chemistry and maintaining an A in that class along with above average, to average grades in my other courses: World History, Trigonometry, and English.

In addition to playing football I had the added responsibility of participating in the honors program, which meant that I would have more class work, homework and higher expectations than the other non-Major Work students. I needed to be involved in something in order to avoid thinking about my mother and grandmother. I worked out a very effective schedule that allowed me to balance my academics with my athletics so that neither one would suffer. I could then put forward the most effective effort for both. I would, unlike a lot of my fellow Rebels, take advantage of my study hall. Instead of being overly social, I would crack open my textbooks and begin my homework to lessen the amount I had to complete after practice. I had an uncanny ability to shut out all of the noise and clamoring voices and focus on the task at hand. If I had any questions or issues with my homework I would simply lay those aside until the next day so I could await an explanation by the teacher during the review or ask a question if I didn't believe I received any clarification. If I didn't have any homework I would use the time productively by reading over what was discussed earlier that day in class. I would also use the time to study for an impending exam. Thus, I would review notes I had taken in class, as well as the note cards I created to help me recall the information I gathered from the lectures as well as the textbooks.

I learned how to study under very unusual conditions, wherein I would have to try to concentrate amid my father's verbal and physical assaults upon my mother. I would have to complete my homework and studying during the time when natural light was present due to our electricity being shut off. I would at times have to study with extra clothes on to avoid being distracted by the cold, when our heat was shut off due to nonpayment. I learned to ignore my stomach that was growling louder than a lion and hunger pains that felt like my stomach was a wet mop that needed to be wrung out, when there was little to no food, and keenly focus on the educational tasks at hand. Thus, a little noise in study hall was nothing. I was able to persevere through difficult situations so that I could be the student I and my teachers expected even in light of my athletic abilities..

When it came to sports I made sure I was one of the first people at practice, be it football or track. , which was a few blocks away from the school at Dove Park, a local community park. The junior varsity and varsity used the worn field area that was less than fifty yards in length. The little grass that was present on the field in August would be trampled and reduced to rubble by November. The landscape changed from green grass to dingy dirt. I would arrive and complete some pre stretching activities before practice. I would also be able to toss the football around, either with the starting or second string quarterback if I was fortunate. On the other hand I would normally have to request the unskilled lineman to throw a few passes. I always wanted to be prepared, whether it was school or on the field. I have found that the best way to be prepared is to practice, study, listen, question when unsure and to ascertain what your weaknesses are and find out how to improve them, to determine what your strengths are and do what's necessary to maintain them.

I surmised that success occurs no matter the situation if you follow this particular precept: Consistent, Productive, Repetition (CPR). You have to perform the same actions in a calculated, frequent manner in order to master that skill. The actions you perform must be effective and not with just a goal of getting through the motions simply to get it done but instead with the laser focus on increasing your understanding of how to perform the skill at the highest possible level. Lastly, repeating the latter two actions over and over and over again makes an indelible mark on your mind and body. The latter actions will culminate in the skill your trying to master becoming second nature. It will be like tying your shoe laces. When you are first taught how to perform the act you are nervous, unsure, uncomfortable and completely ignorant to the process. However, after a number of times of consistently, correctly tying your shoe laces over and over again for days, weeks and months and eventually years it has been imbedded on your brain. Your mind and body react in tandem when you decide to tie your shoe laces and you can actually tie them blindfolded. Why can't you use the same method towards your academic studies or towards a skill in the athletic arena or skills necessary for advance in your profession? I did employ the above mentioned method in my academics and athletics.

After football season ended, I tried out for the track team. The reputation of the John Adams high school track team proceeded itself. It was one of the most revered programs, not just in the city or region, but in all of Ohio. While the team had only won one state championship, Coach Claude Holland produced some of the best track runners to ever grace the local tracks in Greater Cleveland. Coach Holland and his family's prowess on the track and field community was legendary. His mother was a former Olympian, his brothers were highly recruited athletes from John Adams and he himself was one of the most talented middle distance runners of his era. His abilities earned him a college scholarship to the

University of Cincinnati. His love for kids from the neighborhood and his desire to see young people reach their full potential, brought him back to Cleveland to coach, and I am so grateful for him. Coach Holland doesn't look very intimidating to the average person, who doesn't know who he is or know of him.

He had a very slim build with piercing eyes and a very stern voice. It was not a voice that was piercing nor was it annoying or would have been confused with Barry White. He was very confident in his own skills and his teaching abilities. He didn't believe in allowing his athletes to settle for mediocrity. He pushed our bodies beyond what are minds believed we could accomplish. He not only shaped us as athletes but he shaped us as men. He would discuss issues of personal hygiene, personal conduct, avoiding sexual activity but if we were sexually active he strongly encouraged protection. He talked about being responsible young men, he talked about his own marriage and how much he loved his wife and how long they had been together. He discussed how he used his college education to make a better life for himself and his family. He didn't believe in making excuses for anything.

We practiced in our hallways and made a makeshift track by using garbage cans at the ends of the longest hallways in the school. He had measured the hallway to equate with the distance we would have to run on an actual track. We were expected not to just compete but to win. He passed that way of thinking down to the upperclassmen, which then relayed that to the underclassmen, like me. One of the juniors came to me after seeing me run during practice, and knew I had a bright future and said "You don't want people to say you're a good runner for a sophomore." "You want them to say you're a good runner period". He along with the coach made me work even harder at practice. There was one other event that made me push harder than the other athletes, as well as being a life lesson that I recall now when I face a difficult task and want to make excuses for not completing it.

One day we were doing intervals at practice preparing for an upcoming indoor meet. Coach Holland had placed the garbage cans at the end of the hallways. We were running timed six hundred meters in the hallway. I believe that there were two groups of four or five people in each group. The rules were, if you didn't meet the required time you would be required to run with the other group. I was in the first group and I took off and led the entire way for that particular interval. Our group, however, hadn't run it at a pace such that if something unusual happened we would have more than ample time to make it. Unfortunately, as I was turning the corner for the final lap and headed towards the finish line for the first interval, my shoe came off. Instead of continuing through the line and making the time I stopped put my shoe on and jogged over the line. It was clearly obvious that I would have made the required time but for my shoe snafu, since I was leading the pack and my other teammates were following close behind they all made it.

I crossed the line and Coach Holland didn't say anything so I assumed that he and I were on the same page. He quickly ordered the other group to the starting line and then told me to join them. I was shocked and despite my expostulation regarding my shoe he was not influenced to alter his decision. He simply said "If it were a track meet would you have simply stopped and not completed the race?" I knew then that there were no mulligans in track! I complied and lined up and ran with the other group in the required time frame. I was then forced to run with my own group as soon as I finished with the second group. I think that's the day I developed another lung because I had never participated in any workout that tough. The running was the culmination of a practice that included sprint workouts and Coach Holland's killer six inches, wherein he required you to lay down on your back with your legs together and then lift your legs no higher than six inches off the ground and hold it until he directs you to put your legs down. My stomach muscles were screaming for Coach Holland to say down. While I appreciated the workout after and during competitions, I knew they were a necessary evil to get an expected end. He was not only preparing me for unfortunate situations that arise on the track but those that arise in life. I already had experienced unforeseen challenges that made achieving my goal tougher with respect to my life prior to arriving at John Adams. Coach was reinforcing for me and teaching others, that your failure to be prepared can cost you. I should have had my shoes tied tighter and the issue with my shoe detaching from my foot during the race would never have materialized. Additionally, I should have not made any assumptions that substantial completion would be acceptable. I recognized that failure to see something through to completion can cause you to miss out on other rewards (Rest was the reward I missed out on that day).

NOMADIC LIFE CONTINUES

There was some more instability in our life, even after my Aunt Mary came in when grandmother passed. My aunt was telling me how to pray and how to get some of the things that were going on in my life under control. This time I wasn't really going to church that often, because my aunt didn't go that regularly. My sister and my aunt didn't have a very good relationship. I wanted to know what the issue was, but I can't even venture to say what that relationship was about, and what caused so much tension between my aunt and my sister. Like I said, my older cousin Anthony treated me like a younger brother. I guess maybe life in general took a toll on my sister. She just could not handle what was going on and so she wound up running away. The tension came to a boiling point after Christmas.

My aunt, who had been accustomed to providing for just her two children on her salary now had two more kids. Christmas was a time for my sister and I as make up for what we didn't get during the year. We saw it as our parents trying to atone for the things they did during the year; it was symbolic for us. I don't think my aunt realized how imperative that holiday was for me and my sister because we received what my sister and I fashioned as lumps of coal. We may have received two or three gifts while my aunt's two children were showered with gifts. I internally questioned why we received little compared to my cousin, but I was also not too concerned because I knew that my aunt was not getting much help from my father.

My sister may have been more impacted by what happened at Christmas. I believed she saw it as the final straw that broke the camel's back and she decided enough was enough and she didn't want to live under Aunt Mary's rules anymore. She ran away from home and for several hours refused to disclose her location. I was a nervous wreck because at that time she was the only blood relative I knew that lived in Cleveland. She was only thirteen years old, she was a female, she was petite and she didn't have much money. She had decided to travel to

Cleveland Heights and spend the night with my Aunt Joann and indicated that she did not want to live with my Aunt Mary any longer. My father was located and he sat down with both my aunts and they all decided that living with my Aunt Joann would be in our best interests. Thus, we were about to change homes and schools once again.

Our move was a huge burden on my Aunt Joann. While she resided in a beautiful spacious home on Clarendon in Cleveland Heights, she had an adolescent son, her three teenage daughters, along with her two adult daughters and their significant others, and her grandchildren, and my "Uncle" John, who had been living with her for quite some time and now she was adding her brother's two kids. They had established a good family relationship. That was big family and it was a four or five bedroom house, with another room that could be converted into a sixth room, it had to be at least 11 people in that house when my sister and I were added. Eventually – my cousin and her husband left and got their own home, but it was still fairly crowded.

Brian and I had to share a room and that was fine because I missed my little cousin. We got a chance to bond, and I got chance to have a little brother I never had. He and I used to fight a lot, and I used to antagonize him, give him a couple punches and wrestle all around. I got a chance to help a little bit on homework. Also going outside with him, teaching him how to play ball, swing, and provide a little protection for him, I liked being his big cousin/big brother. My sister got a chance to hang out with her cousins in our age group, Maya, Kristee and Nikki.

Our new home was situated in a new community and on a quiet street, ones where I was not accustomed to living. I didn't have to worry about hearing ambulances or police sirens going up and down the street.   It was also a multicultural street something I hadn't experienced since my mother moved us from Lincoln Avenue in Cleveland Heights more than thirteen years ago. We saw people of all colors, and all religions, sexual orientations on our street as well as throughout the entire city of Cleveland Heights.

I enjoyed my time living with Aunt Joann. My Aunt Joann was pretty strict, wherein she imposed chores for everyone and expected us to perform them timely and competently. She believed in punishing either by whipping or taking away privileges, or both when someone misbehaved, didn't do their chores, received poor grades in school or failed to listen. She wanted me to spend time with John to learn how to be a responsible man, since she was keenly aware that a positive male role model had been absent for most of my life. My primary responsibilities were to watch and help my cousin Brian, take out the trash and complete my school work.

My arrival at Cleveland Heights High School wasn't as smooth as my arrival with my Aunt Joann because I had spent many nights with my Aunt Joann and my cousins on numerous occasions prior to our permanent relocation, and they treated me like one of the kids. When I first came to Cleveland Heights High School, I received opposition from some of the staff members when I requested to be placed in the honors program. I was coming from the Cleveland Public School system, a system they perceived to be academically inferior. I, however, believed that after they reviewed my standardized tests scores and grades from the previous schools I attended they would change their opinion. Eventually, I was allowed to enter Cleveland Heights High Schools Gifted and Talented Program without taking the required examination. Most of the children who were in the program had taken a test while in elementary school and their performance placed them in the program. I was exempted from taking that test and some of my classmates were disturbed by that fact. I didn't know if their issue with me being in the program was due to their belief, that I lacked the requisite intellect/talent to compete with those students or if they believed that race had something to do with my ability to usurp the normal process. I didn't care what their opinions were; I just wanted to go to class and to perform up to the best of my abilities.

I quickly learned why Heights, especially their advanced classes, had such a stellar academic reputation; the work was arduous. I was thankful that I started school shortly after the second semester began and was fortunate that the major work program in Cleveland Public School system was in line with Heights Gifted and Talented programs syllabus. Accordingly, many of the foundational things I would need to know for the second semester at Heights, I had already been exposed to at John Adams. Additionally, the grades I possessed in each class at John Adams were transferred to my corresponding classes at Heights. Thus, I wasn't punished nor rewarded for my transfer of schools mid-semester. I say the work was more difficult because of the pace, the type of material we read and analyzed and the manner in which the work was graded.

The teachers expected the gifted and talented students to understand and absorb all the material immediately without much discussion before we moved onto the next lesson. Teachers generally offered help either, after class or after school. Most students would not stay after class because they didn't want others to believe they weren't smart enough to figure out what the teacher was saying, or comprehend the reading on their own. They rarely went after school because of other after-school activities.   I was one of those students who tried to figure it out on my own initially. I, however, despite being very shy was not afraid to ask questions during class. I didn't care what the other students thought; I wanted to understand everything I was expected to know before I left the classroom, because I knew my teacher would not be available when I was completing homework. Also, there was some foundational information that I hadn't received because I was coming from another school district, so I needed to catch up to the other students.

Since I needed to catch up I found myself struggling in some of my classes- Math, World History and English. Struggling for me was different than what struggling was for other students. I considered getting C's as struggling while most students would consider D's and F's as struggling. I hated getting C's on any quizzes, tests, papers or any assignments. Since my grades transferred I started with an A in Chemistry, but B's in World History and Math and a C in English. As I explained , the workload was different and the grading was harder as well. Where I would receive an A for a particular project or answer, Heights' standard was tougher and thus would yield a C+ or B- at best, and for the same thing I would have received an A on in my previous school.

Instead of complaining, making excuses, or throwing my hands up and saying that I couldn't do it I simply altered my routine. I changed my routine by talking less and studying more during my study hall. It wasn't too difficult since I didn't know that many people but my problem was not talking to the guys it was talking the girls. I hadn't ever been in a school with so many beautiful girls and it was virtually impossible to completely concentrate, when a girl walks by who has the body of a twenty year old but is only fifteen or sixteen. I stopped talking and stopped staring at those young ladies and did more work. They probably thought after a while I was a little nerd and I didn't care because my school work was one of a few things that set me apart from the other students. I didn't mind missing a favorite show on television to study a little longer. I didn't have the other distractions some of the other students may of experienced. I asked more pointed questions from my teachers and other students. I did extra work beyond the required homework so that I would be exposed to everything on the test. I took copious notes which aided me in preparing for exams and quizzes.

Although Cleveland Heights was an academic juggernaut, it was also, like John Adams, a high school powerhouse in track and field. In fact, their lone state title at that time in track was a tie between Heights and Adams in the late 1970's. There was much rancor when people heard that a student, who ran track, had transferred from Adams. I was unaware of the rivalry between the two programs. So when I transferred and joined the track team one of the members of the Heights team said sarcastically, "Oh he's from Adams, he must run the 400 in 45 seconds." Everyone laughed, even me because we all were aware that 45 seconds was near or better than the world record in the 400 in 1987. My main events were the 800, long jump and triple jump, I only ran the 400 on relays when I was asked and I wasn't even one of the top 800 runners when I was at Adams.

Actually, when I was at Adams I participated in the 800 and the mile relay on the B teams. I did participate with the varsity team or A team as a long jumper. I surprisingly, was the top jumper when Coach Holland held trials for participation in the first annual Cleveland Metropolitan School District, Jesse Owens Indoor Track Championship which was held at Baldwin Wallace College. I got the chance to compete against some of the fastest and most athletic young men, not just in the Cleveland but many of them were ranked as some of the best in the state of Ohio. I was nervous when I walked into the massive field house because it was much larger than the other indoor tracks, were we ran for the first few meets prior to the city championship.

I think I sprinted the warm-up laps, even though I was only supposed to trot, as a result of my nervous energy. I eventually made my way over to the long jump pit area and saw my name listed on the roster of other jumpers. I was excited because I would be given the opportunity to help my team win a city championship. I, however, quickly learned that I needed more training than I received. Our school was devoid of any indoor facility or alternative training resources to assist the field participants. I did a long jump a few times during the summer track meets but I had never jumped during a school meet, so this was an entirely different experience. While most of the other city schools were in the same predicament in that they lacked the necessary tools, the athletes from the other schools were older and had a chance to practice outdoor, which I wasn't able to do until the spring.

As one would guess I did not fare well against the other bigger, faster, more athletic and more experienced jumpers but I enjoyed the opportunity nonetheless. I did have some personal satisfaction because I jumped further than the student who had been labeled our best jumper before the jump trials were held at the school. More importantly I felt like one of the guys, like I belonged. I was a member of one of the most elite track programs in the city and state for that matter and knew under Coach Holland tutelage my skills would greatly improve. I was an unusual combination because my running events were middle distance events but I also possessed sprinter speed and springs in my legs that helped me leap further than anyone else on my team.

I, however, arrived at Cleveland Heights as maybe the third or fourth best jumper on the team and one of the potential top 800 meter runners. I participated in all of the track meets except for the Mansfield Relays and the State Tournament meets. Since I wasn't one of the top two competitors I was not afforded the opportunity to compete at the District Championship with the chance to move to the Regional and then State Championship. I worked extremely hard in an attempt to displace the guys who were ahead of me in the long jump and the 800, but due to splitting time between the jumping training sessions and the middle distance training sessions I was unable to concentrate on just one. While some people would have grown frustrated by the situation and simply given up I decided to work hard and vowed to make sure that I was one of the top two competitors in one of the two disciplines for the next track season. Mr. Mann, the head coach for the boys track team, saw the potential I possessed and kept tabs on me. He persuaded me to run summer track and I decided to run with Coach Holland's Rebel Track Club. I knew he would challenge me and he didn't care that I was a member of one of John Adams' fiercest rivals; he simply wanted me to realize my greatest potential.

I needed track and my academics to help me cope with the transfer to Cleveland Heights High School because I was inept when it came to adjusting to the social life at Heights. Cleveland Heights was a large suburban city outside of Cleveland and was the symbol of diversity. The student population was made up of approximately 55% African American, 40% Caucasian and 5% other. The majority of the students, of all races, had both parents working in the home. The majority of them lived in sturdy beautiful expensive homes either in Cleveland Heights or University Heights. The majority of them had attended Cleveland Heights or University Heights schools throughout their educational careers. The students wore the most expensive and stylish clothing be it jeans, shirts, sweaters, jackets, coats, sneakers and/or athletic shoes.

The African American student's parents were the beneficiaries of the civil rights movement and therefore were college educated and had well-paying jobs. I didn't have the designer clothing, my hair wasn't cut as often as the other guys, I didn't wear the latest sneakers like Nike Air Jordan's. I didn't use cash to purchase my lunch instead I produced a lunch card that indicated I was receiving lunch via the federally subsidized lunch program. I felt embarrassed, I felt inferior to those students and I assumed that they thought less of me because of my economic status. All those factors made me feel insecure and socially isolated. I felt like I could compete academically and athletically because I had some personal control over the outcomes in those areas, but with respect to my social environment I didn't control my economic status, where I lived, what I wore, how I ate or how I looked. It made me withdraw in the cafeteria and I frequently ate by myself. I would on occasion eat with some of the track athletes or some of the students from my classes—usually Caucasian. I didn't get invited to any of the parties nor was I fortunate to receive the phone numbers of any of the girls that I was physically attracted to either. It was a dismal four months before the end of my sophomore year but in addition to track and my classes there was one bright spot—Mrs. Parran

Mrs. Parran was the guidance counselor at Cleveland Heights High School. I looked eye to eye to Mrs. Parran, thus illustrating her above average height for a female her age. While I didn't know what Mr. Parran's age was, I gathered by her wire rimmed spectacles and the vast number of gray hairs mixed with her streaks of black hair, that she had been in the educational system for quite some time. Her petite frame was able to carry the hopes and dreams of thousands of Heights high students. She was fully aware of the challenges that I faced prior to walking onto the Cleveland Heights campus. She had an opportunity to review my academic transcripts but also had a little personal family history as well. She could count and noted that my educational journey had taken me to ten different schools prior to Cleveland Heights. She could also review my standardized test scores as well as my grades and realized that I was a good student.

During our initial conversation she never made any negative assumptions or passed judgment about my abilities or future aspirations. She just wanted to know how she could help me become a better student and better citizen. She was concerned about ensuring that I made the right choices–academically and socially, so that I would put myself in the best position to attend college. She knew that I was capable of thriving at college and encouraged me to continue with the normal courses that other students took who were preparing for college and not work after high school graduation. She assisted me in completing my schedule for the remainder of my sophomore year and for my junior year. She also suggested that I speak to the school psychologist because of the emotional trauma that I had suffered over the last three years. She saw me as a diamond in the rough and it was her responsibility to dust me off and help shape me into a gem that would be attractive to any institution of higher learning.

I was very reluctant to speak to the school psychologist because of the negative stigmatism that is attached to people who see a "shrink" by others in the African American community. I was so concerned about the perception others would have of me that I didn't tell any of my family members or my friends. The school psychologist was also able to help me cope with so many things that were impacting my sanity. In less than five years I was now living under the supervision and care of a fifth "relative or friend", I was in my sixth school in the same amount of time, I had loss three family members in the last two years and I was just emotionally spent. I would sit and talk with him for at least one period at least once a week. The sessions gave me an opportunity to vent, to question, to listen and to be healed; they were very therapeutic. I received the opportunity to express my frustrations in a forum that I knew the information would not be used to embarrass or hurt me emotionally. I got a chance to relieve some stress by pouring out my heart and soul and trying to find a way to forgive. I got a better understanding that I was not the cause of many of my predicaments. I also started a path towards forgiveness for my mother and father. He, along with my spiritual leaders, were helping me eliminate the anger, frustration, pain and depression that resulted from my previous childhood trauma. I'm glad that I didn't ignore the help that was offered because of the apparent negative stigmatism.

The school year ended with no fanfare. My summer was uneventful, wherein I simply tried to stay in shape for football. I had attended the football meeting at the conclusion of the school year and received the workout information that was distributed by the coaches. Coach Kerry Hodakevic was the head coach and had been in that position for three or four years. He was a pretty intense guy who would scream, yell and get in your face if he thought you were dogging any drill, exercise or especially during the game. His intensity did not subside at the meetings where he expected everyone to focus on words and to apply what he was saying at the appropriate time. He looked like a former star high school linebacker with broad shoulders, beady eyes, intense stare and a muscle frown. His arms looked like someone stuffed tennis balls in his biceps.

He talked about dedication over the summer and coming in prepared to win the league championship because of the stalwart seniors we had returning for the next school year. We had several defensive and offensive players that would play Division I college football after high school. Coach Hodakevic was excited but he had no idea who I was. I did not stand out as some physical specimen that he saw bouncing through the hallways. There was no story in the local paper about a standout football player from John Adams transferring to Cleveland Heights. I was able to hide without any expectations from anyone and thus no pressure. I could simply slip in unnoticed and then show them the skills I possessed.

Soon the end of the summer approached and my family threw me a surprised birthday party, I was turning sixteen years old. My Aunt Joann bought me a cake that had a football on half of it and a track shoe on the other half, I loved it. My cousin Anthony, Alesica and all my relatives that lived with my Aunt Joann came over to celebrate with me. I really enjoyed my sixteenth birthday party and then I went to sleep only to have to begin two a day practices for the football team the next day.

I woke up early that morning and walked to Cleveland Heights High School. We had moved during the summer so my walk to the school was a little further than usual. When I arrived at the school I was among more than 75-80 kids waiting for a helmet to be distributed. After the helmets were distributed, we were required to complete some drills and some tests to measure our progress during the summer. We had to run a time trial that had a standard for our particular position. We were also timed in the forty yard dash as a way for the coaches to determine where if any place they could find some speed. I was still able to remain somewhat anonymous because I didn't play for Heights football team the previous year and most of the football players didn't take any of the gifted and talented classes therefore most of them didn't know me.

I was in a little quandary because cross country practice began shortly before the football two a day commenced, and Mr. Mann was looking for me. He left several messages at my aunt's house trying to locate me but I refused to call him back because I wanted to play football. Mr. Mann was relentless because he knew I was a good runner and simply needed a better foundation, like cross country, to make me stronger and therefore able to compete at the highest levels with most if not everyone. I was stubborn, however, because I had done so well with John Adams junior varsity football team and thought I could compete with the guys at Heights. Mr. Mann got wind of the fact that I was trying out for the football team and showed up for that first day.

I spotted him coming through the gates while I was sitting in the bleachers after having completed the mandatory timed trials. I was sandwiched behind two huge offensive line prospects that blocked out the sun and therefore shielded me from Mr. Mann. Mr. Mann approached the area and whispered to coach Everett Heard, who was the assistant coach in charge of the defensive backs but also the girl's head track coach. Mr. Mann tried in vain to find me and as he moved closer I simply slid over behind the kids causing a solar eclipse and would move in the opposite direction when Mr. Mann moved in one direction. Mr. Heard then said, after a few minutes of watching his colleague's futile efforts, "Is there a Michael Ryan here? "MICHAEL RYAN" he said louder and more fervently . I acted as though my birth name was anyone other than Michael Ryan and ignored both Coach Heard and Coach Mann. Coach Mann eventually turned around and headed towards the fence, got in his car and left the area. I felt a sense of relief because at least for that day Mr. Mann would not be back. On the other hand I was somewhat upset at Coach Heard because he was so unimpressed with me that he didn't even recognize me. When practice did finally start, however, people began to notice me alright.

As practice began I started to get some attention because of the types of acrobatic catches I was making. The coaches would whisper to themselves "Ryan", "Who the hell is this kid and where did he come from?" My receivers coach was a former wide receiver in high school and college and knew a great deal about the sport and the position. He was able to hone the natural skills most of us had, with the technical skills we would need to develop to play football at the next level; he was built like a mini tank. He looked like small grape fruits had been surgically implanted in his chest and biceps. His triceps and his calves were huge as well. The best thing I liked about him was his ability to teach. He made practice enjoyable and fun. He was not a tyrant; he allowed us to grow and respected our limitations, but he always pushed us to go beyond what we thought was impossible.

He began to give me more and more compliments after a few two a day practices. My receivers coach liked my speed and Coach Hodakevic would see my speed when we ran gassers after practice. My receivers coach applauded my catching ability by mentioning how I kept my eyes on the ball even after I caught it and the fact that I ran good routes. He commented on my ability to memorize the receiver, tight end, and quarterback responsibilities. I believed that if I did my job and knew where everyone else was supposed to be I could help my quarterback if the play broke down. I could indicate to the quarterback, who happen to be the only other African American male in my gifted and talented classes that played football, or other teammates that we were lined up incorrectly.

Since I was an unknown at the beginning of the camp I had to work my way up the list of receivers, déjà vu with Mr. Hill in sixth grade again. The older more experienced defensive backs would not even guard me, assuming I would not provide the type of competition they needed to get better. Due to my hard work and perseverance I eventually made it to number two on the depth chart and was doing everything in my power to remove a very formidable top receiver Milton Morris better known as "Chip". Chip was one of the top athletes in the state of Ohio. He was an all-star in football, basketball and track and field. If we had run a traditional offense then Chip and I both would have started. We, however, ran an option offense which required three running backs instead of the traditional two and therefore one receiver position was eliminated for the majority of the offensive plays.

It was simultaneously, advantageous and disadvantageous because on one hand when you were the only receiver on the field the quarterback had limited options if the play was a passing play. The disadvantage was that with the option offense most of the plays were running plays and thus we were thrown the ball sparingly. When Chip was thrown the ball he was pretty spectacular. He was approximately 6'2" or 6'3" and weighed between 170 and 180 pounds with an outstanding vertical leap. I saw him out leap defenders on a routine basis and snag balls that most people would have deemed impossible to catch. I only saw a few weaknesses– his route running and his quickness but other than that he was a handful to guard. He was a bright, confident, classy, respectful and a good role model for younger players. I liked him because he brought out the best in everyone around him even when he didn't realize it.

I say that because about a week after two-a-days began, there was this buzz about the new receiver, me, putting pressure on Chip. Chip and I had a chance opportunity to go head to head on the field during a drill. The drill called for the defensive back coach, Coach Heard, to signal the receiver to run a certain route with Coach Heard acting as the quarterback. The defensive backs were required to guard the receiver and prevent the pass from being caught. They could not cause pass interference and were required to play good defense. The drill lasted for about five to ten minutes. Most of the receivers and defensive backs alike got an opportunity to display their individual skills, approximately five or six times due to the number of receivers we had in camp.

Chip would initially line up and complete a route as a receiver and one of the other defensive backs; he would then switch lines and play as a defensive back since he played both positions in any given game. He and I had never faced one another during that first week. Chip, unlike the other defensive backs, knew that I was a good receiver so he didn't balk when we faced one another. Thus, when my turn came up and Chip's turn came up to be a defensive back, all the receivers and other defensive backs stopped goofing around and paid attention to the duel. One person even yelled "ITS NUMBER ONE VERSUS NUMBER TWO."

I could feel my heart in my stomach and it felt like it was going to jump out because it was beating so fast and so hard. Coach Heard gave me the signal for a comeback, which required me to sprint fifteen yards, plant and pivot and come back five yards toward the sideline. It was the perfect call because most of the defensive backs knew about my speed and thus Coach Heard was trying to test Chip's ability to adapt. Defensive backs are taught to stand five to six yards off the line of scrimmage if they are not pressing a receiver preventing them from leaving the line of scrimmage. They are taught to give a receiver a yard or two more if he thinks that the receiver possesses some speed. I don't know how far Chip was off the line but he was well aware of the fact that I had very good speed. He saw me run down catches during receivers drills and saw me run gassers during conditioning. He wasn't going to let me catch a long pass on him, like I had done to some of the other defensive backs that day and thereby embarrass him.

He was the number one receiver on the team and I would have to learn to accept my place. Thus, it was no surprise that when Coach Heard yelled "HIKE", which was a direction for me to begin the play, Chip saw me take off full steam ahead and he then turned his shoulders and began to run full speed to catch up to me. I, however, had already made up his five or seven yard advantage by the time I had gotten yards away from the line of scrimmage. My shoulder pads were clapping as my helmet stayed steady with each stride. I eventually passed him and stopped on a dime with the grass flying up from the bottom of my cleats as Chip went flying by and I then slanted towards the sideline, all by myself as Coach Heard whizzed the pass to my outside shoulder for an unabated catch. Chip was standing at least ten yards down field. That experience taught me a valuable lesson that I employ even today and that was to have confidence in your abilities, notwithstanding the daunting tasks that lay ahead of you.

I not only won Chip's respect that day but the other defensive backs and receivers as well. The other receivers stop complaining about me being the number two receiver, even though I was new to the system. Some of them even advocated for me to take over the number one spot. The veteran defensive backs who initially shunned me, were now clamoring to face me to see if they could shut me down or at a minimum get some experience so that they would be better prepared for the type of receivers they were going to play against in real game situations. Some of my teammates also began to say that there should be a change at the top of the depth chart for receiver or at a minimum altering the offense, so that Chip and I could play alongside one another but Coach Hodackevic was stubborn and believed he had the running backs to make life difficult for opposing defenses that would try to stop his wishbone offense.

I ended camp nearly eight or nine prongs above where I started. I don't recall the number of receivers we began camp with but it was numerous. I was proud of my accomplishment, having come into an unfamiliar situation and found a way to excel beyond anyone's expectations. While I didn't accomplish my ultimate goal, to be the opening game starting receiver, I was a full participating player on the varsity squad. That gave me more benefits than I possessed at the beginning of camp. I had a very odd number assigned to me when camp began, a number that most starting receivers did not wear, because I was not expected to make the varsity team, let alone see significant time. I, however, was advised that since I was going to be getting significant playing time, relieving Chip because of his double duty, starting as one of the two kickoff return men, back up punt returner and also the second receiver for our two minute drill, I had the chance to change my number. I did just that and took the number that another player was assigned, number 8. Unfortunately for me the numbers had already been sent to media outlets and when my picture appeared in the local paper, another player got credit instead of me.

I wasn't upset because everyone else knew that was me and not the other player. I felt like I belonged for two reasons, the ability to change my number and the fact that the coaches had given the media my name as a player who would provide significant contributions, to the success of the team that year. I was elated and felt like I was on cloud nine and couldn't wait for the opening game against Euclid High School on a hot Friday night in late August.

STABILITY EQUALS SUCCESS

I was experiencing overall elation because not since I moved with my Grandma Lula during the latter part of my sixth grade year, did I feel a sense of stability again. I was enjoying my life with my Aunt Joann, her boyfriend John and all my cousins. I stayed in contact with my cousin Anthony even though we no longer lived together. My father was still pretty much absent from me and my sister's life, leaving my Aunt to raise us, we saw him very sparingly. Accordingly, John became the immediate male role model in my life and he was a great one.

John loved children, at least I imagined that he did in order to begin and maintain a relationship with a woman who had four school age children and then added two more, when my sister and I joined the clan. He was patient, respectful and tolerant. He was the second John that had significant impact on my life; my Grandfather John Tomlinson was the other one. You knew when he was upset and his patience had run thin because his voice would boom even louder than normal and his owl like eyes would bulge even more. John never spanked me or threatened me. If there was some correction I needed, he or my Aunt would do it in a calm and respectful manner, treating me like an adult not a child like my Aunt did when I was much younger. He was never condescending and he valued education. His value for education was implanted by his mother who taught in the Cleveland Public School system for many years. He himself was a graduate of Virginia Union and was a former athlete. He liked the fact that I was a student athlete and supported me in both of those pursuits. He was an excellent role model, in that he went to work every week day and came home at night.

I don't recall a time that he and my Aunt Joann's discussions became so heated that it boiled over to fisticuffs. He would spend time with me and all I saw him doing was going to work and then coming home every day. If he wasn't coming home and just giving us the chores and doing work himself, he was coming with a bag in hand because Aunt Joann had just went to the store. She was getting money and food stamps for my sister and me as public assistance. John was working as well to provide this wonderful, wonderful living environment for two kids who had been through hell. While a whipping may have been the order of punishment when I was younger they both saw me, my cousins and my sister as young adults. The punishment would be denial of certain privileges or extra chores, which to a teenager seems like a ton of bricks has fallen on your head.

I complied with all their requests to avoid any punishment and I didn't want my aunt to see me as a burden. My sister and I were already a drain on their household with two additional mouths to feed, to protect , to worry about and to nurture. If things got tough we knew that our status would be tenuous so I did everything within my power to make sure that I did not do anything that would be embarrassing to her or anyone else in the family, I didn't get into any trouble at school or in the community. I didn't ask for money, I asked for things I needed, I listened, I completed my chores in a timely manner, I didn't have a smart aleck response when asked a question, I willing provided copies of my grades and progress reports and I just tried to stay out of the way.

I was very fortunate to have Aunts, like Mary and Joann, who incurred an additional responsibility when they had no legal obligation to and no moral obligation when it came to me. They, however, saw me and my sister as a package deal. She was blood but the day I was born, and probably before then, I was considered a part of the family. My Aunt Joann didn't do more for my sister than she did for me. She gave her as much attention, affection and guidance as she gave me. I'm glad she was prepared to step up and make sure my sister and I were not placed into the custody of the Department of Children and Family Services. I cannot envision what would of happened to us if we had become wards of the state. I don't know if I would have finished school, avoided any of the streets, drugs or alcohol addiction, jail and/or an early grave. I don't know if my sister avoids having numerous children, being on the streets, homeless, becoming a drop-out, drug or alcohol addiction and alienation from me. It may have been hard for foster care parents to accept two teenage children with the issues that my sister and I faced. I'm glad that my aunts didn't let it get that far.

Clearly, that was not an indictment on the child welfare system. In fact, the child welfare system's goal is to place young people in situations where they will thrive; preferably with family. The general perception of the child welfare system at that time was similar to what I stated above. I, however, know that the child welfare provides shelter, loving family substitutes, education, independent living, support and resources to help children move into adulthood without struggles and challenges they met as infants, toddlers or adolescents.

PROSOCIAL ACTIVITIES BUILDS CONFIDENCE

After four weeks of football practice opening night finally arrived. The game was played at Euclid High School stadium. Euclid was traditionally a top public school football program like Cleveland Heights because it was the only high school in the Eastern Cleveland suburb. The school produced some very talented student athletes over the years, none more famous than the kid who was a freshman running back for the team that night, Robert Smith. I arrived at the designated time to put on my cleats, padded pants and jersey. I wasn't nervous when I boarded the bus more so anxious because this was my first varsity football game. I wanted to make a good impression on the coaches so that they would trust me more in other situations.

We loaded the bus and drove towards Euclid high school. The sun was nearing its setting point as we were traveling to the school, but hadn't quite set yet. We arrived in approximately 30 to 40 minutes after leaving Heights. As I got off the bus and stepped down on the pavement my legs felt like spaghetti because they were so weak from nervousness that built up during the bus trip. I followed my teammates to the locker room and immediately began to put on the remainder of my uniform. I made sure my cleats were clean and my helmet had been shined since this was the season opener. I wanted to look good when I got out on the field. The coach advised the skilled players and special teams to be out on the field first to warm-up, so that's why I was dressing faster than the other players.

I didn't need any external stimulation, like the Walkman some of my teammates were using, because my heart and mind were making my body go one hundred miles an hour. I ran through the tunnel that leads to the field and onto the field with the other skilled players. Chip and I initially took turns catching punts and then caught passes from our first and second string quarterbacks. I was simply in awe of the massiveness of the stadium. I had been on

Heights' field for our pre -game preparation, the day before our first game but never in this setting. I had never experienced playing varsity football under the lights and it was intoxicating for me. Eventually the entire team joined us on the crayon green, immaculately manicured grass field and we began our game day calisthenics. Coach Hodakevic would come around and engage the starters and or significant contributors by yelling, by slapping our helmets or pulling the face masks to get us riled up.

We had practiced extremely hard those few weeks before this game, as well as the other off-season work we completed we also had a ton of talented players at every position and felt that a win was a just reward for all our hard efforts. We quickly lined up and prepared for the singing of the National Anthem when only a few moments after Euclid's team ran onto the field. I knew I had arrived when the band played, the Star Spangled Banner and I was standing there about to participate in my first official high school varsity football game. It was bittersweet because no one from my family attended the game. Nevertheless I went on as though the stadium was filled with my family and friends. I was glad to be involved on the kick return team and I got the first chance to get the nerves out by catching the ball and running it for minimum good yardage, for my team or simply blocking for the other kick returner.

During the game we ran the ball more than 75% of the time. Coach would call a pass play when teams were expecting it, on third down and long. Despite that prediction he sent me in on one play while Chip was still in the game and took one of the three running backs out. The reason he needed me in the game was because we were in the midst of a long drive towards the other team's goal line. He didn't want the momentum to stop, so I knew he wanted me to be the sure handed person he had been bragging about during training camp. I lined up on the opposite side of Chip, who was getting double teamed, and then took off at my quarterback's second hut. I went ten yards and faked to the right towards the sideline and then cut across on the yard line, two yards deep of the first down marker. I turned my head as I was making the cut and Quarterback James Harris saw my eyes and I saw his and he drilled the ball towards my hands and I reached out and pulled the ball into my stomach area.

I was immediately tackled by the linebacker. I also saw them move the yard marker, as well as heard the referee yell "First Down." I didn't catch any more passes that night but I did earn some respect from the quarterback who began to trust me a little more. The majority of the time I was in the game to replace Chip and most of the plays were for one of the three running backs and thus it required me to block or attempt to make a block in the alternative run the guy who was guarding me away from the play.

I talk about my experience playing football because I beat the odds playing this game as well. I was a skinny kid who weighed significantly less than most of my teammates. I was approximately 5'6" if that, and I was one of a handful of black males in the advanced classes at the school and I became familiar with the football system in a three week period over training camp. Additionally, there are hundreds of thousands of kids who never got an opportunity to play high school varsity football and yet here I was, one of the most least likely kids, playing at a suburban school and getting more than sufficient time on the varsity squad. I was unknown before camp started, I was not a physical specimen, I hadn't played in the lower Cleveland Heights/University Heights school system. I didn't have any family legacy in the athletic programs in the lower schools or high schools and yet I had started at the bottom of the depth chart and then found myself standing with my hand over my heart listening to the Star-Spangled Banner and getting prepared to take the field. We would eventually lose that game as well as our next three games because of the level of talent we played against. Robert Smith, a freshman that year, would eventually become Mr. Football for the State of Ohio and star for The Ohio State Buckeyes and Minnesota Vikings. Our next game pitted us against the future Heisman Trophy winner Desmond Howard from St. Joseph High School. St. Joseph was loaded that year because they also had a future pro quarterback named Elvis Grbac.

I received excellent news before our third game of the year when the coaches named me the starter over Chip. The coaches apparently were teaching Chip a lesson at my expense. He was told that he would not start because he was acting too carefree and lazy when he knew a pass was not coming towards him. He was displaying very little, if any effort when running plays were called and therefore opposing defensive backs were making key reads on when a running play was coming based on Chip's refusal to play at 100 percent. I was the first receiver on each drill, on the 7 on 7's, during the first team versus first team, and the pre -game preparation.

I wasn't sure the coaches would keep their promises and I believed that Chip would actually start. So imagine my surprise when after the kickoff return, I went out with the first team and Chip remained on the bench. He did start on defense after we stalled on three plays and he eventually returned to his starting role with much vigor. He was plowing down people such that he was exposing himself to some potential unnecessary roughness calls. I, however, still had one of my best games. We had been working on a reverse in practice since the summer. They allowed me to run it because Chip didn't have the quickness to get around that corner and up the field. The first time we ran it on our first team defense; I made a number of the proposed stars looking for their jock straps. They were diving at air trying to catch and tackle me. I could hear them yelling at each other "GET THAT LITTLE MOTHER FUCKER" "DAMN HE FAST AS HELL." "I TOLD YA HE COULD ROLL". Thus, when we ran it in the game our defense was on their edge of their seat anticipating a touchdown.

After the quarterback gave the vocal sign to hike the ball, I turned left and ran left towards the quarterback who then handed the ball off to me. I took the ball and cradled it like a new born baby and then ran as fast as I could towards the sideline, I put my left foot down and faked like I was going into the sidelines and then pushed off my left foot and headed into the heart of the defense, with a linebacker swiping at my feet. I then planted my right foot in the slippery mud and then faked right and headed back towards the sideline, I saw one person to beat but had to slow down to wait for the blocker which never came. Thus, I was eventually tackled after gaining eight yards instead of sixty (60) and scoring a touchdown. I did, however, have two catches in that game. In fact one of the catches was for a long first down during our two minute drill with both me and Chip on the field. The drive we had that night was one of the more successful drives we had all season because we had several receiving threats on the field.

It was me, Chip, William Hunter (Tight End), Van Ward (running back) and Willie Smith (running back) and we were able to stretch the defense. I almost recorded my lone varsity touchdown, on that night but the ball was thrown behind me. I had separated from the defensive back and was five yards in the end zone. Our regular quarterback was out for that series so the back up a young, strapping sophomore, Melvin Tucker, was replacing him. Mel was probably a little nervous himself, since he was doing double duty as a starter on defense and thus I believe didn't want to mess up. Mel threw me several good balls that night the one, however, that he threw towards me when I was in the end zone was a little short. I was forced to act like a defensive back by stopping jumping over the shoulder of the real defensive back and knocking the balls out of his hands. The picture that appeared in the local paper depicts that very scenario and makes it look like I was the defensive man attempting to prevent the receiver from catching the ball.

Insult was added to the injury when the paper, as I stated earlier didn't receive the updated information about the number changes, printed the caption below, the picture and stated that Allen Christian knocks down the ball intended for the Lake Catholic receiver The photographer obviously was not paying close attention to the game because the player from Lake Catholic was a defensive player. Nevertheless, we still wound up losing the game. I would only play in one more game after the Lake Catholic game and that was the game against Lakewood. I was not very productive in the Lakewood game, no catches, nor too many positive yards in kickoff returns.

After the Lakewood game we prepared to face one of our arch rivals, Shaker Heights High School. Shaker was also an outer ring suburb of Cleveland, Ohio. Cleveland Heights and Shaker competed at every level, culturally, academically and athletically. The stocking houses in both communities were enormous and elegant. They both were open to diversity,

Cleveland Heights slightly more than Shaker but both were considered to be progressive communities. They usually had an equal amount of National Merit Finalist from the PSAT test. Thus, one can readily tell how intense the rivalry was and I unfortunately would not be able to fully experience it because of a freak accident at practice.

I was standing at one end of our practice field with the kickoff return team in front of me and the kickoff team was lined up in normal formation in front of my blockers. Our kicker put a charge in the ball and it sailed approximately forty to fifty yards in the air with me awaiting its descent into my arms. I cuddled the football into my right arm and started right and then jabbed step and cut to my left, then I ran up the middle of the field all the while trying to avoid blockers. I was able to make it twenty five yards from where I initially caught the ball and then I saw that one of my touchdown escorts had pancaked one of the kickoff players and they were both sprawled on the ground. I couldn't go left or right without being tackled and knew that the coach was about to blow the whistle but I wanted to score. I half-heartedly tried to jump over the two players that were sprawling on the ground. As I did that the one player from the kickoff team grabbed my leg as I was in mid-flight and tripped me up, causing me to hit the ground with a loud thud on my right side. I immediately felt like I was dying. I couldn't catch my breath and my ribs were in excruciating pain. I was able to get off the ground with the assistance of one my teammates and the trainer. I walked back to the training room very gingerly. I was more upset about missing practice more than anything else because I thought that my performance in the last game would increase the coach's confidence in me, and give me more opportunities to contribute to the team's success.

I, however, couldn't improve my chances by getting hurt. When I arrived in the training room, I saw that the situation was more severe than just the run of the mill incident of getting the wind knocked out of you. The trainer thought it was more serious as well because when he asked me to take off my pads, I initially couldn't put my arms above my head to remove my pads without out a pain that felt like someone was twisting all my eternal organs, aside from my heart, and trying to squeeze all the blood and air out of them. It took me almost five minutes, when it normally took me no longer than five seconds to get my shoulder pads off. My Aunt Joann discovered what happened and quickly drove me to the emergency room. The doctor examined me and I recalled the diagnosis being "Bruised Insides". I am quite certain that was not the medical term but that was the easiest way for a teenager to explain to his relatives, friends, coaches' and teammates the injury. I was also restricted from practicing or playing for an entire week.

When the following Monday's live practice began I was very energized because I had missed the last practices including the game against Shaker. I returned when we were going against our most bitter rival-Shaw Cardinals of East Cleveland, Ohio. The rivalry was more intense with Shaw than Shaker. We were strongly discouraged, by coaches' and upperclassmen alike, from wearing anything red either to practice or during school that week. We couldn't mention Shaw by its name and had to refer to it as "The school down the hill." This rivalry extended beyond the sports and academic teams. It had become violent over the years and thus while most of our games were at night, the games involving Shaw and Heights were always held at 11 a.m.

Some assumed that because the trouble makers were usually out all night they would be unwilling to get up at the earlier time and come and disturb the tranquility that existed in the stands. Some of the older players informed me that Shaw and Heights males fought constantly and that it was reason for the consternation between the schools. Shaw males believed that Heights males were elitist and uppity while Heights males did want to be generalized in that fashion and thought otherwise which led to the fights.

I was energized to not only be on the practice field but to play against Shaw. I had watched a film of one of their games and saw how fast, big and athletic most of the players appeared on film. Our coaches informed us of their strength, discipline and how difficult a match they would be for us. The Shaw High School Cardinals were always a formidable opponent that we respected but never feared despite their ability to produce potential

Division I, football talent year end and year out. I began practice like I ended it a week ago—working on special teams. Chip and I were back fielding punts but with no blockers and the cover men merely getting off their blocks at the line but not putting any direct hits on the punt returners. I was always Chip's backup for punt returns if he ever got hurt in a game.

During this practice session our punter made several punts, some I was able to wrestle away from Chip, because of his starting status he took more repetitions than me and ran up and caught more of the better kicks. He would leave the ones that went off the side of the punters foot or were low to the ground for me to scoop up. I was becoming increasingly frustrated, that he would not permit me to catch any good kicks and when the coach signaled that we had one more kick, I called for it before it even left the punters foot. I thought that since this was the punters last punt of the special session he would make it one of his best for the session. Actually when he kicked the ball he didn't get enough lift on it and therefore his ball didn't travel that high or far and required me to sprint from my position, which was forty yards from the line of scrimmage.

I kept my eye on the ball without surveying the field for the punt team players. The ball traveled twenty yards in front of the punter, which caused me to sprint from forty yards back. I was able to lower both my hands as the ball descended from the sky, but was not able to pull the ball up and one of the punt team tacklers, saw me fumble the ball, and then proceeded to pounce on the ball just like it was a true game situation. In his efforts to grab the muffed punt, he dove head first after the ball not realizing that I was only able to get one leg off the ground. After I saw him leading with his helmet towards my knee. I jumped with my right knee yet my left leg didn't get off the ground in time. Carlos Warner, a junior defensive end, struck my left leg right above my knee cap, with such force that my leg went from a straight position to curl within an instance from the collision. My leg was hurting but not too painful; I, however, was unable to straighten it.

My coaches' had just viewed this scene last week and didn't want any de ja vu. I even overheard one coach chime in a frustrated unconvinced voice "Is he hurt again?" A few of my teammates helped me off the field but I refused to go to the trainer's room and simply sat on the practice sidelines until practice was over, which was about an hour and half. Two of the receivers let me hold onto their shoulders as I literally hopped on my right leg with my left leg curled from the practice field onto the sidewalk and eventually into the locker room. The coaches called my aunt and told her about my injury. They did not think that my injury was severe because of the fact that I was able to bear some weight on my left leg during briefs stops on my trip from the field to the locker room.

It took me longer to strip off the football equipment than the prior week. I feared that my injury would decrease the number of games I played that season but I did not think my season was over. My aunt was unable to pick me up from the school so one of the coaches took me home. I felt really uncomfortable on my ride home as the pain continued to intensify with each bump, stop and jerk. As I tried to alight from the car, I knew something was seriously wrong and told my Aunt Joann I probably needed to go to the hospital. My aunt called my father, Allen Douglas, and advised him I needed to be transported to the hospital and she couldn't do it. He arrived within a half an hour and took me straight to the hospital. As I waited for him and during my trip to the hospital, I began to become more pessimistic about my beliefs regarding the lack of a fracture. I was pretty quiet on the drive to the hospital, since I was now in agonizing and I hadn't spoken to my father in weeks. He seemed to be concerned because he asked me how did it happen and what was the level of my pain. I gave him a complete description of how I injured my leg and asked him to drive like he normally does, with disregard for his safety and others, so we could get to the hospital faster; He readily obliged.

My father drove me; ironically, to the same hospital where my mother died because I think that was the one we had been using when we lived with my Grandma Lula. I was a little concerned even though I knew that the physicians and nurses didn't do anything wrong, it was still a little eerie to be receiving treatment in the place that couldn't help keep my mother alive. I only waited a few minutes before I was hauled off to the x-ray room. The x-ray technician was devoid of any bedside manner and roughly placed my left leg on the x-ray machine in several positions, to get an accurate picture of the injured area. The doctor, after viewing the x-rays came back to the emergency department private room and said "Well, Michael your season is over. You broke your femur bone." He explained to me that I broke my femur right about my knee that I would need a cast that stretched from my thigh to my toes.

He also added insult to injury when he said "It's a strong likely hood that, based on the area of the break, you will not be able to play football or run track anymore, let alone walk normally again." Nobody tells me I can't do anything, so I vowed from that day to get back to the field and to play. My father actually for the first time in a long time tried to act like a parent and forbade me from playing football again. I, however, became very emotional and told him how much football meant to me. Amid my sniffles and my high pitched voice I begged him to reconsider. "Please don't take football away from me. It helps me keep my competitive edge in class, it has been one of the things I used to cope with so much of the instability that I've experienced in my life. I experience success everyday on this field either by way of team victory, me catching a pass during the game or practice, me making a good block, me gaining yards on kickoff return. I learned how to trust and how to ensure that people have confidence in me. Lastly, I have made so many friendships that I hope last a lifetime."

I eventually persuaded him to withdraw his requirement and he stated emphatically" One more serious injury and you're done." I agreed and went to sleep because the medication they gave me to relieve the pain was quite different from the kind I would get out of our medicine cabinet.

When I woke up the next afternoon, I noticed that I had a cast on my leg that stretched from my hip to my ankle. This was a huge blow for me since I had been very active from the earliest I could remember. I was always running, jumping and participating in any sport related event. I was now restricted to crutches, beds, wheelchairs and to watching. It just felt surreal that I was now limited with respect to my physical abilities. I had to depend on other people and I wasn't accustomed to being in that position. I was accustomed to being very independent and getting things myself. I had to rely on other people, to trust others to help me with the most mundane tasks: making the bed, running bath water for me, helping me maneuver around the house and around school.

I think I made my biggest mistake when I tried to go back to school shortly after I was released from the hospital. There were several reasons why I decided to go back. First, I was taking Physics my junior year and there was a required lab portion for me to complete. I could only complete that portion by physically being in the school building. Second, I had already registered for the Pre Scholastic Aptitude Test (PSAT) and wanted to get a good score in an attempt to qualify for the scholarships that are given for Merit and National Merit Finalist. Thirdly, I really enjoyed the classes that I was taking and I didn't want to miss the opportunity to learn from the teachers I had that year.

I was able to take the PSAT, after getting a ride from a family member, from my aunt's house to the high school. I had my two pencils and my mind ready to take the test. I, however, didn't take any pain medication because I assumed that it would put me in a fog and I wouldn't be able to remember the necessary information to perform well on the test. I had just been released from the hospital a few days before the test and I didn't realize how the lack of pain medication would affect me. About an hour into the test I just felt a sever throbbing in my leg. I tried things to reduce the pain by moving my leg and body in different positions but nothing seem to work. The pain became so severe that I missed certain parts of the test because it was just too unbearable to sit. I just got up and walked on my crutches for a few minutes as those precious minutes to complete a certain portion of the test just withered away like leaves on a tree during an Autumn day in Maine.

I couldn't afford to wait so I returned to the classroom and tried valiantly to finish the test. My mind was more concerned about the throbbing pain rather than the analogy, I was asked to complete, or the answer to a Trigonometry question. I eventually completed the test, the physical one and the written one, and once I arrived home took the required pain medication, went to sleep and prayed I did well enough to garner a scholarship or at a minimum high academic recognition.

I was able to get a few rides to school but soon my daily rides would cease and that caused a huge problem for me in my Physics class. I could easily maneuver through the high school but found it extremely difficult to gain access to the Science wing, where my Physics class was taught. I would have to use my crutches to travel from the main building to an elevator, to get to the Science wing but it would take me more than twenty minutes to get to the Science wing. I would be exhausted on both trips because there were stairs that I would still have to climb even after I got off of the elevator. It was extremely difficult but I didn't want to get a reduced grade in Physics because I couldn't complete the lab requirement. I also really enjoyed Mr. Quail's class because he was very intelligent and he loved to teach. He seemed to get a jolt, when we were able to grasp a concept and then apply it. Our abilities would be manifested in our test and quiz scores or by our successful completion of an experiment and we had plenty.

He challenged us to not accept being average. He knew we were considered the brightest kids in the school and so he expected us to complete our homework, class work, tests, quizzes and experiments, like we were the top students in the building. He set the bar high and all of us tried to surpass it every day. Mr. Quail was not alone, Mrs. Stewart -Lumpkin, my English teacher and Mr. Emerson, my History and Government teacher and Frau Jewel, my German teacher just to name a few ,did exactly the same thing and wouldn't accept anything but our best. I didn't want to lose that and I knew by accepting my counselor's recommendation for tutors I would be missing opportunities to absorb their knowledge and experience. I was stubborn and wouldn't relent until it got really cold and snowed in early November.

The sidewalks were slick as grease on a tile floor because of the ice and it made the road to school treacherous, for the able bodied kids and thus almost impossible for me in my condition. Yet my cousin and my sister decided to help me walk to school that morning. My sister was concerned and said that maybe I shouldn't walk and instead she offered to bring my homework home. I said, "Yeah, you just can't bring home my Physics lab. I need to get in there so I can do those experiments or I won't receive an 'A' on the test or the class," and they said, "Fine. Okay we will go with you." Well, they had walked with me to the school on a prior occasion, which by the way was 15-20 minutes from our home, when both my legs were healthy so it took me about 30-45 minutes with the crutches.

My sister was on one side of me while my cousin was on the other side. My sister and my cousin alternated holding my book bag as we walked down the street. We had been walking, talking and laughing for approximately ten minutes when I put the crutch on a piece of ice and the crutch slipped, I then lost my balance and tried to put my broken leg down on the ice which then led me to lose complete balance and I fell on my rear end. My sister and cousin were unable to catch me as they were both petite and the ice caused them to struggle in aiding me in getting on my feet and back to the house. I met many challenges before like erratic moving, unconcerned parents, tragic occurrences and other physical threats that were barriers to me receiving the quality education I deserved and it was a broken leg that would be the one thing that derailed me for a short period of time. Everyone respected my desire to go to school despite the obstacles I faced but I finally relented and knew I had to accept my counselors' recommendation and requests tutors.

The Cleveland Heights/ University Heights Board of Education provided the tutors at no costs. I received the necessary education for my math, physics, at least with the non-lab portion as well as my other classes, U.S. History, German and English, which included classwork, homework, writing assignments and tests. The tutors were aware of where the classes were, with respect to their positions in my text books. The only area I could not make up was Physics lab. I had to accept an incomplete in Physics because the missed lab work would have significantly reduced my grade so I decided to take Physics my senior year. It wasn't a setback because most students never took Physics at all at Cleveland Heights.

I had three tutors: one taught math and Physics, one taught German and History and another taught English. They would come three times a week and we would spend approximately one hour on each subject. I enjoyed the special attention and used it to my advantage to ask piercing engaging questions, that helped me better understand the material and I was hoping would be me in a better position when I returned to school. I saw this as an advantage because the tutors that came to my house were actually teachers, in the district who were teachers in other schools or former teachers from the district. They knew that I was a student who was serious about my studies and I prepared diligently before they arrived for each tutoring session. I was able to concentrate despite the fact that I was surrounded by more distractions than most students experience like: access to a television, the chance to wake up just in time for the tutor to appear, the refrigerator being in very close proximity and the fact that my bed was only a few feet away from the dining room table. I was able to make substantial progress and not regress with respect to my grades. I completed tests under my tutor's supervision with no assistance and performed fairly well considering my lack of in class participation. I was able to return to school, after the cast was removed, without being behind in my classes, except for Physics, thus I remained on track to graduate with my class in June of 1989.

When I did return to school I walked with a recognizable limp that I soon was able to discard and began walking with a limp free gait. I was able to accomplish the latter by shear will and a very deliberate training schedule to strengthen my leg. I started off just jogging several one hundred meter intervals. I did that for two weeks and moved up the distance to two hundred meter intervals for three weeks and then four hundred meter intervals. After my leg got a little stronger, I began running half-speed repeating the above routine, until I was running the above routine at full speed for five to six months after my cast was removed. I also began lifting weights to increase my upper body strength but also to get my left leg back up to equal strength as my right leg. I was orchestrating all the physical therapy on my own, the running, stretching and the weight lifting.

I was received no health care in the form of suggested training methods, doctor prescribed physical therapy or school trainer therapy. My health plan, Medicaid (Federally funded program for low income families and children), did not allow for such post cast treatment.   Accordingly, I wound up injuring other parts of my lower body because I was overcompensating for my weakened leg, to avoid placing stress on the previously injured part. I severely strained my quadriceps muscle in my left leg shortly before training camp started for my senior year. Nevertheless, I continued to work my way back and eventually was prepared to fulfill my dream to play professional football.

My dream to play professional football which was inspired by a player of miniscule stature, similar to mine, Gerald the "Ice Cube" McNeil. Gerald had played football in the now defunct United States Football League (USFL). He was one of the fastest and most exciting players in that league. H starred alongside Jim Kelly, the Hall of Fame quarterback from Buffalo Bills of the National Football League (NFL) who played with Gerald in the USFL, as one of Kelly's most reliable receivers. When Gerald came to the Cleveland Browns he was a punt and kickoff return specialist whose speed was intoxicating for the fans and a huge headache for other teams. He was listed at 5'9" 170 pounds but most people said that listing was generous and he actually was 5'7" and weighed maybe 160 pounds. While the Browns tried to be deceptive about McNeil's weight they didn't have to be deceptive about his speed.

Gerald would run pass players as though they were standing still but the fans were always concerned, that if one of the Behemoths ever struck him he would break apart like a fist crushing a toothpick. Most of my teammates compared my speed and physical stature to that of McNeil. I even nicknamed myself "Popsicle." I thought that with some training, physical growth and the opportunity to get better, I could play professionally like "The Ice Cube." I worked assiduously in the classroom, on the track and on the field to ensure that I would be eligible and ready for the start of training camp. I didn't let the girls distract me, or the fact that I wasn't able to garner special information from my teachers during their in class lectures. I was behind some of the other players because I was coming back from a serious, near crippling injury. I put forth the work to get back to my pre-injury speed of 4.59 in the 40 yard dash, which I would have been able to best if I hadn't broken my leg in that particular position.

STABILITY INTERUPPTED AGAIN

While my junior year ended better than the beginning, my sister and I were given some very disturbing news from Aunt Joann. She informed my sister and me that she was moving back to Cleveland. My Aunt Joann and her fiancé John had dissolved their relationship. He moved out of the home and with him moving out, the money that he provided to pay for the expenses for the home, which they were both renting on Bainbridge, vacated as well. Therefore, she could no longer afford it by herself. She said she was going to have to move to a much smaller residence in the City of Cleveland that would make it very difficult for my sister and I to live comfortably with my aunt's family. Neither my sister or I was in favor of moving to tighter quarters and transferring to another school. We knew full well that my father's lifestyle was not conducive to providing the care and supervision that two emotionally damaged teens needed. I was in a quandary because I was trying to make arrangements for summer football workouts with Cleveland Heights. I was also trying to schedule my college entrance exams at Heights and I was trying to make decisions regarding what college I would devote my life to for the next four years.

Most of that was now in limbo because I didn't even know if I would be attending Cleveland Heights for my senior year. My Aunt Joann eventually contacted my mother's mom, Grandma Edna, who was living in New York at the time and she agreed to come back to Cleveland to take care of me and my sister. I was both happy and anxious to know that my Grandma Edna was coming. I hadn't maintained that much contact with her since Grandma Lula died but she had obviously been in contact with my aunt. I wasn't sure if she would be willing to find a home in Cleveland Heights and thus not disturb the sense of stability my sister and I had established at Cleveland Heights High School.

My grandmother, unlike my Aunt Joann, didn't have a definitive place to stay and accordingly we didn't either. She called her old boyfriend, Linell Lovelace, who was residing in an apartment that was restricted to older citizens. In fact, she moved in with him, prior to Aunt Joann's actual move out date, which meant that I was very aware of the situation we were going into. Mr. Lovelace lived in a one bedroom apartment that had a tiny living room, kitchen and bathroom. It was a small apartment for one person let alone three additional people, two being growing young adults. My Grandmother was very resourceful so while she was looking for a home, because she was well aware of the fact that the small apartment was too tight, she was able to secure a very good position at the Cleveland Clinic.

My Grandma Edna, despite not having a high school diploma, was hired and worked as a surgical technician for years when she first moved to Cleveland via Pennsylvania. She is one of the brightest, most articulate, most read people I've ever known. She completed the necessary training but never attended any vocational school, college or university to acquire a degree. While she did receive her General Equivalency Diploma after attaining the age of forty (40) and completed several classes at New York City College also known as the "Poor Man's Harvard, she continued to work in the medical field and Cleveland Clinic was gracious enough to give her a job to help support her grandchildren who desperately needed her.

I think my grandma jumped at the opportunity to help raise me and my sister as a way of dealing with her own heartache, over the loss of her son and daughter. Here she would have the chance to help mold two of her daughter's children and help them realize their own dreams. She essentially was rescuing them from being placed in the custody of the Cuyahoga County Department of Children and Family Services- Foster Care. I think her overriding desire to right some wrongs super ceded the independence that she was enjoying, because her legal obligation to raise children ended with my Uncle Michael's death, and my mother and Uncle Chuck becoming adults. She said and still says even today" We cannot have any more lost generations in our family." She knew there was a possibility that if my sister and I were compelled to enter Foster Care we would have been subject to being the second lost generation, unfortunately like her children.

We were living with Mr. Lovelace when my Uncle Chuck arrived. He decided to stay with a friend because there was clearly not enough room for any other human being at Mr. Lovelace's apartment. I would sleep on the floor and let my sister sleep on the tiny, uncomfortable love seat, while Grandma and Mr. Lovelace slept in the bedroom which was five feet from the living room. The entire apartment was no larger than 200 square feet. Crammed would have been an understatement about the area in the apartment but beggars couldn't be choosy. The refrigerator and stove were standard sizes but they were sandwiched into a small compact area. There was a round table with several chairs that was meant to sit one person comfortably and another in an emergency, but clearly not four. When we ate only one person could sit at the table while someone ate in the bedroom and my sister and I usually ate on her bed (the love seat).

My sister and I were not overwhelmed by the situation; we had been in worse predicaments in the past. I knew this too would pass because everything else had worked out for our good. I knew that the Lord continued to have his loving arms of protection wrapped around us notwithstanding, all the turmoil we experienced. I found solace in the fact that I believed it couldn't get any worse (although realistically it could get worse) if I continued to be cooperative, if I continued to display good manners, pray and apply the lessons I learned in church. If I continued to have a laser focus on my academics, continued to use sports as a vehicle to success and combine the two areas to further my education. I wholeheartedly believed the latter philosophy would allow everything else to take care of itself.

My Grandma did not receive any compensation for her first week of work because she started on an off-week for pay and thus it extended the time for us to live with Mr. Lovelace. I was still working out with the Heights football team while my Grandma was looking for homes in Cleveland Heights without little to no luck. In fact, my Uncle Chuck was able to secure a third floor apartment in Cleveland Heights before my Grandma was able to find other accommodations for us. My Grandma was fortunate to receive an offer to rent a home on E. 130th between Buckeye and Kinsman in Cleveland, Ohio. The owner was a member of our church, Cleveland Church of Christ.

The church was a life support system for me. When we started living with my Grandma she insisted that we begin going back to church. I had not been attending church regularly when I lived with both aunts and the year between my mother's death and my Grandma Lula's death. It was a confusing time for me during that period, because I was angry at the world and more honestly angry at God. I had loss two of the most important women in my life. My mother, who loved me, nurtured me to a point, was responsible for my earthly existence, which had flashes of good parenting and the potential for doing something spectacular but was taken away at an early age. My Grandmother Lula, the strong matriarch, the loving, giving, proud, unselfish angel, was also relieved of this sometimes seemingly hard life journey at the tender age of fifty-six (56).

We moved from one aunt to another aunt and now with my Grandmother Edna. I simply asked why so much? My questions were answered in simplistic terms every time I stepped into the sanctuary at Cleveland Church of Christ on E. 105 in Cleveland, Ohio. Bishop James Haughton Sr. and his son now Bishop but then Elder Lincoln Haughton, were wonderful models of good Christian men. They loved the Lord, their family and the parishioners. I indicated earlier that the church was like life support to me because each sermon provided additional breath, for me to continue to fight on. A hug or a hand shake from the Bishop James Haughton, Elder Lincoln Haughton, a Church Mother or a Deacon was like a jolt that the defibrillator gives to a person whose heart had stopped pumping.

My heart, and the emotion inside of it was turning cold, but each time I received some encouragement and understanding via the word of God I felt that energy and my heart began to warm again towards other people and towards God.   Elder Lincoln Haughton once preached a sermon where he used the passage of scripture that detailed a situation where Jesus and his Apostles encountered a blind man. The Apostles thought that the man's disability was his fault, or that of his parents. Jesus quickly stated that it was done so that God, meaning Jesus, could get the Glory when he was healed.

I took that and ran with it. I then had the answer to why I was so troubled, why I had so much heartache, and confusion, because God wanted to get the Glory. When I was able to survive this part of my life journey, I could witness to other people. I stop fretting over bad news from that point and realized "troubles don't last always," and that "things will work together for the good of them that love the Lord and are called according to his purpose." Those were all Bible verses that stuck in my head and were some of the many that help me restore my relationship with God and my family, including Allen Douglas my "step"-father. Those verses and sermons also gave me the desire to forge on knowing that "I can do all things through Christ who strengthens me" I felt somewhat invincible since the things that we supposed to derail me from my goal hadn't worked.

Thus, I wasn't greatly impacted even when we experienced our next set back. The house Grandma had rented was located in an area that had been ravaged by drugs, gang violence and rampant disrepair, with respect to the housing stock. Most of the home dwellers in that area were leasing via the Housing and Urban Development Section 8 subsidy program. My Grandma Edna saved most of her initial earnings so she could afford to pay the security deposit and first month's rent for the home. I was a little disappointed because it meant that I would have to change schools again but it would be to a school that I had left two years ago, so I knew most of the kids that I would be graduating with in the spring of the following year. Additionally, I wanted to have more living space so going from a one bedroom apartment to a much larger dwelling was a welcomed outcome.

The home was a wooden frame, two family with the owner residing in the top half of the two family dwelling. It had a living room that was the size of Mr. Lovelace's entire apartment, a nice dainty kitchen, dining room, very nice bathroom and most importantly three bedrooms. This would be my first time in a single bedroom since we first moved to E. 116th Kinsman, 9th grade. I was pretty excited. We went over to the home to help my grandmother clean. I washed windows, base boards, I helped sweep, I helped mop the floors and vacuum. We also brought a few of our packed personal items and set them in our respective rooms. I think all of us were happy that we would be moving to more spacious accommodations and couldn't wait until the official move in day, which was only a couple of days away. My Grandma was in the process of getting all the necessary utilities. We left that afternoon after working diligently and took the black case which contained my mother's ashes and placed it on the mantel in the living room.

My grandmother was anticipating moving into the home relatively quickly and contacted, the Illuminating Company to have the electricity turned on in her name. She, however, was given some disturbing information, they couldn't turn it on. She was informed that the owner of that property owed a substantial amount of money to the Illuminating Company and they refused to turn the electricity on in her name. My grandmother was confused because when we went to the property a few days before she received this disturbing information the lights were working. The Illuminating Company then advised my grandmother to retrieve her security deposit because they were on their way to the property to investigate the owner, for fraudulently acquiring electricity.

In fact when we returned to the property we saw, via the Illuminating Company technician, how the landlord and her relatives had illegally siphoned electricity from the street light to her property, the downstairs suite which my grandmother rented and the upstairs suite where she resided. My grandmother politely asked for the return of her security deposit, she did not trust this woman or her relatives and felt that this was not the proper way to begin a business relationship. The landlord agreed to return the security deposit and first month's rent my grandmother had provided but claimed she would do so in a few days. We returned to the property to retrieve the few belongings we had stored in the home when we went to clean the place, particularly my mother's ashes.

As we entered the suite we noticed that many things were in disarray and some items were actually missing. My grandmother asked the landlord and she initially acted coy with respect to my grandmother's inquiry, about whom if anyone had been in the home. The landlord eventually admitted that her son may have gained entry to the property and that he was a known drug addict and thief, and stole items in the past to pay for his habit. He didn't know which of our items were valuable or invaluable but just took items because they looked like they were worth something. Unfortunately for us he thought my mother's ashes, which were encased in a black wooden box that had a metallic looking finish, possessed some street value. The box did not have any gold or silver trimmings or any jewels surrounding it. It was plain looking but priceless to me and my sister.

The landlord's son stole the lasting symbol of my mother. We couldn't go to the cemetery and place flowers on her grave, or pick the grass around the grave stone; we couldn't go and view the headstone that had her name, date of birth and date of death eternally etched in the rock. We couldn't go and find some peace simply by visiting her site. The box provided us the opportunity to engage in the latter things on a daily basis if we so chose to do so, but the young man robbed innocent young adults of those opportunities. When life kicked me and my sister it was like a martial arts black belt with steel boots on kicking us in the stomach. My grandmother's confrontation with the landlord about the whereabouts of my mother's ashes, her other belongings and her security deposit were to no avail because the landlord never returned either one.

Eventually my grandmother simply decided to look for other places to reside and saved her money in the interim. We, however, were slated with the strong probability of living with Mr. Lovelace in those cramped quarters for quite longer than we initially anticipated.

CHALLENGES RESURFACE

August 1988 was one of the hottest and driest summers on record in the Greater Cleveland area. We went weeks without any significant rain fall which made playing football hazardous because instead of grass we were playing on virtual baseball infields all over the football field. The heat caused me to receive numerous scrapes on my legs and to also miss several weeks of practice because of a pulled quadriceps muscle.

I was dealing with the inability to play, and the uncertainty of playing because of the devastating injury I suffered a year ago and the fact that my grandmother hadn't found affordable and descent housing for us in Cleveland Heights. One reason why she couldn't save enough money quick enough is because she had to provide food and clothing for me and my sister; she was giving my Uncle Chuck money; and the she needed to pay for transportation costs. She was driving this beater of a car that we had to pour water into the radiator after every stop and we had to put cardboard on the floor of the vehicle to stop the exhaust fumes from seeping back into the car. We had to avoid the temptation of putting our feet on the ground to stop the vehicle Flintstone fashion. We carried gallons of water in the car like some people carry gallons of gas in the car. Water was a very precious commodity for our family because it was as imperative as gasoline. Nevertheless, we had adequate transportation to our school functions and grandma's money source.

My image of my Uncle Chuck was impacted based on some unfortunate incidents that occurred during his hiatus in Cleveland. I at one time idolized my Uncle Chuck. He was a former star athlete, high school graduate, college educated, handsome ladies' man and what I surmised a wonderful dad as well. He had left California based upon issues he was experiencing at home. He was separated , from his wife Aunt Gina, and left my cousins Little Chuck and, Lauren, there with their mom. He was an agent for a company that recruited employees for high end employers also known as Head Hunters. He did a good job for the company; I mean my uncle was pretty smooth. He had a natural charm that could talk a hungry man out of his last dollar.

He was so persuasive and so smooth he could encourage an Atheist to purchase the Bible. That talent translated to his position where he acquired jobs for other people. He made a great living, but used most of his earnings on feeding a terrible drug habit. The same type of things that my mother was into, my Uncle Chuck was as well. My Grandmother Edna was particularly devastated and hurt since both of her children were addicted to drugs. My Uncle Chuck had moved into an apartment, which was in Cleveland Heights. It was a one room efficiency and he was doing well for a period and he would come over and visit us. We lived right down the hill from his one room efficiency. After the good period (no apparent drug usuage) ended Uncle Chuck became desperate.

My grandmother had been saving money for a new place for us to live. She, however, never got the opportunity to use the money she had saved due to Uncle Chuck's actions. She had located an affordable home in the Cleveland Heights school district and she went to retrieve the money for the deposit and first month's rent. She, however, could not find the money after she feverishly looked for it. She knew Mr. Lovelace hadn't taken it, but my uncle had been visiting us back and forth. He was over there at times, when my grandmother wasn't at home, just talking to Mr. Lovelace and he knew about the money. My Grandma Edna eventually discovered it was my Uncle Chuck that took the money. When Uncle Chuck stole the money, he also stole our opportunity to move from this one bedroom apartment, where again, my sister and I didn't have a bed. Two teenage kids, me being a senior in high school and she a sophomore, it was difficult. But yet and still we were going to find a way to persevere.

One day after discovering that Uncle Chuck had taken the money, I talked to Grandma. I just didn't understand why so many bad things seemed to happen to us. I thought we were cursed and she said to me while she was sitting there cutting up some celery, "One day can change your whole life." A couple of days later, we received a check in the mail. The check was back pay from the Social Security Department from my mother. My mother worked, I wouldn't say a long time, but within her 28 years of living. She had worked a certain portion of time, such that she qualified for benefits for her children. None of the individuals who actually were our guardians during that period, even attempted to try to contact the Social Security Administration Department about that possibility.

Maybe because they just assumed that my mother was so strung out that she didn't work at all. But my grandmother was cognizant enough to call them and get the proper documentation sent and the check that we received from the Social Security Administration was three times that of what my uncle had taken from my grandmother. My grandmother used a portion of the money to buy more reliable transportation and she also found property on the border of East Cleveland and Cleveland Heights that we assumed and was told was in the Cleveland Heights/University Heights School District. We moved to the Cleveland Heights apartment a few weeks later.

I was excited because I would move from sleeping on the floor to sleeping on the couch. My grandmother had a room and my sister had a room, but I could sleep in my grandmother's bed at night during the week because her shift was 11 pm to 7 a.m. and during some weekends when she visited Mr. Lovelace. Plus, I didn't really need a bedroom knowing I wasn't going to be in the apartment too much longer since this was my senior year and I was anticipating leaving for college. I had the opportunity to play a complete year of football without any serious injury. I only caught ten passes that year, but I had over 300 yards in just those ten passes. I started all ten games that we played that year. I received my second Letterman award so that was pretty exciting. I had the opportunity to visit two college campuses, Allegheny College and Clarion University during my senior year.

I was also able to finish my Physics class that I had to take an incomplete in the previous year, due to the complications caused by my fractured leg. I was in my second year of

German and things were going pretty smoothly. At that time, we didn't have too many interruptions. No deaths to be concerned about and I was just experiencing the ups and downs of a normal teenage life. I didn't have a real steady girlfriend. There were a number of young ladies that I was interested in, a young lady by the name of Robin who I had pretty, strong feelings for, but a young lady that I liked a lot, Stacy McIntosh, who eventually would become my niece's Godmother.

She was a sophomore, so she was a younger lady. I just wish I had my license at that time, I could have driven her, but we went with her sister, her sister's friend, Stacy and I. I was just so shy and just so green regarding relationships with young ladies that I don't even think that I kissed her goodnight. Stacy was a real nice young lady, but I really didn't have too many long relationships in high school, if any. I was just too concerned with trying to get to college. It wasn't feasible or conducive for me to commence any relationships since I was moving from school-to-school and home-to-home and family member-to-family member. There was one other young lady, Tracy Dent, and then of course Tammy Roston. Those were some of the other young ladies that I tried to forge a relationship with when I was in high school, but none of those situations, ever resulted in any consistent substantive long term relationships..

Although my social life was lacking I was doing extremely well academically and athletically. Actually the class that I enjoyed the most was American Government with Mr. Emerson. I remember him because of his strong distinctive New England accent. His hair was as white as the driven snow. With that strong accent, he made you think that you were sitting right there at the Boston Tea Party and he made History and Government fun. It was in that class where I think I developed this passion for wanting to understand how our government was formed and how it functioned to help its people. The term " ...A government for the people and by the people...", which we first thoroughly discussed in American Government class was one phrase many law school students claimed piqued their interest and desire to pursue a career in the legal field. I, however, did not develop any passion or interest towards becoming an attorney because of the negative impact that the law and courts had on my psyche. I just recalled countless times I have watched my loved ones being escorted out of court or into court with handcuffs because of their unlawful behavior. While I was thankful for the work that law enforcement did to protect me from harm and danger I was hurt that my family had to be punished for their failure to conform their behavior to a set of reasonable standards established by law. I did reconcile my desire to be protected with my disappointment in the legal process because of the emotional harm that was inflicted by its results.

My introverted personality caused me to be somewhat of a loner off of the athletic field. Accordingly, I had few friends who weren't athletes. I think a huge part of my lack of development in making friends came from the constant change I experienced in my pre-adult life. I couldn't establish real long lasting friendships because of the instability. Also, I know that the trauma I experienced cause me to be less trustworthy and to be particular about the people who I let in my inner circle. Thus, it was no surprise that the person I did develop a strong bond with was a football player.

Big John Stanley is what every called him. It was not an oxymoron he was one of the largest kids at Cleveland Heights High School-6'7" and nearly 300 pounds. We looked like Mutt and Jeff as we walked on the field, down the hall and around the city as I was all of maybe 5'6" 140 pounds. John and I were more alike than some may have known or believed at first impression. He and I both suffered injuries that kept us from playing all of the scheduled football games during our junior year. We spent several days on the sideline just talking about life, family, school and of course girls. I discovered that he too was not being raised by his biological mother since his dad had custody and he was living with him and his stepmother. John wasn't a pretentious conceited suburban kid. In fact, John had spent his early childhood in neighborhoods similar to the ones I lived in that were filled with violence, hopelessness, danger and poverty. He didn't use his size to intimidate but would respond with anger and retribution if someone tried to cross him. He was a bright young man and very interested in his future beyond high school. Accordingly, avoiding going to class, getting suspended through failure to attend school or disrupting class or the school, or being involved in criminal behavior were things that John avoided like the plague. The latter characteristics are the things that made us good friends; he and I exhibited the same hopes, dreams and came from similar backgrounds. We were both humble young men that fervently believed that if we worked hard, kept our noses clean and remained faithful to God (John's dad and Step mother were ministers) we could write our destiny.

I spent a significant amount of time with John and his family over the next fourteen years. I became a member of the family. His aunts, his cousins, his dad and stepmom all accepted me without any reservations. I remember countless times eating at Aunt Jean's house with Robbie, Tracy and Lana. I recall the times we spent at Tammy, John's sister's house, eating, drinking, laughing, talking, dancing and joking. John was a good friend but still not one that I could reveal all of the challenges that I faced prior to our meeting. I still didn't trust him or anyone else with such private, embarrassing and painful information. Kids can sometimes be cruel when armed with information about other kids whether they are doing in jest or to really be mean and insensitive. I was ninety-nine percent sure that John would never use the information as ammunition against me but that one percent kept me from entrusting him with that delicate knowledge.

I believed that John and I would attend the same college. We were both being recruited by the same type of schools Division II and III college programs. I think we had fair senior campaigns on the football field but nothing to attract any Division I programs despite our unique talents (My speed and John's size). The aspirations I had of playing professional football or at a minimum Division I college football ended at the beginning of that camp and was solidified during the season as I was only successful catching ten passes and no touchdowns. John failed to meet expectations as a dominant defensive lineman and did not garner any Division I offers. He, however, was able to attract the attention of a Division III program but they wanted him to switch sides. He was recruited as an offensive lineman and went on to become an All-conference lineman at Bethany College. There were two colleges that I was particularly interested in and the latter two demonstrated reciprocal interest in me:

Allegheny College and Clarion University. At the conclusion of my senior football season Allegheny's coaching staff, after reviewing film of me, invited me for a weekend recruiting trip in Meadville, Pennsylvania. I humbly accepted but the beginning of the trip got off to such a rocky start that I thought that it was a bad omen.

AT THE THRESHOLD OF ONE GOAL

It was the second semester of the 1988-1989 school year at Allegheny College and thus it was winter time in northeast Ohio and Western Pennsylvania. I had on a large coat, with a turtle neck and warm shoes, as I picked up my bag containing clothes, shoes and necessities for three days and two nights in Meadville. My grandmother and my sister internally weren't too eager for me to leave, however, their smiles were as wide as the ocean and you couldn't detect their trepidation. I on the other hand wasn't nervous and was more excited to find out more about the school that had shown so much interest with calls from the coach, visits to my school and review of game tape. They made me believe that they were very interested in me attending Allegheny and helping move the program to unprecedented heights.

My grandma, with my sister in the back, drove me to the Greyhound Bus Mini-Station that was located in Maple Heights at the South Gate Center approximately twenty minutes away from our apartment. After arriving we said our good byes and I waived believing that I was on my way to Meadville, Pa. I, however, realized after traveling for thirty minutes toward downtown Cleveland that we were stopping at the downtown Cleveland main station. I assumed that the bus was just picking up other passengers at the downtown terminal. I, however, along with other passengers was ordered to depart the bus because that was its last stop. I asked was there a connecting bus that went to Meadville, Pa and the driver advised me that no buses traveled to Meadville. He claimed that the closest city where Greyhound traveled was Erie, Pennsylvania.

I was extremely confused and questioned the ticket my grandmother purchased that read Cleveland to Meadville. I called my grandmother after about an hour debate with the clerk. My grandmother, unbeknownst to me, and my sister believed that I had boarded the bus and was near the Ohio Pennsylvania border. My sister would later tell me she and my grandmother were both crying after I got on the bus. In fact, there was a bus that went to Meadville, PA, that left while I was debating with the bus driver. So I called the coaches to advise them that I wouldn't be getting off the bus that was scheduled to arrive in Meadville. They really wanted me to come and visit so the assistant coach advised me to get a new ticket to Erie, PA and he would drive up to Erie, pick me up and take me to Meadville.

I figured that they must have really wanted me to attend Allegheny if they were going through that much to ensure that I made my recruiting trip. I called my grandmother and my sister and let them know what had transpired before I left Cleveland. I would have to wait for the Erie bus for about another thirty minutes. I finally got off to Allegheny, or at least to Erie, PA after a long wait. The bus was massive and my small frame was swallowed by the cotton seat. The smell from the upgraded Porta Potty permeated throughout the bus and it didn't dissipate even with the closing of my eyelids. Once I did reopen my eyes all I could see was grey grass that had yellow dotted and solid lines painted on it. There were branches devoid of life with snow glistening off of the leafless branches. It appeared that we drove for three or four hours and then we pulled into the port in Erie, Pa. I unloaded and sure enough, the coach was there and he placed my bags in the car and we traveled down U.S. route 79 from Erie to Meadville, PA. We arrived in Meadville and we were greeted with snow and bitter cold as we entered the city limits. Snow was scattered over the city like grey hair over the head of an elderly man. I said, "Boy, oh boy, I thought I'd be able to get away from the snow, having lived a majority of my life in Cleveland, Ohio" which is known for its cold, harsh winters.

Allegheny College was a good feel, I liked the place. I got the opportunity to watch a basketball game after meeting some of the current and prospective football players. I also had the chance to eat at one of the best dining halls and the food was fresh and delicious. I thought if this was what we ate on consistent basis this was definitely the school for me. I toured one of the best dorms and eventually slept in a room that was located in the dorm reserved for upperclassmen called Ravine. The dorm room looked more like an apartment and what was unusual about me staying there is that the football guide I had, didn't direct me to his room instead I stayed with four basketball players. Ravine was located in a remote area of the campus but with the most modern and update living quarters of any of the other dorms on campus. It a large bathroom, the four shared instead of sharing it with thirty guys. The dorm room was impressive and I saw myself three years from then, being in one of those dorm rooms. The dorm rooms and the food weren't the only things that impressed me during my stay.

Allegheny was the quintessential small college campus with rusty old tiny buildings that contained the quaint confined classrooms. The student to professor ratio was something I had never experienced since I came from a public school environment, where there were 20 to 25 students per teacher as compared to Allegheny's 12 to 15 students per professor. There clearly would be more intimate connections between the students and teachers, which would raise the bar for both teacher and pupil because neither one could hide when difficult questions and issues were raised. The professor and student were held more accountable for their actions and inaction's. The opportunity to learn, debate, listen and to alter one's view, as well as develop a world view all existed at this wonderful institution and I wanted to be a part of it.

The cafeteria wasn't the greatest since there was no wide variety, with respect to meal choices but it was much better than the choices I was afforded at high school. The buildings were all within five minutes walking distance and there was no rigid set time to be in any class, if you missed that was to your disadvantage because the professor began class with or without your presence. Most of the school's aesthetic qualities were concealed under the snow and ice but the pictures I saw convinced me that in the fall and spring this would be a beautiful place to absorb all of the education and life experiences Allegheny had to offer. Allegheny was a small Liberal Arts school where I could just develop and I knew that this was a Division III school, I wholeheartedly believed that I would get a great opportunity to play football as well. I didn't know how good Division III Football was or this team would be but I was intrigued and impressed.

Allegheny didn't have a difficult time persuading me with respect to their academic superiority over other schools I was considering, but the social life was suspect. I say suspect because the school was small and there was a very small pool of people, small campus and it was located in a small town. I was duped into believing that the college students themselves created a nice party environment, when I was taken from frat house to frat house during my one stay. There were very attractive young ladies, of all races, at the parties. Most of the older people were drinking alcohol or drunk. The music was loud, the floors were wet from the beer that spilled while people were dancing and I enjoyed every minute of it. My ears of course were ringing so loud that I could hardly hear the guy that was my guide for that night. The last party I attended that night reminded me of home with a little bit of college life included. The music had a familiar hip hop beat, the majority of the people danced with some rhythm and then I heard and saw something that was quite different. I saw a group of young men, dressed in an all-white jacket with royal blue Greek letters, stomping their feet, and moving their hands, to the beat of the music and one person yelling "BLUE PHI" and the other guys responding "YOU KNOW".

It was my first time ever witnessing stepping by a fraternity. In fact I was so naive about traditionally African-American Greek organizations I went home and told everyone that I saw the fraternity called "Blue Phi". Actually the fraternity was called Phi Beta Sigma and if I had known the Greek alphabet I would have figured that out because the Phi, Beta and Sigma were prominently displayed on the fraternity members jackets. I left that weekend thinking that Allegheny was very beautiful, serene and challenging. I knew it would be a place for me to grow , to learn and to help me change. I had to go and visit other colleges. I wanted something to compare Allegheny to before I made a decision on what the best situation would be for me, so I decided to also visit Clarion University that also happened to be located in Pennsylvania.

Clarion University was a Division II school, which meant that unlike Allegheny College they could offer athletic scholarships to their student athletes. Myself, Will Hunter, a high school teammate, and Carlos Warner, another teammate, were all invited to visit Clarion one Saturday afternoon. The ride to Clarion was similar to the ride to Allegheny, rural and tree dominated but a little longer drive because Clarion was north of Meadville. Carlos and Will really enjoyed the presentation by the coaches. The coaches also liked them more than me because they were much bigger than I was and provided more potential to meet the weight expectations that the coaches had for Division II football players.

The coaches were intrigued with my speed and my ability to catch the football but were concerned about my small stature and didn't think I could withstand the rigors of Division II without some significant weight and muscle gain. Allegheny also liked Carlos and was trying to get me to persuade him to, at a minimum, visit the school. Allegheny was about an hour and forty-five minutes away from home. Clarion was approximately two hours and a half away from Cleveland. So for me, Clarion was losing with respect to proximity. Division II programs yielded a better opportunity to play professionally. Some pro scouts do venture out to Division II schools, especially if a prospective player does exceptionally well. Since Clarion was a state school the tuition was not as expensive as Allegheny's and that was another factor that would figure into my decision on whether or not I would attend Allegheny or Clarion or any other school where I had applied.

After the assistant coaches escorted us on our tour, we then had an opportunity to meet with the head coach. He was the archetypal football coach, tall, wired like he had drank five cups of caffeinated coffee in five minutes, stringy dirty blond hair, glasses with eyes that pierced through his glasses. Clarion was also a small campus. It was a little bit larger than Allegheny; Where Allegheny had approximately 1,900 students, Clarion had nearly 6,000. We stopped and ate at the cafeteria and the food was not impressive enough to convince me, without more, to choose Clarion over Allegheny. The coaches also inquired about our grades and our scores on the ACT. I didn't know what Will and Carlos received but I knew that my grade point average and my ACT scores were well beyond the minimum requirements for freshman student athletes at Division II colleges.

The second to last place we visited before concluding the tour was the stadium. The coach said, "Imagine this stadium full to capacity on a Saturday afternoon in November. We are facing our arch rivals– Indiana University of Pennsylvania." "Will and Mike, it's fourth quarter and we are down by six points with only a few seconds on the clock." The coach's voice began to rise and he continued saying, "The quarterback drops back and then scrambles as he eludes a pass rusher and then finds you Mike or you Will, in the back of the end zone and drills the ball between two defenders." His voice then significantly decreases and he states in an emotionless voice, "One of two things happen. If you catch the ball you instantly become a legend in the history of football at Clarion University. Or, if you drop it you will have to find the largest hole to crawl into until spring practice begins the following year." That scenario energized me and a part of me wanted to the chance to become a part of Clarion University lore and another part of me was still thinking about the chance to play earlier than my junior or senior year and the chance to graduate from one of the finest academic institutions in my region of the country. The coach quickly took us back to his office and spoke to us individually.

The coach was very candid about my opportunity to play. He said you have to gain more weight and your neck has to get bigger because he was afraid that the hits I would take would from the massive defensive players would make me susceptible to a major injury. He liked my ability to catch the football and was even more intrigued when I revealed my ACT score. The tenure of the conversation quickly changed when he informed me that I had qualified for a scholarship that would release me from my obligation to pay any tuition for the duration of my time at Clarion University. He saw a huge opportunity to get a football player without using one his scholarships and he used every advantage at his disposal.

The only thing I would be required to pay was room and board for four years. The other grants I was eligible to receive~ Pell and Ohio Instructional Grant ~ would have relieved any balance I owed for room, board, school fees and books. I would have left Clarion University, having played football or not, with a degree and no bill. This was the best situation that I had put myself into. The hard work I put forth in the classroom, on the track, in the weight room and on the football field was paying off. I was putting myself in the position, even though I hadn't been accepted by Allegheny yet, to choose between two very fine institutions. Allegheny had the better academic reputation and a more national recognition than Clarion. I would have a better chance to play football at Allegheny much sooner than I would at Clarion. Allegheny offered a more intimate connection with faculty than Clarion did and it was closer to Cleveland.

Clarion on the other hand, if or when I got on the field, got me closer to my dream of playing professional football. Clarion was larger than Allegheny, whereas I do something idiotic there and not many people would know, unlike at Allegheny there would be no place to hide. Allegheny costs would be significantly more than Clarion, the social life was quite different than Allegheny's, the money I would have garnered from Work Study would have gone directly into my pockets because everything else would have been paid. Work study at Allegheny would have been a part of the remaining tuition, room and board, books and/or fees that I owed thus I would not have received a benefit with Work Study at Allegheny compared to what I would receive at Clarion.   My financial aid package coupled with the scholarship due to my high ACT score would have resulted in a surplus for me each year if I attended Clarion.

All of those things were going through my mind while I was sitting across from the coach at Clarion. He then said to me because he saw I was in quandary, "Michael the two most important decisions you will ever make in your life will be where you decide to attend college and the woman that you marry." The coach had three letters of intent with our names on them waiting for us to sign. I asked if my signing of that letter of intent would prevent me from choosing to play football at another college. He informed me that the signing the letter of intent would only stop me from playing at any other Division II college' without sitting out for a year. I then thought about all the pros and cons of both institutions of higher learning, what the coach said and my options and I signed the letter of intent to play college football at Clarion University. I was relieved that two schools were interested in me for both my academic and athletic talents.

I drove home excited to share the news with my sister and my Grandma Edna. I just needed to make sure I ended my senior year strong and maintained my good academic standing. I didn't need to visit any other schools, my choices would be limited to Allegheny or Clarion. I informed the Allegheny coaches about what happened during my trip to Clarion and they made arrangements to try to persuade me that I would look better in their blue and gold rather than Clarion's blue and gold.

Allegheny Head Coach Peter Vass and Offensive Coordinator Ken O'Keefe weren't going to give up on me without a fight. They came west to visit with me at our apartment. They were sitting in my living room showing me and my grandmother the highlight tape that had been produced featuring Allegheny College and more particularly the football program that attempted to further encourage me to become a Gator. My Grandma almost blew my opportunity when she revealed to the coaches that I had suffered a broken leg the previous year. They both looked in amazement but still left with the desire for me to attend Allegheny and become a member of the Class of 1993.

Now the ball was in Allegheny's court, Clarion had offered the scholarship and my acceptance would then be a foregone conclusion. I didn't know what Allegheny would do at that point. I was able to get a head start on my negotiating skills by calling the coaches from Allegheny and trying to persuade them to put some pressure on the Admission Committee, to make an early decision on whether or not I would be accepted to Allegheny College. I could have expedited the process if I had filed the paperwork for early admission decision. I had skipped that process because it took me so long just to get all of my documents together. This included the essay, application, application fee and the funds. Despite the coaches efforts it was virtually improbable that I would receive an early admission decision and no amount of artful persuasion was going to allow me to enter that group. So I called them less frequently to inquire about any and all updates.

After I had signed the letter of intent for Clarion its admission office began to send more information about classes and social activities as well as a the exact financial commitment the university was making to me for tuition for the next four years. I was patiently awaiting my admission letter from Clarion and praying that Allegheny would expedite their process. I would diligently check the mailbox each evening when I came home for Allegheny's and Clarion's decision. Clarion sent their response to my request for admission before Allegheny. I didn't have the same anxiety or excitement to read their letter because I presumed that if I was eligible to receive an academic scholarship from them then I would easily qualify for admission to their university. So I opened the oversized envelope to find information about my acceptance and the procedures I had to take to complete the admission process. Then after a few weeks of growing impatient with the lack of a response from Allegheny I went to the mailbox in mid-March of 1989 and low and behold there was a thick envelope that had been sent by Allegheny College. My heart was beating so hard that my eardrums nearly burst from its thunderous boom. I had been advised this was one of those years that Allegheny was limiting the amount of available spots for freshman and I would be fortunate to receive a letter of admission since they were being very selective.

I opened the letter with some trepidation and joy. I would be devastated if Allegheny had denied me admission and ecstatic but not surprised if the letter was positive. I pulled out the first of many documents and it read: "We are pleased to inform you that your application for admission to Allegheny College has been accepted." They congratulated me on being a member of the Class of 1993. I was overcome with emotion after reading that letter because it was vindication for me refusing to give in or give up. My eyes filled with water like a well after a torrential downpour. It was validation for me that God's words were true: "It will work out for the Good of them who love the Lord and are called according to his purpose." All those things that had happen were meant for my destruction but the Lord found a way to ensure that they would work out for my good. I was fulfilling a promise I made to myself while watching my mother get beat by my father, witnessing my parents alight from their bedroom high off Heroin and watching the police take my father to jail on Christmas day. I was fulfilling a promise I made to myself while being moved from house-to-house, school-to-school and neighborhood-to-neighborhood. I was fulfilling a promise I made to myself as I saw my mother's lifeless body lying in her casket and only a year latter to make another promise when I watched my Grandmother Lula being laid to rest at Calvary Cemetery. I promised myself that despite all that was seemingly against me that I would do the unexpected-Graduate from high school and attend college.

In 1989, only 72% of African American males had received their high school diploma or G.E.D. African American females faired a little better because 79.4% of them had reached the same level of success during high school. These numbers are drastically different when comparing African American males and females enrolled in college during the same year. A mere 19.6% of African American males were enrolled in college, while only 26.8% of African American females reached a similar pinnacle. Accordingly, when one considers all of the challenges I faced my chance of being included in that 72% was very low. Moreover, my probability of being included in the low 19.6% rate of African American males enrolled in college was even less likely. I wasn't supposed to make it this far, instead I was supposed to be in a predicament. Yet, I was overjoyed, relieved, and anxious to be able to have this wonderful opportunity. In fact, I would be the fourth person in my family actually to attend college. My Great Uncle Jimmy had gone to college, James Gohanna was an alumnus of University of Pittsburgh... He parlayed that into a job with the city of Philadelphia, for years actually receiving the award for employee of the year. As I mentioned before my Grandma Edna attended New York City College. My Uncle Chuck attended Hiram. My Uncle Carlin Ryan attended the University of Iowa on a football scholarship after starring with Joe Namath as his running back at Beaver Falls High School.

I was even more ecstatic a couple weeks later, when I got the financial aid package because I received the Pell Grant and I was also receiving a significant amount of money from Allegheny. Allegheny gave me a huge lump sum of money that I did not have to pay back; it was like lifting a two ton crane off a Fiat. The Pell Grant, the Ohio Instructional Grant and other loans made it very tempting for me because now I had to make a difficult choice.

I wouldn't be eligible for the financial aid from either college but for an incident that peeled back another layer of my life. In the spring of 1989, I needed my social security card in order to register for the selective service, which was a requirement in order to receive financial aid for college. My Grandmother Edna did not have my social security card. I had to retrieve a new one from the social security card administration office. I went in and completed the application to the best of my ability. I say to the best of my ability because when I was asked about my father I did not put the name my mother gave me, because Allen was in the picture at the time I was born, and Bruce was missing in action.

I approached the case worker and handed her my application, she perused it and entered the information in the computer. She then stated "I'm sorry I can't issue you a replacement card because the person you listed as father doesn't match what was presented to social security administration when the original application was filed." So, I gave her the name my mother gave me several years ago and she quickly responded "that's wrong as well." I told her " Listen Ma'am. I'm not trying to be rude or play games but I'm simply trying to register for the selective service so that I can get financial aid for college and I have no idea whose name is on the list but I am Michael John Ryan." She looked down at me with a wide small and her peppered grey and black hair tilting out of the window towards me and said " I'm going to process your form and you should receive your card in a few weeks." I said thank you and asked as I walked away, " Can you tell me whose name is listed in the computer," and she said without hesitation:" Richard Solomon." I said under my breath, "Who the hell is Richard Solomon? Why did mommy tell me it was this Bruce dude?"

I asked my Grandmother Edna after returning from the social security office if she knew who Richard Solomon was and she squeezed her eyes together, as if she was thinking hard. I told her the problem I encountered at the social security office. I ended up revealing the secret, my mommy told me and my sister to keep for so long and that was that, my sister and I knew that Allen was not my father.

My grandmother knew all along that Allen wasn't my father, in fact I recalled that she was the one who provided the information to be placed on my birth certificate. She however, did not know who my real father was until that moment. When I told her my mom claimed it was Bruce, she said "No it can't be him because he was short and fair skin." She said it had to be Richard, because while she only met him the one time at Thanksgiving I possessed his mannerisms, I was darker than my mother and I was much taller than Bruce. She then said, "Now that I think about it you do look like Richard!" I was shocked, upset and emotionally drained because I didn't know if she was being duplicitous. I didn't understand why the deception was so deep.

I wish I had an opportunity to develop a relationship with my biological dad when I was younger. I know that I didn't possess the maturity to understand the complex relationships that had been created between me, my mom, my biological father and the man I knew as my father, but I was never even afforded the opportunity to navigate that situation. Allen didn't want any confusion and he wanted to ensure that he kept my mother under his control. He couldn't allow the man who was the father of his woman's first child to re-enter her life. I assumed he believed that my biological father would definitely upset the apple cart, and there could be competition for my mother's affections.

Richard looked quite different from the man I thought was my father for the first eleven years of my life. Allen Douglas and I did have several physical characteristics in common: our shoe size, 11, our height, 5'9"- 5'0", our thin frames and attractiveness, the comparisons, however, ended there. He was much lighter than me and had a ton of facial hair.

Allen and my mother's, adult and adolescent family members knew full well that I was not Allen's child, even though he was the first human hands that I felt; besides the doctor of course. That must have been a warm nurturing picture of a man's large hands holding a football size, insecure and fearful bundle of joy. That picture's proper place is on nothing less than a Hallmark's card. If only that protective, loving, caring, model would have been perpetuated throughout my childhood, then there would probably not be anything to special about my life that was inspiring.

So I was dealing with all of those emotions and trying to make an informed decision regarding my college choice. My college decision was pretty much between two places: Allegheny College and Clarion University. I was just making sure that I could finish up my classes at Heights and do well. I was also a little bit perplexed about the Prom. Football had ended and of course, I wasn't running track that year so I had a lot of free time to sit back and think about the things that I was able to overcome and to anticipate what college would be about. I was going to have to get through one more social event and I didn't know how that was going to go and that was the Senior Prom. This was my final year at Cleveland Heights having only been there for two and one quarter years and so I didn't really know a lot of the seniors in my class. I only had an opportunity to actually congregate with them on a very small basis in limited areas like the lunch room, study hall or gym class. But even with the young ladies, again, I wasn't one of the more popular guys and I did not have that much money, if any, of course, so I didn't dress as well as some of the other young men. I was going to be scrambling, so I thought, for a Prom date.

My confidence was so low because I didn't know how to engage in conversation with girls. I was really attracted to many of them but as we said in my neighborhood I didn't have much ability to attract them to me. I was so distraught I once asked my Grandma Edna was I ugly. She of course said no but she said "Not only are you not ugly but you're fine." What do you expect you come from good stock." She and I both laughed. She then said "Michael you're a very handsome young man and I'm not saying that because you're my grandson." "A lot of people will give you things simply because of the way you look." I said why are girls not attracted to me and she said "Some women are intimidated by smart men and despite your good looks they may be reluctant to start a relationship with you." I then responded, "How am I going to ever get married?" She laughed and said "Don't worry you'll meet someone, probably in college who will respect your intellect and be physically attracted to you as well." I needed somebody before college because Prom was fast approaching.

The summer before my senior year I did convince a family friend to allow me to escort her. Elizabeth Norman had beautiful hazel eyes, she was really fair-skinned, red-boned and a nice figure due to her years of running track. She was my sister's teammate, a junior, a track star, very popular and very sweet.

Right before Prom, I had to also make sure that I could drive and I hadn't acquired my driver's license. I took the student driver class a few months before prom. My father, Allen Douglas, gave me a portion of his personal injury claim since Grandma Edna paying rent, expenses for the Prom car, my tux and the tickets.

I had to make a choice about the school I would be attending because the deadline to advise either school about the decision was fast approaching. I didn't want to flip a coin but it was that close. My grandmother wanted me to attend Clarion because it was the least expensive university but she also knew how much interest Allegheny and the coaches had shown in me and knew that my heart and my mind were leaning more towards Allegheny. I went to church and prayed about the decision and asked that the Holy Spirit lead me to make the right choice. Two days later I received a letter in the mail inviting me to an awards ceremony near the end of the school year that would follow prom weekend. I had completed an application for the Jon Lewis Scholarship that is given to a senior student at Cleveland Heights High School every year.

The scholarship was administered by Peter B. Lewis, who was at the time the Chief Executive Officer (C.E.O) of Progressive Insurance Company. I apparently was one of the top candidates for the award, thanks in part to Mrs. Parrin insistence. After receiving the invitation I had a feeling that I would get the scholarship and that could then defray the costs for Allegheny.

STUMBLING BLOCKS TURNED INTO STEPPING STONES

Graduation at Cleveland Heights is a little different than most schools where Valedictorian and Salutatorian are given the opportunity to give a graduation speech. Heights also gave the opportunity to four speakers and something I was not aware of until my Uncle William Tarter told me. So I decided to audition for one of the four senior speeches. There were a number of people that actually wanted to be one of the senior speakers and I didn't realize that it was so competitive. The audition took place after school in a classroom across from the library. Before the audition, I wrote a two to three page speech and asked my Uncle Bill just to critique me on my presentation and the substance of the speech.

Uncle Bill just happened to be one of the English teachers at the school, he did just that, he critiqued me about my speech, and gave me some helpful hints about my grammar, voice projection and word selection. I then went in and auditioned and they loved me. They didn't know who I was before the audition primarily due to my short presence in the Heights school system. Some of the judges may have considered me to be an interloper since I was unknown to most of them. Despite the disadvantages I entered the room with I let my voice and words speak for me. I had partially memorized my speech which made my delivery more powerful and it had a resounding effect on the judges. They heaped praise and adulation upon me after I concluded and indicated that I would be selected as one of the speakers for graduation. I would thereby continue my streak of speaking at each promotional ceremony (I didn't count Whitney Young because I was only there a few months and I had already been promoted to high school from Central to East Tech). Additionally, my speech was so impressive that the judges selected me to be the final speaker of the night amongst the four.

I had one other important event to attend prior to graduation and that was the senior awards ceremony. It was there I would discover if I was the recipient of the Jonathan Lewis

Award that Mrs. Parrin had strongly urged me to seek. The Peter B. Lewis Foundation gave $3,000 every year to a Cleveland Heights High School student to go towards their post high school educational pursuits. You would get $1,500 your first semester of college and they would give you the other $1,500 your second semester of college.

The scholarship was named after Jonathan Lewis, Peter B. Lewis' younger brother. Both of the Lewis' were students at Cleveland Heights. Peter B. Lewis was obviously a Heights High School graduate but Jon Lewis did not graduate. The reason why he didn't graduate was because he died from a tragic car accident. He was sitting on the trunk of a friend's vehicle and he fell off that vehicle, and somehow it began to roll and it rolled over Jon Lewis, killing him. So Mr. Peter B. Lewis, who was the founder and former CEO of Progressive Insurance, which is nationwide, created the scholarship on behalf of his younger brother. Millions of people know about Progressive Insurance and the commercial with the white dominated scenery and the famous brunette customer service representative. Many people benefitted from the generosity of Mr. Peter Lewis. Instead of simply hording the profits he received from the many people he insured under Progressive Insurance Company Mr. Lewis famously gave a significant portion away to many causes and thankfully he did not forget about his alma mater.

There were a number of Heights High School students who applied for that particular award. I don't know what the criteria was for the award but Mr. Parrin told me to tell them about my story; about the obstacles that I had to overcome; about my grade point average and the other extra-curricular activities that I participated in at Cleveland Heights. In addition to being on the football team and having run for the Track team, I was also in the German Club, so I was very diverse.

My grandmother, sister and I all arrived early for the awards ceremony. The ceremony was held in the Cleveland Heights auditorium which was not completely full because it wasn't sports awards but instead academic awards. Awards were given to those individuals who were in the National Honor Society, people who had received National Merit Finalist status due to their scores on the SAT and other academic awards. After about a half an hour into the presentation of awards a very slim, tall, Caucasian male, with glasses, balding and spattering of gray hair, with a dark sports coat, white shirt and dark neck tie, walked onto the stage and grabbed the microphone. He introduced himself as Peter B. Lewis and began to speak about how proud he was of the previously mentioned award winners. He then spoke about his connection to Cleveland Heights. He talked about his time as a student at Cleveland Heights and then segues into talking about his brother.

He reiterated the story that I spoke about earlier and I was profoundly moved by it to the point that I shed a few tears. Peter Lewis then began to talk about the scholarship and that it is awarded to a student who exhibits great character, intelligence and one who has higher educational goals beyond Cleveland Heights. He then began to make descriptions about that year's recipient and the descriptions are very familiar. I have a very sinking feeling in my stomach at this time because I am nervous that he might call my name and also scared that he might not. My nervousness was quickly relieved when he said "...and this year's recipient of the Jonathan Lewis Scholarship award is Michael J. Ryan." I turned and looked at my grandmother, who was smiling from ear to ear because she had been contacted prior to the award ceremony and knew I had been awarded the scholarship; boy she knew how to keep a secret. I got up and hugged my sister and my Grandma Edna, giving her a kiss on her cheek. I then walked briskly to the stage, shook Peter B Lewis' hand and accepted the certificate that advised me of my award. I didn't receive the money, the first $1,500.00, until late July early August.

I was extremely excited because this was another validation of the hard work and energy that I had put forth from preschool to twelfth grade. It showed that I could avoid the distractions and still excel. It illustrated that I could avoid the temptations of easy money, the party life and the street life and obtain money that would aid me in reaching my goals. I didn't have to expose myself to the risk of death, robbery or the relinquishing of my liberty in my attempts to put myself in a better financial state. After I received the scholarship award it validated my decision to attend Allegheny. The financial aid package they offered was great in comparison to the quality education I was going to receive, plus the Jonathan Lewis scholarship would reduce some of the costs, meaning that I wouldn't have to take out as many loans. Also, my Grandma Edna didn't have to pay anything either that first year which was a blessing for both of us.

Graduation was again an opportunity for me to demonstrate to the people who didn't have any idea who I was and those who did some other unique characteristics and special things about me. The graduation ceremony had to be one of the largest and longest in the history of Cleveland Heights High School. We had speech after speech from administrators, faculty, and members of the Board of Education and then the student speeches. The three students who spoke before me did a great job and received loud applause after they completed their speech. They all were neat in their appearance and read comfortably from either note cards or a typed sheet of paper. I on the other hand always have to be different. I wanted my speech to be memorable and I wanted it to impact the students, faculty, parents and friends. Thus, when I approached the podium, I didn't take any note cards or sheets of paper with my speech or key words to remind me of different subjects to discuss. Instead I approached with all the confidence I obtained over the years from the church, classroom, football field, track and most importantly my ability to survive and recited my speech from memory. I had been practicing from the time I was selected to be one of the senior speakers and I knew that my other colleagues wouldn't be attempting to read theirs without some assistance.

It was an excellent advantage for me because instead of looking down periodically, I could look into the faces of the sea of people who were attending the graduation. I say sea because there were over six hundred graduates along with faculty, staff, parents and other relatives. It was so large that we held the ceremony at the Cleveland Convention Center as opposed to the high school auditorium. The gist of the speech was to motivate Heights High students. I thought that many of my classmates were highly intelligent and the world was waiting for them to offer cures, to provide healthcare, to build up the infrastructure, to create new inventions, to provide legal advice, to just be more than the average productive member of the community. I believed that I would have a huge impact on the world and based upon what I witnessed from many of my classmates, I thought many of them had those same capabilities.

I didn't want them to settle because they had the high school diploma. I talked about how we should not pay attention to outward appearances, but the inward spirit. I spoke about how Heights High students shouldn't rely upon public assistance; I spoke about how Heights High students should always aspire to be something more than average. I wanted them to know it didn't matter what race they were, how much money or property they possessed nor what was their last name. Instead what mattered was what the desire in their heart. I repeated a phrase that my old football coach, Everett Heard, used to say to the smaller players who would display courage by going up against the larger players "It's not the size of the dog in the fight that matters; it's the size of the fight in the dog." I altered it a bit and said "It's not the size of the person in the fight that matters but the size of the fight in the person that makes the difference." That phrase was applicable to my life because I wasn't a strapping young man, I didn't have the huge shoulders to carry the load of the tragedies that befell me. Instead I was this skinny kid, with a passion for learning, good intellect, and a descent athlete, and fierce competitor that refused to be denied. I had more fight in me than all the former heavyweight champions of the world. My voice was loud and commanding as I used the tools of raising and lowering my voice and different times to emphasize certain words and phrases. My words and presentation resonated with everyone in the building and I could feel the electricity going through my body outward to the audience with each word. As I concluded my speech, nearly all six hundred of my classmates rose to their feet, along with many of the parents, friends and relatives, they gave me a thunderous standing ovation. I was excited because it was nothing more than validation again of the hard work, I put in towards the speech and the struggles I endured that was the impetus behind the speech.

ALLEGHENY COLLEGE

My summer of 1989 was interesting. I had actually gotten a job through Coach O'Keefe working for Mr. Charles Reimer. He was an architect who earned his own firm located in Downtown Cleveland. His beautiful home was nestled in a very secluded area of Chagrin Falls. I was hired to fill a position a recent Allegheny graduate and former Allegheny football player vacated due to his television camera job.

Mike Parker was an African-American male about 6 feet 240-250 pound a pretty put-together fellow. One of the quickest guys that you've ever seen who was his size based on the conversations that I had with other players as well as the coaches. Mr. Reimer extended opportunities to young men like me and Mike because he was an Allegheny Alumnus and a former member of the football team as well. Mike's physical stature allowed him to complete certain tasks that were very difficult for me. I was paid the same amount of money but the work grew more tedious and tougher as the weeks elapsed. I would go to the property at least twice a week ,to complete the jobs of mowing the lawn, cleaning out the pond, cutting wood, replacing light bulbs, raking, turning over the earth, etc..

The frequent trips to Chagrin Falls also began to wear on me and my Grandma Edna, especially when my Grandma had to drive me because she needed to use the car, so many times I would be stuck just waiting for her to return even after I had completed the assigned tasks. I quickly learned that manual labor would not be something I would make a livelihood out of, if I could avoid it. I had a hard time taking the lawnmower and placing it in an area from the top of the hill so that I could cut the grass without falling into the pond; it was pure torture at times. I was also paranoid because deer would just creep up behind me and stare at me with the look that said "What the hell are you doing out here in this neighborhood?" I was a city kid and was not accustomed to wild animals parading through the neighborhood unless it was foaming at the mouth, barking and showing its large canine teeth.

Mr. Reimer was a very patient and thoughtful man who believed that manual labor built character. I didn't need any character building; I just needed some money so I could have a few dollars in my pocket when I began my freshman year at the beginning of August. I eventually quit my position with Mr. Reimer but before I did I had the opportunity to meet one of Mr. Reimer's neighbors, who substantiated my decision to attend Allegheny. His neighbor was an executive at one of the large businesses in Cleveland at the time, a name I don't recall today. Mr. Reimer, the neighbor and I were all outside when the neighbor stated, "So I hear you were admitted to Allegheny?!" I responded that I would be entering Allegheny College, as a freshman in the fall and the neighbor was completely taken aback. He shouted with a sense of shock and surprise and said with a sense of amazement "YOU GOT INTO ALLEGHENY!" I said with a little indignation, "Yes I did." He said, "No offense but that is a great college.

You have a wonderful opportunity to graduate from one of the finest educational institutions in the Midwest. People will see Allegheny on your resume and immediately recognize you as bright and outstanding student. My son applied to Allegheny but was denied admission and I wished he would have been accepted. Good luck!" I had been battling internally with my decision to choose Allegheny and the loans over Clarion and a clear and free education but that conversation with the Caucasian, corporate executive, whose son was not adequate for admission to Allegheny lead me to believe I had made the right choice.

In addition to working I was also preparing for my first college football camp. I knew that I would have to make a standard time for the half-mile before I could begin practicing with the team. There was a standard time for certain positions since it would be completely unfair to make the offensive lineman meet the same time of the more skilled and presumably faster players like wide receivers- the position I was recruited to play. I was also supposed to complete a strengthening program: lifting weights and doing calisthenics and plyometric drills to increase my speed and agility. Lastly, the coaches wanted to make sure that we participated in other activities that would make us more prepared to play college football: running routes, catching passes, learning or improving our blocking techniques and other things that would help us become better football players.

I begrudgingly did a small portion of the latter mentioned activities. I would run maybe once or twice a week when I should have been running at least four days a week. I had a lackadaisical attitude because I had run track since the seventh grade and had easily met the standard that the coach insisted the wide receivers make before participating in football related drills. I lifted weights maybe once a week when I should have been lifting at least three times a week. I ignored most of the agility and speed exercises. I believed that since I had played football in the top Division of football in Ohio that it equated with Division I football for college and accordingly I didn't need to prepare that much for Division III football. The players I met during my initial visit to Allegheny were much smaller than the players I met at Clarion and thus I didn't believe I had to get much bigger because I assumed they were inferior players and in an inferior division. I was arrogant because I had been recruited by a Division II team and because of my speed and catching ability I thought I had the real chance of contributing as a freshman or at least a sophomore at Allegheny. Additionally the coaches' intense recruitment was a sign to me that I was wanted and that I could come and help immediately.

Instead of working hard to prepare for camp I spent too much time with a female friend. She was one of the few young women I had any intimate relations with, prior to college. I was very green, naive and she was more experienced than I. She taught me a little about how to treat women. She helped guide me along a beginner's course of sensuality for women at Allegheny. I was no Don Juan but she made me feel like I him. She saw beyond my lack of money, lack of a prominent name, and my lack of being a thug or perpetrating as one. Our relationship was more physical, so we didn't talk or need to talk as much as other couples. They say hindsight is 20/20 and I regret to an extent the type of relationship I had with that young lady. I assumed that she was fine with the arrangement because she never asked me to take her to the movies, dinner, or lunch. I never purchased her a gift and she never did any of the latter things I mentioned for me. I feel ashamed that I simply saw her as an object, someone who I could call up at any moment, when my hormones were on fire. I shouldn't have treated her quietness as disinterest in doing something other than being intimate. I wouldn't want my daughter to be involved in a relationship similar to mine and I can't use my youthfulness as an excuse or justification for my behavior. If I had the opportunity to go back in time this would be one of many things I would change.

I tried to spend a good majority of the remaining time with my Grandma Edna and my sister. I talked to my Grandma Edna about my anxiety regarding leaving and not returning home until November. It would be the longest period of time that I would be separated from my sister since I lived with Pat in Euclid and my sister lived with Grandma Lula. I wanted to impress upon her that I would be fine since Allegheny was only less than two hours away. I was more happy because it was at least two hours away and she couldn't just pop up on campus; although my Grandma Edna was not very   attached to me and my sister since she believed in letting her children, and now grandchildren, find their own way. She helped me purchase a number of items that I would need for campus: sheets, pillow, clothes, class supplies and other miscellaneous materials.

My sister and I didn't go out to dinner, or to the movies or to the mall during the time before I left because she was a little busy working and the free time she had she spent with most of her friends. We had a relationship where we didn't talk as much unless we needed one another. She knew, however, that whatever and whenever she needed something from me I would drop everything and make sure I could get it for her. We share a bond made out of blood, tragedy and triumph and don't necessarily need to talk all the time for the other one to know that they are loved. I told her that I would miss her and she reciprocated and asked when could she come and visit. I told her she was always welcome and I would find someone she could stay with while she visited. Neither one of us cried when we discussed me leaving because we both knew eventually that was going to happen. We didn't reminisce about the past nor did we discuss the future. It was an unspoken understanding of how the turmoil we experienced built us to be where we were in life. College wasn't a surprise but an expectation for both us. I was blazing the trail for her just as I had done for most of her life. I gave her a standard to reach for and she did it. She didn't want to let me down and I made sure that I didn't let her down. If we didn't have each other I think that neither one of us would have made it. I inspired her and she was my motivation.

I slowly but surely packed all my clothes, books, instructions and everything related to football and prepared for the special trip to Allegheny College. Then on or about August 4, 1989 my sister, Grandma Edna, Mr. Lovelace and I all packed up into a car only a few days after my eighteenth birthday. The trip did not seem as long since I was not required to stop at some of the other small towns we traversed when I traveled by Greyhound earlier in the year. We listened to the radio and talked briefly and candidly during the two and half hour trip. It was two in half hours because we drove I-90 East to Erie, Pennsylvania and I-79 South to Meadville, Pennsylvania; mostly highway. I was the only person in the vehicle that had seen the campus and so Grandma didn't know how intoxicating the atmosphere was at Allegheny College. She described it as similar to many of the small towns in Pennsylvania. She was a Pennsylvanian and was comfortable with the small town and felt Meadville was a safe place. She was concerned about the financial handcuffs I would have when I graduated. Plus she was not too happy with me turning down the free ride I was getting from Clarion University.

She gazed at the beautiful old buildings that were located on campus. She commented about how beautiful the full blossomed trees were and the overall landscaping of the school. My sister simply said it looked nice and small and that I shouldn't have any trouble getting around at school. Mr. Lovelace simply said "wow" as he observed the same scenery as the rest of us. Most of his amazement didn't come from just the aura of the college grounds but also his astonishment that little old Michael was attending such a prominent school. We drove to Baldwin Hall, the dorm designated to hold all the football players for training camp. My roommate was Steve, a senior wide receiver from Boston, Ma. He was built like a Mack Truck where he stood 5'9", 200 lbs and his biceps were three times the size of mine.

He was a veteran and knew the system very well and was chosen to help guide me through the process. He was the most coveted receiver at Allegheny and had been personally recruited by Coach Voss and I assumed I was the heir apparent. Most of the players were paired with players of the same position and there was an upper classmen paired with a freshman. Steve and I spoke briefly and then he escorted me and my family to the picnic that was taking place at the Student Center. While the picnic was for all the football players, the coaching staff and the player's families, the majority of the families were related to the freshman players. There was a ton of food as one would expect at a picnic for a group where the average person weighed more than one hundred and eighty pounds. We had and endless supply of hamburgers, hot dogs, chips, juice, salad and fruit. During the picnic I saw two familiar faces that I was surprised to see and hadn't seen since ninth grade at Whitney Young Middle School: Stanley Drayton and Darren Hudson.

Stan and Darren both attended, graduated from and played football for John Marshall High School. Stan was a standout running back and defensive back in the Senate League and actually had been recruited by some top notch Division I and II programs but chose Allegheny. Darren was a very good receiver at John Marshall and thus provided some competition for me. Stan and Darren were also very good track athletes and thus I would have a chance to forge a good bond with both of them if we all decided to play football and run track at Allegheny. After a few hours of eating and talking I noticed for a brief period my Grandma Edna had disappeared. I assumed that she had taken a stroll around the campus since she admired its aesthetic qualities so much. Eventually she returned and she and Mr. Lovelace and my sister said their good byes. They individually gave me a big hug with Grandma Edna's being the longest.

I wrapped my nervous and slim arms around her waist and gave her huge kiss and whispered in her ear "I'll be fine. I will try to call and if I can't call I will try to write. I love you and thank you for everything you've done for me and my sister." Mr. Lovelace would later tell me that the reason why Grandma disappeared was because she went to cry in peace since she didn't want me to see her and then both of us be emotional in front of the other football players; she was saving my masculinity. She said with a trembling voice and eyes watering and tears shaking on the bottom of her eyes but not dropping "I will miss you. Make sure you write me and I think you made the right choice. I love you!" She then quickly entered the car and told Mr. Lovelace and my sister to hurry so that I could spend some time with the other players.

After they left, we got an opportunity to talk to a lot of the guys. The freshmen got together and conversed and then we walked around to each of the different rooms. We had a 9:30 pm curfew lights out curfew, because we would have to be up at 7:00 a.m. and it was a requirement that everyone eat breakfast, at least get up to go over to breakfast. Everyone had to attend breakfast and after we went to breakfast, it was to a meeting; a meeting with your position coach and/or the entire offense or defense, whichever one you were on, and then to the field. But that first day we had one large team meeting during breakfast and we were then given instructions on the testing we would endure and then a final meeting with the head coach at the end of the testing.

At approximately 6:30 a.m. while I was still sleeping, a loud blasting sound boomed through the hallways and bypassed the metal dorm room doors right into my eardrums. The frightening horn blared so loud I thought the coach was standing next to my bed. I was so scared that I jumped up out of the bed with my heart feeling like it was going to jump out of my chest. My roommate, who was already up because he knew about the horn, simply laughed and smiled and said, "Make sure you're ready for breakfast." That was the wakeup call that we would get every single morning for camp.

I immediately put on my sandals, grabbed my shower gear, went into the community bathroom, showered, brushed my teeth, put on my training clothes and went to breakfast. After breakfast, we returned, I grabbed my other gear and I walked this time up to the field. The field was located approximately three miles up a hill from the dorm. Thank God that the actual practice facility, once we got to the field was down a hill, but we had to walk up the hill after practice. I mean, Pennsylvania, it should be nicknamed the "Hilly State" because of all the hills and mountains that are present throughout the region. Nevertheless, when we got up to the field after walking that distance, we had to complete the skills testing.

I trained during the summer, but obviously I hadn't trained hard enough because by the time I completed the half mile time, which was below the expected time for receivers, I did not have enough energy to run the forty yard dash at my fastest and most productive time. I was not aware that the forty yard sprints would commence immediately after the 800 meter dash and thus had little to no time to recover. My legs felt like there were one hundred pound ankle braces on them. I could barely lift my legs when I walked over to the area where they were staging he forty yard dash. I think they had me clocked at somewhere around 4.8 and I normally ran it, at least before I broke my leg, in the low 4.6's near 4.5. My slower than expected forty (40) times startled and disappointed my coaches. I was utterly ashamed at my forty (40) time because I knew that my failure to take my summer training more seriously had now put me in a very awkward position. I purposefully underestimated the amount of work and energy I would need to compete for some playing time at this NCAA Division III program. I let my recruitment from Division II schools give me a false sense of security and I was embarrassed.

I initially internally tried to justify my slow time due to running the half-mile prior to the forty, but if I knew I could make any excuses and simply accepted the consequences for my failure to prepare. It was a huge lesson for me in making sure I was prepared no matter the subject. It could have been for practice, for a game, for a track meet, for homework, for a writing assignment, for a test, a job interview, job project or even for a date. I didn't want to underestimate anyone or anything else again. What hurt me here, however, was first impressions are too difficult to alter and thus in my teammates and coaches eyes, who believed I had come to help the receiving core move from good to elite, I was a bust. The final skills tests, the route running and catching, sealed my doom. I was a bundle of nerves because I had performed poorly on the forty and I wanted to impress the coaches with my catching ability. I, however, dropped two passes, two other passes were thrown out of my reach and the one pass I did catch was caught with the assistance of my face mask.

I was shell shocked but I figured that I would be placed close to the bottom of the depth chart but be able to move myself up after a number of practices. I went to lunch a little distraught but felt more relieved after the afternoon session because we completed routines that tested our athletic ability: shuttle runs, back pedaling, stop and turns. I did extremely well according to the coaches and I awaited the decisions of the staff on where I would play and where I would be initially slated on the depth chart. The assistant coaches had an opportunity to observe us doing the skill session, our half-mile time, our 40 time and our participation in the agility tests and then they made a choice, with the head coach's input, about what position they recommended we play and our position on the depth chart.

I was called into Coach Voss' office and he didn't waste any time because he had to speak to all the first year players. He facetiously said, "Mike, what position would you like to play?" He was aware of what position he wanted me to play. I responded " I want to and came here to play receiver." He said matter-of-factly, " I believe that you would better serve the team playing a defensive back. Your performance on the agility skills was consistent with how many of the defensive backs on the team did. Now if you want you have the option of playing wide receiver and being placed at the bottom of the depth chart and the option to play defensive back with the more of an opportunity to advance and get on the field." Instead of having faith in my abilities, instead of remaining steadfast about my hopes and dreams of playing receiver in college, instead of standing up to the coach I relented and agreed to play defensive back. It was the beginning of the end of my football career. When I left that office my passion for football remained in the office with Coach Voss. I was embarrassed and lacked a genuine interest to play defensive back. They say hindsight is 20/20; I should have stood up for myself then. I should have said, "No, I want to continue playing receiver. I don't want to play safety." Yet, because I declined to say anything, I accelerated my retirement from football.

I was miserable the entire year at safety. I was on the scout team helping the offense and I never got the opportunity to even, at a minimum, travel with the varsity team to away games. The team could only take a certain number of players to away games. If you didn't go, then you were, at least in my eyes, deemed to be a scrub. I had fallen pretty far after having been a starter for a Division I high school team to being an afterthought on a Division III college team. I just couldn't fathom it and I was not energetic like I should have been, and I admit that I was my own worst enemy. I could have taken advantage of the situation, I could have gotten stronger during the season, became more knowledgeable of the defense, but all that didn't interest me anymore..

I was simply going through the motions after a few weeks into the season. I started off during training camp, the preseason and the initial start of the regular season working diligently to comprehend the defense language, to grasp the skills needed to play defensive back, to demonstrate to the coaches that I would be a valuable member of the special teams at a minimum. I studied the defensive playbook non-stop to ensure that even if I wasn't physically prepared at least I would be mentally prepared if and when I got an opportunity to play. I tried to win each gasser, sprinting the entire length of the field, I was near the beginning of the line when we were doing drills, I tried in vain at times to tackle guys who were more than fifty pounds heavier than me. As the season started, however, I was never selected as the week's best non-varsity player and accordingly was never given an opportunity to travel. In fact, the year ended without me sniffing the chance to travel with the team to opposing stadiums. I did get a chance to play on the junior varsity team recording only a few tackles all year.

Additionally, I got a chance to dress for home games but again the closes I stepped on the field of play was during warm ups both before the game and halftime.

I was contemplating not even returning the next year, but I'm the kind of person that doesn't like to quit. So, after the season concluded I focused on getting faster by joining the track team and I participated in the offseason agility and strength program. While football and track occupied a significant portion of my time, nothing was more arduous and time consuming as the work I was required to complete for my courses.

Allegheny was quite different from any other learning environment I had been exposed to when I was in school. Allegheny was different because they taught you how to think critically. We didn't have a lot of multiple-choice tests. Instead a majority of the classes I took that first semester required many essay type responses to questions both in quizzes and exams. We were given essay type questions in subjects like Math, Astronomy, Computer Science and other similar disciplines that one would find odd to be required to draft lengthy word filled answers to. The requirements were in addition to the expected essay questions and research papers that we wrote for writing type courses.

Allegheny compelled me to overcome my issues with grammar. My grade school nemesis of English resurfaced again. At Allegheny I had to draft papers and although grade school introduced me to King James English my home environment made it extremely difficult to master. There wasn't really an emphasis on subject-verb agreement at my home. There wasn't a focus on whether the comma or semi-colon were in the correct place. I used phrases and words that were clearly incorrect usage in the English language. No one took the time to correct me either because they didn't know or because they didn't care. I struggled from the first time I went to school until my latter years in high school. My writing was impacted by the way I spoke. I couldn't grasp the correct grammatical terminology and application because I was so accustomed to one area. The old phrase it's hard to teach an old dog new tricks applied to me. I was so accustomed to the old way, the way I grew up speaking, that the new tricks were just difficult for me to master. While I didn't have any difficulty with reading or comprehension my ability to articulate my understanding or opinions regarding information I read or learned was agonizing at times for me. The fact that I didn't have a large vocabulary also impacted my ability to write as well as I needed to at Allegheny.

Allegheny College focused on improving, or enhancing ones communication skills. They believed that if you possessed the ability to speak and write exceptionally well you could perform at a superior level in any profession. I believe that Allegheny assumed that a majority of the students had exceptional comprehension and analytical skills but felt that if they could not effectively express those conclusions that they reached from what they learned or read then their skills would be wasted. I quickly learned that in order for me to do well that I would need to improve my writing and oratory skills.

I was assigned to English 101 based upon the assessment test I took upon arriving at Allegheny. It was the lowest English class you could take and I was ecstatic because I saw it as a way to get off to a good start. Most of the students either didn't perform well on the assessment test or had been placed in that class due to their placement in Allegheny's Freshman Assistance Program. I was not a participant in the Assistance Program but a number of the students I knew were a part of the program. They actually came to campus before most of the other students and took what amounted to remedial classes to acclimate them to Allegheny and increase the retention rate amongst the freshman students. I was disturbed to discover, however, that most of the students were African-American. Nevertheless, Professor Diane Goodman was a Godsend for me in that course. She was an excellent, patient and understanding English professor.

She was not disparaging regarding our low level skills but I think took the challenge of conforming us into better writers and speakers. She encouraged our class participation, which helped develop our public speaking skills. She made very meticulous remarks on my writing assignments, that were extremely helpful to me in understanding the things I struggled with grammatically before I arrived at Allegheny. I received a very good grade at the end of the semester in that class. I also received a very good grade in Astronomy despite fighting to stay awake most classes because I took the 8:00 a.m. course. I wanted a lot of classes in the morning so that they wouldn't interfere with my football practice schedule or my work schedule either. I nearly fell asleep in my Astronomy class because it was so early and there were many times we had lab and my professor was compelled to cut the lights out so that the room would display the Milky Way. It was at times too serene, coupled with my professor's monotone voice, the darkness and early hour made it difficult for my eyelids not to feel like someone had placed tablespoons of salt on them. I was able to gain a ton of confidence from my two grades in those classes to help me continue to strive for excellence in my other courses. I did so well in my first semester courses that I received the distinction of being placed on the Athletic Honor Roll.

DELICATE BALANCING ACT

In addition to the challenging academic program, football and eventually track & field, I had to balance my social life and my employment as well. The social life at Allegheny was different from other larger colleges and universities due to the small campus and small surrounding community of Meadville, Pa. Since a majority of the students were below drinking age freshman, sophomores and most juniors were restricted to attending parties on campus or at homes that were being rented by older students. Allegheny was diligent in its efforts to reduce underage drinking and the opportunities to engage in it by monitoring the activities at the Greek parties and student homes. Many students assumed, but it was never verified that they also collaborated with the State Liquor Control Board when the latter raided parties. The fraternities did as much as possible to limit the people who had access to alcohol but they couldn't control members who would pass alcohol to under age students. The same safeguards were in place in the homes that students rented but there were occasions when students in my class were clearly inebriated.

I have to honestly state that there were instances where I was influenced by my peers to drink and to drink heavily while I was underage. I would go to the parties and since I was an athlete I knew a number of the other athletes that were in the fraternities and they were more than willing to pass me a couple of beers at no cost. I would drink and dance from the start of the party to the end and then try to find some young lady to take back to my room or go back to her room. I was clearly engaging in some dicey behavior in drinking and intimate encounters, but I believed that was a part of the college experience. I was young and didn't think I was subject to being arrested for drinking and so I took huge risks. I was fortunate, however, when I decided one night not to drink and simply had a few sodas before I went to a house party. The house party was eventually raided by the Liquor Control Board and I was not arrested because I hadn't been drinking. The experience of seeing individuals my age, some students and non-students, being given citations for court appearances made me less inclined to engage in that type of behavior until I was of age.

The alcohol high wasn't worth all the other problems that could follow. Alcohol had a negative impact on my conditioning, there were times that I was sick and my felt like there was a mini-man in my brain with a jack hammer. The alcohol was costly because I would have to pay people extra money to get the alcohol since I wasn't old enough to purchase it. If I had a hangover that would impact my study time. Finally, I couldn't fathom what if anything I would say to my grandmother if I was arrested and then expelled from school for underage drinking.

Since drinking would not be a priority for me in my social life my attention turned towards the women. I didn't have many experiences with many women prior to college. I had a few girlfriends but no long relationships. I was pretty naive and green when it came to women, since I didn't have too many positive male role models to teach me how to attract and keep a woman. I think that may of helped me because most of my experiences came from listening to the female relatives in my life about what men did or didn't do for them. I acquired a respect for women that most of my peers didn't possess because of their backgrounds. I knew what things to say, to do, what to say to them and when to do the acts. My first interaction actually wasn't even with a student from Allegheny but instead from a young lady who lived in Meadville.

I met her at a party that the Allegheny sponsored for the beginning of the school year. She had a small stature, with chocolate smooth skin, a beautiful smile, a very hilarious laugh, and adult size hips on a high school junior. She was a very smart young lady who was enthralled by me and I liked her as well. She introduced herself and I told her my name and she called me by my first and middle name each time we spoke from that point on: "Michael John." We danced that night to several songs and we exchanged numbers as well. I was a little concerned initially because she was not a college student, and I didn't want my friends embarrassing me by accusing me of robbing the cradle, since she was two years younger. While at that point we were two years apart she would turn seventeen before my birthday and therefore I was actually not much older than her.

After about two weeks she and her friend, who was interested in one of the guys who lived down the hall from me, and came to our dorm. Her friend went to my friend's dorm room and she came to mine, we sat and talked for a while before we made our way over to the bed. I took a huge risk that night when I engaged in sexual act with this young lady without protection, after initially trying to use protection with no success. Neither one of us was virgins but we both lack the experience and thus made it a very awkward situation. I was thankful that my roommate made friends and decided to stay out for the rest of the night. The young lady and I spoke and met on several other occasions, with me making the same mistake of not using the proper protection. I was asking for a potential disease or an unwanted child by continuing to engage in that pattern of conduct. I was fortunate each time that I didn't acquire either one. I mention this experience as a way of trying to elucidate the importance of first thinking about abstaining from intimate relationships until your married or in the alternative using protection. I was blessed not to have become a father or a statistic during those episodes in college. If I had the opportunity to do it again I would have made better choices and not taken such a huge gamble with my future and my life.

This was quite different from my pre-college relationships because in college I didn't need to work as hard before the relationship became physical. I didn't understand it and frankly didn't care because my needs as a vibrant healthy hormonal young man were being met and I only needed to smile, wink and whisper a few sweet nothings in her ear either on the phone, or in person and she was like putty in my hands. At the time I didn't take her feelings into account and simply thought she expected the same thing without any significant attachment. In fact I was told by many of my peers don't get attached because she's a townie and they just want to latch on to a college man. I knew Na-Na wasn't like that because she was very bright young lady, who could have if she applied been admitted to Allegheny. Instead she attended and graduated from a college in Ohio located south of my hometown Cleveland. Some of the recommendations against engaging in any relationships with women who lived in Meadville were from many of the African American women who attended the college. They would routinely say," If you lie down with dogs you'll wake up with fleas." They were extremely nasty and I think, without any direct claims, because they were jealous because our attention wasn't directed towards them. Nevertheless, Na-Na and I mutually decided it was better to end our relationship but we remained good friends even after she graduated and began her college career in my home state.

The extent of my relationship with that young lady would become common place with respect to other relationships (if you could call them that) I had with other women while I was a student at Allegheny. I didn't know if it was like that because of the types of women I sought or because of the women that were available. During my four years at Allegheny there was never any one woman who I met on campus that I eventually became intimately involved with that I considered a steady significant other; all of my relationships were purely physical. It's not something I'm extremely proud of because I admit that I used women but in turn they used me as well. I assumed that because I was upfront with all of them by stating that I didn't consider it a relationship simply because we were intimate that I was justified in not calling them, or moving on to try and sleep with the next woman. I bought into the theory that most of the upperclassmen ascribed to and that I was advised not to engage in long term relationships because most of the women didn't intend to be monogamous. I had a warped approach to engaging women on campus and believed that caused me to have an unsavory reputation due to my smash and dash attitude. During my freshman year I went from having virtually no experience with women on an intimate level to a male whore because of the number of relationships I started and ended in such a short time span.

I engaged in some very unsafe, immoral, respect deficient behavior with young ladies both from town, prospective students and students. I made no commitments and was using my charm as a way of obtaining intimate relationships with the women of my choice. I didn't discriminate, wherein the young ladies were black, white, tall short, thin robust, young and some even a few years older than me. I, however, unlike some students, didn't let my social life consume me such that I couldn't manage my other responsibilities.

CHALLENGES CONTINUE EVEN IF PLACES CHANGE

My financial aid package required that I participate in the work study program. The money I earned made up the difference from the grants, loans, scholarships, money from my summer job and the financial assistance my Grandma Edna gave me from my sophomore through senior year. During my freshman year, unlike most athletes, I wasn't able to secure a cozy job and was relegated to working in Brooks Dining Hall. My duties consisted of placing food in the serving area, replacing items in the salad bar, monitoring pop an ice dispenser while replacing them when they were depleted. I also mopped the floor after the hall closed. But the most unpleasant duty was washing the dishes. For the 3-4 days a week I worked that job, I left each day with calluses on my fingers. My fingers felt like the skin was peeling off like a banana skin peels off of the fruit inside.

I learned a valuable lesson performing that job because I understood the hard work that individuals who are employed in in the service industry endure every day. I witnessed dedicated, hardworking, respectful and courteous individuals (who trained me, protected me and were proud of me) come to work per their schedule on time and without complaints (at least not to me). I say proud because many of them were African American and they could only dream of being a student at such a prestigious institution of higher learning. I would hear some students speak in a condescending tone towards the workers and I would respond in a defensive manner on behalf of my co-workers. While I wanted to respond in a vitriolic manner I instead was frank and stated that my co-workers deserved the same type of respect the students expected from them. They were good people who didn't deserve to be denigrated by a few elitist pretentious young men and women who only who saw them as the help and therefore inferior and not deserving of their respect. I would work in the cafeteria for both my freshman and sophomore years and enjoyed my time.

I not only interacted with many from the small African American community during work study but also in my social life, more particularly the historically African American fraternity Phi Beta Sigma Inc.

The Sigma's were the only historically African American fraternity on our campus and the majority of them happened to be football players. I was intrigued by their camaraderie, the fun they had partying, the strolling they did at parties (stepping) and the royal blue and pure white colors they frequently wore. I was unaware of the history of fraternities and more specifically African American frats. I mean I had never experienced a real, true fraternity life. The closes thing I knew about fraternities derived from Spike Lee's movie "School Daze."

I attended a smoker, which was an introduction of the fraternity to prospective candidates. The smoker was very brief and simply included introductions by the current members of the fraternity, a brief history, the estimated length of the initiation period, the estimated costs, the sacrifices we would make and the benefits of being a member of such a distinguished group. The following were factors in my decision on whether or not to pursue membership in Phi Beta Sigma: finances, my Grandma Edna's hatred of fraternities and my lack of knowledge about the other historically African American fraternities. My Grandma Edna told me that one of her friends went to college and pledged a fraternity only to return home "crazy" in her words so she opposed my initiation. The brothers indicated that they would help us organize fundraisers to pay for the initial fee. The big brothers were eventually able to assuage me of my concerns by persuading me that the only real good choice I could make from was Phi Beta Sigma as opposed to Alpha Phi Alpha, Kappa Alpha Psi, Omega Psi Phi or Iota Phi Theta.

A few days later after deciding that I would begin the process, we jogged around campus singing the fraternity songs that "Crescents" (Pledges for Phi Beta Sigma) were allowed to sing. After the initial night I began to have reservations about being a member of a fraternity. I could not sacrifice my time, personal dignity, money and respect to the degree they indicated I would have to in order to become a member of this storied organization. Furthermore, my friends Lorice and Suzanne were discouraging me from participating because of the stories they heard about the heinous hazing that supposedly took place in fraternities. So I essentially quit. I hadn't ever voluntarily quit anything in my life that I started. I just knew at that time being a part of Phi Beta Sigma was not in my near future. I regretted the decision I made during the second semester of my freshman year. Quitting would become an ugly trend for me regarding groups or and or programs at Allegheny.

One of the things that attracted me to Allegheny was the Educational Program they offered to students. The program allowed students to acquire a Master's in Education in only five years as opposed to the normal six year period (4 years of undergraduate and 2 years of graduate school). I had intended on becoming a teacher in the public school system and felt Allegheny's program would provide me with the best preparation. Unfortunately, during the second semester of my freshman year we were told that Allegheny would no longer provide students with the opportunity to acquire their Master's in Education because it was the only graduate degree the college offered and it wanted to move to an exclusive four year degree institution. I was upset and at a crossroad because I thought about leaving school but instead, after speaking to my advisor, choose not to pursue an Educational tract and thus quit my pursuit of an Bachelor of Arts in Education; in retrospect the latter was the best decision I ever made for my future.

I came back to campus after a very productive summer of working, starting a relationship, running and lifting weights, I was prepared to be a more effective member of the football team. There was a change in leadership wherein Coach Voss had accepted an assistant coaching position at the University of Notre Dame and Coach O'Keefe had assumed the head coach position, his first time in that new job. I was hoping that Coach O'Keefe would see Coach Voss error and switch me back to the offensive side of the ball. My body had noticeably changed in that there was more muscle in my chest, arms, legs and neck. While I looked more like a defensive back my heart was still on the offensive side of the ball. I came into summer training camp in the best condition I had ever been. I had grown approximately 2 to 3 inches and I was "in love." I became reacquainted with a young lady I faintly knew at Cleveland Heights High School. I came in focused on being a back up to our starting free safety or at a minimum playing on special teams if I couldn't move to receiver. Coach O'Keefe never considered switching me and so I went all out during camp. I was able to make some spectacular plays both during drills and as a member of the scout team against the first team offense. I did so well there were times that I was invited to play with the first and second string defensive players against the offensive scout team. I had worked myself into being able to play during our first scrimmage with the second team defense. I was actually on the field, not in a junior varsity game, playing college football. I thought I did well but the coaches had another assessment. I would never see the field again in live action against another team. The latter occurred because the coaches never gave me another opportunity, injuries to my back began to restrict my ability to perform at my highest level and then the final straw was leaving me off the traveling squad. I thought I had at a minimum earned the chance to travel with the team but again just as I did my freshman year I was relegated to listening to the game on the radio. I then, after consulting with my Grandma Edna, made one of the most difficult decisions in my life- I quit playing football.

I first told my position coach that I no longer wanted to play. I told him the same reasons I just mentioned and he tried to persuade me to remain on the team and keep working hard and I would eventually make a significant contribution to the team. I wasn't persuaded. I then went into the office and had a very long conversation with Coach O'Keefe. He was the one that recruited me the longest and hardest. He had spoken with my Grandma Edna on many occasions and developed a rapport with her. After he listened to me give my reasons behind leaving he simply asked " Did you talk to your Grandmother about your decision?" When I told him yes he then said "I wish you would stay but you have to do what's best for you."

I experienced feelings of embarrassment, guilt, frustration and envy after I cleaned out my locker and handed in my practice uniform and equipment. I had never voluntarily quit playing my favorite sport. Despite being outweighed by most of my teammates and opponents I found being able to win those small battles help develop my character off the field. I surmised that if I could make a catch over someone much bigger, if I could tackle someone much stronger, if I could beat guys in wind sprints that were faster than I could clearly be successful in other endeavors concerning my life even if it appeared as though I should fail. I assessed the situation and determined that I could not benefit any longer from remaining on the team. I felt that notwithstanding all of my efforts I was not going to be promoted from the scout team even though most of my classmates and younger players were being afforded the opportunity to travel; I was left at the school listening to the game on the radio with the female fans. My embarrassment turned into envy as the team performed beyond expectations resulting in a National Collegiate Athletic Association Division III Football Championship. I quickly put that decision behind me and focused on continuing being a contributor to our Indoor and Outdoor Track and Field team and so I could still be a part of a winning program. Additionally, I would be able to devote more time to my studies, the true reason why I chose Allegheny in the first place.

I always had reasons why I quit until after my second opportunity to pledge Phi Beta Sigma arose. Dean of Pledges (D.P.) Paxton told us whenever we made excuses for not being prepared or being on time for a set or a study table "Excuses build bridges that lead to nothingness." It was a paraphrase of a much longer quotation but it's meaning wasn't changed by the abbreviation. It still meant that excuses were unacceptable and that I needed to make sure I was meeting expectations and not relying on reasons for not being prepared, aware or on time. It would be a theme I would implore throughout the pledging process and in life. If you are prepared then excuses aren't necessary. Me and three other pledges began the long arduous path toward the "Burning Sands." We were required to complete certain activities that taught us the history of Greek organizations, more particularly Phi Beta Sigma, we also learned how to be brothers and work in unity to achieve a common goal- crossing over from pledgee to Brother. I wasn't successful in achieving that goal of crossing the spring of my sophomore year, due to circumstances beyond my control, which centered around most of the other pledgees deciding to quit. I did "cross" line and reached the "Burning Sands" and became a member of Phi Beta Sigma Fraternity Incorporated in the Spring of 1992. So, while I may have quit football as well as initially quitting pledging Phi Beta Sigma, I remained committed and loyal to Track & Field as well as my academics at Allegheny.

I believe that the reason that I was able to effectively reset and balance track, work, academics, while maintain a social life, and disappointments was due to my faith. My faith was the foundation that allowed me to persevere when things went awry and kept me grounded when things were going well. I needed to rely on my faith after deciding not to pursue a career in education. Mr. Hill's influence on me was not significant enough to persuade me to leave Allegheny and find a comparable program at another institution of higher learning. Instead, I followed the advice of my advisor and took a class called Civil Liberties with Professor Robert Seddig. It was the turning point in my career and truly demonstrates how God orchestrates your life.

I had always enjoyed and done well in classes that had some type of governmental component to them and this class was no different. I received a more thorough and extensive understanding of the first Ten Amendments to the Constitution also known as "The Bill of Rights" during this course. Professor Seddig's exuberance and his ability to explicate the law helped me develop a different perspective about the law. He spoke eloquently and passionately about freedom of speech, freedom of religion, freedom of press, unreasonable search and seizures and other related Bill of Rights. I once saw the law as being destructive, in that it destroyed my family by incarcerating my "step" father, uncles, cousins, and my biological father. Instead after his course I saw the law as being a champion of those it sought to protect, namely the public. I received a very high grade in that class and decided that I would pursue a career in law. I went to my advisor and asked her which courses I should take in order to prepare myself for law school. She surprised me and recommended that I take more classes with a writing component. She had spoken to a number of law school professors and they indicated to her that while the law school students had the mental capacity to understand the curriculum they were unable to adequately compose their understanding on an exam or in a legal writing project. Accordingly, she felt that I should take courses that would improve my writing ability. I was literally frightened by the idea of taking more courses that emphasized writing due to my lack of any productive writing proclivity. Despite receiving an A in the introductory English course I was not confident in my abilities regarding the higher numbered courses. I, however, trusted my advisor and realized that in order to become a great lawyer I would need that foundation. Moreover, I believed the more effort I put into a weakness I would eventually be able to turn it into a strength.

My grades suffered from my decision to take courses more heavily concentrated in writing. I, however, made a calculated sacrifice by not majoring in an area where I was receiving high marks–Political Science– but taking enough of the latter courses to offset the mediocre grades I received in my writing courses in an effort to improve my writing ability. I knew that a lower grade point average (G.P.A) would be viewed unfavorably by law school admission committees but I ascertained that my Law School Admission Test (LSAT) score along with my essay would convince the committee of my ability to do well in law school. The highest grade I ever received in an English course aside from my introductory course was an A in a beginning Journalism class. The majority of the classes I took with a writing component resulted in a C. I was dejected at times because I felt that I was working hard and didn't deserve the disappointing grades but I was willing to give up immediate gratification for a future blessing.

I wrote essay after essay, paper after paper and read book after book. I noticed a marked improvement in my writing and the reduction in comments from my professors. I became less of a procrastinator regarding my papers so that I could devote more time on editing before I turned homework, or papers into my professors. I got progressively better on each test, paper and eventually in class participation. My grammar mistakes decreased, my writing became more complex and I noticed the latter in the former of higher marks. I, however, plateaued at the high C level despite my strenuous efforts.

Track & Field was going well but could have been better if I wasn't dealing with injuries and still trying to recover the speed I lost when I broke my leg in my junior year in high school. I was able to participate in our Indoor and Outdoor Conference Championships. Allegheny had never won the NCAC Men's Track Championships but with Stan, Darren, Andre Perry, myself and a number of veterans we were able to capture the championship and keep a stranglehold on it for three consecutive years.

I was dealing with minor issues at home and minor disagreements on campus at well. Sometimes I would not have enough money because our work study pay checks were only distributed once a month. If other students had been under the same pressures that I was they may not have been able to survive let alone thrive under the same circumstances. I am a very visual person so I wrote the phrase is bold letters "TROUBLE DON'T LAST ALWAYS," and each time there was a setback I would color in a part of one of the letters. I noticed that I never got to Always in either year. I was able to see no matter the circumstances God would never let them accumulate to result in my destruction.

While my G.P.A wasn't where I imagined it would be but it was at the level that the scholarship I was offered at the conclusion of my freshman year would be continued the following year. I had received a letter from the Office of Financial Aid in late May of my freshman year requesting that I stop by the office before I left to go home for the summer. The Director of Financial Aid invited me into his office and stated that they had been monitoring my grades and that they had just received funds from an alumnus and that I fit the criteria. If I had declined the scholarship it would have increased the amount of money I would have been required to repay in loans following my graduation from Allegheny. Accordingly, I was receiving the Nancy Sutton Scholarship, Ohio Pell Grant, Allegheny Grant and other government backed loans. My Grandma Edna would sacrifice and pay the small balance that was left, minus work study.

I enjoyed the opportunity that I was afforded at Allegheny in terms of the classes I had taken, not only the English classes, but my Political Science classes, my Economics classes and, my Math classes. Whatever class it was, it was a professor in there that challenged me. Challenged me to think outside of conventional norms. Challenged me to believe in myself, have confidence in my abilities to communicate in writing or orally. Allegheny wanted to make sure that once I graduated I would be able to effectively communicate my position on any given subject. The latter skills easily translated to those needed to be an effective litigator who argued before judges and juries. Also, my writing ability would be crucial in helping me convince judges and senior attorneys to follow my line of thinking when I drafted motions and memorandums of law.

In high school Math and Science were my favorite subjects not English because they required that you use a formula to ascertain the correct answer. It didn't matter what numbers you inserted into the formula as long as you followed the formula you should get the correct results. Even when you are half way through the process and it seems as though the answer appears to be inconsistent with what you know if you stay with the formula, and you don't make mistakes in the calculation, you will end up with the right answer. I applied the same philosophy to my life and other subject areas in and out of my college classrooms. I continued to use a formula of hard work, patience, law abiding and faith and things began to work out for my good. Even when it appeared that the results would be unfavorable, I stayed the course only to see the unexpected be realized.

POLITICAL BUG REKINDLED

Allegheny did not simply offer me challenges in the classroom, on the field and socially but also in the more expansive classroom–the political arena. My introduction to politics with Mr. Charney's wife, C.J. Prentiss' campaign was simply the appetizer for the experiences I had my freshman year at Allegheny. My initial exposure to the political climate of the college occurred at a meeting I was invited to attend by and with Derrick Paxton, my fraternity brother. The upperclassmen along with some sophomores were embroiled in a battle with the administration over the college's refusal to divest in companies that were in South Africa and thereby supporting the apartheid that existed in that country. I was startled when I walked into a classroom in the basement area of one of the academic buildings because most of the students were wearing black. I asked Pax, if this was the right place and he assured me that we were at the correct meeting. There was no agenda and the participants just spoke freely about their disdain for administration, their reluctance to listen to the students and supportive staff members and protest ideas. The protest ideas ranged from sit-ins at the administration building to marches and then finally someone made a comment that left me feeling uneasy–They wanted to blow up a side of one of the buildings in order to get the administration's attention. Although most of the other participants laughed at the comment and dismissed it as frivolous, I instead made my way to the exit. I decided at that point I did not want to be a part of any organization that could cause harm to people or property.

A few weeks later a different group of students planned to take over the administration building. I had gotten an opportunity to meet and mingle with these students and felt more comfortable with them and their intentions. Thus, approximately thirty people walked to Bentley Hall, where President Daniel Sullivan's office was located, and sat against the wall on the bottom floor of Bentley Hall. We displayed signs and sang songs similar to those that were performed during the Civil Rights era in the 1950's and 1960's. We also added some other ones like Public Enemy's "Fight the Power" to our selections. We camped out until well after the building officially closed. Security dared not move us because we were college students exercising our fundamental rights of free speech and freedom of assembly in the very building our tuition was paying to maintain. We were eventually joined by some of the administrators, namely the Director of Multicultural Affairs, who empathized with our protest but could not initially persuade the administration to at a minimum hear our concerns. The administration eventually changed their stance when the local media showed up and began interviewing students. The news of our protest went regional since I got word from back home that someone saw me on television protesting Apartheid at Allegheny College.

We would have to stage two more demonstrations to finally convince the trustee board to find more moral acceptable ways of increasing and protecting the College's largess endowment. First, we disrupted the trustee board meeting by banging on the doors, pounding on the windows and drafting letters to the board members to reconsider their initial positions, which were to continue investing in those companies because of the positive financial returns the college was experiencing. Second, and probably the most effective plan, we distributed literature to the prospective next freshman class and their parents during the visit day in the spring of 1990. The Board noticed the significantly low number of students who had applied, been accepted and had forwarded their deposits. The literature had the impact of influencing open minded students and their parents that supporting an immoral, archaic form of governlment, was against their democratic principles and beliefs. The student and their parents felt that the former could receive a quality education without the stigmatism of Apartheid being connected to their education.

I saw the power of the Latin term" e pluribus Unum", which appears on money and is a Latin phrase that means "out of many one." I saw the power of the collective we and the fact that persistence and creativity is what led to the board of trustee's being influenced to alter their initial course. I saw how one finger in your hand can be controlling and powerful but when you make a fist the power to influence and to strike if necessary becomes greater. I learned a lot about how to work with different personalities and how to create strategic plans that don't initially seem to make sense but when you see the big picture you recognize both the past and the inevitable conclusion.

My political participation was restricted to protests from outside but during my sophomore year I was elected to serve in our Student Government Association. I was chosen by my peers and represented the area where my dorm room was located that year-South Hall. I was one of a few minorities who were even interested let alone who had the courage to run and then serve. I brought concerns about safety, quality of food, racial and gender equality and college costs to the attention of our president. He then took those concerns back to President Sullivan and they had dialogue regarding what if anything the college could do to improve the areas of concern. It was not a position that demanded a lot of time, we met one Wednesday a month and we always had the ability to speak to an officer of SGA if we had other inquires. I only served one year because my junior year I was thrust into the position of president of the Advancement of Black Culture (ABC).

This organization was formed to primarily address the concerns of the African-American students at Allegheny; social, economic, academic, retention and athletic. The organization, however, evolved such that it was not only concerned with the latter mentioned items but also the history and the perception others possessed about African American people and its culture. I was elected vice president at the end of my sophomore year but moved into the presidency when the person elected president didn't return to Allegheny in the fall. I wanted to ascend to the presidency but not in that manner. I was hoping to gain some experience from the vice president position and thereby have some knowledge and familiarity when I was voted in as president. Nevertheless, I took the position with some eagerness and tried to maintain a sense of normalcy for the organization. I made sure we had regular meetings, I encouraged people who were not active in the past to participate more frequently. We were able to start a paper bank so that individuals could get ideas about how to write certain papers or research projects, with the disclaimer that they could not plagiarize. We organized the Black History Month celebration and was able to convince KRS-1 a noted hip hop artist, poet and scholar to come and speak, and not perform, regarding the importance of higher education for those who talents had been suppressed for centuries. I believe, however, that I was destined to be in that position because of the incident that changed the entire community at Allegheny College.

Me, "Butch", my house mate' Todd's cousin, Sean Todd's brother and Mike Penn (A college classmate), decided to go to one of the many parties that were being held around campus. It was nearing the end of winter and on the verge of spring and thus it was a little nippy that night. Prior to leaving Butch and Sean, who were both older than twenty-one, had a few beers. I had just returned from a date and wasn't interested in drinking while Mike had a few but was by no means intoxicated. We decided to go to the "wrestlers" party which was located at the captain of the wrestling team house located a few blocks from our house. When we arrived we met at the door by an unknown individual who was asking us for money to purchase a cup in order to gain entry. We politely indicated to him that we didn't want to drink and we weren't going to drink but just wanted to socialize, particularly with the females that were inside. While we were in discussions with him Mike was able to slip through, mainly because some of the players from the baseball team, which he was a member, momentarily distracted the gatekeeper. Eventually, we saw Mike inside and stated that our friend is in why aren't we allowed to go inside. He simply said no money no cup no entrance. We understood, even though the general policy for campus parties was that if you weren't going to drink you could still enter but without a cup they would refuse to serve you. We started to call Mike's name so that we could leave and find another party but we were standing in the doorway. Then, the captain of the wrestling team, who also happened to be a member of one of the prominent fraternities on campus, came to the door and said "Didn't I tell you Niggers you had to leave." I was shocked, intensely angry and ready to physically assault him if he had not been on the other side of the door. Todd's relatives, who grew up in one of the toughest suburbs (That may be an oxymoron) but they quickly sobered up and began to incite the wrestler to step outside to answer for his derogatory and uncalled for remarks about us. I knew this individual, having been an athlete and sharing the same facilities with him for the last three years. I had never heard any racial animus spewing from his mouth before, but I was incensed by his statements. More epithets were voiced by the wrestler and others involved along with threats of violence, which caused the frightened females to call the police. I then informed all of those who had walked with me to disperse because we knew if the police were called and we were there when they arrived the probability of us being arrested would increase exponentially.

Most of us walked back to the campus house enraged. I was more calculating than angry about going back to the wrestler's house and seeking revenge. Thus, I called all the members of ABC lead by the thought "Out of many one" and advised them of the incident. I tried, to no avail, contacting the Director of Multi-cultural affairs and to make him aware of what transpired. Some of the people I told were very upset and wanted to respond with violence. One person, however, made signs and placed them strategically all over campus in the early morning hours. The signs advocated violence: "I'm going to get my shotgun and kill all the Honkeys I see!" There were signs saying " Black Power" with a blackened fist prominently displayed on the white background. It sent the campus into panic alert. The Director of Multicultural Affairs tracked me down later that morning, with all the signs in tow and asked, "Mike, what the hell happened?" I relayed to him what had transpired as well as other incidents of racial violence, threats and insensitivity by students, faculty and staff. I told him something needed to be addressed otherwise this was nothing more than a ticking time bomb.

A few days later I was able to meet with President Sullivan and he intensely listened to our grievances and concerns surrounding racial issues we were experiencing at Allegheny. My main focus, however, was on how the college would treat this incident with the wrestling captain. He assured us that he would be given due process and put through the normal disciplinary process. We were also able to convince President Sullivan to take off the rose tinted glasses and recognize there are members of the Allegheny community who do not like each other simply because of the color of the other person's skin.

The meeting with President Sullivan resulted in a committee whose purpose was to research and determine if a Racial Harassment Policy would be feasible at Allegheny. We met at least twice a month before the end of the school year and then again at the start of my senior year. We discussed Constitutional protections versus personal safety and peace of mind. We discussed possible sanctions for violating the policy. We also discussed why it was necessary and how it should not be used as a way to stem thoughtful, academic and pertinent discussions in the classroom and in the college community. We also spoke about the process that would be used to adjudicate complaints that alleged violations of the policy. We reviewed other policies from colleges, universities and some businesses as well and incorporated our concerns and desires into what we felt was appropriate for Allegheny College. While I didn't have the opportunity to see the Racial Harassment Policy come to fruition since it was not completed and adopted until after I graduated, I was able to see one proposal materialize.

The racial event revealed some very deeply rooted hostilities between the students who reflected the majority at Allegheny and those who represented the greatest percentage of the minority population at Allegheny. There were misconceptions, outright hatred and at times unawareness of the others culture. The majority of the students who attended Allegheny had never had a class with an African American student let alone, live with, eat with and shower with them. The quote "Ignorance is bliss" was clearly unacceptable at this juncture of the lives of the young future leaders who were attending Allegheny. Accordingly, the college devised a plan to provide more education about the African American culture and issues surrounding racism, tolerance and inclusion. Allegheny would begin its evolution by acknowledging Dr. Martin Luther King Jr. holiday. On previous occasions Allegheny was not lawfully required to adhere to the holiday based up on the fact that it was a private institution. Nevertheless, this incident was the impetus behind forging a new understanding and more dialogue around the issue of race. Allegheny saw no better example of someone who fought for racial equality, inclusion, tolerance and respect for the intellect of the African American people than Dr. King. Classes were only permitted to be held in the morning and the afternoon was devoted to small group discussions, led by faculty and special guest speakers, discussing the same issues previously mentioned. Students were encouraged to attend the special sessions as well as the general session that had a keynote speaker. I thought the celebration was brilliant because I wholeheartedly believe that in the area of race relations education was the bridge to finding common ground and solutions to the racial divide.

My zest for politics did not end at the conclusion of my junior year. I was fortunate to secure employment with my fraternity brother, Tyrone Freeman's, employer Service Employees International Union. Ty worked as an organizer. He was responsible for influencing individuals who were state employees in Georgia to form a union and thereby negotiate with the state for better wages and benefits. I inquired about the opportunity to work in their legal department and he purportedly had secured the position for me. Ty, who was originally from Pittsburgh, drove to visit family and then headed west to retrieve me and we then drove to Atlanta, Georgia. A few days after arriving he and I went to his office only to be informed that their legal department, all of one attorney, preferred interns that were already in law school. Thus, the position went to a young lady who was in her second or third year at Boston University's Law School.

I was then relegated to being the political coordinator for the Georgia State Employees Union /SEIU. The union was endorsing candidates that had not only been supportive of their efforts to unionize but also of the issues that were important to the union: wages, working conditions, health care, promotion, discipline and other work related issues. The union supported one incumbent but was backing two upstarts. One candidate was considered by most to be a carpetbagger due to his recent relocation to Milledgeville, Georgia from New York. The other candidate was a community organizer and felt a passion for being more involved as a representative as opposed to working on the outside with or against the representative.

My job was to provide assistance to the three candidates in any way shape or form they requested; therein lied the dilemma. The incumbent candidate had a committee and had run numerous successful campaigns throughout his more than fifteen years of service for the Georgia House of Representatives. He, however, was under a lot of scrutiny due to comments he made the last two years regarding the African American community in and around Milledgeville, Ga. He was a Caucasian state representative that was in his late sixties and hadn't recognized the gains African Americans made since the 1950's. The "carpetbagger" was running against an incumbent who had placed significant barriers in the union's path with their struggle to unionize more state employees.

I was instructed by both the candidates and the GSEU staff, more particularly Grant the Director, to sit outside on the island that separates incoming and outgoing traffic to the largest state agency located in Milledgeville and distribute the three candidates literature and ask for their vote and support for those candidates. I was met with angst for a number of reasons by many of the people. Some disliked me because I was representing the union and they were a part of the administration. Some had a disdain for me simply because I was a young African American male. Some of them made very rude, disrespectful and racist comments towards me as a way to discourage me. It did just the opposite by making me more assertive.

I would carefully run towards cars with the flyers in hand and my GESU shirt, or candidate shirt prominently displayed. I would not only be there prior to the morning shift I was also there when everyone was leaving. I put the union and candidates signs on the island or near the entrance to the driveway for the state agency. I would ,whenever possible, engage in productive conversations with people who had not made up their mind and discussed issues they had and tried to assuage their concerns. Sometimes I was successful and other times I probably did a disservice to the candidate the union was supporting. I recruited members of the union to help with other campaign activities like canvassing, phone banking (phone calls) and sign distribution. I did the latter work Monday through Friday and then drove north to Atlanta every weekend prior to the summer primary.

On the eve of the primary, I felt good they we would have at least one victory out of the three. The entire staff joined me on the eve of the primary helping to secure voting polls with signs and people to pass literature out during the primary. I was exhausted that night and actually only slept two to three hours the day before I awoke and headed to my assigned polling place. When I arrived that morning I was met with the same type of dislike and disdain from some voters that I experienced at the state agency. I would walk and converse with individuals all the way to the door leading to the voting poll. I was eventually instructed by an official board of elections poll worker that I could not stand within 100 feet of the polling place if I was going to distribute literature. I got into a number of shouting matches with voters who disagreed with the candidates that the union was supporting. I was eventually moved to a slower paced polling location because I was told that I would be arrested if I didn't adhere to the 100 foot limitation. I eventually was relieved of my duty and returned to my apartment and then we traveled to Atlanta to watch the results. I wasn't shocked by the outcome. The incumbent we supported was defeated by a candidate who was more progressive, less insensitive to minorities and while they didn't initially support the union they eventually did based on what happened in the other two races. The one candidate who was unknown received a percentage of the vote that required an automatic runoff. Lastly, while the carpetbagger did not win he garnered 45% of the vote as a virtual unknown without roots in the community. He did so well that the incumbent representative stated on election night that he would work with the union from now on. Since none of the candidates I did most of the work claimed victory that night (The runoff candidate eventually lost) I assumed I did a terrible job. Ty, however, called me after I returned home and said "Mike. You did an awesome job. In fact they are thinking about hiring you as a political consultant once you graduate. Are you interested?" I said, "No thank you. My first option is law school and if that isn't available I'll think about other opportunities." Ty then said as he was ending the call, "The union was really impressed because you were able to assist a virtual unknowns to get nearly a majority of votes in the rural area of Georgia against an established incumbents during their first run for office. It was virtually unheard of and they wanted to tap your brain frat." My initial disappointment turned to elation but I needed to finish my senior year at Allegheny and so I declined and returned back home with the political bug having morphed into a butterfly.

COLLEGE LIFE COMING TO A CLOSE

I returned from Georgia armed with new experiences, knowledge and a readiness for my senior year. I was single, had just turned twenty-one, and had been practicing for the LSAT (Law School Admission Test) by taking previous LSATs in order to best gauge the time I would need on the actual test I would take in October. I went to visit Willie Cooper, who was always involved in his community, so we could discuss some of the hotbed political issues that were germinating in Cleveland, Ohio. He invited me to a local community center to speak to a group of young people about the importance of education, making good choices and being a part of a group-fraternity- that was positive as opposed to being in a gang. Willie was impressed by what I shared with the kids and he asked me to come by his house for a few minutes. Those few minutes would have a significant impact on my love life.

While waiting for Willie to come from his room his younger sister walked into the door. She was petite, fair skinned, and had beautiful black piercing eyes. We spoke briefly and then Willie and I left. When we returned Willie indicated to me that his sister, Shandell, was interested in me. I was intrigued by her as well. We decided to go to the movies that night to get to know each other a little better. During the drive to the movie and back to her apartment that she shared with her mom, we talked extensively about family and our dreams. She was a junior at General Motors Institute in Michigan. She was studying to become an engineer. She was a very bright young lady who grew up in the hood. I had found what I considered to be a rarity: someone who was attractive, who was smart and who was from the hood. I thought I found the female version of myself. We talked for hours after the movie and then due to the strong connection we had engaged in some intimate acts on our first date.

After that night we spent the majority of the summer together. We would talk on the phone for only a few minutes before I would get in my Pinto and drive thirty (30) minutes from

East Cleveland to Lakeshore Avenue in Cleveland. I spent so much time at her apartment that her mother could have collected rent from me. I slept over numerous nights because our time to be together was shortening as the end of August was approaching. I never had such strong feelings for any woman before I met Shandell. She and I both were concerned that the distance would be a barrier to our relationship surviving. We had initially decided to break up. I, however, changed my mind and convinced her to do the same. I left for Allegheny before she went to General Motors Institute (GMI) and believed that if we could survive a long distance relationship then we could survive anything; I was sadly mistaken.

Our relationship began to deteriorate as soon as Shandell returned to GMI. She was back in familiar territory and around some of the same guys she had relationships with over the last two years. I was resigned to be committed to her despite the distance and the new faces that were on campus at Allegheny. I was not interested in them and maintained my focus on graduating, doing well on the LSAT and Shandell. I thought about her daily and tried to talk to her at least four to five times a week. I became concerned when during the second week of school she was not answering her phone even though it was late at night and early in the morning. She would not return calls until the next day or days later. She had ridiculous excuses for not contacting me or calling me days later. The most telling sign that the relationship was doomed was when the picture that I had of her on my desk would constantly fall off the dresser despite it is placement in a secure place and no wind from natural or manmade mechanisms.

I was dealing with circumstantial evidence when I was at Allegheny regarding Shandell's infidelity but my visit to GMI solidified my concerns. First, I should have known that it was going to be a regrettable trip when my car broke down on the Ohio Turnpike right before I was about to enter Michigan. My grandmother's boyfriend Miles, had to drive from Cleveland, and give my battery a jump. Instead of turning around and going home I continued onto GMI. When I arrived Shandell introduced me to all of her friends and then we headed to her single dorm room. We had a nice time together especially since it had been a few months since I last saw her. After a few hours she got a call and left me in her dorm room for hours. In a day in age where cell phones weren't prevalent I was unable to contact her. I was incensed and when she returned she acted as though her actions were appropriate. I left that next day and returned to Allegheny with a different perspective about our relationship. I didn't call as often and wasn't too worried if she didn't return my calls anymore.

The straw that broke the camel's back occurred the night before the biggest test of my life to that date. Shandell and I agreed that she would come to Allegheny for the weekend as my guest for my frat brother, Tyrone's wedding. The wedding ceremony followed the administration of the LSAT. I agreed to meet Shandell in Cleveland and then we would drive my car back to Allegheny instead of her driving all the way from Michigan to Pennsylvania. I arrived at her mother's apartment with enough time remaining for her to arrive and our drive to Allegheny College, get something to eat and for me to get some needed rest before the LSAT test that next morning. I waited, and waited and waited nearly four hours. I had resigned to leave and return back to Allegheny without her. Instead I let my passion for her outweigh my common sense. I was willing to forgo my future by putting my mind and body at risk of being exhausted for an exam that I needed to do well on in order to convince law schools that I possessed the aptitude to perform at law school.

She appeared at nearly 10 p.m. even though she was scheduled to be there no later 5 p.m. I drove back to Allegheny furious. I was mad because we had to buy fast food instead of sitting down and eating at a restaurant. I didn't have a coat or jacket or a hat because most of my clothes were at Allegheny and the temperature fell late that night causing me to develop a migraine headache because of congestion and a slight cough I incurred from the frigid night air. We arrived back at Allegheny at 1:00 a.m. due to not leaving Cleveland for another hour after she arrived. I hardly spoke to her during the trip aside from small talk. She lied about where she was and I didn't care. I tried to get some sleep but I was anxious about the exam and generally perturbed by her demeanor and nonchalant attitude.

I woke up the next morning and my head was hurting so bad that it felt like it was going to explode. The cough went from being slight to mildly severe. I took a few aspirins but didn't want to ingest too many for fear that I would fall asleep during the test. I entered the South cafeteria to take the exam with other students but I was so under the weather that I can't even recall how I was able to finish the exam. I was fortunate that I had prepared by taking some of the previous tests, as well as reading some of the test strategies that were offered in the LSAT preparation publication. My stomach started to hurt along with feelings of nausea. The latter feelings didn't stop even after the test and continued through the wedding and then finally reached the zenith when I vomited in Burger King. To Shandell's credit she took care of me for the rest of the night. I, however, knew that when she left that would be the last time she set foot on Allegheny campus as a guest of mine. I was still upset that she put me in such a predicament without any true sense of remorse. She apologized for being late but I felt that if she truly cared about how the test would impact my future she would have beat me to her apartment that day.

I drove her back to Cleveland the next day and she drove back to Michigan and I headed east back to school. The calls became more infrequent and the feelings I possessed before began to diminish and eventually it all came to an end during Thanksgiving break. We hadn't officially ended our relationship but when she called another man while I was at her apartment with me obviously in earshot and told him "I love you", I became incensed. I felt betrayed, disrespected and embarrassed and knew that our relationship was at a irreparable state. We did briefly try to rekindle the relationship during the Christmas break. I spent a few days with her prior to Christmas and a few days after. We both, however, knew that New Year's Day would usher in a new status of our relationship–Over.

The experience with Shandell taught me not to allow people to distract me from my goals no matter how impressive they look or sound. I should not have been so connected to her that I lost sight of my true purpose. I wrapped myself around her and my desire for pleasure that I completely discarded logic for what was masquerading as love. My grandmother gave me some sage advice after I had been mopping for a few days when I realized that Shandale and I were not going to get back together, we weren't going to get married and raise children and grow old together. She said "People who love you won't hurt you." Maybe she did love me at some point but her last actions indicated otherwise. I realized that her presence in my life was as purposeful as the other difficult challenges that I faced. I was destined to encounter many obstacles to be a witness to others on how you overcome, no matter the situation. Additionally, I had to experience Shandale in order to prepare me for my true love– Robin Jeannette Nelson.

MEETING THE THREE INITIAL LOVES OF MY LIFE

It was January 2, 1993 a day after New Year's Day and I was still in no mood to socialize with anyone but John knew that I needed to get out and meet some "new people" at a local nightclub called the "Splash." It was Reggae night and most of the college students were still home and I conceded after his relentless requests for me to get out of the apartment.

John, me, and his cousins Tracy, Lana, Robbie and Sheila all trekked down to the "Splash" for some drinking, dancing and good times. The "Splash" was not a spacious club and if more than hundred people were packed inside the Cleveland Fire Department would have to come and shut the place down due to overcrowding. When we arrived John and I stood in the middle of the club next to a few tables and just talked and gawked. I could only see some of the tantalizing women as they approached because it was so dark in the club my view was restricted to two feet at best. I, however, was able to see a vision of beauty located near the door where more lighting was present, both from inside the club and the light that fell from the street lamps. I saw this gorgeous, coco brown skinned young lady with a beautiful smile who was dancing by herself. She wanted to dance, and the dance floor was not that big. If you wanted to dance, you had to make sure you got on the floor pretty quick or you would be dancing on the stools. She saw me staring and then returned a look that said "I'm interested." After a few moments I got enough nerve to walk over to where she and her friends were standing. I didn't introduce myself, she wouldn't of heard me anyway because the music was too loud, and so I merely grabbed her hand and led her to the dance floor.

We danced for approximately twenty (20) minutes. It was something different about this young lady than all of the other women I had been involved with or attempted to court. I had never been as assertive with other young ladies as I was with her and I doubt that any other woman would have responded in the same manner that she did. Despite my years of athletic training and dancing at other clubs I couldn't keep up with her. She was smooth, sexy, and exotic in her dance moves. I hadn't ever danced with someone who had as much rhythm as Robin. Due to the deafening volume of the music Robin and I talked sparingly. We talked more with our bodies and our eyes. I decided to go sit down before Robin was ready to stop but I asked her if she would save me at least one more dance before the night was over. As she walked away I watched her thin, 5'4" inch sexy frame go towards her seat with a smile on my face and butterflies in my stomach.

I walked briskly back to where John had been standing and he said "I saw you on the dance floor. I guess you haven't let the grass grow underneath your feet." I smiled and said " Nobody has ever did that before. I hope she doesn't find some other cat and dance with him all night." As soon as I got the last two words of the latter comment out of my mouth a guy came up to Robin, hugged her and then looked towards me and John. Robin had purportedly said something about me to this individual. I assumed that he was her boyfriend due to his continued concern with what we were doing a few feet away from them. He eventually began to put his arm around Robin for most of the remainder of the night. When she went to the bar to get something to drink he followed her, she only danced with him when she did get back on the dance floor. I was disappointed because I believed that she was single and I was attracted to her and wanted to get to know her better.

After a few hours the DJ states "Last call for alcohol" thereby indicating that the club was about to close soon. The other sign was the fact that they were playing a slow song to let people who were dancing fast and hard now get an opportunity to get close and cozy. I was dancing with John's cousin Tracy, who was about my mom's height so I could see over her head and I watched Robin dancing with her conjoined twin whose shoulder she could see over due to his short stature. Since she couldn't hear me I mouthed to her
"You played me. You promised me another dance. " She smiled and lit up the entire club and then responded to me by putting up three fingers, then two fingers then one, then made a zero with her thumb and pointer finger, then another single finger, then five fingers and then

finally six fingers. I realized that she was signing me her number (321-0156). I then mouthed the word

"Do it" and put up one finger and pointed to my watch which when interpreted meant "Do it one more time." She obliged and I was able to memorize it. The dilemma I had was that I did not know her name and so I wrote the number on a napkin and wrote "Cutie Pie" underneath and would find out her name when I called her. Robin was more resourceful and approached me as we were getting ready to leave the club with a piece paper with her phone number and name.

I was so enamored, or thirsty as the kids would say, with Robin that I called her about an hour after we left the club. I actually called her from John's Aunt Jeanne's house because I couldn't wait until I got home. Robin didn't answer the phone instead her niece named Tara, who I realized was a young lady I knew when I lived in Longwood, answered and began interrogating me like relatives do when their loved one meets someone new. She asked, "Who is this?" I said, " Michael Ryan." She then responded "Ugh, Michael Ryan?! What are you doing calling my aunt?" I then responded in a concerned voice asking "Your aunt? How old is she? She didn't look like an aunt in the club! " Tara and I spoke for about ten or fifteen minutes just catching up on old times.

Eventually Robin regained access to the phone and we started what would be normal for us, hour long conversations on the phone. I discovered that we were both Cleveland Heights High graduates. She was a year older than me but our birthdays were similar; Mine was August 1st and Robin's was August 10th. I also found out that she served as my cousin, Zonequa's (aka Nikki), "Big Sister"/mentor when my cousin attended Cleveland Heights. In fact, during our conversation Robin recalled numerous times dropping Nikki off at my Aunt Joann's house. Additionally, she recounted a few times when she came in at stayed for a while and introduced herself to my aunt, other cousins and even my sister. It was ironic how during those occasions I was never at home. More often than not I was at school for some athletic or academic event that required me to sacrifice late afternoons and sometimes evenings. I essentially kept missing the woman of my dreams each time she stepped foot on my family's property. Robin and I both later surmised that God didn't want us together then because it may not have evolved into a long term marriage. We were both naïve, young, energetic and not ready to be tied down to just one person for the remainder of our natural life when we were in high school.

While most would say that even if I didn't meet her at my home surely I would have seen her in Cleveland Heights High School. Actually, it was not out of the realm of possibility that one could be unrecognizable by other members of their graduating class at Cleveland Heights due to the sheer volume of children that attended the school. My graduating class from Cleveland Heights was almost 700. Robin's class was close to 800. So there were almost 3,000 kids in Cleveland Heights High School. I know that it was all in God's plan and I was destined to meet the love of my life on that day on that night and under those circumstances combined with the other ironic connections we had to each other prior to our first encounter. I had prayed for a woman like Robin. A woman who was strong, independent, classy, intelligent, beautiful, respectful (She didn't let me even kiss her until our third time meeting/date) loved the Lord and could sing. She is all of the latter and then some.

As I stated earlier we spoke about a number of things during that hour or two hour conversation but family was the main topic of the discussion. Robin not only spoke of her immediate family mother, father, siblings and nephews and nieces but also about one she was responsible for caring for- her daughter Lauren. I heard the slight hesitation in her voice when she told me she had a daughter. I was an attractive, young African American man, single, no children, college educated, and waiting on decisions from law school admission committees. I was in no wise intimidated or fearful of the challenge of dating someone who had a child or of the long distance, a mere 100 miles. There was something special about Robin that no matter what hurdles that stood in the way of initiating a relationship we found ways to conquer each one.

We tried to spend every free moment we had together before I had to return to Allegheny to complete my final semester. Robin wanted me to meet her mom and Lauren so she invited me over for dinner. Prior to my arrival Robin prepared me for her mom and Lauren by giving me some tips. She told me that her mom loved to cook and talk so I should be ready to eat and engage in conversation. She also told me that her mom was very opinionated and didn't hold anything back. I noticed that upon entering the home, when I walked in and introduced myself to her and shook her hand she said hello and immediately questioned me about the earrings I had in my right and left ear. I had a diamond stud in one ear and a small gold hoop in the other ear.. She said, "Hmmm… Do you think you are Janet Jackson or something?" I chuckled and said, "No ma'am it's just the style." Ms. Doris Nelson waddled back to the kitchen to finish cooking.

Next, after taking my coat Robin led me to the living room and invited me to take a seat on the couch. She then went into the kitchen to help her mom and Niece Tenisha with the food preparation. In less than a minute, the most beautiful, chocolate skinned, with gorgeous brown eyes near two year old with tons and tons of energy came into the living room and sat right on my lap. She told me her name was Lauren and I couldn't stop smiling at her rapid, intelligent speech and her adorable smile. I was pleasantly shocked by her behavior towards me because Robin had forewarned me not to take offense if Lauren isn't friendly. She said, "Lauren doesn't like strangers and rarely would allow anyone, even family to touch her. So don't be offended if she acts standoffish."

I think Robin's mom started to like me more when she saw how attached Lauren had become in only a few minutes. Lauren climbed onto my lap and sat down, and I put with my arms on her back so she wouldn't fall due to her sitting sideways on my legs with her legs dangling off the side of my legs instead of the front. After a few more minutes of conversation Lauren asked me, "Do you want to see me ride my horse?" I saw the tiny plastic riding horse sitting in the corner of the dining room and said "Sure honey, go ahead and ride it." She jumped off my lap and ran to the horse, straddled it and commenced to ride the horse so hard that she was literally raising the horse off the ground with each time she would pull back and then move forward. If not for the wall that was in front of the horse she would of rode that horse down South Taylor into Shaker Heights, the adjoining city to Cleveland Heights. I screamed "Someone come and get the baby! Robin, please come quickly before she hurts herself." I went from a place of comfort and peace with her on my lap to panic and fear when she started riding the rocking horse. All the ladies in the kitchen came running into the living room only to see Lauren engaging in her traditional past time- scary rocking horse riding! They all laughed and assured me that she would be fine. Soon thereafter we sat down to eat the salad, rolls and the spaghetti that had been prepared. We started off with a prayer, well I was asked to start the prayer. I thought I did an admirable job but learned years later that they compared it to Ben Stiller's prayer in the movie "Meet the Parents." They were appreciative that I prayed but were laughing inside to spare me any embarrassment. The food was delicious and the conversation was wonderful. My soon to be mother-in-law was not convinced that I was in college; the first impression I left with respect to my earrings had a lasting effect on her!

Robin was different from the other women I had been involved with in any type of relationship- one night stands, a few weeks, months or years. We did not rush to become intimate partners. Two weeks of being with anyone was the maximum for me but her desire to make me wait separated Robin. I was convinced she was special. In lieu of the intense physical contact we substituted a lot foundational necessities such as talking, laughing, spending quality time together. We were becoming friends before we became lovers, which helped cement our relationship. Her other qualities that I mentioned made her unique and intriguing for me. I was hesitant about revealing to her how she made me feel and how enamored I was about her. I relished the long phone conversations we had while I was at home and those that continued when I went back to Allegheny. We stayed on the phone for so long that we both would begin to start breathing hard and eventually snoring only to be awaken by the other person. As Gladys Knight use to sing "Neither one of us wanted to be the first to say good bye." When I did hang up I anticipated her call each night. I didn't try to engage in any games, waiting for her to call before I did, I was passed the juvenile stage. I also didn't buy into that old adage that the next relationship following a break up from another one was simply the rebound relationship and thus no future. I dismissed those ideas and was all in as was Robin.

Robin visited me at Allegheny numerous times. She and my sister, who was dating Todd Jones one of my best friends at Allegheny, risked life and limb by traveling to and from Meadville in the snow, rain and many times at night. At times they would bring Lauren and Karese, my niece, to visit as well. I did not have any reservations about her visiting because I was devoted to her even though she sincerely believed that I had a woman or women on campus. While I was once considered to be what the kids now call "runners" my running days ended when I met Shandell and even more so when I met Robin. I began to focus more on completing my senior comprehensive project, preparing for indoor and outdoor track, completing and trying to excel in all my senior courses and preparing for life after graduation. The latter things along with trying to maintain this wonderful newly developing relationship kept me focused and undistracted from peripheral things that were at Allegheny.

Robin was slowly but surely becoming my best friend in addition to being my girlfriend. I began to trust her more than I had ever trusted anyone who wasn't considered to be family. I possessed those feelings notwithstanding what occurred in my most immediate past relationship. I was able to suppress those non-trust feelings and direct my attention to the positive things Robin was bringing. She was encouraging, she was understanding about the time I had to devote to studying, track and work, she spent her hard earned money on gas, and food when she visited. Additionally, she did something that no other woman had done for me in quite some time, she purchased me a pair of tennis shoes/sneakers that I badly needed. The shoes I had were old and worn. I was using glue and tape to keep them together. Shoes weren't the priority for me, instead buying books and food were the tools I needed to graduate. While it appeared that she was infallible I later learned something that made me momentarily question whether she was the one for me.

Robin had confided in me that Lauren's biological father had passed away in a motor vehicle accident. I wholeheartedly believed what she said and had no reason to doubt her because neither he or his family were ever present. I began to question whether he was dead when Robin showed me pictures of him and his mother. The picture she showed depicted him in a uniform that inmates at Mansfield Correctional Facility wore. I knew those uniforms like the back of my hand due to the number of times I saw my father, Allen Douglas, in those same plain beige uniforms with the similar background. I inquired about the picture and asked "Did he go to prison before he died?" She dismissed my question by changing the subject. She eventually told me the truth that Lauren's dad was not dead but was in prison. She assumed that I didn't want to be involved with her anymore because she knew how much I valued honesty in a relationship. She explained that she even told Lauren that her daddy was dead because of the circumstances surrounding their separation. I accepted her explanation and we moved on. I saw it as minor indiscretion and when I weighed it against all of the other wonderful things about her I felt great about continuing our relationship. Some people would have seen it as a warning sign and decided to terminate the courtship. I on the other hand saw it as a moveable roadblock on our path to something better. I suspected that both of us would make other mistakes on the path to fortifying this relationship. I wouldn't want her to end it over a minor indiscretion of mine. More importantly, I could sympathize with Lauren, where I too had a dad who was incarcerated and another man stepped in to take his place.

The issues with building a honest and loving relationship with Robin did not and I would not allow it to overshadow my commitment to completing my senior year on a strong note. I worked tirelessly on my Senior Comprehensive Project (Better Known As "The Comp" at Allegheny). I wished I had completed it during the fall of my senior year instead of the spring because I missed so many opportunities like missing the chance to sleep at regular hours of the night. Instead there were many nights and early mornings that I was spending at Pelletier Library modifying my Comp. I was also working, practicing and completing work for other courses. The majority of the courses were in English and thus I was writing so much that my dreams were filled with books, computers and words.

While English was the major focus of my courses, I did have a chance to participate in a political science class that prepared me for my future profession. Each year Professor Seddig has a class where the students prepared and argued a current United States Supreme Court case. One group is selected to play the attorneys for the original petitioner and another group is selected to play the role of attorneys representing the respondent. Professor Seddig chose my group to be the petitioners. We had to research not only the true case but the other cases that dealt with the issue of freedom of speech. The case was "Simon Schuster vs. The State of New York."

The State of New York had enacted a law making it impermissible for a convicted felon to profit off his or her crimes. We argued just as the attorneys in Simon argued that No means no. The First Amendment states:

"Congress shall pass No law restricting freedom of speech or freedom of the press," along with other unalienable rights. We argued that denying an author his or her right to obtain profits from their own words would discourage them from writing and thereby "chill" their freedom of speech guarantees under the first amendment. We made that argument to a panel of our classmates who had been chosen to act as Supreme Court Justices. I was excited about debating points of law as questions were being hurled at us by our classmates similar to what the Justices do to attorneys who appear before the U.S. Supreme Court. It was a fascinating experience that left me wanting to be a litigator once I got the opportunity to practice law. The latter chance would not come unless I was accepted into law school so that was what I was impatiently waiting to hear.

Notwithstanding my desire to attend law school I wanted to make sure I had options. Accordingly, I applied for a position at State Farm Insurance Company as a Claims Adjuster. I was offered an interview after completing the application process and was eventually offered a position with the Meadville office. I, however, had not heard from the three law schools I applied too and reserved my acceptance of the position until I knew what the status was of my law school applications. Ohio Northern School of Law, Case Western Reserve School of Law and Cleveland State-Marshall College of Law were the only three places I applied. I initially applied to Ohio Northern because of its proximity to Michigan based on my misbeliefs about the longevity of my prior relationship. I applied to the other two law schools because of their reputations for producing outstanding lawyers for the Greater Cleveland community (Cleveland Marshall) and nationally (Case Western Reserve). I did have one favorite and that was primarily due to the relationship I had established with a Dean from Cleveland-Marshall.

I met Dean Melody Stewart, now one of the judges for the 8th District Ohio Court of Appeals, during my sophomore year when she visited Allegheny and set up a booth discussing the law school. There were other universities that were present but I was intrigued by one of the few African Americans in the student center and she happened to be representing my home town law school. I merely perused the other law schools but stood and had a long thorough conversation with Dean Stewart about the advantages of attending Cleveland-Marshall. She made such a huge impression on me that I accepted her invitation to come to the school during my Christmas break and visit a few classes. In addition to sitting in on a contracts and civil procedure class I received a full tour of the small law school that was tucked into a building on the corner of East 18th and Euclid Avenue in Cleveland, Ohio. I loved the exchange between the students and faculty as well as the quaint and austere of the law school building. Additionally, she was a huge proponent of the Legal Careers Opportunity Program (Hereinafter referred to as LCOP) which was geared to helping non-traditional (minorities-African Americans, Hispanics, Women and older students) students successfully navigate the law school system and graduate with the ultimate goal of bar passage. We exchanged numbers and I kept in contact with her on a monthly basis.

As April was fast approaching and I hadn't received any communication from either law school I began to call Dean Stewart on a weekly basis. She assured me that the committee was doing their due diligence in deciding what approximately 300 students out of more than a 1,000 applicants were worthy of the chance to one day be called graduates of Cleveland-

Marshall College of Law. She also indicated that the odds were even tougher to be admitted to the LCOP program. I inquired if I should take the LSAT again because of the physical condition I was in when I initially took the exam and she assured me that my score was sufficient and it along with my grades and other characteristics would be given proper consideration in the committees' evaluation of my application. I stopped worrying and began to pray. I held onto the old adage that I learned at Cleveland Church of Christ through Bishop James Haughton and Elder Lincoln Haughton that "If you are going to worry then don't pray. If you are going to pray then don't worry."

Then one day in mid-April I called home, which I had been doing periodically, and asked my sister if I had received any mail. She looked on the table and in the kitchen and didn't notice any envelopes addressed to me and said "No." Robin happened to be on the phone with me when I called and I asked my sister to go downstairs to the mailbox and see if there was anything in there for that day. She sat the phone down and Robin and I began to pray. "Lord Jesus, we pray in your name that Michael's prayers are answered today. We pray for your favor regarding the decision from the law schools he applied too. We pray specifically for a yes from Cleveland State University-Marshall College of Law. In the name of Jesus." All the while I could hear the apartment door open and my sister's shoes echoed off the hallway walls and she walked briskly to the mail box. I could hear her enter into the apartment and close the door behind her with a slight push on the door. She retrieved the phone and said "You got an envelope from Cleveland State-Marshall College of Law." "I said is it thick or thin?" She said "It's thick Mike!" I knew, just as I had did with the acceptance letter from Allegheny College, that it takes less paperwork to tell you no than to welcome you to their university.

I asked her to open it and read what it said. I heard her say "Congratulations you have been admitted to Cleveland State University-Marshall College of Law for the school year commencing August 1993. " She read some more lines but I was oblivious to all of those things. I was the kid who was neglected, abandoned, and whose parents abused drugs. I was the kid whose male role models had been incarcerated. I was the kid who experienced his mother's death due to a drug addiction induced disease. I was the kid who saw his "grandmother" literally die in his arms. I was the kid who was trekked from school to school and neighborhood to neighborhood and who refused to give up. I simply was the kid who faced adversity and never gave up. I didn't think suicide, homicide or genocide (Selling drugs in my community) was an effective option. I bolstered my faith by accepting my lot and fighting like hell to make my life better. The weapons I used were my faith, education, athletic prowess and my respect for the law and those who had authority over me. It was because of those things that I was able to climb over the mountainous like challenges that life brought me and stand in a place only me and God knew and believed was possible.

I was elated with the news and simply cheered as loud as Robin and my sister did. I, however, cried like a baby who had been hungry and wet for hours after I hung up the phone. I thanked God so many times that day for giving me a chance to do something magnificent. I promised the Lord, myself and my family that I would work assiduously to insure that the Cleveland-Marshall College of Law Admission Committee didn't make a mistake in selecting me to be a member of the Class of 1996. Additionally, I was given the opportunity to further my legal education as a member of the LCOP. LCOP afforded students the chance to begin our law school education a few months before our other classmates. We were introduced to legal writing and our required criminal law class. The introductory program gave us the chance to hone our skills and essentially reduced our first semester course load by one because we wouldn't have to take Criminal Law since we had it in the summer. It gave us a distinct advantage over our classmates but it also helped non-traditional students avoid the pitfalls that led to a reduction in the retention rate of those students in previous years. I didn't care how I got in I was ecstatic that I had been chosen. I told everyone I could that I saw that evening about my admission into law school. To many of my friends it was a no brainer that I would be admitted. I was appreciative of their confidence in me and then afterwards I increased the intensity of diligent work in my studies and my Comp to ensure I completed my time at Allegheny on a positive note. I stood in the middle of the courtyard at Allegheny as the least likely kid, based on my circumstances, to be on the precipice of a law school education. The American dream was still alive and well in me.

CULMINATION OF A DREAM INITIALLY DEFERRED

My college graduation day was fast approaching along with my impending law school education. I believed that I was an atypical pre-law school student because I didn't possess a childhood dream of being an attorney. I heard countless stories from many of the pre-law students at Allegheny and others who were, had or were preparing to take the LSAT regarding how they wanted to be a lawyer since they were in elementary school. Some spoke about watching a lawyer on television and being enlightened about a particular episode that led them to seek a career in law. A few of them spoke about relatives who were attorneys and how they wanted to follow in their footsteps. I on the other hand possessed an aversion to the law and courtrooms due to my family circumstances. My desire to become a part of a profession that had impacted me emotionally was unusual to say the least.

My passion was for teaching. I knew I could have a profound impact on the next generation of leaders in society by being the navigator of their educational success. I knew how much impact a dedicated, concerned, conscientious and intelligent teacher could have over students because so many of the teachers I was blessed with provided the latter example for me. The teachers made school fun, interesting and challenging. Moreover, school was a refuge for me. It was the one place I could excel without the distractions of home and community. My teachers gave me confidence and thereby boosted my self-esteem and made me believe that I was special. I am forever grateful to Mr. Bruce Hill, my sixth grade teacher at Miles Park Elementary Additionally, Mrs. Ballard, Mrs. Ashford, Frau Jewett and Mrs. Stewart were four new "moms" I acquired that had showered me with praise and encouragement both during and after my classes with them. Mr. Quinn in Physics, Mr. Emerson in U.S. History and U.S. Government didn't allow me to rest on my laurels with good grades but pushed me to do better on the next exam, project or lab. I wanted to be able to have the same effect on kids they had on me and education would be my vehicle. While I was unable to obtain my Master's in Education, Allegheny was an initial disappointment.

After four years the initial disappointment evolved into utter gratification when graduation commenced. Pomp and Circumstance was truly the proper way to describe Graduation day for me at Allegheny. It was a mild day, which was perfect because if it was too hot or too cold it would have been miserable. May in Meadville, Pa is a far cry from May in Miami, Florida but you couldn't tell me it wasn't the brightest, warmest day that I had ever experienced. I was very excited and emotional because of this day. I had family and potentially new family celebrating this auspicious occasion with me. My Grandma Edna, my sister, my niece Karese, Robin, Lauren, Mother Nelson, my Great Uncle Jimmy, my Great Aunt Brenda, my father Allen, cousins and other relatives made the nearly two hour trip for some and four hour trip for my Uncle Jimmy and Aunt Brenda to watch me walk across the stage and fulfill a dream of mine and theirs. My Uncle Jimmy was the only college graduate in my immediate family so everyone else was living vicariously through me. I didn't mind at all being the representative for the family.

I was a first generation high school graduate of my immediate family (Mom, Dad, Step Dad, Grandmothers) and now a college graduate from one of the best private liberal arts schools in the Midwest. So my name wasn't the only one that belonged on that diploma. My mother's, my fathers', my grandmothers, my sister's, my aunts, my uncles, my teachers, my friends from the projects, friends from Miles Avenue, my friends from Kinsman Avenue, and the pastors' of the churches I attended. They belonged there because they are the ones that help shape me. Their actions, good and bad, developed the character and intellect I would need to do the unexpected- An African American male from the projects, with a terribly dysfunctional family, graduating from a prestigious institute of higher learning where only 4% of the school population resembled him. I was about to enter an elite group because only 12.6% of African American males between the ages of 20-26 years old had obtained a Bachelor's Degree from college.

My stepfather, Allen, was so excited that he stood at the bottom of the stage on the side where I exited after receiving my diploma from President Sullivan, and grabbed me, and kissed me on the cheek. He said, "I'm proud of you, especially after all the things that me and your mother put you through." "I'm sorry," he stated all the while wiping tears from his face, but not prior to the ones that he left on my cheek that mixed with mine.

I wasn't supposed to be in that audience, on that stage or in that school. In fact, if you look at my situation and compare it to many children who have had similar circumstances I was more likely to be dead, or a high school dropout, or in prison, on drugs, or a dead beat dad. I instead wanted to break the cycle of failure that seemed to follow those closes to me. The college diploma was a symbol of faith and hard work fulfilled.

After taking pictures and talking with some family, friends, professors and administrators Robin and I headed to my dorm room to retrieve the rest of my packed items that I didn't take when I returned home after the semester ended. I spent most of my senior week at home with Robin instead of with my classmates.

I took the boxes to the car and drove down Pelletier street towards North Main Avenue and then to Park Avenue, which is U.S. route 322. I then drove west passing the Arby's that was on left side and the Taco Bell on my right, for the umpteenth time. I was closing one chapter of my life and starting a new one with a more positive and stable foundation. Allegheny had allowed me to mature physically, emotionally, mentally and socially. I grew four to five inches and gained nearly thirty pounds during my four years. I was able to survive countless one night stands, a few heart break losses from committed relationships, my favorite Uncle-Charles Ryan II (Uncle Chuck)- death and the financial stress of not having a lot compared to the students whose parents were paying a majority of the tuition.

I learned a lot during my tenure at Allegheny. I was able to analyze problems and craft solutions through critical analysis. I was then able to verbally articulate my assessment and conclusions, while also being able to write eloquently and persuasively. Living, and being educated with individuals of different cultures taught me how to relate to people who didn't look like me. I was able to dispel myths that others had about African American men and they were able to help me do the same with respect to the ignorance I had of other cultures. I was indebted to Allegheny and all those who are associated with that wonderful institution of higher learning. I never regretted the decision I made in May of 1989 when I chose to attend. It was May of 1993 and now I had tangible proof of my good decision.

Allegheny provided more than just a tranquil place to learn, mature and develop it also shielded me from the tragedies that had befallen me during my pre-college years at home. I didn't have to contend with the utilities being turned off, or hear the crashing sounds of metal prison doors, or the blaring sound of a first responder siren. Additionally, the only gun shots I was privy to while at Allegheny were the ones emanating from a television.

When we arrived home there was an intimate celebration of my achievement with family and friends. We had a few hors d'oeuvres' and punch but no large celebration. I publicly thanked my Grandma Edna for her unconditional love and support. I also dedicated my Allegheny diploma to her since I had dedicated my high school diploma to my mom and Grandma Lula. I then said my law school diploma will be for me. Robin and I left and went to the movies and had our own private celebration. I relaxed and reflected on the day and the last four years. I felt blessed and satisfied but ready to work to make some money before law school began in a few weeks.

Going back home presented new challenges after I completed numerous applications but was unsuccessful in obtaining even an interview in my first few attempts at employment. I was advised by most employers that I was over qualified for the position I sought. I did get past the application stage when I sought a position as teller with a local bank. I took the bank teller test and performed well which led to an interview. The interview, however, did not go as well as I expected. I was sure that the interviewer was impressed, probably too impressed, and asked me an honest question about where did I see myself in five years. I said without hesitation, "In a courtroom practicing law." Accordingly, I was not surprised when I was informed that I did not get the position. I decided to contact the Temp Agency I worked for during one summer after returning home. They found daily and some weekly positions for me just so that I could keep a few dollars in my pocket until I started the LCOP program at Cleveland-Marshall Law School.

ONLY IN AMERICA

In the first week of June 1993 I confidently walked into my Criminal Law class that was half of the requirement for the LCOP program; the other half was legal writing. Our class was located on the second floor of the law school. The professor's desk was a few feet away from both doors that allowed ingress and egress to this particular room. There were three rows of tables that ran the width of the room and they were situated in a stadium like style wherein they ascended upwards on a slant with the professor's desk representing the "field." It gave him or her an opportunity to survey the entire room and negated any person's attempts to evade detection and accordingly avoid participating in the classroom discussion. I strolled into the classroom with my Phi Beta Sigma majority white with royal blue outlining hat atop of my head. I was also wearing a Phi Beta Sigma shirt that was mainly royal blue with white outlining. I was approximately ten minutes early and noticed a mixture of students. There were approximately 20-25 students in the LCOP. Most of them were part-time students because of their current family and occupation status. Our class was representative of the Great American Melting Pot theory because there were African American men and women, women who were young and others more seasoned. There were Caucasian men and women and again some young and then a few more seasoned. It was an interesting mix of race, gender and age but talented, articulate and bright people. The brightest of us all was Professor Fred White.

Professor Fredrick White functioned as a teacher, mentor, inspiration, and motivation for me and my classmates. I say the latter notwithstanding the fact that he embarrassed me on the first day of class. As I explained earlier I walked into class with my hat and neglected to remove it when I sat down. He walked into class after me, a few minutes before it was scheduled to begin. He took attendance for formal purposes but I believe also to find out my name. After discovering who I was he directed his attention to me and in a stern voice stated "

Mr. Ryan, hats are not permitted to be worn in my classroom." He then made another statement that let me know he had a good sense of humor, "Especially Phi Beta Sigma hats!" He then smirked and laughed. He was not an imposing man, being that he was approximately 5'5" at most but he had a very commanding and persuasive voice; he got your attention. I was impressed and proud of Professor White because he grew up in Cleveland, went to Columbia for undergraduate and law school and returned back home to give his talents to other aspiring lawyers from his home city.

I hadn't met many other older African American men in academia like Professor White. I hung on his every word both about the law and about life. He said to all of us if we have significant others who we knew couldn't and wouldn't understand the lack of time we would have for the next three years then we should sever those relationships because they would prevent us from being successful in law school. I didn't have to worry about that with Robin. She never minded when I studied at her house or went home to study. She wasn't jealous if I went and had a study group with my classmates during the summer or during the regular school months.

I read, and read and read some more and that was just for one night of homework. The average night of homework consisted of a minimum of 30-50 pages per course, pages in conjunction with analyzing each case using the IRAC method. Professor White, who was a member of Omega Phi Psi Fraternity (Another reason why he pointed me out in class that first day), impressed upon us the need to be prepared for each class because we never knew who was going to be called on to expound upon the cases we read the night before. He urged us to read, to apply the IRAC (Issue Rule Application and Conclusion) analysis to our legal case studies. He urged us to use our common sense and logic in deciphering why a jurist or a group of jurist came to a conclusion regarding a certain matter that became law. He taught us to be humble by suggesting the only thing that separated a lot of lawyers from lay people with respect to understanding how to successfully win a case was the fact that "We know where the books (Statutes & Case law) are and they don't."

Criminal law is one of the least difficult courses and one of the shortest accordingly most first year students only take it their first semester. We, however, squeezed ten weeks of work into eight along with the legal writing component. While once we successfully passed the criminal law portion of the LCOP program we were still required to take a class for Legal Writing during our first year. The material we were studying was at times, fascinating, enlightening, gruesome and bizarre. We read about different degrees of murder, about assault and battery, trespass, criminal common law (Law created by judges) and statutory criminal law (law created by the legislature). We read and discussed cases that showed how sexism was a huge part of the law in the past. The law has evolved when in the past a man was able to avoid a murder conviction if he killed his wife and her lover while viewing the latter two parties in the act. The latter was considered to be sufficient provocation. The latter protection, however, didn't apply to the wife if she saw the reciprocal instead she would have been convicted of murder. I learned that it's illegal to create devices (Boobie traps) that can cause harm to would be trespassers. We read cases about individuals who were stranded and in order to survive they began to eat those who perished in order to avoid their own demise (even though cannibalism was illegal). They were applying the principle of necessity as a defense to the charge of cannibalism. There were many more cases and statutes that we read in a four week span that was preparing us for our mid-term.

I walked into the mid-term with an extreme amount of confidence. I had prepared fairly well for the exam by using my notes, flash cards and being quizzed by family to give me the assurance that I would do well on my first official exam. I sat down and began the test which was a mixture of multiple choice questions and essays. Professor White believed, unlike many of the law school professors, that essays weren't the exclusive way of measuring a law school students understanding and retention of the law for that particular subject. Additionally, he was also helping to prepare us for the format we would encounter at the Bar Examination. I went through the multiple choice questions with precision and poise. I, however, was a little leery about some of my responses and after I completed the essays went back to the multiple choice questions and changed some of my initial answers. Well when I went outside and compared them to my classmates I discovered that I should have just went with my initial conclusion. I still did well, because of my essay, but I would have done much better.

Four weeks later I had the opportunity to redeem myself for our final criminal law exam. I had studied with my classmates, as I was invited to be a part of an "elite study group" based upon our conversation after the mid-term exam wherein I knew most of the answers and discovered and discussed the right issues on the essays. I also did a lot of my own independent study employing the same methods I did for the mid-term. I did not change any of my answers this time on the multiple choice questions. I read the questions and marked my answers with alacrity and confidence on the multiple choice portion of the test. I then read the essays and began to write fluently and effectively regarding the issues and applying the law to the fact pattern provided by Professor White. I knew that I had nailed each issue and articulated the correct conclusion. I was shocked, however, when I received my grade- C+. I had only missed two of the multiple choice questions and was surprised that I did that poorly on the essays to reduce my grade to a C+. I eventually received my bluebook back, which is the apparatus law school students use to write their essay answers to the legal dispute provided by the professor. I saw the score and then the heading across the first page " I can't read this!" I had mistakenly wrote my essays in pencil instead of pen. At 22 years old I had better eyesight, even with my corrective lens, than Professor White. I recalled, but completely forgot during the test, that he advised us prior to the test to bring both a pencil and pen. The pencil was for the multiple choice portion because the answers were calculated by a computer while the essays had to written in ink so that he could see the writing. I had made a colossal mistake. I was devastated and relieved at the same time. I initially believed my average grade was due to my lack of understanding and inability to regurgitate what I knew on paper. Instead my grade was a reflection of my inability to follow the rules. Professor White noted on the exam that the areas where it was legible lead him to believe that I had a very good understanding of the law and how to apply it. Unfortunately, there were too many areas that were illegible and thus the rationale for the poor but not zero grade. I left Professor White's office with a renewed confidence in my ability to comprehend, analyze and articulate my legal conclusions both orally and in writing.

After the LCOP class ended we had a few weeks until school started. I used the time wisely by spending more days and nights with Robin and Lauren. I also split time with my sister, niece and Grandma Edna at the new home my grandmother purchased, which was approximately ten minutes away from Robin's house. I was preparing Robin and my family for the limited time I would be able to share with them while I was attending law school. Professor White had stressed the latter and then it was reinforced by one of the Dean's of the law school during the orientation. The individual told all of the nearly 300 first year students" Turn to your left and then turn to your right. Odds are that those two individuals will not complete the program and graduate from law school." I immediately said I was going to be one of the hundred or so graduates come May 1996. I would not succumb to the stress, pressure, anxiety or the tremendous amount of work that law school can produce and require respectively. If I was able to make it through the tumultuous times I experienced when I was younger then surely law school would be a piece of cake!

Cleveland-Marshall was far from being a piece of cake. I had some difficult classes, some not so difficult classes and some classes that at times were a combination of challenge and comfort. I received marks as high as an A in Secured Transactions and Family Law, to C's in some of the more basic courses like Contracts, Torts and Evidence. I received B+ only points away from A's in Constitutional Law, Property , Criminal Procedure and Products Liability. I took courses that would help me in any specific area of law that I chose to enter like: Statutory Construction, Labor Law, Arbitration, Bill of Rights, Client Negotiation and other interesting courses. I was able to maintain a very good grade point average as well as balance home life and my relationship with Robin.

I have always found a way to balance what would appear to be chaos for other people. The latter ability may be due to the fact that I was surrounded by chaos so much as a child and never let it affect me such that when I was immersed in so many obligations I found a way to thrive. Accordingly, I opted to apply for a part-time position toward the end of my first year in law school. First year law students, were strongly discouraged to avoid obtaining employment during the first year of law school. Myself and other first year students from Marshall were allowed to begin working since the second semester was nearing a conclusion by the time we were hired.

I acquired a position as a Mediator with the City of Cleveland Prosecutor's Office. My attainment of the position was ironic since three years before that date I had ventured to the office in search of some legal related work as an undergraduate student. I met with the then Director of Mediation, Ann Feighan, who was at the time the outgoing Director. She advised me and John, my best friend from Heights, that although we had excellent resumes the office only hired students in law school for the Mediator positions. I left the office three years ago with the intent on returning with the one last criteria to get the job-law school student. Accordingly, when I did return with that title the office considered my current status, my prior interest, along with my application and completion of the interview, I was hired and began my professional legal career.

I was responsible for conducting the initial intakes for citizens who were seeking some legal redress for alleged criminal behavior. I had to input the information verbatim, along with evidence, if any and witnesses statements if any. I would have to make an assessment regarding whether a crime was alleged to have been committed and what level. If it was a felony I was instructed to advise the individual to contact the police so that a Detective could conduct an investigation. If it was civil in nature then I would advise the individual to small claims or recommend that they seek legal counsel to help them with their legal controversy. If it was a misdemeanor I would then take the information I gathered and seek the counsel of one of the esteemed Assistant City Prosecuting Attorneys regarding whether official charges would be filed or the matter would be set for a mediation hearing. I would get Petitioners who had very little evidence to ones who would bring bags of pictures, torn clothes, letters, broken glasses, and other evidentiary items. Sometimes the Assistant Prosecuting Attorney would simply evaluate the evidence on their own without my input. There, however, were several who would ask me to analyze the situation and give them my opinion. They weren't just evaluating the sufficiency of the evidence but also the probability of the individual being convicted of the offense.

I was learning the skills that prosecutors used in determining credibility of witnesses and the evidence they assessed in determining whether justice is served by prosecuting this matter or finding another alternative-mediation or a terse letter to cease and desist the alleged unlawful behavior. If the prosecutor agreed to file charges I was then responsible for generating the paperwork for the prosecutor and alleged victim to sign. I then gave the alleged victims instructions regarding how this process would unfold. I gave them my card and advised them if they had any questions they could call me and I would forward them to the prosecutor that was assigned to their case. Another option was for the prosecutor to decline to file charges and instead hold a mediation hearing.

I would inform the alleged victim and then schedule the matter for a hearing. We would send a notice to the other party and hope that they would show, although they weren't legally required to attend. The letter did, however, indicate that failure to show could result in charges being filed. There were several Mediators when I worked and we would alternate on days when hearings took place. The mediation hearings always occurred after working hours in order to make it convenient for people. I would conduct the hearings in an Assistant Prosecutor's office because they had more space. I would advise the parties that I was not a lawyer but would give them a chance to voice their concerns. I advised them that nothing stated in the hearing could be used against them as a way of getting them to be candid and hopefully leading to a resolution of their dispute. I would have people who would yell and scream, which would cause the on duty police officer to make their way to the room. I was able to alleviate the situation and avoid an arrest of any of the parties by either talking in a very austere tone when necessary or a calming tone depending on the parties and the allegation(s). I was able to develop my communication skills and demeanor. I found ways to address people's concerns without being arrogant and condescending. I would advise them of what the law was in certain areas and they would listen. A majority of the mediations ended amicably and without further incidents. There were a few parties who found their way onto a court's docket because they refused to adhere to the advice I had given them.

There were other times when the Assistant Prosecutor, however, believed that neither charges or mediation was warranted. I was then charged with the unenviable task of telling this individual that our office would not be doing anything officially about their complaint(s). This was the most interesting part because I had to use my communication skills to explain why the decision was made and to insure that I made it out of my office unharmed. I never had any close calls because I walked into the office with an air that I wasn't someone they wanted to physically accost.

I enjoyed the things I learned regarding the different misdemeanor laws that people were prosecuted for by the city of Cleveland and the State of Ohio. I became very familiar with the criminal procedure from the initiation stage until the plea or trial. I became familiar with the resolution process because I would use my lunch hour or days when intakes were slow to watch the Assistant Prosecutors dispense justice in one of the thirteen courtrooms in the Justice Center that are designated for the Cleveland Municipal Court judges. I watched the pre-trial stage when litigants and or their attorneys tried to determine what evidence the prosecutor possessed and the strength of that evidence. The litigant would then decide based on that whether to plea, ask for another pre-trial or a trial date. If the matter was a moving violation or other minor misdemeanor I would get a chance to see a trial. I watched the Assistant Prosecuting Attorney perform an opening statement that included what they believed the evidence was going to show, who was going to testify and why they believe the judge would find the person guilty beyond a reasonable doubt. The defense attorney or normally the person would be Pro Se, acting as their own attorney, would then counter with their own statement refuting the city's ability to make its burden of proof. If the individual was unrepresented they would just waive opening. The prosecutor would then question the officer about the alleged facts in a succinct and common manner. The defense attorney would attack the officers recollection of the facts, their eye sight, their attentiveness if any that particular moment, the sufficiency of the radar gun. If, however, the person was Pro Se, most times their questions wouldn't be relevant but instead were personal. The officer stopped them for reasons non-related to the offense. The officer could be doing and should be doing better things than issuing them citations for speeding when people were robbing, burglarizing homes and selling drugs. Some, however, had very legitimate claims and were able to convince many of the judges that the city didn't meet its burden of proof.

I was able to visualize justice working on behalf of the city, in its attempt to keep the citizenry safe and the accused in that they were given due process in their efforts to defend the accusations that had been made against them. I saw how the system worked and was more intrigued when I would go back to law school because the law was living and breathing for me. I wasn't just reading words, a ton of them nearly 100 pages total a night because of all my classes, I saw the words being applied to everyday situations. It was fascinating and only increased my desire to expedite my legal education so that I could become a member of the legal profession and really fulfill the passion I gained at Allegheny in my Civil Liberties class.

My first year of law school ended without any fanfare. I successfully passed all my classes by an acceptable margin no D's no F's. I was never in danger of being placed on academic watch. I point out the latter because I met and communicated with a number of former students who voiced their displeasure with the law school and some of the professors. They felt that the primary reasons they were no longer students at the school was based upon race, gender and socioeconomic status. I would later learn from both African American, Caucasian and female Deans and administrative staff that their failures were due to poor grades and nothing more. Law schools across the country have instituted mechanisms to reduce discrimination and/or favoritism towards students that was not based on merit by requiring students to use an ID for their exams instead of their names. The professor purportedly doesn't know the students name, for purposes of the exam, until after the grade is assigned to the particular number. The professor may need the name to add points for participation when appropriate. The professor, however, generally only relied on the exam or exams for the final grade. Accordingly, many times a person's success or failure in law school hinged on one exam. If you do well you get an excellent grade and you move on to the next year. If you do poorly you put yourself in a position of being removed from the school and ending your dream of entering the exclusive association of Juris Doctorate holders. I mention my encounter with the disenchanted former students to demonstrate how difficult law school can be. It requires intellect, diligence, foresight and determination. I was imbued with those characteristics both based upon external events and an innate desire not to give up hope.

I entered my second year with even more confidence and was eager to learn more unique perspectives, philosophies about the law as well as more black letter law that would allow me to be better prepared for the bar examination as well as the actual practice of law. I had continued to work throughout the summer but there was one special thing that had occurred in the spring that was life changing.

Robin is and will always be one of the greatest things that ever happen to me, outside of being saved. I say that because it was her influence that lead me back to the church and allowed Jesus to take my heart and mind and mold me into the man that I am today. I saw how much she loved God and how she had been blessed despite some unpleasant circumstances in her life and I wanted that and more. I would travel with Robin, Doris Nelson-Robin's mom, Lauren and her brother Jeffrey to Akron, Ohio to her sister Linda Wright and her husband, Pastor Abraham Wright's now Bishop, home on Saturday nights. Pastor Wright was the pastor at Greater Temple Baptist Church a small building with a vibrant congregation. He was clearly one of God's many mouthpieces. God placed a word inside of him that he delivered to the people that convicted us and gave us hope. God used him to reinforce to me, even though I know he didn't directly preach to me, the fact that he (God) never left me alone through my heartache and pain. His words let me know that God had been ordering my steps all along. His words let me know that what Satan meant for bad God meant for my good. His words let me know that it would all work out for the good of them that love the Lord and are called according to his purpose. Pastor Wright was instrumental in me becoming more intimate with God and making a decision that would impact the rest of my life.

The first decision I made was accepting the call to become a Deacon at Greater Temple Baptist Church. I had spent a significant amount of time with Pastor Wright and the other Ministers and Deacons at the church and saw how on fire they were for God; I wanted it. I felt that I owed God based upon the fact that so many people who had been in similar situations like mine and yet they couldn't testify about the manifold blessings that had been bestowed upon me. I felt that the least I could do was to serve God is a leadership role in the church. Thus, I increased my personal reading of the Bible. Since we were traveling to Akron on Saturday nights I had the ability to attend Sunday School and thereby receive a more thorough understanding of the Bible, via the assistance of both Pastor Wright and Minister Eric Bufford, the men's Sunday School teacher. The more I read about God, the more of an explanation I received regarding the word of God, my receipt of the Holy Spirit all influenced me to try and change my lifestyle. My lifestyle had still consisted of partying, being less than truthful in certain circumstances. Prior to Robin and Shandale I dated several women simultaneously without making any commitments, drinking alcohol and other behavior that is frowned upon by the church. I made great strides to change but the one thing that was very difficult to change was the strong physical attraction I had for Robin.

Robin was not only smart but one of the sexiest, most beautiful women I had the honor and pleasure of calling my girlfriend. While I can now say it at the time we were engaging in pre-marital intimate acts that was against the teaching we were under. Pastor Wright, because of our candid talks, was aware of my desires cautioned me personally and from the pulpit about the image I was portraying to the congregation and others in the community.

I didn't want my image to be tarnished nor people discouraged from accepting Christ because they saw me as a hypocrite. Thus, I began to discuss the possibility of marriage with Robin in order to gauge her opinion. She was initially not as interested as I was in getting married. Aside from Pastor Wright's conversations and his sermons, I had never felt for any woman like I did for Robin. I had butterflies in my stomach every time I knew I was going to see her. I couldn't wait to hug, hold, kiss or caress her. I spent so much time with her I couldn't imagine not spending the rest of my life with her. She was all that I wanted in a woman: she loved God, she could sing, beautiful, sexy, smart, compassionate, great mother, supportive and loyal. Why wouldn't I want to marry her. I believed, but she later told me that was untrue, that her hesitancy with me was due to the fact that she was waiting on someone else better to come along. I wasn't sure but I was becoming impatient and refused to discuss the issue of marriage anymore for several months.

Shortly before my first year exams were to begin the entire church went to New York for a revival that Pastor Wright was leading. I had to study and thus I couldn't join them in New York. Robin, Lauren and Mother Nelson went with the church and I stayed home and cracked open the books and my notes. I spoke to Robin after they arrived and didn't speak to her again until the day they left. Our lack of communication didn't come from our intentional acts of trying to avoid contact. In fact, I left several messages on the number that was given to me. Those messages were never returned. Robin did call my grandmother's phone, this was in the day of no cell phones, but no messages were forwarded to me. I assumed that she had found some new beau in New York and she believed that I was gallivanting around town with another woman and using my exams as an excuse to be unfaithful. When Robin and I did talk the day they left New York we cleared up the confusion. However, the old adage, absence makes the heart grow fonder made Robin realize that she didn't want to live the rest of her life without me.

A few weeks after she had returned from New York, she and I were walking into the grocery store. I grabbed her hand like I normally did and, even though I had vowed not to bring the issue of marriage up anymore, asked her would she ever consider getting married. She responded "Yes." This was a shock because only a few months ago she chimed numerous times that she really liked our relationship as it was. She told friends " Oh, I'm not getting married right now. I'm too young." With eyes wide open as an Owl I then asked her "Well Robin, would you ever consider marrying me?" She said,

"Definitely." My next few words came out like a track runner tripping over their shoelaces as I feverishly stated, " I, I, I, I, want to knowww are youuuuu serious?" I was nervous at this time. I stopped and said, "Don't go into the store!" I then said with conviction, with my eyes watering, and my head dripping with perspiration " So does that mean you will marry me?" Her next comments were five of the greatest words any one had ever spoken to me,

"Yes. I will marry you!"

I grabbed her tight around her twenty some inch waist, pulled her close to me such that even air had a hard time passing between us and then I kissed her softly and gently for what seemed like eternity. I could have flew back to her house on a cloud. I walked through the grocery store the happiest man on earth. I couldn't remember what we came to the store to purchase and I didn't care at that point. I wanted to get home so that I could tell someone else about the second greatest decision I had made in the last few months. We decided, however, to delay telling anyone of our decision. We wanted to choose a time when there was a large gathering of family and friends. Accordingly, a few months later we told everyone one day after church when we had a huge dinner at one of my fellow Deacons homes. Tears of joy flowed from all of the women both family and church members. Congratulatory handshakes and pats on the back came from the brothers and other family members. While I wanted to marry Robin as soon as possible I wanted to make sure that I had completed the majority of my law school education before I took on the awesome responsibility of being a husband and father. Thus, I convinced Robin to wait until after I finished my second year of law school before we got married. She acquiesced and then began to prepare the wedding of a lifetime.

While Robin was raising Lauren, working and organizing our wedding I was helping her as much as I could with Lauren, working and beginning my second year of law school. I was told by the more experienced law school students that my second year would be better than the first because the first year they try to scare you, the second year you chose the classes you want and the third year they bored you too death because you want to simply take the bar and begin practicing. I did take a number of elective classes that were interesting and helpful. Secured Transactions, Products Liability, Employment Law, Criminal Procedure, Statutory Construction and other specialized classes. In addition to taking the less generalized courses I also applied and attained a position as a law clerk with the City of Cleveland's Civil law Department.

My position at the Law Department gave me the opportunity to use my writing skills to analyze civil legal issues and draft memorandums and motions for and on behalf of the lawyers at the civil section of the Law Department. I was able to gain a significant amount of experience and knowledge with my position as a mediator and intake officer with the criminal portion of the Law Department. My responsibility, however shifted when I began as a clerk for the Civil Division. I was expected to complete assignments regarding different areas concerning municipal law: car accidents involving city property, excessive force complaints against the police, building and housing, economic development and employer/employee relations. I changed buildings from the Justice Center to City Hall. I went from the more modern spacious mammoth building to the more quaint, five story archaic building with the spectacular architecture. I loved seeing the beautiful and dynamic paintings on the walls and ceiling of City Hall. I was mesmerized by the atmosphere of Cleveland City Hall and the Rotunda area knowing that the law for this great city was made and enforced by those who traversed those halls each day and days before I was born. I was amazed that I now had the opportunity to weigh in regarding how the government would proceed regarding difficult issues that were presented to the law department.

I spent a vast majority of my time in the law library just as I did at Cleveland-Marshall, at Allegheny, at Cleveland Heights and in the Longwood Projects at the mobile library. I would research both the law supporting a particular issue and cases that held an opposite view, if any. I would analyze the law and apply the applicable facts and generate my opinion. Many of the city attorneys accepted my opinion and would substitute it as their own or would ask for me to complete more research if they believed I hadn't provided a concrete opinion or legal foundation to support their point of view. It was exhilarating to have the attorneys accept my work and simply apply their name and disappointing but also a learning experience when I was directed to go find more case law. I actually became known in the office as the case on point locator. I worked diligently to find cases that could be used by the attorneys to support their arguments that had facts and law that were uniquely similar to the facts in their respective cases. I also got a chance to observe trials, participate in arbitrations by drafting questions and observing the City attorneys. I drafted motions that were filed in Court and granted by a judge. I was thrilled to know that judges were persuaded by my legal arguments and satisfied with the grammatical and analytical form of my motions.

I PUT A RING ON IT

My proposal lacked any of the traditional requirements: I hadn't asked Robin's father's and/or mother's blessings, I didn't get down on one knee, I didn't take her to a fancy restaurant or a park or Lake Erie, I didn't even have a ring and yet she still said yes. I wanted to correct at least three of those things and the first was to acquire the ring. Robin and I had went shopping shortly before her birthday and she saw a ring that she really liked. It was a non-traditional engagement ring wherein instead of one diamond there were a cluster of diamonds shaped like half oval. She was adamant about purchasing it as a birthday present for herself. I, however, convinced her to keep her money and buy something else other than jewelry. I told her she had enough jewelry and didn't need much more and so we continued shopping. A few days later I went back to the same store and put a down payment on the ring. The more than thirty small diamonds sparkled brighter than sunlight that reflects off the window when the sun rises in the morning. I had saved the minimal amount I was making as a mediator and I would use some of the same amount I was making as a law clerk to pay the balance. The ring was the best investment I had made; even better than the down payment I made for Robin's car but tantamount to the one I made for my education.

After I made the last payment on the ring I brought it home and showed it to my Grandma Edna, my sister and my father, Allen, who was living with us at our new home in Cleveland Heights. They were enamored with the ring and all of them said how beautiful it was and how fortunate Robin was to have me. I took the ring and hid it in a safe but memorable place in my room. I asked Grandma Edna and my sister to come to Greater Temple with me on the Sunday after I secured the ring so they could be there with me when I presented it to Robin. They had visited the church before and so their presence wouldn't spark any curiosity from Robin. Sunday came and service was performed in the normal fashion. I, however, had asked Pastor Wright after he had made a request for people to join the church to allow me to speak before church officially ended. I walked up to the front of the church and while it only took me thirty seconds the path seemed to measure one hundred yards and it felt like it took five minutes to arrive and grab the microphone. I grabbed the microphone and garbled my first words which was to thank my grandmother and my sister for coming to church. I then said " When I was being recruited by Clarion University the head football coach told me that I would make two important decisions in my life. I would have to decide where I would attend college and who I was going to marry. Well I have already graduated from Allegheny College and now I want to marry Robin Nelson." Robin was sitting in the back of the church with her shoes off seemingly unaware of what I was doing. I then asked her to come up to the front and then said " I can't ask you to marry me without a ring and I have it with me today." She hurriedly put on her shoes and trotted up to the front of the church. She hadn't seen the ring since the day she wanted to purchase it. I opened the box and took out the ring and simultaneously grabbed her left hand. I had to pause for a few seconds in my attempts to put the ring on the third finger of her right hand because my hand was trembling. I actually grabbed my right hand with my left hand to stop the shaking and then I gently placed the ring on her quivering finger. I had to wipe the tears from her cheek in order to kiss her. The ring was validation for me but it was merely window dressing for Robin. She knew that I intensely loved her and that I was adamant about marrying her and she didn't need a ring to begin or continue with planning our wedding. The ushers passed out so much of the Kleenex that they had to resort to using the tissue from the rest rooms because so many people were crying. I admit it was emotional for me as well.

Reality began to set in that I was going to be the head of a household relatively soon. I would be a husband and father without a lifelong good example of either one. The only males who I knew in my immediate family that were married were my Uncle Chuck Ryan, my "Uncle" Bill Tarter , "Uncle" Eugene Sanders and my Great Uncle Jimmy Gohanna . "Uncle" Bill and "Uncle" Eugene were the only ones who lived in the Greater Cleveland area. Despite Uncle Bill and Uncle Gene living in the area I had little contact with them, similar to what I had with my uncles that lived out of the state. I didn't get a chance to watch their daily interactions with their wives to gain some knowledge of how husbands should treat, respond to and generally relate to their wives. I was unacquainted with what was necessary to sustain a healthy marriage. Additionally, the men who were supposed to provide care, comfort, guidance, protection and support as a father for me did a less than stellar job. I had no positive direct knowledge or experience of how to raise a child. A lot of the things I did prior to being married and shortly thereafter was by trial and error; I was blessed with a forgiving and patient wife.

I did learn some responsibilities that were akin to those that husbands and fathers are generally required to meet prior to taking my vows. I shared in the responsibility of taking and picking Lauren up from daycare. She would persuade me every day to take her to the convenient store located a half of mile from her home so that I could buy her a snack before dinner. I could never turn down one of the cutest little girls I had ever seen. As I stated before I supplied the down payment for the car Robin purchased that gave both of access to a vehicle that she didn't have to share with her dad. She wanted her own car and I needed something reliable to drive to and from law school so I wouldn't have to take public transportation every day. On occasion, I would drive Robin to work, drop Lauren off at school, take the car to Marshall, return to pick Lauren up from daycare and then drive later to pick Robin up. She would either drop me off at home later and come get me in the morning or I would take the car and be there bright and early to engage in the same routine. We shared money for meals, if she needed something extra on bills or vice versa we could rely upon one another. We assisted one another just as spouses did, which helped lay a good foundation for the beginning stages of our marriage.

I was different from most grooms because despite my busy schedule I was excited to be an integral part of the wedding planning. Robin didn't have to exhort me to fully participate I actually asked what did she need me to do. She made sure that those weren't just idle words emanating from my mouth and she put me to work. We went to several greeting card shops looking for the right wedding invitations. After the fourth one, we finally arrived at American Greetings shop in Randall Park Mall, located in the Village of North Randall, Ohio.

Randall Mall once one of the most vibrant, patronized malls in the country with a number of high end retailers located throughout the two story and more than 1.5 million square foot complex. It had deteriorated to a degree by 1993 but what still operable with a few retailers hanging on by threads. We were thankful that American Greetings was still there and active. We walked in and headed straight to the invitation section and began reading the pre-written invitations. We must have read over thirty while we were there and more than a hundred total over the days we had been searching. Ultimately we had gotten so tired that we both laid on the floor next to each other with our legs sprawled in front of the shelves that held the other cards with the invitations in our hands being held a few feet away. We would read the invitations to each other and then comment on why we did or didn't like that specific one. I then found one that started with "Today I marry my friend...," we both immediately knew that was the one we were going to send to family and friends. I was also involved in helping pick out the menu for the wedding, I was responsible for the size of the wedding party because I wanted my friends, my sister and my cousin Chucky to be in the wedding which then required Robin to match the men and so she, despite her desire for a small party, had to recruit some more friends to shell out money for a dress and shoes. We both discussed and made calls regarding the limousine company we were going to be using. Robin, however, was responsible for the honeymoon arrangements I trusted that she would find the most beautiful, serene and exotic place for us to begin our life journey together. Our wedding would not have been possible without the generosity of Robin's wonderful father, Robert Nelson.

Tradition generally requires that the bride's family pay for the wedding and the groom's family be monetarily responsible for the rehearsal dinner. Well my family didn't have much money but we were able to scrap up the funds to provide for a very bountiful dinner. Robin's dad gave us the largest donation towards our wedding but it was in lieu of him being present to give his baby girl away. His donation came by way of his insurance policy that was presented after his untimely death at the youthful age of 59.

Robert Nelson was truly a legend amongst his family and friends. He was one of two boys amongst a number of siblings who were born and raised in Mississippi. He was an imposing man before his illness standing at no shorter than 6'6" and weighing three hundred plus pounds at his heaviest weight. He was affectionately and respectfully called "Big Rob" by family, friends and foes alike. I simply knew him as Mr. Nelson. Our first encounter was again not the typical way an individual wants to greet their potential son-in-law.

Robin and I had decided to go out to a club or getting something to eat one night, this of course is around the time she and I initially started dating. She said she needed to stop by her dad's house before we went out. She was driving her dad's truck that had a stick shift. When we arrived at her dad's house she left me in the truck and indicated that she would return shortly. Despite having met her mom already I was wondering why she didn't invite me to meet her dad but I wasn't too stressed about the situation and just sat patiently in the truck for her to return. I saw her dad come out on the second floor porch and peer over the bannister into the vehicle. He made a remark to Robin. I then heard some raised voices that appeared to be a male's and a few female's. Moments later Robin, her dad, and Robin's stepmother came storming through the first floor, of a two family home, door onto the lawn next to the truck. Robin's dad, with his Fred Sanford like house coat, which was cloth and multi-colored, and his grey hair that was split by the smooth bald portion of his scalp in the middle, and his wire flame glasses, began to yell at Robin. I alighted from the truck in an effort to protect Robin and to attempt to diffuse the situation. I walked towards Robin and her dad, without saying a word reached into his bathrobe and retrieved a revolver from his pocket. Before I could say or move any further he placed the gun on the left side of my temple as I was facing him and standing next to Robin. The metal was cold as ice and caused my legs to feel like they were seated in cement. I didn't move one inch, actually it was not even one centimeter. I didn't want him to sneeze and accidently discharge the gun. Millions of thoughts flashed through my mind but the one that stuck more than any others was Lord please protect me. Please don't allow this man, who I don't know, to shoot and kill me over my desire to protect Robin. While Mr. Nelson was holding the gun to my head he said "And who is this motherfucker? And what are you trying to prove?" Robin came to my aid and said in the midst of her tears " Daddy no don't shoot him!" "Please daddy put the gun away. He's not going to try and hurt you." I just stood there paralyzed and praying that irony would not strike wherein I was able to avoid death despite growing up in so many violent neighborhoods and a violent home and yet I would be a college graduate and first year law school student and then be the victim of a senseless act of violence. I knew Jesus was talking to Mr. Nelson along with his good common sense because he put the safety back on the gun, returned it to his pocket. He apologized for placing the gun to my temple but also chimed in "You need to be careful and not just walk up on elderly people who don't know you or your intentions." He was absolutely right. I probably didn't exercise good judgment by approaching him in what I should have known and what he perceived was an aggressive manner.

His apology included some very sage advice, which was his style. He was known for being a very perceptive man that gave his honest opinion about any and all situations. I unfortunately would not be privy to his wise words on a consistent basis due his illness and then eventual passing. He died in February of 1995, six months prior to our wedding. He missed what he had longed to do, walk his baby girl down the aisle and give her away. I think, however, he was satisfied with me and confident that I would be able to provide for his youngest daughter. He knew I was in law school and assumed that I would successfully pass the bar and be given the opportunity to make a substantial salary. Accordingly, the statement he made to Robin, years before we met, prior to giving her some money came to fruition " Boy, boy, boy... You better marry somebody rich!"

I was far from rich but my life with Robin would make it seem like I was rich. Mr. Nelson's passing dampened Robin and my ability to enjoy all the festivities surrounding planning for the wedding because the person that was supposed to walk her down the aisle wasn't going to be there. I think that was extremely hurtful for her.

The church, the reception hall, the tuxes, the dresses weren't the only lose ends that needed to be cleaned up before our wedding. I had to deal with an issue that was raising its ugly head and I didn't want it to negatively impact my life with Robin. My sister and Grandma Edna had some reservations about me marrying Robin. My Grandma Edna said, "Michael you need a fulltime job in order to care for a family. Why don't you wait until after graduation." I responded that, "I didn't want to wait, and by my faith I believe we'll be fine." I knew she meant well and she just believed money problems could be detrimental for a young marriage. My sister didn't say anything overtly but I could tell based on her body language that she wasn't too amused with my decision. I really believed that they were opposed to the idea of me marrying anyone, let alone Robin. It was the three of us against the world, four when Karese arrived four years before my impending wedding. Thus, I believe there was a little separation anxiety. I know that was the case for me and my sister because we had been through so much together and we have survived and thrived because we relied upon one another. Despite the fact that I would only be a few minutes away I might as well have been thousands of miles away because I would not be available to fix something at home, to give or get advice, to baby sit, to eat (Grandma loved to feed me) or to hug or be hugged. I would be spending holidays with my wife and daughter and not always with grandma, my sister and Karese. I wrote a letter to both my sister and grandma and told them that I loved Robin immensely and I was going to marry her with or without their blessing. I wanted them to eventually accept her and Lauren as a part of our family. Once I broached the subject with them their comments, attitudes and behaviors changed. Thank God because we couldn't of had such a wonderful wedding day without them.

August 12, 1995 arrived with high anticipation. Me and some of my groomsmen, John Stanley (Best Man), Chucky Ryan and Michael Penn all spent the night at Deacon Jimmy Ashford's home. There was no bachelor party, John and Robbie took me out to a special club weeks before the wedding date, similar to the wild parties that are depicted in the movies. Instead, we ate pizza, talked, listened to some music and then played cards before we settled in and went to sleep. I slept really well that night, unlike Robin. She told me she hardly slept because she didn't want to wake up late and miss her hair appointment. I, however, believed she was a little nervous about settling down with me for the rest of her life. I couldn't wait to arrive at the church and put my tux on and get the ceremony started. All of the groomsmen had fresh new haircuts and mine made me look like I was five years younger. The waves in my hair were flowing so freely you could place a boat on my head and it would not have a hard time making to my forehead without a paddle.

I had been telling everyone that I wasn't overly nervous because nervousness would indicate an uneasiness, doubt or uncertainty. I, however, felt and believed that I had found my soul mate and thus I had no reason to lack any confidence in my decision. The anxiety I did feel stemmed from becoming the leader of a family and being required to care for, nurture, protect, provide for both Robin and Lauren. The anxiety came from trying to find the proper balance between leaving the family that nurtured me and cleaving to my wife. The anxiety came from not having a home, a permanent job and trying to support a wife and daughter with a part-time gig and financial aid. I was praying and believing God even more prior to this date and asking that he give me the wisdom I needed so that I would not fail as a husband and father. All of those concerns began to weigh on me but they didn't outweigh the enthusiasm I had bottled up inside that was just waiting to explode like fireworks on the Fourth of July.

We all got dressed in shorts and shirts and grabbed our tuxes, shirts, bow ties and shoes and headed to the stretch pure white limousine that was waiting outside to take us to the church. As we drove through the streets of Akron, Ohio on our way to Greater Temple Baptist Church my mind reverted back to the last time I was in a limousine, when we were traveling through Cleveland, Ohio on our way to the Crematory where I would last see my mom's face in the flesh. The onlookers peered the same way that day as they had done more than ten years ago trying to see if there was someone famous in the car. I, however, didn't have a sense of something ending but instead a joy that something spectacular was about to commence. I had no tears of pain nor of joy for that matter, at least not yet. My heart was not weighed down but instead was full of electricity because I had been able to convince this woman whom I loved to trust me with her heart , body and mind forever. I wished the limo driver could get to the church faster but we didn't want him breaking any traffic laws. We arrived at the church and hurriedly exited with our belongings because the limo had to travel about five miles up the hill to my sister-in-law and brother-in-law's apartment where Robin and bridesmaids where all congregated. Robin had actually stayed in Cleveland the night before in order to get her hair washed, permed and cut early the morning of the wedding.

As we waited for the ladies to arrive me and my groomsmen used the Pastor's office to change. We were able to transform from shorts and shirts that were more appropriate for a game of basketball to me in my all white tux and them in their black opal tux with the black pearl bow tie and the white tuxedo shirt. We all looked like we could double as members of the Great Britain Royal Court. My chocolate skin was accentuated by the all-white tuxedo, the white tuxedo shirt, the white bow tie, the white socks and the white shoes.

Robin's intent was to have the same philosophy with her wedding attire. Her dress was pure white with diamond like beads streaming throughout the dress, more pronounced however on her sleeves and neck. Her veil was white but transparent enough that I could see her beautiful brown eyes as they sparkled when the sunlight hit them and I saw a rainbow in them as the light reflected off of her tears. I couldn't see her eyes until after her my brother-in-law Ted Williams walked her down the aisle. Ted was the appropriate substitute for her dad Mr. Nelson. I wished, however, that Mr. Nelson had been given the opportunity to present his daughter to me. He was a difficult person to impress but I believe that prior to his death I had earned his respect and trust to take care of his baby girl like or better than he did and that's what a father looks for in the man to whom he will entrust his daughter.

I was supposed to see her sooner than I did but my nephews Steve Doaty and Gaylon Clark II got lost coming to the church. Once they arrived we had all my groomsmen: Mike, Chucky, Phillip, Gaylon, Steve and my best man John. Robin's bridesmaids were beautiful: my niece LaWanda, Yvonne, my sister, Tammy , my niece Toni and Joyce as the maid of honor. The ladies were all dressed in a silk fuchsia dress that covered ankles but exposed their backs, shoulders and arms. They would need the manmade air conditioning due to the 95 degree (The temperature inside the church was set on blazing due to a lack of central air conditioning).

Pastor Wright did not adhere to our request to keep it short and instead took the opportunity to address a church full of people about the importance of marriage and family. I appreciated it to an extent because I hoped others who were married or contemplating it in the near future did so too. He addressed topics, albeit in a microwave fashion due to a restraint on time, that dealt with what life time commitment to each other meant, and not to in-laws. Prior to his conversation my good friend from law school John Deas, with the help of my brother-in-law Jeffrey Sims on the piano, sang Stevie Wonder's "Ribbon in the Sky" My nephew James Jackson, dressed in his Air Force uniform, with the dark blue pants and jacket, loaded with patches, medals and other ornaments indicating his rank, he had a low fade haircut and a stern face with no signs of a smile in sight was responsible for pulling the runner down the aisle. Our twin nephews, Justin and Jason Evans, followed James down the aisle as the ring bearers. Shortly after they concluded my Niece Karese Ryan and her partner in crime my Baby girl Lauren walked down the aisle in their matching, puffy white dresses and white patent leather shoes. The flower girls didn't drop flowers as tradition usually requires but instead handed out roses to the family and friends on both sides of the aisle that were sitting on the end of the pews.

Pastor Wright's words rang loud in my ears, mind and heart like woofer speakers. I virtually yelled my vows to Robin so not only could she hear but that everyone else who was there could be a witness to what I said and hold me accountable when I didn't live up to those promises I made. Robin and I were very sincere about our commitment to each other, to Lauren and to our future children. We spiritually sealed our marriage with Communion with our Lord and Savior Jesus Christ and then we physically sealed the marriage with a long, French kiss that had our guests expressing their satisfaction with a chorus of oohs and awes. We would later receive our friends and family as husband and wife and then leave to take a plethora of pictures at local garden in Akron.

The wedding reception was held at Tangiers which was an inconvenience for some family but they sacrificed for Robin and me and endured the long day in Akron. Instead of the traditional wedding speeches, Robin and I were roasted by her family, my family, and of course my friends from college. One of my friends from college didn't realize that Robin and I were going to be roasted when he accepted the invitation but he relished the moment when he was asked to speak during the wedding. Andre Perry, a college classmate and track teammate, walked feverishly from his table toward the microphone and belted out a name that I believed was buried deep under the hallowed halls of Allegheny College. Andre said while he laughed in between sentences, "While everybody is talking about Robin's family nickname of Bobbie Jean we had a nickname for Mike as well. We called him the "Mole."" There was some spattering of laughter but not much until he revealed why they called me the "Mole." "He got that nickname because we would rarely see him during the day. But come nighttime, usually between 11 p.m. and 2 a.m. , he would be coming back from one of the women's dorms with a back pack on." "We knew he was studying really hard!" Andre strolled to his seat amongst a room full of laughter.

We didn't want to do anything that would make us seem hypocritical and therefore discourage people from seeking God so there was no open bar. We did, however, engage in other reception traditions: John and Joyce gave speeches, Robin and I thanked all of our guests for sharing this special day with us and I took off her garter belt in a most ingenious manner. I convinced Robin to go along with an idea that I got from watching another wedding reception. I sat Robin in the middle of the dance floor and then I bent down on my knees directly in front of her. I threw the bottom portion of her massive gown slightly in the air in order to place my head underneath but not high enough for others to see what only I and her OB-GYN would see. I then tickled her leg for a few moments and then resurfaced from under her dress with a pair of my boxer shorts in my right hand and I raised them high above my head instead of the small circular piece of cloth- the garter. There was a loud roar of laughter from the family and friends who had stayed despite the fact that we didn't have any dancing. I eventually returned underneath Robin's dress and removed her garter with my hands and then held it in my mouth. We did end the evening with Robin throwing her bouquet and I threw the garter belt.

Our honeymoon was a seven day unforgettable adventure. We decided to travel to Montego Bay, Jamaica at stayed at the Sand Castles hotel. We swam in the crystal clear Pacific Ocean, ate exotic food, shopped, climbed the Dunn's River Falls, survived the bus trip on the road to Ocho Rios and grew closer in those seven days. We, however, also couldn't wait to leave because we also experienced a fire, being bitten my numerous mosquitos all over our bodies, we had numerous room maintenance issues, staff entering the room during intimate moments and the airlines attempt to keep us in Jamaica due to our inability to provide our original birth certificates that were being housed in Cleveland City Hall. We had one of the craziest honeymoons on record but I wouldn't have changed anything since I experienced it with the love of my life-Robin.

I wanted to include a chapter or two about my courtship, wedding and honeymoon with Robin to further illustrate how I was the least likely guy to be involved in this type of relationship. The one relationship I watched as a child was rift with violence, disrespect, lack of trust, lack of true commitment (No marriage) and a lack of public displays of affection. I was doing something that I hadn't routinely seen, other than on television and one cousin Sonny, and yet it felt natural and right. I knew that my future didn't have to be a repeat of my past. I was able to move from those memories and make some great ones of my own.

FINGING MY BIOLOGICAL FATHER

After we returned from the honeymoon I told Robin that I was interested in recommencing my efforts to find my biological father. I had made some attempts when I was in college, however, they proved to be unsuccessful and it was just a curiosity that would never diminish or disappear until I found him alive or dead. I had visions of my father being a wealthy man with a huge house located on acres of land with another family. I had dreams of him meeting me and taking me to his home to meet my siblings and me being welcomed as though I had lived my entire life with them. I imagined being driven to his home in a Mercedes Benz, with a horseshoe drive, and large white pillars in front of the house that held up the three story home. I saw the massive chandelier that hung from the ceiling with a thousand lights and gold glimmering like the Sun. I saw a table fit for a king with a white metallic like cloth trimmed in silver that had the finest china and a bountiful amount of food spread across a table that sat more than sixteen people. I saw myself being immersed by family with hugs and kisses as well as being bombarded with questions. I had those dreams as kid once I discovered that Allen wasn't my biological father but as time passed and I got older and more mature my dreams of that type of meeting faded. I nonetheless wanted to meet the man who was partly responsible for me being given a chance at life.

Robin and I retrieved the phone book and began calling all the Richard Solomon's in the phone book. I dialed the number and there were four rings, my mouth was dry, my hand was shaking due to the anxiety I was feeling anticipating someone picking up the phone. After the fourth ring there was a click, but it was only to suggest that I leave a message. The next few numbers I called were disconnected. I wasn't getting a little discouraged but at the same time my nervousness was decreasing for every call. I then called the next number and on the second ring a wonderful older female voice answered. I asked her, "Is this the home of Richard Solomon?" and she said "Yes. May I help you?" I then told her, "My name is Michael

Ryan and I'm trying to locate my father. His name is Richard Solomon." The woman then chuckled and said "Honey, I seriously doubt that he is your father. He and I have been married for twenty-five years and we have seven children. If he had any other children I would have known about it!" I said, "Ma'am thank you and you're probably right. I hope I didn't get him into any trouble." She assured me that he wasn't in any trouble and that was because she could tell my ethnicity by my voice and said in so many terms that her husband Richard Solomon could not have been my father! I then decided to make one more call after looking at the address for the last name listed in the phone book. The address was West. 25th, which is where some housing projects are located for those who could only afford subsidized housing. I dialed the numbers with some trepidation and anxiety. The phone rang twice before there was a male voice on the other end. He had a very deep, distinct African American male voice and said "Hello", I then responded "Is this Richard Solomon?" He said "Yes. Who is this?" I then said, " My name is Michael Ryan. Do you know a woman named Marguerite better known as Peggy?" He then said, "Michael? My son Michael?" I was overcome with a rush of emotions. A few tears flowed from my eyes, my heart was beating so fast it felt like it would jump out of my chest and I was breathing so fast it felt like I had just completed a hundred meter dash. Robin grabbed my hand and clutched it so tightly that my hand seemed to blend into her hands. She put her other arm around my shoulder. I got myself under composure but I was still very nervous and didn't ask many questions. Instead he suggested that we meet and I acquiesced.

We scheduled a time for me to come over to his apartment building and I drove there by myself. Robin asked if I needed someone to go with me but I informed her that I needed to do this on my own. A few days later I drove over to the west side of Cleveland. Ohio. I traveled past Longwood projects as I drove down Woodland and then drove past Tri-C and eventually past Public Square. I wasn't too anxious until I started to approach the Detroit-Superior bridge because after I drove over the bridge I would be only yards away from the notorious West 25th High Rise. It was known as a place where crime, drug dealing and drug using was rampant. I wasn't concerned since I had grown up in that environment for most of my adolescence; my wife's uneasiness about the area was another factor in my decision to go alone. As I got to the bridge my heart began to race, thoughts of what my biological dad looked like began to form in my mind. I wondered if he was taller or shorter than me, if he had the same complexion, did he possess a slim athletic build like me. I knew that my vision of him being this affluent person was less of a possibility after speaking to him and realizing that he was living in subsidized housing. Nevertheless, I was excited to meet him because some people who are similarly situated to my circumstances never get to meet their biological dad. I had a chance to ask probe, to see, to hug, to detract to run the gamut of emotions that some only wish they could. He was alive and well, in his right mind and he could provide some answers to some very burning questions. After crossing the bridge I eventually made it to the apartment building. I searched for his name on the intercom system and pressed his apartment number. He answered and then buzzed me upstairs to his apartment. My heart was racing like a NASCAR engine at the Daytona 500 as I walked towards the door after getting off the elevator. I got to the apartment door and knocked semi-violently on the steel doors. I could hear his feet dragging across the floor, as though he were limping, to answer the door. He opened the door and the first thing that protruded out at me was his brow. It looked as though someone had taken my brow and placed it on his head. We were both very slim but with a recognizable athletic build. You could tell that he had muscle definition but not much fat surrounding the muscles, just like me. His ears were miniature as well and looked like they belonged on a child's head not a twenty-four year old or a forty-eight year old. Despite the fact that he had a walker he was still taller than me even as he bent down a bit to walk around the apartment. My biological dad's disability resulted from being injured on his job. He relayed to me that suffered a "stroke" while working that caused his injuries. We would later learn that it wasn't a stroke but instead was the beginning symptoms of Multiple Sclerosis (Better Known as MS). As I ventured inside I saw pictures of uncles and aunts that I would meet years later. The one picture that stood out among all of them was my brother's- David and his family. David was standing next to his wife Thelma and my niece Latanya was just a baby. My brother's entire body frame took up the width and length of the picture frame. My dad first response when I walked inside the apartment was "You're short!" I thought he was comparing me to himself, and while I was shorter than him it wasn't by too much. He was approximately 6'3" and I was about 5'10". He was actually comparing me to my brother. I asked him "How tall is Dave?" and he responded "He's at least 6'8" and maybe 6'9" 280-300 lbs." While he may have questioned if I was his son based on Dave's gigantic build he couldn't deny the "Solomon Brow", the dark complexion, the smooth texture of the skin on our face, lack of facial hair, the protruding but sexy full bottom lip and our similar builds was a dead giveaway.

We sat and talked for an hour, mostly about my mother and how they met. He had heard about her passing but didn't think it was appropriate to come to the service. He didn't discuss why today was the first day of our lives that we had met. Neither one of us broached the subject. I did discover that he was one of ten kids and that I had a combined eight uncles and aunts and one aunt who was murdered before I was born. We talked about my paternal Grandmother Gloria Solomon and the love and compassion she had for my dad and his siblings. Ironically, when I told my dad my birthdate he informed me that was my grandmother's birthday as well. I told him about my wife, my daughter, my sister, niece, grandma, my mother-in-law and brother-in-law. We spoke about sports and he told me stories of his legendary prowess on the football field. I then told him I must of inherited his football skills because I was a good player until I broke my leg. There were times when the conversation was awkward but we found a way to break through by looking at photo albums or making small talk. We were both reserved and quiet by nature and so it was challenging at first. I then questioned him about whether his quietness was mistaken as weakness by any of his friends or enemies. He revealed to me a trait which I then knew, even though I already concluded when I walked in the door, that he was my dad wherein he stated that "I am generally a quiet guy and I don't initiate or agitate situations but if someone keeps aggravating me I will retaliate and finish it."

After about an hour of talking I asked him for some pictures. He let me have three pictures: one with him by himself; another one with my Uncles Harrison Solomon and Anthony Solomon and then the picture with my brother Dave, his wife and my Tanya. He then walked me downstairs and to my car. I didn't say his name or call him dad at any time nor did he refer to me as son. We were trying to fill each other out. We both, however, reached out to the other simultaneously with open arms to give each other a hug. He then said "I want to see you again. It will get better." I said "I would like that very much!" I got in my car, honked my horn and drove off. I was committed on that day to making the effort to cement a good relationship with my biological dad. I, however, didn't want to impact the burgeoning relationship I had with my father (stepdad) Allen who wasn't aware that I knew he wasn't my biological father (At least I didn't tell him I knew). When I drove out of the parking lot, little did I know it would be more than three years before I would see my biological dad again. Law school, graduation, preparation for the bar, my biological dad's health worsening all lead to our inability to reconnect.

HARD WORK EQUALS JUST REWARDS

I admit that I wasn't one of the top students at Cleveland-Marshall College of Law's Class of 1996. I, however, was also not a part of the bottom 10% either. I worked diligently in each of my classes and I didn't earn anything lower than a C in any of my classes. I was able to secure some high marks B+ and A's in other courses that was noticed by individuals in the financial aid office. It was almost like De ja vu wherein the financial aid office at Cleveland-Marshall was staying abreast of my progress just like they did at Allegheny. My hard work and good results caused the financial aid office to recommend me for the Louis Stokes Scholarship. My name, along with my transcript was submitted to the scholarship committee and I was deemed a recipient of one of the 1993 Louis Stokes scholarship awards. A few weeks later I also received the prestigious Cleveland-Marshall Alumni Association Scholarship which was given to a select group of third year law students out of a large applicant pool.

The money was a blessing because Robin and I were struggling financially with just her paycheck and my part-time employment at the City of Cleveland's Law Department. Robin and I were responsible for paying a portion of the rent and the utilities for the home we shared with Ma and my brother-in-law Ted. We had the additional requirement of paying for Lauren's preschool as well. The fees I needed to pay for my bar examination package (The fee to take the exam along with background check fee and other related fees), along with the bar preparation course were going to add to an already stressful situation. I could see and feel the frustration mounting on Robin and knew that we needed a blessing. Normally scholarships are awarded before the school year begins and then applied to your tuition and thereby reducing the amount of financial aid (grants or loans) you are awarded or need respectively. My scholarships, however, were awarded after my financial aid packages had been completed and distributed, accordingly I was able to use the money to help defray costs we had accumulated at home and to pay for the items I needed post-law school to help me prepare to pass the bar examination. It was just another demonstration of me being able to take advantage of God's favor by working hard to put myself in the position where God could bless me.

The scholarship money made going home a little easier. While Robin never made any direct statements expressing her dissatisfaction with our money situation she did state on several occasions "I can't wait until you can work full time." "We need a place that we can call our own." Those were phrases that let me know that my focus should be shifting from school to work. I, however, had a few more milestones to reach before I could collect a reasonable salary as an attorney. First thing I needed to complete was law school. I had begun studying for my final exam in my last semester courses well before the Cleveland Marshall Alumni Association Award Reception. I, however, studied in earnest after I received the award and the money was deposited into my account. I didn't have any trouble with my final courses and prepared myself for graduation.

Graduation day at Cleveland-Marshall School of Law was more formal and exciting than Allegheny. I enjoyed this graduation more because it was at home, I had the support of a my wife and daughter not my girlfriend and my baby and I was in a select group being one of only four African American males and the youngest of that group. In fact, the 2000 Census statistics illustrated that only 4.8% of the more than 19,000,000 African Americans over the age of 25 had acquired an advanced degree. More specifically, only 2,855 (7.2%) of the 39,920 people who were awarded a Juris Doctorate in 1996 were African American.

Law school combined with a new marriage took a toll on me and that was evident in the weight loss. I was already a slim man but looked emaciated on graduation day. It, however, didn't detract from the megawatt smile I had all day long. I had a fresh hair cut that faded my sides with the waves flowing at the top. I had my black leather shoes, with holes in the bottom that I wore out running for the Regional Transit Authority (RTA) bus when I was going to law school and/or work. I put on one of the suits my friend, Alfred Miller's, dad gave me. Robin was a vision of beauty. Her caramel skin glistened when it reflected off the brilliant orange skirt suit that she wore. She looked like an attorney's wife.

The graduation was held at the beautiful Palace Theatre that was located a block away from the law school. While my name was not in lights the marquee did mention Congratulations to the Cleveland-Marshall College of Law Spring Class of 1996. The interior of the building was immaculate. It had the architecture reminiscent of the old European theaters. The first floor had a huge ceiling with beautiful woodwork. We assembled outside the theatre doors talking, laughing and relaxing before our big moment. Due to my last name I was situated on the second floor of the theatre and would have to walk down the massive white winding stairs in order to get to my seat for the ceremony. Standing in that line with me were sons and daughters of lawyers and judges along with not just first generation college graduates but law school graduates as well. On that day you couldn't tell us apart. Education was the great equalizer and that was most evident on that wonderful day. I was given the same tools, the same opportunities, the same discretion, the same assessment and was able to achieve the same result~ Juris Doctorate. I patiently sat until they called our row to approach the stage. I had an extra skip in my step as I approached the stage and everyone could see it. The person who crossed the stage before me received a spattering of applause. When my name was called, however, a thunderous ovation ensued that startled Dean/ Professor White and me as well. His eyes enlarged and he and I both rapidly turned our heads towards the second floor seating area. He started to chuckle as did I and he commented " Are all of those people your family?" I said, "Yes". I was only expecting to see a few of my family because we were given a limit on the amount of tickets we were allotted and thus when I saw my cousins and aunts along with Robin, Lauren, Ma, Grandma Edna, my sister, Karese, my father Allen and other family and friends I was elated and nearly snatched my diploma due to my understanding of the significance of this event. I was not only a representative of my family but also of the neighborhoods where I grew up. Not only did Michael John Ryan make it but Mount Pleasant, Miles Avenue, E. 116th off of Kinsman, Inglewood (California), Union Avenue and the Longwood Projects made it too. I carried the hopes and dreams of the older people who only wished they had a chance to achieve the level of success that I did. I also was the reality for those young people who lived in the impoverished areas that I just mentioned; They had no more excuses.

After the ceremony Robin and I made a brief appearance at the reception that was sponsored by the law school because Robin was pestering me about going to retrieve a desk one of her co-workers was gifting me for graduation. I was amazed by the fact that none of my family had come to the reception other than my cousin Sean Ryan from Beaver Falls, Pa. He had parked his car at my Grandma Edna's house and rode with someone else to the ceremony and we were giving him a ride back to the house with two detours. Prior to going to get the desk from Robin's colleague I told my wife, since I wasn't having any celebration, to stop at a local restaurant to get my favorite dish- Barbeque Ribs. Robin was urging me to move faster and I was oblivious as to why since the desk wasn't going anywhere without me and Sean moving it.

We eventually drove into the front parking lot where she worked and she distracted me from looking towards the right side parking lot. We parked the car in the back of the building and she tried to convince me to wear my graduation cap, but I refused indicating that it would get in the way of me being able to move the desk. I did relent regarding my robe and said I would show her co-worker my robe and then take it off to move the desk. We walked up the stairs and turned the corner and there was a huge shout
"Surprise!" and all of my family and friends who had attended the graduation or missed it but wanted to share in the celebration was present. I was so surprised that I was sprawled over the top of a garbage can with my mouth wide open in amazement.

My wife was the orchestrator of the entire event. She secured the usage of the cafeteria, she ordered the food, the cake, organized the family and designed the deceptive plan to get me from the law school reception to my own surprise one. Pastors Paul Carrington and Beverly Johnson, dear family friends, came to celebrate along with my cousin Cherellee, my cousin Chucky from California and other significant family members and friends. I thanked my wife profusely both publicly and privately for her love and efforts. I then reminded everyone that this was only the second step. I had successfully completed one step, passing the multi-state professional responsibility exam, before graduation. I, however, had to successfully complete the final and most grueling step- passing the bar examination.

My preparation for the bar examination began with me requesting and receiving a leave of absence from my law clerk position with the City of Cleveland. I was advised and accepted the advice of learned attorneys regarding making passage of the bar a priority. Many of my advisees urged me to stop working and to treat my preparation as a job. I did exactly as they suggested. I would get up at 8 a.m. and study for an hour. I would then wake Lauren up, wash her up, get her clothes ready for the day, feed her and attempt to braid her hair. I would then allow Lauren to either play with her toys or watch television. I would then return to studying for another hour or two. I would take a break and make Lauren something for lunch. She and I would then walk to one of the two parks near us. I held her hand pretty tight but also had earphones on listening to tapes I had made going over the material I needed to remember for the bar examination. Once we arrived at the park Lauren would run to the sliding board. Once she was bored with that I put her in the swing and pushed her for close to thirty minutes. I would push her slow then fast. I would take the swing and push her forward while maintaining control of the swing as I bent underneath the swing and then extended my arms up to place Lauren high in the air. I would then release the swing and allow her to travel higher and faster to her delight. We would then return back home with a few hours left before her mom returned home from work. Prior to her mom returning I would sit Lauren on my lap and read the study guides to her while at the same time soaking the information in for my own edification. Once Robin came home Lauren's only complaints concerned her hair, which Robin redid a few times and what she ate for breakfast. There was one occasion when I accidentally poured a huge pile of sugar on her oatmeal. Lauren said "I'm not eating that!" and became suspect about most of the things I fed her that summer. Normally I wouldn't have been the primary caretaker for Lauren but my mother-in-law had traveled to North Dakota to visit with my sister-in-law, Vera. It gave me and Lauren time to bond and taught me how to balance being a parent with taking care of other important responsibilities. When Robin came home it wasn't a study reprieve in fact I then left to attend a new bar exam preparation course. I went to the evening review for four hours a day Monday thru Friday. I would cut my studying to three to four hours on Saturday and nothing on Sunday so I could allow my mind to rest. The West Bar Review wasn't as established as Bar-Bri, which was the more preferred and had a higher success rate than most bar review courses. I had an opportunity to review both programs and compare their costs and despite the relatively small margin of costs of West Bar compared to Bar-Bri I felt more comfortable with the former program. I liked West Bar because of the time, in the evening, as well as the national law school lecturers that were assigned to teach each course. Additionally, West Bar had several practice tests that were conducted close to the actual exam, which was also a difference between them and Bar-Bri. The practice exams, which included the essay portions as well, were timed and gave us the ability to get better acclimated to the time pressures along with the intellectual challenge the exam presented. When I returned home from the West Bar exam preparatory I implored the same tactics I used to study in elementary, middle school, high school and college. I would read over the material I just reviewed for approximately twenty minutes. I would then take a five minute break and watch television or simply rest my brain and do nothing. I would then review the study sheets I had prepared that had most of the important information I believed that would be on a test. I would study those sheets by repeating the information, line by line, at least five times. My philosophy would be to engage in that process for twenty minutes and then relax between five or ten minutes and then go back to studying for another twenty minutes. I used flash cards, I read my notes, I enlisted Robin to quiz me, I completed old bar exams and I would write the answers to the questions.

After approximately two and half months of studying for the Ohio Bar Exam the day for me to travel to Columbus had arrived – July 29, 1996. It was the day before the first day of the bar examination and I wasn't overly nervous or excited about taking the exam. I knew that minorities, especially African American men, didn't fare well on their first attempts at passing the bar exam. Additionally, the minimum passing score had been increased from 375 to 406. I would not let those facts deter me, because I felt that I had adequately prepared myself for the exam by studying extremely hard and praying at the same rate. I had successfully made it through my bar exam character interview that was the last hurdle to taking the test. Now I would be given the chance to demonstrate to the examiners that I was worthy of being a part of one of the greatest professions in the world.

I persevered through two and a half days of the most grueling academic exercise of my life. I was thankful that the Olympics were on because they were, because of the American victories in 1996, a relief to the stinging migraine that I had from all the reading and analyzing and writing that I had to complete in those two and half days. So instead of studying like a number of other Bar takers had told me that they were doing, I decided to study a small amount and relax and rely on what I did to prepare before I arrived in Columbus for the exam; if I didn't know it then I wasn't going to learn it in one night.

The bar exam was one of the most taxing events in my life. I was challenged mentally and physically by the process. For all three days we began at 8 a.m. and ended at 4 p.m. except for the third day we ended at noon. We did receive a one hour lunch for the first two days. The exam covered the basic legal subjects: Criminal Law, Civil Procedure, Criminal Procedure, Contracts, Torts, Evidence, Property, Constitutional law, Business Associations and some Tax law. The latter subjects were assessed via the most grueling multiple choice exam I had ever taken as well as essay questions. The first day was all essay questions, and the vast amount of writing that I had been compelled to complete over the last seven years made me very comfortable drafting those responses. I, however, left the second day, whose primary focus was on the multiple choice questions from hell, with the worst headache I had ever experienced. If I wanted to study for a significant period after the second day I couldn't because my head was pounding like there was a small man inside my skull with a large snare drum with huge sticks striking it as hard as he could and as rapidly as he could. I woke up the last day with renewed energy because I knew it was the last day, it was only half a day, there were no multiple choice questions and it was my twenty-fifth (25) birthday. I completed the exam and felt that I had done well enough to pass. My fellow LCOP classmates: John Deas, Russell Tye and Anthony Stevenson, all African American men, had met before the last night and all had a sincere belief that we would pass it. John, Russ and Anthony had been studying with each other as well as other groups. I, however, did most of my studying alone. They had some doubts about my ability to pass because of my isolated studying habits. I assured them that I would be fine and that I didn't intend on making reservations for a hotel in February 1997 for the next bar exam.

When I returned home from taking the bar exam things were less stressful. I began working forty hours as a law clerk with the City of Cleveland's Civil Law Department; albeit at the same rate when I was only working twenty hours due to work study restrictions. I did not qualify for the outstanding public servant medical benefits but at least I was providing more financial assistance for my new family. I also was more friendly, more approachable, I socialized more often with family and friends. I just felt like a three ton weight had been lifted once I completed the exam. I was able to spend more time with Robin and Lauren and build the foundation for our family. Robin and I began discussions about moving to a home that we could call our own. We would travel throughout greater Cleveland looking at homes that were for sale or land that was available in new developments. It was exciting for me because I generally knew about renting. I knew homeownership would be a huge change and a lot of responsibility but I was prepared for it. While I was nervous about the pending bar results I wasn't overly anxious or petrified to discover how well I did on the exam.

The summer seemed to drag on for months in 1996. I wanted the end of October to arrive at break neck speed. I was given more responsibilities at the Law Department. I was drafting more motions and of course forwarding the completed motions to the attorneys I was assigned to assist so they could sign them. I was preparing questions for depositions but not allowed to ask them because I was not officially licensed. It was frustrating on one hand but also gratifying because they were trusting me to research, analyze and then make decisions similar to what the attorneys were doing. The administration was giving me the experience I needed to hit the ground running when I successfully passed the bar. I enjoyed the time I worked at the law department and had the chance to work under some very talented attorneys. Ron, whose last name escapes me, looked like Clark Kent. Although, he was not a superhero is intellect was on par with them. He had a very acute intellect regarding tort law and municipal corporation responsibility. He assisted his section chief on many of the law suits filed for abuse by the Cleveland Police Department (Section 1983 Cases- Federal Cases) I learned a lot about case preparation, negotiation and civil litigation from Ron. My two favorite role models were Lessie Milton and Joe Jerse. They were two of the best civil litigators I had the chance to observe. They were tough labor negotiators on behalf of the City and Mayor White relied upon them to find case law to support his positions. I watched them dismantle witnesses in arbitration cases. I completed tons of research and wrote memorandums of law regarding issues I researched on their behalf.. They provided critical feedback that made me a better legal writer. They were very honest regarding weaknesses I displayed but also very encouraging when I did well on an assigned project. Lessie was so enamored with my progress that she was on a campaign to make sure I got a job at the law department once I passed the bar. I appreciated the help that Lessie, and I believe Joe as well, was providing but my desire was to begin my career as an Assistant Prosecuting attorney either with the City of Cleveland or Cuyahoga County.

I wanted to begin as a criminal prosecutor because I was well aware that I would be given an immediate opportunity to engage in litigation. While I enjoyed research my true desire was to stand in a courtroom and argue cases before judges and juries. It was the competitor in me that drew me to litigation. Me versus another or other trained litigators was similar to battles that I waged on the football field and the track. I wanted to use my skills to display my intelligence but more importantly to speak on behalf of my client, the people of the State of Ohio/City of Cleveland, when a wrong had been committed by a member of our community. I began my legal career as a mediator in that very office and was influenced by many of the attorneys there like Ed Buelow, Brian Fritz, Richard Kray, Pinkey Carr, Antia

Laster-Mays, Lou Bonacci , Rueben Sheperd, George Pace Jr and the Chief at the time Carolyn Watts-Allen. They were a group of outstanding professionals and they taught me a lot in the year I worked as a mediator about being a prosecutor and it was one of the factors I considered in pursuing a career as an Assistant Prosecuting Attorney for the City of Cleveland.

I could hardly sleep the night before the bar results would be released. I was like a kid on Christmas Eve waiting for Santa Claus to arrive and give me the best present I have ever received. I may have gotten three hours of sleep and had tossed and turned all night. The results would be available by phone starting at 7 a.m. I applied my Grandma Edna's sage advice, "Expect the best but prepare for the worst," by taking the day off of work. Many would say the odds were against an individual like me being able to rise above all of the chaos I experienced as a child to become an attorney. If I were placed in a line up with other test takers and they read my bio I would be the least likely person to be in the same position as my counter parts. I wasn't supposed to be the person representing anyone, actually I was supposed to be the one needing representation. I stood on the doorstep of history for my family and my community. My success would be a model for so many people who were hopeless, who lacked self-confidence, who had been dismissed because of life circumstances. I thought about the times when I could have given up because the work was too tough. I thought about the times I refused to go out and stayed at home study, I remember the times I was being influenced to sell drugs or rob someone so I could get money to eat or buy needed clothes or shoes and I declined. I recalled the times I wanted to give up on God but I remembered that he refused to give up on me.

I got out of the bed at 6:50 a.m. and located the number that we were advised to call. I made sure that I didn't disturb Robin because it was so early in the morning. I gingerly walked down the stairs so that I could call without any interruption. I sat on the edge of the couch in the same place I did when I first spoke to my biological father and dialed the number at approximately 6:55 a.m. I got a busy signal. I hit re-dial and got another busy signal. Clearly, other people had the same idea that I did. I then waited a few minutes and hit re-dial again. No success busy signal. I hit re-dial a few more times all to no avail busy signals each time. I then waited another two minutes and noticed it was approximately 7:10 a.m. and I hit re-dial and I heard the other line ring. A wonderfully pleasant young woman eventually answered the line and said "Good morning. Can I have the name of the person you are inquiring about?" I said with a scratchy but confident voice "Michael John Ryan from Cleveland, Ohio" She took a few seconds to locate my name and said with a cheerful voice "Congratulations you passed!" I said "Thank You" while trying to contain my excitement. I then sprinted up the stairs, where Robin was already standing, and yelled to the top of my lungs, having no regard for Ma, Ted or Lauren who were all still asleep "I passed. I passed. I passed the bar exam." I grabbed Robin around her waist and kissed her, with bad breath and all right on her lips. I swung her around and she said "Congrats Mike. I'm so proud of you."

After alerting the entire house about my accomplishment I phoned my Grandma Edna and my sister and they were very happy and both stated "Congratulations! I'm so proud of you." My sister also added, " Were you expecting any other result?" She has always believed in me and is astonished when I don't accomplish something. My next phone call was to the Cleveland Prosecutor's office. Athena Cobb, the office manager, answered the phone and upon me stating my name said "Congratulations Mike!" " I guess you want to talk to Ms. Allen correct?" I said, " Of course I would love too." I was eventually connected to Mrs. Allen and she also expressed congratulatory remarks but was more concerned with giving me a much better reward for reaching my goal- a job. She scheduled a day for me to come down and interview for one of the vacant prosecuting positions. There were only two African American males who held the position of Assistant Prosecuting Attorney for the City and one of the First Assistant to the Chief so he rarely appeared in court.

I believe that my hiring was a foregone conclusion. I had served as a mediator in that very office and was well aware of the complaint process. I knew about the review prosecutor's had to engage in regarding allegations of criminal mischief. I had a very good rapport with all of the prosecutors and as I stated earlier I really wanted to cut my teeth regarding litigation in the prosecutor's office. I was hired and became only one of three African American male prosecuting attorneys. I was a symbol of hope for many that walked into the courtroom and saw me there, with complete autonomy regarding my cases, making decisions and analyzing criminal cases. Many were proud to see me in that position both because of my race and my age. I was twenty-five and fresh out of law school and excited about the work.

I quickly became disenchanted because of the volume of individuals who looked like me that were consistent participants, as parties, in the varied criminal cases I was assigned to prosecute and review to determine whether charges were appropriate. I did not give people favorable treatment, giving a hook up, because of the similarity of my culture with their culture. Nor did I exact unreasonable or unfair compromises or demands regarding pending cases in the courtroom I was assigned to for a three month period for those who weren't from a similar background. I had some power but I chose not to abuse it and used it as a tool to teach. I became involved in community events that discussed educating individuals about the criminal process. I knew the way I could engage the community and thereby make a dent in the dockets without jeopardizing my livelihood was through participating in the community events as well as participating in career days at schools throughout Greater Cleveland.

My initial training as an official prosecuting attorney was completed by the First Assistant George Pace, Jr., who was, and still is, an outstanding litigator. George taught me how to make sure I knew all of the strengths and weaknesses of each case. It would require me to read through the complaints and tickets, which would be voluminous, the day prior to the pre-trial. I made what I thought was a good impression on many of the defense attorneys that represented their clients by providing a thorough explanation of the facts while not giving the entire theory of the state/city's case. George taught me how to negotiate cases whether the state/city had a strong or weak case. I quickly learned that my job wasn't to simply try and secure a large amount of convictions but to ensure that justice was served. At times that meant dismissing matters because they were wrongfully charged. It meant reducing a charge to one that properly fit with the facts deduced from conversations with the complaining party, witnesses, physical evidence or lack thereof and the alleged offenders' claims. I wanted to make sure that people who were wrong received the an appropriate and adequate retribution for their conduct. Sometimes that meant a fine and court costs while at other times it meant the same along with a suspended jail sentence and probation. It, however, at other times meant that the person should be removed from society for an extended period of time to remind them we live a society of rules and they cannot cavalierly ignore those rules and not think that there were consequences for their behavior.

George was also instrumental in helping me develop my jury trial style. He taught me the technicalities of preparing for a jury trial and bench trial. I watched him conduct several bench trials and knew how important interviewing witnesses were before a trial in order to avoid surprises. I knew how to completely dissect police reports and witnesses statements in order to develop questions and prepare for questions that might be asked by opposing counsel. I actually prepared a direct examination for my witnesses as well as questions I thought the defense counsel would ask on cross-examination so I could find ways to counter them and also what to possibly object to as well. George explained how to paint a picture for a jury so as to place them in room, on the street, in the park, at the school or wherever the incident was alleged to have occurred. I kept my opening statements short and only indicated what I thought the evidence would show as opposed to being brash and claiming what I knew it would show; too many times witnesses change their mind, perspective or simply forget. I then put all of those skills together in a mock jury trial a few days before my first official trial. George and I stayed after work one evening and with the permission of Cleveland Municipal Court Judge Salvador Calandra used the actual courtroom to go through all of the stages of a jury trial. After I concluded George expressed his delight in my performance and my development and stated that I would sit second chair at the jury trial and he would lead it for me.

I learned that George was not very forthcoming about his reason for conducting the mock trial, he actually wanted to see if I was prepared. I didn't sit second chair, actually George sat second chair. The only part of the trial that he handled by himself was the rebuttal argument against the defendant's request to acquit the defendant at the close of the prosecution's case. I had interviewed the witnesses weeks before the trial. I had reviewed the police reports and the witness statements and I thought that the charges were appropriate. I did the Voir Dire, selected the jury, the opening statement and I did the direct and re-direct of examination of all of the prosecution witnesses. I was initially nervous when I began the Voir Dire-asking questions of the potential jurors to determine their ability to be fair and impartial. The nervousness dissipated the more questions I asked and the more smiles I saw on the faces of the jurors who were simply proud to see a young African American male in such a respected position. Their smiles made me feel comfortable and the nods of the heads gave me more confidence every minute. I, however, and more importantly my witnesses weren't as persuasive with Judge Calandra. He granted the defendant's request to dismiss the matter (Criminal Rule 29) without it going to the jury. I essentially lost my first jury trial and learned a valuable lesson- make sure you make the proper decision to charge and avoid making people go through procedures that are unnecessary.

I was in my glory as an Assistant Prosecuting Attorney for the City of Cleveland. There, however, was another event that would surpass all of my other accomplishments-the birth of my son Michael Benjamin Ryan. I had been anticipating his birth far longer than the eight months it took for him to develop in my wife's womb. I was probably the happiest, proudest, most protective, most caring husband and father-to-be in the history of a woman's pregnancy. I went to almost every doctor appointment, I went and purchased the most expensive and comfortable maternity clothes for Robin, to her delight. I begrudgingly went to the store at all hours of the day and night to fetch the most bizarre things for Robin to eat when she was craving something unique. My hands were glued to her stomach from the time she began to show until even after Michael was born because I was so accustomed to putting my arms around her waist and stomach to feel and hold my son.

Michael was making an impression even before he arrived. When we had the ultrasound to find out what the sex was for the baby Michael was seated in his mother's womb, with his hands behind his head, his legs spread apart and his manhood sticking straight up; it wasn't difficult to tell there was a Little Michael growing inside of my wife. Michael would also become restless at midnight, which was an omen for his behavior when he was born, and would kick me in the back, through his mom's belly. I would also request my wife to drink some cold water so that I could see him moving. Each time after she digested the ice cold water, I could see the form of her stomach change. Michael would be moving around and many times we watched his tiny fist make an impression in my wife's stomach and see him stretch her stomach from one side to the other. The entire experience was amazing and life altering for me.

I was more anxious than amazed the day he was born. Firstly, a few days before his birth my wife was at home complaining about not feeling well. My brother-in-law Jeffrey Sims, a registered nurse (Now CEO of one of Ohio's Mental Health Facilities), checked her blood pressure and discovered that it was dangerously high. Robin drove to the hospital to talk to her Gynecologist and when Dr. Schneider re-checked her blood pressure he admitted her. I got the news via Robin's tear filled call to me at work. I left work immediately and reported to Hillcrest Hospital in record speed. After several days of tests Dr. Schneider advised us that for the baby's safety and Robin's he was going to perform a cesarean to extract the baby. Robin and I were concerned because her due date was more than five weeks away. Dr. Schneider assured us that Michael would be fine and he gave Robin a shot to help further develop his lungs. After a few more tests and a review of an ultrasound Dr. Schneider sent me to get ready and Robin was assisted by the medical staff.

On Sunday, September 7, 1997, at approximately 12:30 p.m. the second pride and joy of my life came into this world. All five pounds, four ounces and 24 inches of him came in with a small whimper. He was a little Jaundice because of the early birth but was a beautiful, fair skinned baby, with beautiful jet black eyes and silky black hair. His full lips, like mine, along with his full eyebrows, like mine gave him a distinguishing Solomon look. Lauren gave a wonderful description of her brother to a couple that was waiting for a family member to deliver when she said "I have a new baby brother...but he's white." The couple responded, "We'll is that okay with you?" Lauren said in a matter-of fact tone, "Yes!" The doctor remarked how much Michael looked like my mother-in-law, while my brother-in-law Bishop Abraham Wright said he looked just like me. I was the first family member to see him, to hold him and to kiss him because my wife was unable to hold him because of the surgical procedure. I was also the first person to feed him and to change him and I don't mind revealing that he vomited and urinated on his dad.

We have and will always have a special bond because of those initial and subsequent times. I wanted so much to be a father because the examples I had were so lacking. Lauren helped me be a better dad for Michael and I'm grateful God gave me a chance to parent a girl and a boy. I know that my life would be radically different without Michael and Lauren in it and I cannot imagine that life.

I took advantage of the city's paternity leave and provided care for Michael and Robin during his first few days on earth. Robin was still in a precarious health position and Dr. Schneider ordered her to avoid stress or work for at least a day. She, however, couldn't resist feeding her baby boy and I dare not keep him from her all day. Eventually, I did leave for a few hours to clear up some issues with my docket and then returned for good for two weeks to help raise my only son. Robin and I would trade off in terms of changing and feeding Michael. I was more adept at changing him when we got home and avoided being sprinkled again. I had a chance to place this life that I was responsible for in my arms and give him the nourishment he needed to develop into my dreams and expectations for him. He spent countless hours resting his tiny head on my chest and our hearts would beat in a synchronized fashion. He would fall fast asleep and I would soon follow. Robin would try in vain to detach my arms from around his back but my fatherly grip wouldn't let go until she woke me.

THE YOUNG LAWYER BEGINS HIS JOURNEY

I really enjoyed the opportunity that was afforded me by the Prosecutor's Office to get a lot of litigation experience. Prior to my first jury trial I had to gain some courtroom experience dealing with pre-trials, plea agreements and bench trials. Similar to my first time before a jury I was extremely nervous my first day in court with Judge Calandra. I came into the court and my knees were shaking and Judge Calandra just told me "Relax son you'll be just fine" because he heard my voice cracking. After the first or second defendant I had pretty much memorized the speech we were supposed to give and the requests we were supposed to make if we were asking for the court to dismiss a particular charge in lieu of the defendant pleading to another charge. George gave me the spiel and once I did it for about five or six defendants, he said "You know that's pretty good. You got this down pat." I felt comfortable from that point on. He would come up a few more times to Court to assist me but eventually I was there by myself. And of course, the older attorneys, the more seasoned attorneys as well as the defendant would try to take advantage of me, but , I was adamant in terms of what type of agreements I told them what they could plead to and then they would go and talk to their client and then we would negotiate from that point, if at all. There were some things which, I didn't want to plead down; like Domestic Violence cases. Only because we had an office policy of not dismissing those and so we were going forward on a number of those matters to trial or if the parties did not come, then that matter would be dismissed and of course, that was fairly frequent.

While my initial trial was unsuccessful I did get my first guilty verdict for my second jury trial. I believed that each case was very important and I was very conscientious about each case, from traffic case to domestic violence. I, however, was very troubled by the allegations levied against the defendant in my second trial. He was an older but not yet elderly African American man who was accused of trying to lure a pre-teen into his car. The incident occurred a few steps away from the child's home but her mom could not protect her. I applied the skills George taught me in preparing for this trial. I didn't want the same result as my first trial. I interviewed all the potential witnesses. I, however, had my good friend and mentor Pinkey Carr assist me with the young victim because of her apparent fear of males because of this very incident. I reviewed the police reports, the witnesses' statements and the defendant's statements. I went to the scene of the incident and drove from that area to the location where the defendant claimed he was at the time of the incident. I timed the route to determine how long it would take to support my claim that he had enough time to commit the act and get to the location of his alibi. I drove through the neighborhood of manicured lawns, painted or aluminum sided homes and trees that were blooming since it was the beginning of spring. Pinkey had established a good relationship with the young lady so I needed her to sit second chair to provide assistance with the trial but also to do the direct examination of the young victim. Pinkey did a phenomenal job. I did everything else except for the rebuttal closing argument. The jury, eight African American elderly women, took only a few hours to find the older man guilty. The judge ordered him to serve ten days in jail, I thought he deserved more. This young lady was traumatized by this terrible act. She began to revert back to childlike behavior- wetting the bed and separation anxiety. She was deathly afraid of leaving the house and when she had to for school or other activities she would only do so with her mother. His two minute action of driving next to her, opening his yellow and brown 1979 station wagon passenger window and asking her to get into his car caused her to fear most men (regardless of color or age). She was able to provide excellent details of the defendant, his car and his clothing. The police located him in an area that was near this upscale neighborhood in the City of Cleveland.

I was able to hone my skills by building my case with each witness and then of course Pinkey's dynamite direct really helped. I was able to tie the defendant, an average sized male, with more grey than pepper as the color of his hair. He wasn't feeble nor was he stout but somewhere in between. He was confident and secure during his direct but very nervous and confused when he was cross-examined. He was caught in several lies and made illogical claims regarding time and location. He maintained his innocence even up and until he was released from probation, which was not until after he served his ten days at the Cleveland House of Correction. When the jury returned their verdict of guilty it solidified my reason for going to law school and beginning my career as a prosecuting attorney. I was able to provide some vindication, some relief and some belief in the system. I couldn't restore this young lady's sense of normalcy or her innocence but I could establish, on behalf of the city, a position of taking crimes like these against our young as serious and of the highest priority.

My third jury trial was not as successful as my second one. Due to the city prosecutor's office policy after three months with Judge Calandra I was rotated to another judge's courtroom—Judge Angela Stokes. It was one of the toughest rotations I would endure because of the amount of time that one had to dedicate to her docket. She was a very meticulous jurist and took a significant amount of time to make decisions on cases and she requested that I participate in helping individuals acquire the necessary rehabilitation to avoid returning to her courtroom; it was her way of trying to reduce recidivism. Jury trials are very rare because attorneys and courts will work together to resolve matters short of a jury trial.

Jury trials are very time consuming and stretch the resources of the defendant (Higher attorney fees) and the court (reduce regular docket & pay juror fees) and thus occur infrequently. Jury trials in Judge Stokes courtroom were a rarity as well despite her perceived position of not allowing many or much of a reduction of the initial charges filed against a defendant. We were unable to reach an agreement that was satisfactory to the court and despite my extensive preparation I had no control over my witnesses. This case went to the jury and they returned a verdict of not guilty and I spoke to them afterwards and they pointed to one incident during the trial that caused them to disbelieve the witnesses testimony. My strategy during direct examination is to stand at the end of the jury box so that my witness will direct their attention towards me and obviously toward the jurors so that they could assess the person's posture, facial expressions, movements, non-movements, voice conjecture, etc. all the factors one uses to determine credibility. During my examination of a third witness I noticed at times, and apparently so did the jurors, that the witness would look to his right side and then toward me and the jurors after I asked him a question and before he responded. What I could not see, but what the judge did see, was the other two witnesses ,who had previously testified, mouthing the answers to the questions I posed to the third witness. After seeing this for a second time to confirm her suspicions, Judge Stokes moved for a brief recess and excused the jurors. She admonished the witnesses and made them depart the courtroom and when we continued with the trial the third witness was horrible. The defense attorney shredded him on cross examination and there was still enough evidence to have the case go before the jury. I was astonished and visibly upset with all of the witnesses because they were completely inapposite of the people who I had interviewed weeks prior to the trial. Ironically, I received a card from the alleged victim in that case thanking me for my fine effort on her behalf. She never apologized for her conduct and it may have been a way to dissuade me from seeking perjury charges!

I would not lose another jury trial as prosecuting attorney with the City. I was victorious in cases involving Domestic Violence, Selling Liquor to Underage Persons, Driving Under the Influence of Alcohol and or Drugs, Assault, Endangering Children and Bribery involving a public official. I would not back away from a challenge while others would seek to plea. I enjoyed exercising the skills I had attained in law school and during my time at the prosecutor's office because they allowed me develop my ability to think on my feet and gain a wide varied experience for the jury trial process. I would need that for my ultimate position (Judge) that I began contemplating during my first year at the office.

I realized that in order to effectuate my goal of becoming a judge I would have to be more involved in the political community. I thus reinvigorated that bug I had let lay dormant since my involvement with the primary election in Georgia as I volunteered to distribute literature for Mayor Michael R. White's re-election campaign of 1997. My involvement was minimal wherein I passed out literature several times in highly populated areas of the city of Cleveland on Saturday mornings. I, unlike a lot of my fellow volunteers, did not simply pass the literature out. I reached out, attempted to shake the constituents hands and indicated why I was seeking their support on behalf of the mayor, answered any questions that I could within reason and knowledge. I did that with each person regardless of race, gender, age, culture, religion or sexual orientation. I was so active that my boss, George Pace Jr. said "Man, you are so convincing I can't wait until you run for office!" Once the mayor was easily re-elected I used the little notoriety I gained to obtain an interview with him for a position in his administration.

My interview with the mayor was unusual to say the least. I was picked up at city hall by his driver and then whisked to his morning meeting spot on E. 105th. When I walked in the mayor was engrossed in a conversation with another individual and I couldn't tell if that person was being interviewed as well. The mayor, all five foot five of the mighty spark plug, with his piercing eyes that were only slightly hidden by his wire-rimmed spectacles, abruptly concluded his meeting with the gentleman grabbed his coat and hat and headed outside. I was summoned to follow as we all entered the vehicle that the driver brought me in and we began driving away from the restaurant. The mayor, without looking back towards me or extending his hand to say hello, began a series of questions to test my intelligence as well as my passion for this highly politicized position. He, had heard of the interview I did with several of his cabinet members and the good impression I had left on them. He wanted to know if I, at the tender age of twenty-six, could handle such a delicate job. I assured him I was ready and he then turned around, shook my hand and said, "I pray that you are because this position could cause you and your family some sleepless nights." I was hired shortly after my interview with Mayor White.

I was charged with the task of leading a division of the Department of Public Safety whose primary requirement was to investigate allegations of police misconduct. The Office of Professional Standards was also required to provide an analysis of the complaints to the Civilian Police Review Board and act as the advocate for the latter Board in any hearings held before the Chief of Police and/or the Director of the Department of Public Safety. As one can tell with all the layers of government involved, highly politicized was an understatement of the position of Administrator for that office. I was able to gain valuable administrative experience while working in that unit. I was the direct supervisor for two civilian employees and quasi- supervisor for three sergeants of the Cleveland Police Department that were assigned to investigate the complaints. I also had the luxury of being able to consult with an attorney from the law department when prickly legal issues surfaced about enforcement of the board's powers and or modification of the latter. The job did in fact cause some unneeded stress but worthwhile experience. I got the opportunity to meet and discuss policy with some of the city's most influential and progressive people. I learned how to manage employees and find a balance between being an approachable boss but one that has high expectations of quality work from his employees. I learned how to sacrifice my time and convince others to do the same in an effort to meet a common goal.

When I arrived there was a huge back log of cases that had been completed but not reviewed by the board. I took the initiative of sternly requesting that the Board and I , along with my staff, break from the tradition of only hearing cases once every three months to twice every two that allowed us to reduce the back log in less than six months. I enticed the Board and the staff by purchasing dinner, either pizza and/ or wings plus something to drink. I also strongly urged them to read the investigative reports, that included my recommendations, before they came to Cleveland City Hall to conduct the hearings and the subsequent case dispositions. I defined the standard they should use when making a determination on a case since they hadn't been informed of what standard if any to use. We were able to encourage more police officers to participate in the process whereas in the past they refused to honor the subpoena's that were sent. The Board began to make more balanced decisions in cases instead of simply dismissing them and finding no fault. They were making more informed decisions based upon not just the written report but also the live testimony of the complainants, the witnesses if any and the officers. More often than not the officers presence gave the Board a chance to clear up any ambiguity in the police code of conduct or some lingering material issue that couldn't be resolved via reviewing it on paper.

My employment at this division taught me a valuable lesson I would need to reassert during my political campaigns- There are never any permanent friends or permanent enemies. I say that because before I became administrator I was the principal advocate for the police as an assistant city prosecutor. The position I held as administrator required me, if I found something improper occurred between a citizen and the police officer, to now act as an adversary against the very group of people I once represented. It was a very awkward but educational position for me to occupy. I also learned how to make balanced decisions. My knowledge about the criminal law and criminal procedure gave me the chance to explicate regarding issues that arose with respect to police functions and procedure. I knew what was right and what was incorrect and vehemently defended those officers that were right and recommended finding cases to have been substantiated when procedures weren't followed.

After a few months on the job I quickly learned why there had been so much turnover. Some of the former administrators were ambitious and moved to higher positions within Mayor White's administration while others just couldn't cope with the constant tugging between police, the administration and the community that the job possessed. I was stressed with the lack of power and focus the office had to truly eradicate misconduct that was being perpetrated by a very few in the police department. I also began to experience unexplained hair loss and possible stress induced ulcers. The mayor's more focused attention to the office based upon an investigative report that showed an increase in the amount of complaints filed just added to my increased stress level. Eventually, the mayor and I came to a mutual agreement that prosecuting was my strong suit despite the changes that he made to make the Office of Professional Standards more relevant and powerful. After a year of fighting on behalf of officers who were vindicated and citizens who complaints were declared true I returned to the prosecutor's office for a brief stay.

My wife was adamant that I should simply quit and start my own practice. I wasn't ready to quit, especially since I was the only one working and I could not fathom placing my wife and children in harm's way to prove a point, where I would be going to a secure position with an expectation of receiving funds for the home on a biweekly basis. If I had ventured out on my own I would have had little capital, very limited resources and only a year and half of experience as a trial attorney. I admit that my wife's faith in me was larger than mine but I couldn't risk putting them in danger of losing everything we worked for to that point. I accepted the transfer and found it very challenging to return to the prosecutor's office.

Many of the officers saw me as a traitor and some of my fellow prosecutors were of a similar mind. They would sneer at me, with their eyes lids squelched and their lips poked out when officers who had been brought before the Civilian Police Review Board were in their office seeking charges. I knew they were discussing me because whenever I came into a courtroom or walked down the hall the officers and those particular prosecutor's would be huddled up and talking and then ceased when I approached. Many of the officers avoided reviewing complaints before me, thus precluding me from making a determination on whether to issue charges. The only time they couldn't avoid me was when I was the assigned night prosecutor and was the only option. I decided to stay notwithstanding the uncomfortable working environment because of George Pace Jr. George had been my mentor and trainer and I wanted to continue to work for and learn from him. However, shortly after I returned he was offered a position with the U.S. Attorney's Office in Washington D.C. I began to make plans then to find another position but I wouldn't leave until I had the other one secured.

In the interim I continued to gain invaluable experience trying cases both as lead counsel and second chair. I was also able to simultaneously observe the Cleveland Municipal Court judges. I gained a better perspective of the very difficult decisions they made on a daily basis. I got a chance to observe up close how they controlled their courtrooms, operated their dockets, how they dispensed justice without being condescending but at the same time commanding respect for the process and the Court (them). I was fortunate to be able to see varying styles; some very serious while others injected some level of levity with humor or attempts at humor. There were many things that I viewed that was pervasive throughout the entire bench: the judges were bright, articulate, conscientious and the majority of them consistent. I saw how they impacted the lives of everyone that was involved in the case: the alleged victim, the accused, the family connected to one or both of them, the advocates, the attorneys and court personnel. The judges wielded a lot of power and for the most part not many of them abused it.

I was the kid who rose from nothing to something. I was fortunate through faith and determination to hold positions where I worked for and conversed with the mayor of one of the United States illustrious cities. My story is only possible in America!

PUBLIC SECTOR LAWYER TO PRIVATE SECTOR LAWYER

I begrudgingly remained an assistant prosecutor until one of the former prosecutor's recommended me to one of the most renowned and prestigious African American law firms in Cleveland- Forbes, Fields & Associates. George Forbes was the principal owner of the firm and considered by many to be the "God father" of the modern day Cleveland African American Political community. Mr. Forbes was formerly the President of City Council and had been practicing law for quite some time. He was the President of the local chapter of the NAACP and he was a former mayoral candidate. He and my former boss, Mr. Michael R. White, were enemies, deep-seated enemies. They had actually been acquaintances and friends for some time especially when Mayor White was originally on City Council. It was my understanding that Mayor White was George Forbes' protégé' and a number of things that Mayor White learned about politics supposedly came from Mr. Forbes. Mr. Forbes was a fierce defender of the issues that plagued the African American community. He fought for minority inclusion in areas of business, education, medicine and government both elected and as civil servants. He worked tirelessly both as an attorney and governmental advocate to make sure that people were treated fairly and properly compensated. He did not believe in handouts and felt that you should work for what you received but he wanted to make sure everyone, especially African Americans due to their exclusion for so many years, would get a fair opportunity to engage in the process. I had several reasons to seek a position with Mr. Forbes: First, I wanted the chance to work in a private practice atmosphere. I had been working in the public sector for the last four years and simply desired a different practicing perspective. I knew that the firm represented a variety of clients: hospitals, community boards, drafted legislation for cities, bond issues for the government, car accident victims, criminal defendants and any general legal issue that walked through the door. I was anxious to expand my legal experience beyond criminal prosecution and felt that Forbes, Fields & Associates would afford me that chance. Second, I would be receiving a pay increase. Thirdly, I would have access to one of the best and one of the most knowledgeable political figures in the state of Ohio. I wanted to tap into his thoughts, strategy, charisma and overall perspective on the political scene especially the judiciary.

I was successful in persuading Mr. Forbes to hire me as an associate attorney in his firm. He wasn't a micromanager but he expected all of the attorneys to work hard and complete assigned the projects in a timely and efficient manner and to zealously and competently represent the clients. It was his name and reputation that was on the line each time one of the associates drafted a memo to a client, appeared in court on behalf of a client or submitted a brief on behalf of a client. I learned that there was no set time we were expected to be at work but 9 was the expected time, unless we had a court hearing then our day would start earlier in that particular court house, and he expected us to be there until 5 or later. I was involved in areas of municipal law, bond work, criminal defense and personal injury. I represented a number of clients who had been involved in car accidents. I represented an individual who was injured walking in a nursing home. I represented a child who was severely bitten and later deformed by her classmate in daycare. I represented criminal defendants who were accused of assaulting a mental health patient and they were the caretaker at the time. I represented a man who was charged with domestic violence regarding his troubled adopted son. I also represented a young lady who was charged with telecommunications harassment that was a love triangle with a police sergeant. I represented a guy who was charged with robbery of a grocery store and when he pulled the money out for his retainer my colleague and I thought we would see some lettuce hiding underneath the bills. I assisted in drafting questions for a deposition involving an employee that was suing one of our clients. I worked with different boards during their sessions which generally occurred after the regular working hours because the trustees were prominent people in the community who had other obligations during the day. I met influential political and business members of the community through my association with Mr. Forbes.

I had a number of newsworthy cases. One involved a young lady who was the defendant in an involuntary manslaughter case. The involuntary manslaughter arose when she was accused of allowing her son to fall to his death from the porch of their high rise apartment. It was child endangering and whenever a misdemeanor is committed that results in someone's death, it can be labeled involuntary manslaughter, and that's what happened. The young lady was participating in the program that required those individuals who were recipients of public assistance to seek employment in order to retain some of the social services: daycare, housing subsidies, health insurance and future assistance if she was terminated from her job. The young lady was a single mother of two very young boys. The boys' fathers weren't consistent participants in the lives of the children. The youngest child's father was supposedly on his way to the apartment when the young lady left for work. When he failed to arrive the kids decided to open the sliding balcony door. They began to jump on the mattress that was located on the balcony floor and unfortunately the youngest child jumped too high and dove head first over the balcony that was more than seven flights above the ground. His three foot, less than fifty pound frame slammed head first onto the concrete and he eventually died from massive brain trauma. The young lady was numb when another associate and I went to speak to her at the county jail. She loved both of her boys immensely and indicated to us and the judge, "There is no punishment that could equate with the death of my child." She was eventually freed and remained on bond until her case was resolved. She eventually plead to the involuntary manslaughter charge but the judge felt her remorse and displayed compassion for this young mother whose heart was broken and needed it to mend so that she could surround her remaining child (and future children) with the love she would have stored up for her deceased son.

I was also privileged to assist on another media case that had an unusual legal component. One late evening at the firm, shortly before we were about to leave for the day, a paralegal transferred a call from a frantic middle aged man. When I spoke to the gentleman he indicated that he had just returned home from the Cleveland FBI headquarters. He had been interrogated for hours regarding the missing money that fell off the AT Systems truck.

He stated that he was a security guard and was headed to work in downtown Cleveland one early morning. He claimed that there was no traffic on the street because he reports well prior to morning rush hour. He claimed that as he was walking toward his office building he noticed several packages sitting in the middle of the road with no apparent owner. When he got a closer look he saw stacks of currency that was wrapped in plastic. He took a survey of the area and then began to haul the three heavy packages back to his car. After he loaded the money in his car he decided to go home and called in sick to work that morning. He then, like most of Greater Cleveland, watched the news on television and read the newspaper that lead with the story about the missing funds. He decided to turn the money in without first consulting with a lawyer after hearing that a reward would be offered for anyone that had information about the missing money. He turned the undisturbed packages into the Federal Bureau of Investigation (FBI) and was essentially advised that he would not receive a reward and was lucky that he was avoiding any charges due to his delay in immediately returning the money.

Me and another associate attorney traveled to Mr. Forbes' home and informed him of the dilemma and Mr. Forbes met with the young man the next day and Mr. Forbes agreed to represent him. Mr. Forbes was able to negotiate with the FBI and AT Systems regarding the reward and AT Systems agreed to fulfill its public announcement regarding the reward. I was requested to join the team representing "Money Man" when two unknown parties made claims to the reward money. They both asserted that they were entitled to the money because they had provided information to law enforcement that was sufficient enough to lead them to "Money Man" just before he turned the money into the FBI.

I was responsible for drafting a legal memorandum that Mr. Forbes would use to argue during his pre-trial conferences with the other reward seekers attorneys and the judge that was assigned to hear the case. The memorandum was effective enough to allow Mr. Forbes to secure the bulk of the reward money for "Money Man." After the firm took its fee and the other monies were disbursed to the two other claimants the "Money Man" walked away with more than $40,000 as a finder's fee for the negligence of the AT System workers. We would later discover that none of the money was marked and was well over $250,000 because it didn't originate from a bank. The "Money Man's" moral compass wouldn't allow him to keep what he clearly knew didn't belong to him. Forbes, Fields & Associates stepped in when we discovered that he wouldn't be properly compensated for his thoughtful moral decision. This was a poignant time for me because it was one of the reasons why I decided to go to law school and that was to protect the rights of the uninformed, the misused and mistreated.

My decision to leave public employment was very important for my future employment endeavors. I needed to obtain some experience as a criminal defense attorney as well as some civil experience in order to make me an effective balanced jurist. Accordingly the time I spent at Forbes, Fields & Associates was priceless for me professionally. It, however, nearly cost me my family.

I ALMOST LOST EVERYTHING

I spent far more time at the law firm than I did in the public sector. When I worked in the public sector I would leave at the normally scheduled time and return at the designated appointed time. I, however, found myself leaving the law firm when the assistance of the street lights. I didn't enjoy the public holidays and instead found myself working while the kids and Robin were at home. I also wholeheartedly believed that Robin disliked me and the love we had built was crumbling. I have been and always will be a very touchy feely person and Robin would prefer her space. My desire for intimacy, not just intercourse, was a product of not having a well-balanced personal relationship with my parents. I believed that the less contact the less the person loved me. I didn't realize, nor did Robin, that I communicated love through physical touch. Robin's inability to understand that caused me to drift away and to believe that maybe she wasn't the love of my life. My perceptions caused me to make some very poor choices that nearly derailed my family from God's intended course for us.

I consulted with the wrong friends and associates and decided that it was better if I moved out. Robin was initially adamantly opposed to me leaving and felt that we should find a way to resolve our problems together and not living separate and apart. She wasn't able to convince me to stay and I left. It was the hardest decision I ever made because I had made a vow to her, to Lauren and to Michael to be completely opposite of the men who were supposed to be role models for me. I left them without nightly protection, I left them without assurance in their safety or the future of our family. I had never spent more than a few days away from Michael is entire life and living apart from him was like having a knife stabbing me in my lungs because I felt like I was suffocating. I did not completely abandon the family because I paid the mortgage, along with sending Robin money for food, utilities, and other essentials. I made sure the insurance was paid on both vehicles as well. I was in no way proud of my actions. I cried myself to sleep many nights. I reverted back to rocking when crying was insufficient to get me to sleep. I also invested in sleeping pills to try and get some much needed rest when the rocking and crying were ineffective. Robin allowed me to periodically visit the home I voluntarily vacated so that I could read to Michael, help Lauren with her homework and/or play video games with both of them. I enjoyed just hugging and kissing on both of them whenever I got a chance. Eventually, I was able to secure an apartment and they came to visit and spent the night with me, which I truly enjoyed. As for me and Robin we became more civil and the vicious name calling and the loud angry conversations in person and over the phone decreased to the point where we genuinely began to question if we should truly end our marriage.

Prior to the dissipation of the animosity between Robin and I, I made the painful poor choice to officially file for divorce. I regret to this day that I drafted the complaint without first making every conceivable step to avoid the annihilation of our marriage. I'm grateful that my wife is and was a praying woman. She wasn't going to contest the divorce proceedings but she did make me think. She said," Do you think God makes mistakes?" I said" No." "Well if that is the case then God didn't make a mistake when he brought the two of us together," she said with eyes wide open and glazed over with water. She then said with tears streaming " I will give you a divorce but I don't think that is God's will for us." This was a completely different Robin that I was accustomed to interacting with on any issue.

Robin is very confident, intelligent, independent and assertive woman, but I started to see someone who would let me love her the only way I knew how, let me help her raise our children, someone who would be receptive to my ideas and someone who would not emasculate me but instead build me up. We began to talk more often and then she invited me for a secret rendezvous at an exclusive hotel. I of course accepted and we spent hours together that was memorable. I still remember her candy sweet breath that met my nostrils with much approval right before her cotton candy lips met my lips. Her beautiful body glistened in the moon and starlight that provided the only illumination in the room after we entered. I was careful not to lay on her beautiful shoulder length and full black silky soft hair. Instead I let her lay on my broad shoulders and my chest that was heaving up and down from spent energy but also anxiety about what this meant.

I was concerned about whether this was just a fling or were we on the path to reconciliation. I thus left after a few hours not realizing that she wanted me to stay the entire night. I called her after I got back to my apartment and she sounded disappointed but not upset. A few weeks later I told her she owed me and she obliged and we met back at the same rendezvous place. She was the one who left early this time and I was left to wonder what it really meant now that she didn't stay. We would eventually have several encounters at our home instead of the hotel. We made sure no one else discovered our trysts; not the kids nor my mother-in-law.

It felt new and exciting and it felt right. The butterflies instead of the bats returned. They were present similar to what I had when we first met, not just when I saw or spoke to her but whenever I thought about her. We acknowledged that we would always love one another and would do the best we could to raise our children but we both wanted to know if we could do it together. I didn't want the old Robin nor did she want the old Mike. The Mike who was overly sensitive, who held things in instead of confronting them immediately, the Mike who would rather communicate through a letter instead of talking to avoid true emotions and hiding behind the words and the paper. We decided that I would move out of my apartment and we would seek counseling. I would be able to see Mini-me grow up on a daily basis not a weekly basis. I could resume my rightful place as his role model. I could continue to give him his baths, help him brush his teeth, help him learn how to tie his shoes, help him learn the alphabet and teach him how to count. I would be able to attend Lauren's soccer games without feeling awkward after it was over when we all surrounded her and told her how great a job she had done. I could provide the protection she needed from unknown dangers that she would encounter as a young lady. I could provide a sense of stability that she would need to thrive. My presence back home was also a testament to Lauren's faith because she was praying I would come home and she anointed my coat pockets with oil every time I came over before I came back home.

The most difficult thing for both of us to do was to forgive the past harms both things known and unknown and not just for the months we were separated but from the time we began dating. I not only forgave but tried to forget everything that I knew or suspected regarding Robin and that I had done so that there would be no barriers to our happiness. I didn't want the guilty stain of our prior comments, deeds and thoughts to prevent us from securing the best possible future for us and our kids. The only obstacle to our anticipated reunion would be my current job.

Unfortunately, my position at the firm was the impetus that led to the deterioration of our marriage and despite the wealth of experience and knowledge I gained from my time there I needed to find another place to make a living and provide for my family. I had lost my contact with God who had been my source of strength for so long. I didn't pray like I did when I was a kid when I would bend down on my knees before I went to sleep and then when I remembered after I woke up. I would ask God to keep me through the night but if he didn't I would ask that I find myself in heaven. If I awoke I would fall back on my knees and thank God for keeping me and to watch over me through the day. Everything I needed I went to God for be it small or large and while I didn't get everything I asked for, God's protection was adequate. I returned to my childlike behavior and my knees began to get sores as I prayed for the restoration of my family and specifically for a job that would help me realize a dream I had possessed since I became a prosecuting attorney. God worked much faster than usual in this instance.

FINDING MY TRUE CALLING

A month after I had returned home I went to Cleveland- Marshall College of Law to visit a few people in the administrative office and to use the library for some research I was conducting on a case for work. As I was leaving the library I saw a board that had job postings. I looked over a few that was asking about associates for a firm that handled bankruptcies. The firm was offering a decent salary with benefits but wanted someone with experience in bankruptcy law. I also saw another classified advertisement for a small firm dealing in general practice but the salary was non-negotiable and less than what I was making at Forbes, Fields & Associates. I was becoming discouraged and nearly left until my eyes glazed over the last posting. The posting was for a Full time Magistrate's position with Cleveland Municipal Court. I was pleasantly surprised to see the position being offered to the general public. Magistrate positions are appointed by the judge(s) of a court for the purposes of assisting the judge in presiding over matters that are generally the judge's responsibility but delegated to the Magistrate. All judges in Ohio, except those that preside over federal cases, are elected. Accordingly, judges are quasi politicians. The Judicial Canons which prescribe the rules that all judicial officers (Judges, Magistrates and candidates for judge), however, make an effort to separate judges from the normal politician in restricting what they can say, who, how and when they can raise money for campaigns and the connections if any that they have with people who might appear before them in any case or controversy. Nevertheless, it was common practice that Magistrate positions were given to those who knew the judges and had worked in the political scene. I was not a part of the political scene but felt that the my perception was flawed if the Court was opening the position to the general public. I met the state law requirement for being a Magistrate solely based on my status as a licensed attorney. The Cleveland Municipal Court, however, had an additional requirement of having a minimum of five years of experience as an attorney. I fell short of this requirement by four months yet I was not discouraged. I felt that my experience as a prosecuting attorney and now the experience and knowledge I possessed from the civil side of the law would serve me well. I would be able to bring a balanced approach to making decisions in both criminal and civil matters. This was the perfect position for me and I was relentless in my pursuit especially since the application deadline was only a few days away.

I was able to timely file my application with my resume firmly attached and was blessed to receive an interview with the Deputy Chief Magistrate Greg Clifford and the Chief Magistrate Michelle Paris. I knew Greg on a more personal basis based upon his involvement with Cleveland-Marshall College of Law. He was one of the first African American attorneys that introduced himself to me at an event that was held to engage the new minority law students from Cleveland-Marshall and Case Western Reserve. Greg was very involved in the community being chair or committee head of several organizations. I aspired to be like him, especially since he was replacing Michelle as the Chief and becoming the first African American Chief Magistrate for the Cleveland Municipal Court.

Greg and Michelle took turns asking me questions about my experience focusing simply on my time as a prosecuting attorney. They became even more interested when I enlightened them about the fact that I had worked in varying areas while being employed with Forbes, Fields & Associates. They were intrigued and I informed them of the criminal defense representation, the personal injury claims, representing hospitals and individuals who had been terminated or not promoted for discriminatory reasons. I believe the combination of my great interview along with my relationship with many of the judges afforded me an opportunity to interview with the entire court.

I entered the judges monthly meeting a tad bit nervous. I have always felt comfortable in the court, especially when I was able to litigate a matter on behalf of my client. I, however, was not required to argue on behalf of myself. I would have to be persuasive enough to convince at least seven of the judges that I was the best candidate for the job. I was placed at the head of the long conference table that had all of the judges on each side along with the court administrator and the deputy administrators. The judges dispensed with introducing themselves because I had appeared in each of their courtrooms during my time as a prosecutor or defense attorney. They simply asked me why did I want to be a Magistrate.

I spoke about the passion I had for the protecting the legal rights of those who are victimized as well as those of the accused. I said that my passion was only partly fulfilled as a prosecutor and then as a defense attorney but would be completely fulfilled as a judicial officer. I felt that my connection to the city would serve as inspiration to those who came before the bench and motivate them to do better. I also interjected that the bench should reflect the make-up of the community and there was a clear deficiency when it came to African American male representation on the Cleveland Municipal Court bench and Magistrate Department; there were only two African American male judges out of the 13 on the bench and only two African American Magistrates out of more than 15.

The judges didn't ask me any other questions partly due to possessing my resume, application, the recommendation from Magistrates Clifford and Paris along with their personal knowledge of my legal abilities. I left the meeting feeling confident but knew that politics would play a role because one of the other candidates possessed more experience and had a better connection with the judges due to family history, practicing before them and both sides of the aisle as a prosecuting attorney and legal aid defense attorney; She was well qualified for the position. I later learned after speaking to one of the judges that there was a fight over me and the other person due to our prior experience (both having practiced on both sides of the aisle), our writing ability (We were both English majors in college) our community activism being equal. She, however, separated herself due to her length of service as an attorney which slightly dwarfed mine and she also had run very good campaigns against two of the sitting judges and thereby developed friendships with them and she was chosen to fill the vacancy.

I had no regrets about the judges' decision because I knew that I was facing a tough battle based upon all the things I just mentioned. I, however, didn't stop praying and believing that God would make a way and I would be able to realize my dream of being a judicial officer someday. I waited for the official word from the Court that I didn't get the job. I didn't want to pursue other options since I wasn't sure if maybe the judges had second thoughts and were reconsidering me or there was another vacancy and they were thinking of hiring both of us. My prayers remained specific and consistent and my faith didn't dwindle. I continued to go to work each day doing my job both believing that my days were winding down at the firm.

Approximately a month after my interview I received the letter for which I had been waiting patiently. I took care in opening the envelope so that I wouldn't tear the letter and be unable to later preserve it. I was confident and faithful that the letter was one of celebration and not mourning. My faith was justified when the first words of the letter stated": *Please be advised that the judges, at their meeting held on.. ..appointed you to the position of General Magistrate with the Cleveland Municipal Court at a salary of $51,949.24 per annum.*" My eyes began to water, my mouth grew dry and my voice cracked as I ran towards Robin to share the good news. I would now sit in the seat of judgment over minor misdemeanors; other misdemeanors that the attorneys consented to; garnishment hearings; driving privilege hearings; small claim hearings; and jury trials where money is being sought for personal injury or breach of contract where the claims were below $15,000. I knew I would not be the final arbiter regarding a matter, all Magistrates Decisions had to be approved and confirmed by a Judge, but I would be the primary person involved in deciding a dispute and the judges would have to trust and rely on me to make the right decision regarding the facts and the law. The judges were entrusting me with a lot of power and I wanted to do everything within my being to convince them that they made the right choice. I was going to be in an important position because an individual's perception of the judicial system is formed by what they see at the municipal level since most people fortunately won't come into contact with the felony court.

By virtue of being appointed I immediately was placed, by society, on a pedestal and presumed to know everything about the law. I, however   can attest that is far from the truth. Although the job brings prestige, and demands respect I was not immediately imbued with all knowledge and foresight about the law and people who appeared before me. It was a learning experience that I was grateful to be able to begin. Additionally, it didn't hurt that I got a raise of more than $11,000 in pay from what I was making at the firm. I took my letter down to our basement and with on one else watching just said "Thank you Jesus" multiple times and my feet stomping simultaneously with my shouts. My steps had been ordered so that I could legitimately hold that position. I possessed the professional and personal experiences needed to properly adjudicate the cases that came before the Court. My race, my age, my gender, my socioeconomic background, while factors I doubt neither one of them was the leading reason I was chosen. I believe it was a combination of things: my faith, my experience coupled with all that I just mentioned and I was the right person at the right time for the right job. The Bible says that "...it will work out for the GOOD of them who love the Lord and are called according to his purpose..." My faith and my hard work worked together for my good. The kid who was so poor that he couldn't go outside when it rained, who fought roaches for crackers, who saw family members being carted off to prison would now preside over courtroom cases. Only in America!

YES WE DID!

The Cleveland Municipal Court was moving toward diversity amongst its classified and civil servant staff therefore how could that not be extended to the unclassified less protected Magistrate Department. I was not only making history as one of a few African American males to ever hold the position of Magistrate I was the youngest full-time Magistrate ever appointed in the history of the Court- I had just celebrated my 30th birthday less than a month before receiving the appointment.

I approached the job with humility, respect, understanding of the law and procedure as well as an expectation for a level of respect. I knew I would be tested by attorneys, by litigants and by staff members regarding my level of expertise, my youthfulness, my compassion, my legitimacy and my ability to discern. I had to respond to attorneys in a respectful but confident way when they challenged me on a particular evidentiary, legal or procedural matter. I would not try to purposefully embarrass an attorney, staff or litigant in open court, as a way of demonstrating the power I wielded. Instead I would calmly tell them how I interpreted the law and the facts of a particular case or situation and that if they disagreed they were well aware of the process to overturn my decision. I would not hesitate to call attorneys who I believe were headed towards a dangerous line and remind them of what the law was regarding contemptuous behavior. I believed my demeanor on the bench led to my reputation of being intelligent, procedurally knowledgeable, even handed, balanced and possessing compassion for both complainants and respondents. I truly believed that I was playing with house money because I got the chance to do something I really enjoyed and I was getting paid a handsome salary to do it. The old adage that if you are able to make your passion your profession you'll never work another day in your life was manifested in my position as a Magistrate with Cleveland Municipal Court.

Most of the public's perception of a Magistrate is an individual who hears the traffic cases on behalf of the Judge. While Magistrates are assigned to hear those type of cases, as I was on many occasions, the vast majority of the time is spent writing decisions. Thus, a Magistrate should possess strong writing and oral skills in order to be effective in their role. I would suggest that many of the people who knew me in the legal profession thought I possessed very good oratory skills. I was required to recite statutes, changes of plea, argue motions, address juries both as a prosecuting attorney and defense attorney. Thus, it was no surprise to many that I was able to "handle" a docket and courtroom. My superiors as well as some of my colleagues, however, were more astonished by my writing ability more than anything else.

Chief Clifford didn't immediately throw me into the fire during my initial weeks as a Magistrate instead he allowed me to shadow both Magistrates on different assigned dockets as well as some Judges. In an effort to keep me busy as well as acclimate me to law I would be interpreting on a consistent basis he asked me to respond to objections and legal questions posed by the Judges. I believe the latter was a test to determine my writing level and whether it would be a hindrance to my survival of the ninety (90) day probationary period. I must have written numerous memorandums of law for the judges and also answered the objections filed by parties that disagreed with the Magistrate's Decision. The memorandums were then reviewed by the Judge to assist them in determining whether to uphold the Magistrates Decision or not. Chief Clifford would not openly comment to me about how well they were written but he stated in a staff meeting, with all of the veteran Magistrates listening, how impressed he was with my writing ability and style. It was comforting for me coming from someone who was both a respected and astute attorney and longtime Magistrate. Additionally, Chief Clifford had graduated from Ohio University with a B.A.. in English like me. Also, one of my colleagues, prior to Chief Clifford's commendation at the meeting, remarked about one of my decisions that"... We need to get you over to the Court of Appeals. Your decision reads like a Court of Appeals decision. " Lastly, the former Chief Magistrate,

Michelle Paris, was reading a memorandum of law that I wrote for a Judge and she just happened to be handling the case for the judge that day. She called me and asked, "Who wrote the memo?" I hesitantly stated, "I wrote it," because I was unsure if she was upset with grammar or content. I initially thought she had issues with the conclusion or the research but she was astonished by the excellent writing and thanked me for the doing such a phenomenal job.

I would eventually develop a reputation amongst the judges for being able to write organized, easily readable, logical and properly analyzed opinions regarding questions posed to them or to me while I was presiding over cases. I took pride in being asked by the judges to conduct the research to a question and then provide an analysis on the research that contained a recommendation. I would then draft a recommended journal entry that the jurist would only need to sign. Accordingly, there were many opinions that I authored that the judges were given credit for and which I appreciated because they showed so much confidence in me to sign the entry without much, if any tweaking. It gave me the assurance that I could decide the cases without the covering of a jurist and my desire to seek office was more solidified.

I wanted to mention the comments I received regarding my writing because they serve as validation for the hard work I put in to reach that level. I struggled with grammar in elementary, middle school and high school. As I stated in early chapters English was initially not fun for me; especially the mediocre grades that I would receive for that course. I, however, devoted a significant amount of my time to reading a variety of materials and practicing my writing to improve my ability to communicate in a non-verbal manner. I practiced by reading newspapers, magazine articles and then writing summaries of the latter items. Additionally, I kept journals and would periodically expound on my present feelings and describing the day events. I didn't let past failures, perceived notions of my inability to write, racial stereotypes or family history to derail me from my goal of becoming an above average writer. Again, I demonstrated through hard work and perseverance that the least likely kid would receive accolades in an area that no one would have fathomed I would years ago.

My position didn't simply entail writing but I was also responsible for handling small claim cases that had controversies similar to what appears on the popular daytime judge shows like Judge Mathis, Judge Judy and The People's Court just to name a few. My colleagues and I were on a rotation and would be the small claims leader every three months or so. Our duty as the leader was to preside over the entire morning docket which included dispersing some contested cases to be heard by other Magistrates, hearing default cases where the other party failed to appear and to hear any remaining contested cases. Our small claims docket was held in the smallest courtroom in the Justice Center. It was so small that I could long jump from my chair that sat high above the podiums and seats that faced the bench, all the way to the last seat in the back row of the courtroom. The courtroom would normally be filled with parties, who came to court to have their dispute settled by us when their efforts proved to futile. The ages ranged from young adults in their early twenties to older more feeble but still somewhat active senior citizens in their late seventies. The majority of the individuals in small claims chose that forum due to the low filing costs, the perceived immediate resolution, and the fact that an attorney is not required to prosecute claims. In fact the Magistrate acts as an attorney and protects the rights of both claimant and the respondent while making sure they are not advocating on behalf of one party and against another. The Magistrate would devote most of the morning and a small portion of the afternoon if a trial was lengthy to hearing small claims but could then focus on completing paper work and drafting preliminary findings of facts for the trial(s) they presided over that day.

I had some very interesting small claim cases that involved varying issues and were ripe for television because of the peripheral issues that existed outside of the initial claim. For instance, in one case a mother was suing her daughter for the value of a computer and for unauthorized charges on the mother's phone bill that the daughter incurred. After the facts were fleshed out I discovered that the true reason behind the suit was due to the mother's disapproval of the daughter's boyfriend. The mother had given the daughter a computer as a gift for graduating high school. The daughter had been dating a young man for whom the daughter was accepting collect calls from the state prison. The mother forbade the daughter from talking or seeing the boyfriend but the daughter declared her love for him. The daughter also, without her mother's permission, continued to accept the collect calls. The daughter decided to move out and live with her father before she headed to college and attempted to take her computer. The mother refused to let her take it out of the home but the daughter was able to successfully remove it when her mother was at work. I was able to get to the crux of the problem and discovered that the computer and phone charges weren't the true issue. I was able to engage in an intervention with them that resulted in them leaving the courtroom in tears, me too, and mom dismissing the claims against her daughter. I impressed upon them the value of family and how courts shouldn't have to be involved in solving minor controversies like this one. They both needed to listen and respond in a civil manner towards each other as opposed to hurling damaging insults towards one another. I needed them to understand their respective roles and when they have crossed acceptable lines. I informed them that my decision would have been to find in favor of mom on the bills and the daughter on the computer because it was a gift and not contingent on the mother's approval of the daughter's love interest.

I also had cases where one neighbor sued another neighbor because they cut the branches that were protruding over into their yard and they wanted the neighbor to pay for the service to cut the branches. I found in favor of the neighbors who branches were cut because while the cutting neighbor had a right to cut they didn't have an additional right to charge for the service to cut the branches, especially where the branches or the extracts from it failed to cause any damage. I heard cases involving minor car accidents; poor performance by auto mechanics and contractors; money damages for breaches of landlord/tenant agreements; former tenants suing for unreturned security deposits; nonpayment of child support ordered by the domestic relations court; breach of furniture agreements; breach of credit card agreements and a slew of other money damage claims.

I was also fortunate to hear the judges personal docket cases. I actually sat and listened to testimony, generally in the judges courtroom and using the same chair as the assigned judge, and made a decision about a person's alleged guilt and about a civil claim that someone filed. I was also given the authority to impose sentences or money judgments and thus preparing me for what would be my ultimate destination- an Elected Judge. The only thing that separated me from the jurist whose docket I was scheduled to preside over was a robe and the fact that I hadn't been elected. The courtroom would be full to capacity since the average case load for most Cleveland Municipal Court judges on a full day would be more than 85 cases. I would approach the bench from an area concealed to the public and the personal bailiff would address the litigants, the attorneys and other personnel or interested parties and state "All rise court is now in session. The Honorable Magistrate Michael Ryan presiding. Turn off all phones and electronic devices. There should be no talking." I would then say "You may be seated" after I sat in the chair. When I initially came out on the bench whether it was during small claims, misdemeanor arraignment, traffic court or a judge's personal docket there were always surprised looks and whispering by those in the crowd. Many people were astonished by my age and a significant number were even more surprised to see a young African American male in that position. Many times after I pronounced judgment someone would say "I'm so proud to see a young man like you in that position.;" they said that even if I gave them a fine and court costs. I would hear red light violations, speeding violations, I was also given authority to preside over Domestic Violence trial, an Assault trial, a Driving Under Suspension trial and Driving without a License Trial. I also had the distinct opportunity to preside over two jury trials as a Magistrate that involved car accidents. I was able to learn how to pick a jury, guide the attorneys in the process, create jury instructions, manage a trial with lay people being fact finder and applicators of the law. I was absorbing every piece of experience I could muster during my time as a Magistrate.

I didn't shrink when I was asked to perform a task that others found arduous but instead considered that if it didn't kill me it would simply make me a better jurist; I wouldn't be surprised by anything because I would of seen everything or something related to it and knew how to respond. Challenges didn't frighten me, because I had been through so many other mountainous obstacles in my past, instead they were the fuel in my ignition that would help separate me from everyone else. I was more than average and it was finally starting to show in the way I spoke, the way I prepared, the way I thought, the way I interacted, the way I approached situations and the outcomes I experience in every facet of my life.

MY POLITICAL CAREER BEGINS

By the beginning of 2003 I had established a good reputation as a Magistrate and capable substitute for Judges who were either on vacation, attending a required judicial conference or tending to some other court business. My past experiences as prosecuting attorney, criminal defense attorney, civil attorney and now nearly two years of working as a judicial apprentice gave me an excellent resume if I decided to seek a position on our Court. In fact due to the retirement of the intelligent, conscientious and long serving Cleveland Municipal Court Judge C Ellen Connally I was contemplating throwing my hat into the ring for that seat. I, however, learned fairly quickly how preparation and timing are the true keys to the start of a successful campaign. I didn't realize how far behind I was in my preparation until I went to a meeting organized by the Council of Sisters.

The Council of Sisters was comprised of long-standing African American women who were members of the Democratic Party that had been a part of the grass root division of the party that worked for numerous elected officials and causes in Cuyahoga County, but more particularly in Cleveland, Ohio. Many of them had worked behind the scenes in helping the late U.S. Ambassador Carl Stokes become the first African American elected in a major U.S. (Cleveland, Ohio) city. They were instrumental in helping state and national Democratic candidates secure overwhelming victories in Cuyahoga County. These beautiful, smart, idealistic, stubborn, and loyal women felt that it was their obligation to vet the judicial candidates who could assume Judge Connally very important seat. It was a seat that Judge Connally had held for close to a quarter century. The co-leaders of this group were Gloria Rice and the late Ohio State Representative Claudette Walcott. Mrs. Walcott was about five feet tall but her voice, conviction and her energy made her appear to be seven feet tall. She was a wife, mother and grandmother that fought not just for the well-being of her family but for everyone that was affected in her district and this state. Ms. Rice possessed the most institutional knowledge about Cleveland politics than anyone else I ever spoke to about the subject. She knew where all the bones were buried, which ones they were and who buried them. I only got an opportunity to get close to these two fine women after I literally bombed at the vetting meeting.

The vetting meeting took place at the African American Museum located in the Hough neighborhood in Cleveland. I was the last candidate to be interviewed and had no idea what this process entailed. I completed the sign in sheet well before they called me in and sat outside and spoke to the other potential candidates and their "handlers" until I was the last one left. I walked into the room and was greeted by stares and whispers similar to the ones I got when I walked onto the bench as a Magistrate. My chair positioned in the middle of a circle and the women seats surrounded me. A majority of them had grey or silver hair and the ones with the midnight black hair only had that do to the miracle of dye. They all had veteran faces whose wrinkles were badges of honor displaying the years of experience and knowledge they had obtained. They asked me my name and then a barrage of questions regarding my experience. I could see them writing profusely on their notepads as I was answering their questions as best as possible. Someone then asked the question that was the clearly the elephant in the room type question "How old are you young man?" The entire room erupted in laughter, including me. I said after catching my breath that I was thirty-one (31) and would be thirty-two by the time I was elected (32). One of the lovely ladies said " You look like you're 12!" That led to a smattering of "He sure does" from most of, if not all of the other women. Someone even shouted "Is he old enough to vote?" They asked me about my organization, of which I had none. They inquired about the amount of money I believed I needed to raise to run a campaign and I answered miserably based on the frowns on their faces and the peering eyes over their eyeglasses toward me. Eventually, they asked me why I wanted to be a judge and that changed the entire atmosphere of the interview.

I told them, " Judges have the power to effect the lives of people more so than any other elected official. They get to determine if someone is guilty, if they are placed on probation, how much if anything to fine them, is someone liable for personally injuring someone, did someone breach a contract and whether or not an individual in incarcerated. Additionally, they have the authority to terminate your life; that's a lot of power." I felt that I had the knowledge, experience and compassion to make fair, just and tough decisions that would provide justice for the accuser and well as the accused. They questioned my ability to relate to what many who came before the Court experienced due to my youthfulness. I, however, told them that "My personal experiences separate me from the other candidates. I'm the son of a teenage mom, and my biological father went to prison shortly after I was born, the man I knew as my "father" was addicted to drugs and alcohol, my "father" mercilessly beat my mother every other month, I lived in the Longwood Projects, my mom died from drugs when I was 13, my "step" grandmother, who was my guardian, died the year after my mom. Despite attending 11 different schools before college I graduated from high school, college and law school. I know what it means to be hungry, to be dirty, to be afraid, to be nearly homeless, to be unprotected and I could empathize with individuals who appeared before me but simultaneously require more and expect more from them because I found an alternative way to survive and they could do the same. "

After that statement the women surrounded me with tears streaming down their cheeks and tissues patting their faces. They were shocked by my testimony but hopeful and energized by what the future held. They, however, couldn't support me because some of them had made a prior pledge to other candidates. I, however, immediately was adopted by all of them and they became my surrogate grandmothers since Grandma Edna was living in Alabama at the time. Mrs. Rice would become my ex-officio political advisor.

I called Mrs. Rice after the event and she gave me some sage advice-"Think about it before you run." I wasn't too discouraged by the vetting process but Mrs. Rice was correct that I would meet challenges trying to secure the assistance of some of Cleveland's political leaders. I was contending with some very difficult obstacles: my potential opponent was well known both in the political and legal community; she had been an attorney for a much longer period of time than me; her father was a very good an respected attorney in his own right; she had held some very high profile positions in the community and was then the arraignment room prosecutor for the County giving her more exposure especially on the more gruesome and newsworthy stories. Additionally, she had run two closely contested races and lost by the slimmest of margins and this was supposed to be her race. Plus, she had done something I was unaware of- secured the support of many of the elected political leaders in the city and I met with the same statement each time I approached them, " I would like to support you but I already pledged my support for someone else." Thus, when I personally walked up to city council members before and after council meetings I got the above response. When I called them on or a representative for the mayor on the phone same response. I'm not the type of person whose has to be continually burned in order for me to realize that the stove is too hot and thus I made a conscience decision to not enter the race. The other young lady went onto win the race with 77% of the vote against an individual who happen to be a Magistrate with Cleveland Municipal Court. My wife and I quietly slid under the wings of Mrs. Rice and Mrs. Walcott and strategized on how I could put myself in the same position as the young lady who had just successfully won election.

Mrs. Rice was clearly heaven sent for me and Robin. I always include my wife when discussing my judicial career because without her blessing and her diligent hard work I would of never ventured into that arena. My wife and I knew that Mrs. Rice was an angel because we were specific in our prayers and asked for God's guidance and support if his will was for me to be elected Judge. Mrs. Rice was not bashful or reserved in her advice and response to our failure to abide by her blueprint.

She was a vault filled with the institutional knowledge of how to effectively win an election and she combined all of that into one acronym-M.O.M. She gave me and my wife the combination by exclaiming that M.O.M. stood for Message, Organization and Money. She stressed that without those three your chances of winning an election are severely diminished. She stated that if you have only one while your chances increased it would still be a difficult battle. She felt that they weren't necessarily mutually exclusive and a good candidate would rely on all three to be successful. For example, if you had a great message and no money it might be hard for people to hear that message if you don't possess the resources to broadcast the message. The alternative would be to have an organization that would assist in spreading the message notwithstanding the lack of necessary funds. I had a great message but was lacking in money and an organization and so our goal was to enhance the message and build the organization and acquire the money.

The message was one that illustrated to the community a completely different image than the one that was portrayed about young African Americans. I knew that in order to be successful I had to alter the negative image that was associated with young African American males. Unfortunately the media—music, newspapers, movies, magazines, internet, etc. painted a picture of young African American males as being angry, unintelligent, irrational, abusive, lazy, indecisive, disrespectful, unmotivated, criminally active and whatever negative terms that were frequently used to generalize a segment of one race. Overcoming that image would be paramount to my success; I had to be seen as a stereotype breaker. I surmised that my enhanced participation in the community would be one factor in altering that negative image. I, however, had already started to be a stereotype breaker even before I contemplated a run for office.

Unlike most college students who were focused on partying and relaxing when they were home on break I would be at some elementary school or high school discussing what steps one needed to take in order to be prepared for college. I went to the inner city schools in Cleveland and then of course back to Cleveland Heights to provide some inspiration and to educate the kids. They saw me as a tangible person and accordingly could visualize themselves in my position in their very near future. I gave them pragmatic advice about how to secure a future in college and they intensely listened whether they were in the first grade or high school seniors.

My work in the community, particularly the schools only increased when I became an attorney. Many schools and community organizations would routinely request an attorney from the prosecutor's office appear for career day. I volunteered each opportunity I got so that I could find a way to show kids it was possible to acquire jobs that they only see people on television or the movies obtaining. I believed in the phrase "They can be what they see," and I made myself present as much as possible. My conversations with the young people blossomed from not just what it takes to be a successful college student but what it took to become an attorney. The kids asked such that they could visibly see and touch someone who looked like them and could thereby envision themselves as an attorney or Magistrate. My community work was not just limited to speaking but also using my intellect to help tutor the next generation.

I was a part of the program sponsored by the Cleveland Metropolitan Bar Association that went into local high schools and tutored the children on the social studies portion of the Ohio Graduation Test. I initially was assigned to work with several other attorneys at one local school but was chosen, a few years later when I became a Magistrate, to help two young men at one specific school~John Hay. I met with the two young men one day during my lunch hour and we spoke briefly about a schedule, my expectations for them and what we were going to discuss to help them pass that portion of the test. They were two very energetic, popular kids who had passed all but the social studies and one other portion of the test and they needed to pass all portions to obtain a certified high school diploma. We all agreed that noon would be the time we met twice a week. I could not meet them any other time as their schedules precluded after school meetings and mine didn't allow early meeting times. I decided to sacrifice my lunch hour for two days a week for approximately six weeks. We would meet in a teacher's classroom and we would review the test preparation materials. I would quiz them on the information, I would use notecards to help them remember the information and I would explain anything they didn't understand. I assigned them homework and expected them to complete it by the time we met. I would also impart some advice to them on how to conduct themselves in class, with the young ladies and outside the school. I revealed information about my family and the fact that I was just like them since I grew up in Cleveland and attended Cleveland Public Schools for the majority of my young life. The young men showed interest and were always respectful but we had a very frank discussion after they failed to meet with me one day.

I had completed my docket, burst through the Justice Center doors on the first floor and barely caught the loop bus to take me to John Hay annex which was located on the campus of Cleveland State due to the renovation of the old John Hay high school. I arrived at approximately 11:55 and went to the area that was designated for tutoring my two mentees. I waited for approximately thirty(30) minutes and they never appeared. I could of left and simply returned to my office and grabbed a sandwich on the way and simply threw my hands up and quit. I, however, was upset, agitated but also motivated and sought the advisor for their whereabouts. The advisor was frustrated and embarrassed by their complete avoidance of the session. I took the advisor's advice and went to the library and they were nowhere in sight. I then began to ask other students if they had seen them and where I might locate the dynamite duo. I eventually found them cuddling with two young ladies. I called out their names in a very frank, low and commanding tone that startled them and the young ladies. I asked the young ladies "Could you please leave so I could talk to the smooth operators." They giggled and hurried out of the lunchroom. I told the guys that I was disappointed in them because they were risking failure for a few minutes of silliness with these young ladies. I impressed upon them the sacrifice I made of my time, energy, lack of food each time I ventured to the school because I care about their success. I indicated to them that if they missed another session I would not return to tutor them and the sad look on their face showed that my threat to not return to tutor them bothered them more than anything else. The two young men, who could easily be my younger brothers, never missed another session. They both successfully passed the social studies portion of the Ohio Graduation Test as well as the math portion and went on the graduate from John Hay with their certified high school diploma.

My community involvement wasn't restricted to high schools I also tutored third and fourth grade students at Daniel E. Morgan. The school was located in a rough area of the city of Cleveland. The latter was evident when one of the receptionist had a bullet graze her hair and lodge into a wall. Despite latter incident, I would continue what I had been doing for years and that was getting up early every Wednesday morning from October to March and providing tutoring sessions first in reading and them math for select third graders at the school. I, through my membership with the 100 Black Men of Greater Cleveland, was assigned one child that I tutored and mentored for the third grade and then the fourth grade until they passed the Fourth grade proficiency examination. Over the next four years, I had three children who successfully passed the exam despite having some difficulties with reading prior to our tutoring sessions. It was magical to see the improvement the children made week to week. I was excited when they were able to write, comprehend and read at levels that others suggested they may never reach. Their confidence grew in their academics and their behavior improved in the classroom as well. I saw a direct correlation between success and good behavior. They would sometimes drag into the cafeteria on a Wednesday morning but by the time we got started you could see their minds working and their eyes large as the ocean absorbing everything we had to say. Our connection with the kids didn't end in March but was extended to lunch that we provided after they passed the examination. Many of them had never been outside their neighborhood but we sponsored a lunch to the Hard Rock Café and they ate and drank heartily. We, the 100 Black Men of Greater Cleveland, were also present to hand out toys immediately prior to the Christmas holiday break. It brought back memories for me when I use to go to the Salvation Army that was few blocks from our apartment in Longwood and I would get a chance to pick one toy for Christmas. Life had come full circle because I was now a part of an event that gave toys to kids whose families, like mine when I was younger, were unable to afford to provide multiple toys for their children.

My community involvement also extended to areas where I possessed professional expertise. I was a constant volunteer facilitator for the Teen Domestic Workshops that were sponsored by the Cleveland Municipal Court and the Cleveland Metropolitan School System and other partners. I was responsible for discussing issues surrounding dating violence with groups of young men. I implored all of them to enter a circle, when space permitted, and we engaged in open, candid discussions about dating violence. I gave them the law as well as practical information on what to do and who to contact if they saw the violence or was a victim thereof. We discussed the difference between healthy and unhealthy relationships. We also discussed the cycle of violence and the punishment both criminal and collateral for those who used violence as a way to resolve conflicts they have with loved ones.

I was also an instructor for Cleveland Municipal Court Mock Trial competition where I helped teams prepare for the mock trial. I gave pointed instructions on posture, on diction, on speech delivery, on writing, on cross-examination, making objections, responding to objections, on opening and closing arguments and of course the law regarding the issues that were raised in the problem for that specific year. I also functioned as a judge for the Mock Trial Competition making sure, however, that I didn't provide a score for the team that I helped.

My appearance at those events was helping to change the perception young people had about themselves and what they could be when they grew up. It was also changing the perception others had about me because I was no longer considered to be just an attorney and then later just a Magistrate but I was also deemed to be someone who genuinely cared about helping our kids reach their expected potential. I felt that giving back to my community was an obligation. I wholeheartedly believed in the old adage "To whom much is given much is required." So despite the sleep I missed out on or the food I failed to eat it was worth it if I could impact someone's life and either motivate them to keep going in a positive direction or knock them off the path of destruction.

My community involvement, coupled with my personal experiences and professional experiences solidified my message. I now needed an organization. My initial organization included me, my wife, my daughter, my son, my mother-in-law, my sister, my niece, Karese Ryan, my brother-in-law Marcus Green, my sister-in-law Brenda Adrine and my brother-in-law Ted Williams. It was a very tight nit group that I could trust and rely on to help me reach my goal. My initial decision was to wait until 2005 to run for the seat that Judge Mabel Jasper would be vacating due to reaching the age limitation of seventy for judges. I knew I would have to begin campaigning in 2004 but an opportunity presented itself that would give me a chance to put this plan to work much earlier than I expected.

Accordingly, my wife and I prayed, spoke to my family, discussed it with Ms. Rice and finally had a conversation with members of the bar and the judiciary with whom I had a friendship with and the majority of them agreed with my decision to put my name on the ballot for Cuyahoga County Court of Common Pleas General Division.

I had a very elementary perception of what a full campaign would entail for the City of Cleveland and was completely ignorant of the enormity of a county campaign; even one for a primary. The easiest part was obtaining the mere fifty signatures to be placed on the ballot. I had to complete the process in a relatively short period because I waited until only three weeks remained before the deadline to file a petition. Once I secured my petition and all of the registered Democratic party voter names were approved I went to the Democratic Party Endorsement meeting held at Euclid High School in Euclid, Ohio. It was home to many of the Party meetings based on its proximity to the freeway as well as the vast amount of seating that was provided and needed when all of the Executive Committee Members got together for this type of event. I was green regarding the entire process. I hadn't contacted any of the Executive Committee members, the City or Ward Leaders or the Democratic Party Officers regarding my intentions; I just appeared at the meeting. In fact I was so oblivious to the process that I nearly paid dues that were only assessed to the Executive Committee members in order for them to be allowed to participate in the voting. I wasn't aware that there was a screening that took place weeks before the large meeting with City and Ward leaders. The individuals in that meeting had recommended my opponent, Peter Corrigan, receive the party endorsement for the seat for which I chose to campaign. In fact the first time Peter and I met was on stage. I actually followed him on stage when they asked candidates for the varied positions to step on stage. No one had my name or even knew who in the hell was Michael Ryan. Actually they

didn't find out who I was until after the chairman asked Peter to step forward and indicated

that he had been recommended by the screening committee and that there was no other

candidates in the Democratic primary for that race. I then spoke up and said, "I'm also a

candidate for that position." The chairman said, " And who are you" with laughter coming

from the audience. I said, "My name is "Michael John Ryan" and I filed a valid petition with

the Board of Elections seeking to represent the Democratic Party for this seat." When I said

my name, Peter's head swung around like it was on a swivel and he looked at me and his face

was like that of a ghost. The precinct committee members overwhelmingly gave him the

endorsement, I don't believe I received one vote.

He, however, was concerned because here was a young African American male, with

an Irish name running for judge. He knew he would have his work cut out for him. He

imagined that he would have a stress free primary and be able to reserve resources and time

during the general election where he was facing an incumbent who was a Republican but was

surprisingly successful in areas of Cuyahoga County where Republicans didn't normally fare

well. While Peter would have to work harder than expected my job would be like lifting a

two ton crane up Mount Everest without a pulley; nearly impossible. Peter's father was already

a long serving judge in the Probate Court for Cuyahoga County. The former longtime serving

Cuyahoga County Prosecutor's last name was Corrigan, there were two other Common Pleas

Court judges with the surname of Corrigan. The Corrigan name was and still is a very popular

and powerful name in Cuyahoga County politics and would take some miraculous work to

overcome that impediment for my campaign. I, however, didn't flinch even when people were

suggesting that I simply bow out and wait until next year's municipal court race. I felt that I

had the right and the experience to be sitting as a judge at either trial court level–Municipal

or Common pleas.

We knew that our organization would be volunteer driven based on the lack of any

financial support. I had two fund raisers and neither one of them yielded enough money to pay for staff. In fact the most I was able to pay for was literature, a DJ (Disc Jockey), food and the venue. My wife was the chief operating officer of the organization. She was responsible for making sure volunteers were at the appropriate locations, the day and times for the Ward Club meetings, the coordination for the fundraisers, making sure literature purchases had been completed, distributing literature to those who agreed to canvass and doing everything I requested regarding the campaign. She and I functioned as volunteer coordinators and applying the advice we received from Ms. Rice we created a volunteer card that we asked people to sign whenever I was discussing my campaign. We had them primarily with us during my visits to the Ward Club meetings.

Normally at the Ward Club meetings, when you are not the endorsed candidate, you are not allowed to speak to the club as a whole, but you may go and speak to individual members or guests prior to and after the meeting commences. I would arrive thirty minutes early and begin conversing with everyone I saw. I would gravitate towards most of the women and strike up a conversation about my candidacy and ask them to vote for me or at least consider me. If they displayed strong interest in voting for me I would then ask if they would like to volunteer and to sign one of the cards, which had spaces for their name, address, phone number, email address, cell phone number and what areas they would be able to provide assistance. I would sometimes meet with opposition from individuals either due to my youthfulness, race, sex or lack of notoriety. I was not discouraged one iota and kept talking and trying to convince people to at least consider me.

My wife and I determined that my message was not being received by the staunch supporters of the party who were attending the Ward Club Meetings because of the policy of non-endorsed candidates not being allowed to speak. We wanted to find a way to get people to really know who I was and why I was the most uniquely qualified candidate. We then had an epiphany, why not put bullets of my testimony on the literature. We went back to the L. T. Squared, a startup printing company that did some phenomenal artwork for my first pieces of literature, and asked the twin African American women if they could modify the literature. I asked them to reduce some of the professional experience and add the personal experience piece and highlight it and put it first. It started to get traction at all the other Ward Club's where I wasn't given permission and some that still allowed me to speak based on the fact that I was a Democrat.

If I wasn't allowed to speak I would approach individuals and ask for their vote and consideration and then point them to the area of the literature that had my personal story. I would then walk away only to see them taking off their glasses to wipe their eyes. The following was the format of the story on the literature":

Personal Story

- Son of a teenage drug addicted mother
- Stepfather physically abusive and addicted to drugs
- Grew up in the Longwood Projects
- Didn't meet biological father until 22 due to him being incarcerated.
- Step father was convicted felon
- Saw his mother die when he was 13 and she was 28
- Grandmother died the year after
- Attended 11 different schools from K-12 grade
- Received Scholarships in high school, college and law school
- Passed the Bar on his first attempt"

The writing was small but powerful and it was causing a buzz among the Ward Club Members in the particular meetings. It was even more impactful when I was given the chance to address the Ward Club because you could see people initially not drawn to me until I started to talk about my personal experiences. Many of the Ward Club members were disinterested because of several factors that would change at each venue. A vast majority were looking at the exterior- African American male who appeared to be in his late teens or early twenties and they simply dismissed me as being unqualified on that basis. Some dismissed me solely based on my age, or skin color, or my grammar (Being too proper).   I, however, could see them begin to search for my literature and begin to read more intensely about my background both personal and professional after I began to speak about my personal life; many of them said it was refreshing to hear a person running for elected office be so open and honest. The personal story was the hook and the professional experiences was simply icing on the cake for many of those who were once curious to those who became supporters. I would see many of them placing my literature in their back pockets, purses, book bags, or coat pockets while they left the other candidates literature on the table. I would be swarmed by the members after I spoke congratulating me on overcoming such difficult circumstances and also asking how they could help. My plea to them was obviously to vote for me but also to spread the word to friends, neighbors, co-workers and family about me and encourage them to vote for me as well.

When I couldn't attend every Ward Club Meeting because some were held on the same night and at the same time my sister, my brother-in-law Marcus, Robin, my college teammate Darren Hudson and other family and friends, would be responsible for representing me at those meetings. I gave them a script to read and allowed them to adlib, where appropriate, so that they could spread the message. They would return with good and bad news and I was just happy that they were returning with any good news. I would ask them to go to areas where African American males judicial candidates didn't always receive a welcoming reception from all the members of particular Ward Clubs in Cuyahoga County. My speakers, however, were like me, bold, committed, confident and accustomed to addressing crowds where none of the people they were speaking to looked like them.

Although the campaign was making headway into the Ward Club's, I was receiving an even greater response from the predominant African American churches. The pastors of many congregations were very careful in not proclaiming their support for me over their pulpit. They were giving most candidates the opportunity to address the congregation regarding our qualifications and judicial philosophy if any. I, however, was given a unique opportunity because my personal story was one of tragedy to triumph that was a central theme of Christianity. It was a story of vindication for a person who was downtrodden. It showed how Jesus' grace and mercy protected me during my tumultuous upbringing. It showed how God's promise over my life never wavered despite the obstacles, Satan's tricks, that were placed in my way. It showed how my unwavering faith along with my determination to work hard was the impetus behind my success. I was able to tell the story of how I was able to overcome and credited God as the primary reason. It was a story that resonated with believers and they held onto that hope for themselves and their children and grandchildren. They saw me as an example for so many and a way to defeat the stereotypes that existed about young African American men. They saw me as the hope for our future generations. They embraced me, prayed for me, protected me and made sure people knew who they supported. I always knew how important the African American church was for political success. I didn't take that for granted and was humbled by those pastors that allowed me to "feed" their flocks. I was grateful to political activist Chris Jones and Michael Fields for helping me gain access to some of the members who had direct connections with the religious leaders and were able to persuade them to allow me to come in and say a few words.

The final activity that I had to participate in before the primary election was the local newspaper endorsement meetings and the interviews before the local bar associations. The interviews with the local papers, The Cleveland Plain Dealer, The Call & Post and the Sun News were succinct but nerve wrecking. I was fortunate that Peter had never been through the process so it was uncomfortable for both of us. He, however, had an upper hand due to his dad's experience but also because he had the Democratic Party endorsement in a Democratic Primary. During each interview session Peter and I were questioned simultaneously regarding our professional experiences. Neither one of has had an extensive history as an attorney, both being Assistant Prosecuting attorneys, Peter for the Cuyahoga County Prosecutor's Office and me with Cleveland. He had been in the Major Trial Division and presided over the same types of cases he was currently prosecuting on behalf of the State of Ohio. I, however, had two unique qualities that Peter lacked- I had practiced general civil law and criminal defense, while his entire career had been with the prosecutor's office. I was more well-rounded and balanced than him. Additionally, when they asked what makes you different from your opponent I repeated the personal story that was on my literature to show my ability to relate to as well as to be a guide for those who come before the court having dealt with tumultuous childhoods or situations as well.

I believe a combination of factors allowed Peter to enjoy two of the major endorsements- The Cleveland Plain Dealer and The Sun Press. The latter two organizations had access to hundreds of thousands of voters through their daily circulations. I was able despite lacking a strong political name, parents who were involved on the positive side of the legal system, lacking the Democratic Party endorsement to obtain the preferred candidate declaration from the Cleveland Bar Association. The latter organization as well as the other Bar Associations that participated in the interview (Norman S. Minor Bar Association , Ohio Women's Bar Association, Criminal Defense Attorneys Bar Association) had all designated me and Peter as Adequate out of the other choices of Not Recommended, Good and Excellent. I felt a sense of vindication wherein it was the attorneys who practiced in the court that extended their approval and recommendation to the voting public. I would be able to use that declaration by the Cleveland Bar Association as well as the write up by the Cleveland Plain Dealer to bolster my campaign as it steam rolled towards the primary. Brent Larkin, one of the Editors at that time, wrote about my troubling past an how inspirational it was for so many, especially those that come before the Court. Despite the glowing remarks the Cleveland Plain Dealer recommended Peter partly due to his more than six years of experience with the same cases he sought to be elevated to preside over.

Election night eve came faster than I expected but we were nonetheless ready. I had been involved in election eve festivities while in Georgia but never to this magnitude. We were well aware that we lacked the funds to pay people what Peter may have paid and what other candidates did pay their staff; even the volunteers got paid during the primary for manning the polls. A lot of the heavy lifting was conducted by family with no expectation of payment other than to help a fellow family member achieve a dream. My wife and I couldn't hire anyone to take the yard signs and place them at the lawful distance from the polling station and instead we received an expedited geography lesson regarding Cuyahoga County. She and I left the house at approximately 9 P.M. with a map in hand and the addresses for some of the polling locations. I had acquired the voting records for each precinct and knew which ones had the most consistent voters and created a top twenty-five (25) list. Robin and I took turns driving on all sides of the Cuyahoga River (Natural boundary between the east and west sides of Cuyahoga county). We would park the car in the area where we saw other signs and then jump out and place my sign in a conspicuous place near another candidate. I made sure I didn't cover the other candidates name or other vital information. My sign was a tad larger than the other candidates and had an Emerald background with lightning white letters bold letters RYAN. In neighborhoods that we knew about and were comfortable with we acted in a reasonably cool fashion in putting up the signs and leaving. On the other hand in areas that were personally unfamiliar but were notoriously the worst places to be after 10 p.m. we were much more deliberate in our approach and literally drove to those spots placed signs in the area and left all in a matter of seconds. Our process would of made the NASCAR racers pit crews envious. As we were on our way to our final stop we called Ms. Rice because we were unsure of the location of the last site we were placing signs at and we knew she could guide us. Unfortunately we never made it to the site because Ms. Rice, once she discovered where we were told us " ...High tail it out of that place...Ya'll trying to get killed." It was approximately 1 or 2 a.m. on Election Day and Robin and I were exhausted. We headed home only to catch a few yawns and prepare for one of the longest days of our lives.

Robin, Lauren, Mike and I all woke up at approximately 5 a.m. and began to prepare the lunches we made for the family members and volunteers who agreed to distribute literature at the most highly populated voting precincts in Cuyahoga County. I then took half the lunches with me and Robin took the other half and we delivered them to the designated individuals. I drove to the polling locations on the Westside and Robin handled those on the Eastside. The campaign poll workers were directed to ask people to vote for me and to provide the modified literature piece that had the Cleveland Bar Association preferred candidate declaration. Additionally, the Cleveland Plain Dealer had printed the results of all the bar associations assessments for the most informed voter to use in making their decision about judicial candidates. I implored them to hand out that literature and stress the Cleveland Bar Association recommendation. I thanked each and every one of them and asked Robin to do the same because while it was not cold it wasn't unseasonably warm either. We had on hats, thick coats and gloves to fight off the elements. I went to the largest two polling places on the Eastside, in Cleveland Ward 10 and the other one was in Cleveland Ward 1. I employed the same tactics I used in Georgia wherein I would approach all the voters I could get to before the 100 foot barrier was reached and extended my hand while introducing myself. It didn't matter the race, ethnicity, sexual orientation or gender. I asked them to read the literature and to vote for me. If they felt perplexed about voting for me I would ask that they simply vote to ensure they had a say in this process.

I would leave one area and return to the other voting polling place and remain there for an hour or two. My last two hours, however, was spent in Ward 10 at the New Avenues voting location. It was located on top of a steep hill that was somewhat symbolic of the struggle that people were willing to endure just to vote. They saw this minor struggle as being elementary compared to the struggle that so many of their forefathers sought that were murdered, slaughtered, shot, strangled and burnt alive all for the purposes of participating in the fundamental democratic process of voting.

I returned home after the polling place closed at 7:30 p.m. The house was full of family, friends, neighbors and volunteers who had also just arrived from their assigned polling place. My mother-in-law, my wife, my sister-in-laws Brenda Adrine and Wanda Clark and other family had prepared some spaghetti, salad and chicken wings for everyone to eat while we waited for the election returns to come streaming in on the television. I dragged myself upstairs to change clothes and put on something more comfortable. I think I completely shocked everyone when I arrived back downstairs with jeans and a cotton long sleeve grey shirt that was had no buttons. I also has white socks on with my tennis shoes (sneakers) and sat down in front of the television to watch the results. I'm sure many people were discussing what happened at the polling locations where they were situated and I'm sure they were very interesting stories. I, however, couldn't recall them due to the fact that my exhaustion was so enormous that I didn't even witness the final voting count. I was awake but fading fast after each half an hour when there was an update. I started off initially only being a few thousands votes behind. The few thousands just continued to steadily grow like grass in a fertilized field where it's rained for forty (40) days and forty (40) nights. I eventually fell asleep when 50% of the votes had been counted and I was well more than 25,000 behind Peter.

I awoke the next morning and since I called off I wasn't concerned about being late for work or the kids being late to school because we simply kept them home for the day. I asked my wife if she knew the final tally but she was as unaware as I was due to the fact that she was extremely tired as well and had fallen asleep shortly after me. I ventured to the store to grab a copy of the Cleveland Plain Dealer. I purchased a copy and went to the Metro section that had a special election area displaying the results. I scrolled down to find me and Peter's race and noticed that he had a little over 90,000 votes while I had 45,000. I saw it as a monumental shellacking.. I showed Robin the results and she was indifferent and simply said, "Maybe next time." I went home a little defeated and returned to work the next day to face the music from colleagues about my epic failure.

I arrived at work with calls to come and see Judge Mabel Jasper, Judge Ronald Adrine and Judge Robert Triozzi. I imagined that they wanted to discuss the results of the election but there was also some trepidation by me because judges usually don't request to see them unless there is an imperative personnel issue. I immediately called Judge Jasper since her name was listed first among the three messages and she asked me to stop by. I walked around the corner from my Magistrate office to her chambers and she summoned me inside after her Bailiff Liz informed her I had arrived. She said, "Did you see the results of the race in the paper?" I informed her that I had and she exclaimed, "Michael you did a marvelous job. I was surprised that you were able to garner 45,000 votes in a Cuyahoga County election especially since this was your first time running." She believed I had a real chance of one day of actually winning a county election without first being appointed. I left her office more invigorated and ready to take on the world. I then went to Judge Adrine's and then Triozzi's and left feeling like Superman; invincible. Both Judge Adrine and Triozzi had repeated the same sentiments and congratulatory remarks that I heard from Judge Jasper. They all had restored my vigor and energy back into my dream of being a judge. I assumed that Peter's massive margin of victory was a sign that I lacked a future as an elected official. On the contrary it demonstrated that I had a future so bright not even Ray Ban sunglasses could blot it out.

PREPARATION FOR VICTORY

I was riding a wave of momentum after the primary, which is quite unusual for someone who lost. I returned to the Ward Clubs, both those that let me speak as well as those that limited my speech because of the Ward Club endorsed candidate rules, and was allowed to address the membership. I simply said I was honored to have received their vote and for those who didn't support me I promised to work harder in an effort to secure their vote the next time I ran for public office. Nearly every time after I spoke, someone from the crowd approached me and said "Whatever I could do to help you in the future please let me know." They were willing to sign the volunteer card and was adamant that they wanted to assist the campaign in any way shape or form. My "Thank you tour" was not just limited to the Ward Clubs and was eventually extended to the community parades and churches as well.

I was no longer a candidate so I couldn't purchase nor distribute literature with my future intentions. Additionally, I couldn't post signs or wear anything that indicated I was a candidate. In fact I simply walked in the parades and said "Thank You" as I walked pass the crowd of people and distributed candy. Some of the people watching the parade would then inquire "What are you saying thank you for?" I would then exclaim "I was thanking people for voting." Not necessarily for me but for participating in the process. They would ask what my name was and I would state "Magistrate Michael John Ryan." I also had a badge that had the same moniker,
"Cleveland Municipal Court Magistrate Michael John Ryan." The name began to reverberate in their minds as well as the Ward Club members and other parade watchers.

The parades gave me the opportunity to distinguish myself from others who may have considered to be a judicial candidate. Society's perception of judges was and still is one of individuals who are not receptive to the public. They see them as being on a pedestal and not accessible. I wanted to change the way people saw judges and judicial candidates and so instead of simply walking in the middle of the street for a parade or riding in a convertible vehicle along the parade route I would run from one side of the street to the next shaking hands with as many people as possible and introducing myself as briefly as I could without being offensive. I was thankful to Mike Fields and Chris Jones who helped me by informing me regarding the locations, times and coordinators of the parades. They also provided assistance for me by running interference if people became too aggressive regarding prior cases or they were instrumental in pulling the women away who held on a little too tight when I was introducing myself. I tried to participate in all of the parades in both the City of Cleveland and the outer ring suburbs as well because I felt that I needed to touch not just those who could one day vote for me but individuals who could influence family and friends to support me that did have the authority to vote for me; I adopted the philosophy of leaving no vote unturned!

The last place I would go for my "Thank you tour" was the churches that I had been blessed to speak at or allowed me to be introduced.

Chris and Mike, along with the Council of Sisters, had liaisons in the churches that permitted me to come back and the Angels of those houses of worship were very kind and acknowledged my presence. I would stay for the entire service and would raise my hands, stomp my feet, sing and clap my hands just like I would do in my own church service at Emmanuel Apostolic Church. It was very rewarding going back to the churches because even though it wasn't as the victor, I knew that they were praying for me and wanted to see me reach my goal. They promised to keep me on their prayer lists and to remember the name whenever I decided to run again.

The general election came and went in the first week of November of 2004 and I began to prepare for a very long campaign for Judge of Cleveland Municipal Court. I, however, would have to deal with another significant loss before the campaign got into to full swing. My biological dad, Richard Solomon, had become very ill.

Over the last year I had become reacquainted with him after discovering, via my uncles, that he was in a nursing home in Beachwood, Ohio. I would frequently go visit my dad, either with my wife and or the kids or alone. I would cut his hair, sit and talk with him, read his Bible with him and discus his childhood and how he and my mother met. I would also contribute to his bad habit by buying him cigarettes. As he got progressively worse I would help feed him at times as well. I was amazed at how life came full circle where he should have been there to help feed me as a child and now I was feeding him. I forgave him for not making a better effort to enforce his rights to raise me. I possessed no animosity, no anger, no frustration, no condemnation for my dad. I had already missed more than eighty percent of my life without him and didn't want to waste time on trivial issues that I couldn't control or change. I was living in the present and in order to provide foundation for my kids about their Grandfather I had to find out who he was as a man and as a father. Unfortunately, our time was winding down due to the acceleration of his Multiple Sclerosis condition. He developed pneumonia shortly before Thanksgiving and before I could see him as the nursing home made the decision to send him to hospice care, he died.

Just as we were getting a chance to know each other and further cement a relationship that had been unable to develop due to a number of circumstances, his life ended. I was sad, disappointed but also relieved for him because he wasn't suffering anymore. He was no longer confined to a wheelchair, he no longer had to struggle to use his one non paralyzed arm, he was no longer required to have others assist him to the restroom, to assist him to eat or to assist him to bathe (although he enjoyed that when the female nurses did it). Even though with my dad's death I was now parentless he left me with a connection to his siblings, particularly my Uncle Harry and Uncle Tony. I also, was able to meet my Aunt Arlene, Aunt Beverly, Uncle Kenny, Uncle Australia, Uncle Don Lee and my Uncle Darryl. I was able to meet other cousins and other family friends. The repast after my dad's Home going service was reminiscent of the scene in the movie "Antwan Fisher" where he imagined sitting at thirty seat table full of food with family and friends waiting on him to come home.

A few days after my dad's service we began our campaign for Cleveland Municipal Court in earnest. I traveled to the Board of Elections had acquired several petitions in order to obtain the thousand registered voter signatures needed in order to simply be placed on the ballot. The Board of Elections allowed potential candidates to turn in triple the amount of signatures in order to ensure that the candidate had a valid number of signatures. Signatures could be invalid if a person was not registered, had not voted in several elections or was a valid signer for another potential candidate seeking the same seat. Accordingly, I had my work cut out for me because I had five other opponents who were seeking the same signatures I was trying to procure.

I held an initial organizational meeting with friends, family, and volunteers. We met at a local library and devised our plan to win eleven months from that day. We were able to convince nearly twenty people, along with me and my wife, to complete the petitions. We needed people to work assiduously due to the sheer volume of the number of valid signatures. Once we completed that task we then needed people to sign various sheets for several categories: parades, help with fundraisers, making phone calls, distributing literature, speaker's bureau, and Sunday camp shipping (combination of campaigning and worshipping). Everyone was very eager to help except for the individual I brought to provide us some guidance as a possible campaign chair.

That individual had managed the successful campaign of one of my friends who was currently sitting as a Municipal Judge in the Cleveland area. The individual came highly recommended but they declined my request to be the campaign manager I think due to our inability to pay the amount needed to secure their services. They did indicate that we appeared to have a very energetic, large and passionate volunteer base that could help us do very well in the race. We had trouble choosing a campaign manager because everyone we spoke to, even those who had been either recommended or sought me out, were asking for amounts that I could not supply. I wanted to spend most of the money we raised on the campaign material since we were operating from a disadvantage regarding lack of name recognition, connections in the political arena and money.

       Once I discovered that the individual was not going to be as helpful as I anticipated I shifted the focus to our strategy regarding the literature. My wife and I had passed out copies of the literature we used for the initial race and the literature we discussed using for this race. We received a lot of backlash from one my "step" father Allen's relatives. She was adamantly opposed to me listing the challenges I experienced that related to my parents drug use and my "step" father's violent tendencies. She felt that it was unnecessary and disrespectful to their memories. She, however, wasn't the first person to raise concerns, I did that internally so many times when I was younger and before I even contemplated a run for elected office. Many of the people in the room felt that my decision to reveal what transpired in my life was a demonstration of humility; something they found was not the reputation of other jurist. Many of the volunteers thought jurist were elitist, arrogant, rigid and conservative individuals. They felt I was unique because of my humility and the philosophy I possessed towards those that came before me of: *But for the Grace of God there go I,* and thought my decision to include the personal information was nothing more than a manifestation of who I truly was as a person. My sister was the last person whose advice I sought on displaying that information out of respect for her because she lived through it as well. She simply said, "Mike it's the truth." I then decided that all of the literature would provide a synopsis of my life experiences for voters to peruse.

       Lastly, prior to us leaving my Aunt Joann's boyfriend Bill had been looking at my literature and asked, "Do you have a campaign theme?" I said, "Not really. Do you have any suggestions?" He then said, "Well, I was just reading your literature and thought this would be a catchy acronym." On both pieces of literature he saw the terms fairness, integrity and toughness but not in that order. He then put them in the latter order and stated that the campaign theme should be " F.I.T (Fairness, Integrity Toughness) to SIT on the Bench" The fit was also used to counter claims that my youthfulness and minimal experience didn't qualify me for the position. I loved it and we began to put the theme on all of the literature, t-shirts and signs.

I had learned some very valuable lessons prior to the meeting with my volunteers. One of those lessons was to secure support from other elected officials much earlier than I attempted to in 2003 and 2004. I, with the assistance of Chris Jones, went to Cleveland City Council meeting every Monday for an entire month. I waited both before and after the sessions to approach each councilperson regarding the open judicial seat. I went to ask them for their support because they possessed a significant amount of influence over their constituents who would eventually become mine as well if I were successful. They were also generally the ward leaders in their respective areas and thus had influence over the executive committee members that would be voting regarding the Democratic Endorsement. I was able to secure commitments from a number of council members that would at a minimum, prevent a candidate from obtaining the recommendation from the Ward leaders to the Executive Committee. I had previously sent letters to each councilperson and Ward leader announcing my candidacy along with experience, accomplishments and why I wanted their support. I had also sent a holiday card and letter to the individual precinct committee persons throughout the city and had individually signed both. My hand felt like spaghetti noodles after signing all those items. Many of the precinct committee persons were astonished, but happy that I took the time to hand write my signature and was just another way of connecting with the electorate.

After my adventure at City Hall concluded I then began to venture out to the ward clubs; all twenty-one (21). I had to use yahoo maps many times to find the ward clubs that were at times tucked away into nooks and crannies in the neighborhoods throughout Cleveland. I was not precluded from speaking since there had not been any endorsement vote either for or against me and the councilperson, especially those that I had secured an endorsement from, were more than willing to allow me to address the club. I was generally given between two (2) and five (5) minutes to give my stump speech, which I had perfected over the last twelve months. I would begin by addressing their initial concern about my age and then delve into my life and personal experiences. I would usually say after thanking the Ward leader": I'm thirty-three (33) years old for those of you who are wondering what is this kid doing talking about running for judge. I have been a prosecuting attorney, a defense attorney, an administrator in the Department of Public Safety in the City of Cleveland. I am currently a Magistrate Judge for the Cleveland Municipal Court and I hear the same cases that I once prosecuted people for as a prosecuting attorney as well as defended people as a criminal defense attorney. I bring a unique perspective to the bench because I have a balanced experience due to being on both sides of the room. Additionally, I have been making decisions as judicial officer for the last nearly four years. I am uniquely qualified not because of just my professional experiences but because of the challenges I faced as a child." I would then simply state the bullet points on the literature and quickly see people retrieve it once I started talking about my personal life. I would then conclude by saying that " My life and professional experiences allow me to be compassionate but also set a high standard for those who may be found responsible for some wrongdoing in my court." I wasn't just impacting potential voters but also the precinct committee people who happened to be at the meeting. I would then suggest, and they would then act accordingly, that they tell someone else about me. I was able to create a buzz, despite the fact that there was a heated mayoral campaign taking place simultaneously with the seven judicial and twenty-one council races.

The buzz intensified when we held the Cuyahoga County Democratic Party Endorsement meeting for Cleveland Municipal Court. My band of volunteers joined me as we ventured to a west side establishment large enough to hold all the democratic party's precinct committee people from the twenty-one (21) wards of the City of Cleveland and Village of Bratenahl. A few weeks before that meeting all of the candidates had appeared before all of the ward leaders and neither candidate received enough votes to get a recommendation from the Executive Committee. I had learned from one of the ward leaders that I fell one vote shy of obtaining the recommendation for the endorsement to the precinct committee people. When we arrived on a cold winter/spring Saturday morning we placed our people, with our computer generated t-shirts,(we brought better t-shirts with the union bug when we raised more money) in places near the entry to the establishment. My volunteers and my wife, Lauren and Mike were cheering and shouting " Michael Ryan, Michael Ryan, Michael Ryan" as the precinct committee people entered one by one into the establishment. Once inside I was able to go around to the areas that had been designated for each ward. I had met and spoke with many of the precinct committee people while I was at their ward clubs. They had grown very fond of me and many simply shook my hand, gave me a wink and a thumbs up and said " I got you Ryan!"

Once all of the precinct committee people arrived, the Democratic Party Chairman, Jimmy Dimora, explained the process and indicated each candidate for the contested races, there were two, would be given three minutes to address the precinct committee people. The individuals wards would then caucus and tally up the vote. In order to receive the endorsement one candidate had to get sixty-percent of the precinct committee people who were present and eligible to vote for them. Sixty percent was nearly impossible due to the fact that there were five people in our race. Two of the candidates were from the west side of the city where the population was mainly Caucasian and the three remaining candidates were all from the east side which was predominantly African American. The ward clubs were also reflective of the cultural make-up of the east and west side communities.; except for Ward 11, which was a mixture and Ward 14 which had a significant Hispanic population. I kept my speech very brief because I had sent numerous correspondences to the precinct committee people well before the endorsement meeting and I had addressed them at their respective ward clubs. After we all spoke they began to take the vote and while many were not surprised to see the African American candidates get split support from the east side many were amazed at the level of support I received from precinct committee people from the west side. They were not concerned about color but saw me as someone who transcended color and would be an asset to the Cleveland Municipal Court bench. I didn't receive the endorsement but I did receive more votes than any other candidate. I was the only one who received significant support on both sides of the Cuyahoga River (The physical line of demarcation for the East and

West sides of Cleveland). One councilman from the west side whose support I didn't have because of his promise to support another candidate before he knew I was in the race whispered to me, "I didn't realize you had such broad support Mike. The next time you run for something please let me know I'll support you." I remarked, " Thank you and I intend on calling you on that promise one day!" I left even more encouraged and determined to work as diligently as possible to achieve my dream.

I was starting to see the light at the end of the tunnel and I was making every conceivable step to make sure the light didn't go out. Not only was I energized but other people were as well. Elected officials, candidates, and precinct committee people themselves were all talking about how I was able to garner votes in areas that African American men were generally unable to secure votes. The damor was slowing growing into a roar.

While clearly buzz wasn't the issue we had to deal with raising money was problematic for several reasons. Firstly, Cleveland Municipal Court judges couldn't promise to bring more jobs, or hire more police or provide more services to the community and therefore people were reluctant to even consider voting for judges let alone donating any money to their campaigns. Secondly, unlike other Court of Common Pleas judges, Municipal Court judges didn't appoint private attorneys to represent indigent defendants. The normal process in Municipal Court was for the Public Defender to provide legal representation from his staff of competent, effective and passionate attorneys. Thus, there was no benefit in donating to an individual who could not help their cause plus I wasn't an established incumbent judge either. Thirdly, the council and mayoral candidates were siphoning all of the money from community members who would traditionally donate to worthy candidates no matter party affiliation or elected office. The letter my campaign sent to past donors, to Political Action Committees for various organizations never received a response. We were all trying to drink from the same well and the water level was diminishing. I decided that we should combine traditional and nontraditional ways of acquiring funds to support our endeavor.

The traditional ways the campaign employed was writing letters to family and friends asking for donations to the campaign. I secured addresses of college classmates, former coaches, friends and family that lived out-of-state. Robin or Brenda would sign the letters, put self-addressed stamped envelopes inside with instructions on the additional information that had to be sent for recording purposes and then mail them across the city, state and country. We didn't receive a lot of responses but the ones that did respond I was more than appreciative. I knew full well that they had no obligation to forgo their hard earned dollars to support me. I surmised they did it based on the impact I had on them during our interactions at Allegheny. Thus, I had a college classmate and former track teammate, Fletcher Brooks, who I hadn't spoken to since graduation send me over a hundred dollars. My old track coach Ralph White also put a substantial sum in the mail to help support the cause. Older alumni from Allegheny also deposited checks not simply because they knew me but because they believed in my candidacy.

I also held a campaign kickoff at senior citizen building on the north east side of Cleveland with the help of two other surrogate grandmothers Doris Jones and Daisy. They were very instrumental in galvanizing support for me amongst elderly residents in the Cuyahoga Metropolitan Housing Authority properties. They wanted to make sure I met the people in their building and I obliged and said the best way is do a fundraiser. We didn't charge anyone to attend but requested a donations in $50 increments up to the maximum individual contribution. My wife, my sisters-in-law Brenda and Wanda, my brother-in-law Ted, my mother-in-law Doris, Doris, Daisy and a host of residents decorated the hall located near the building in green, white and blue streamers, napkins and balloons. We had ordered chicken wings, pizza, we had celery sticks, carrots, tossed salad, meatballs and of course cookies and potato chips as well. I had invited friends, family, neighbors, co-workers (Who actually were permitted to come without paying due to the judicial rules that prevented me from charging those who I may have supervision over once elected), my bosses including Chief Magistrate Greg Clifford and Deputy Chief Joan King as well as all of the judges. Greg was present at the only fundraiser I had for my county court race and was Johnny on the spot for this one too. I cannot recall an event where I needed support, just people to be present, when he wasn't in the crowd. He was a great role model for me and an outstanding role model for young and mature African American men. He and I had multiple conversations about strategy since he nearly missed an opportunity to win a primary for county judge a few years before I became an attorney. While Greg's presence wasn't surprising I was pleasantly shocked to see three judges walk through the door and I also learned that they left a donation to the campaign as well. Judge Mabel Jasper, the matriarch of Cleveland Municipal Court, the person whose shoes I would attempt to fill, Judge Pauline Tarver and my very good friend Anita Laster Mays. I felt a sense of worth knowing that their presence meant a lot to other people because it demonstrated to them that other jurist on this bench had confidence enough to not simply say they believed I would be a good judge but to back it up with an appearance and some resources to help. Our fundraisers were always alcohol free and nothing was different about this one. We did hire a disc jockey to play music of all varieties because of the age and cultural variance we had in the hall. I spoke after an hour had elapsed and introduced the elected officials, other candidates, I thanked my wife, Brenda, Wanda, Doris, Doris Jones, Daisy, and everyone that had a hand in making our initial fundraiser a success. We cleaned up and went home with a little more foundation to start purchasing more literature, t-shirts, bumper stickers, and all of the other paraphernalia that was typically used in political campaigns.

Our next fundraiser was non-traditional, notwithstanding that I was I was advised to have one where I invited attorneys, elected officials and candidates to a venue near downtown Cleveland. I instead choose to invite those same individuals, plus family and friends, to a bowling fundraiser. I thought it was a genius idea because the owner gave us a great deal on the amount we paid to secure the lanes, shoes and parking. My kids friends, their parents, neighbors, volunteers, bowling enthusiasts, people who were initially just coming to bowl and who saw who the fundraiser was supporting came and bowled with us. I bowled a few gutter balls in between my walks to the different lanes thanking people for coming and helping the campaign. When Brenda finished counting and collecting all of the money it was the most successful fundraiser we had during the entire campaign. I say that even though we scheduled another fundraiser where I sent invitations out to attorneys but got very little response.

I was disappointed in the turnout but knew that I wouldn't generate that much from attorneys based on the nature of the court, my lack of connection with the private attorneys and I discovered that one of my opponents had a fundraiser the same day and she had more connections with private counsel and the political community than me. We had one final fundraiser before the voting ended and to no one's surprise it was at the bowling alley again.

We were very deliberate and conscientious about where we spent the dollars we raised because they were limited. Although the bulk of our money was used toward literature we also purchased t-shirts, billboards, yard signs and television spots. We were very fortunate to have help with the distribution of our literature not just from our cadre of volunteers but from George Edwards who became a surrogate grandfather for me. He used his vast grassroots connections to help spread my name like a wildfire in a dry forest in California. George also extended his hand by organizing a meet and greet so that I could be introduced to people like Bryan Flannery and his wife, a past state representative and past state wide candidate. He introduced me to all of the members of the Black Trade Council and several of them after meeting me donated funds to the campaign. George would have his family distributing my literature in and around their neighborhood.

George had a very extensive network but my volunteers and I were successful as well in distributing the literature. I made sure we had more than enough literature at each ward club meeting we attended. We would take the literature to the , community meetings, community festivals, to street club meetings and to the block parties. While some of the places were conventional we decided to go to areas that conventional political wisdom suggested voters didn't go. Grocery stores, night clubs, comedy clubs, high school basketball and football championships, places were the young rising business and political leaders of the city ate and socialized on the near west side and downtown. I was not afraid to go to anywhere or to speak to any group or to distribute any literature in any area of the Greater Cleveland community. My goal was to plaster my face and story in as many venues as possible and thereby inundate my name to the entire public in hopes that I would gain some much needed name recognition without having to mail pieces of literature to every home where a voter lived in the city of Cleveland and Village of Bratenahl.

Me along with my family also went door to door in high voter turnout communities. I did so for three purposes to introduce myself to people, to ask for their vote and to ask if I could place one of my campaign signs in their yard. I was met with utter shock by many voters who said they had never heard of a judicial candidate going door-to-door, I responded by saying that I was an unconventional candidate and my courage along with my credentials not only won me their support but the support of their family, friends, co-workers and neighbors. Robin, Mike, Lauren and Dewayne Davis, my first personal bailiff, were very helpful in my door-to-door campaign strategy. They would go door-to-door and work different sides of one street while I canvassed the other side. Dewayne and Robin would venture out during the day when I was at work.

Robin and the kids were exposed to untold dangers while going door-to-door. On one occasion she and Michael approached a home and the door was open but the screen was closed. When Robin went to knock on the door a huge, mouth foaming, growling dog approached the screen door. Robin noticed that the screen door was ajar and she grabbed a hold of the door and pushed all of her weight against it preventing the dog from exiting the home. Michael did not wait to see if Robin was going to be attacked and ran halfway down the street back towards the car. The homeowner eventually came to the door and called the dog back. I also had a comical run in with a dog as well. I convinced Robin to help me go door-to-door one day after church service. I had on a dress shirt, tie and shoes that lacked a rubber base. I decided to go to areas that had been traditionally ignored by elected officials due to a pattern of disinterest in voting. We agreed to start at opposite ends of the street and meet in the middle. Robin finished before I did due to me engaging in longer conversations with potential voters. As I was leaving one of the porches Robin was motioning for me to unlock the car door. I was confused as to why she didn't simply say out loud "Open the door." Well she didn't say anything because there were three dogs approximately ten feet in front of me and thirty feet in front of her. If she had said something they would have turned towards her. Instead, they began to growl at me, with saliva dangling from their sharp off white teeth. They were midsize dogs with scruffy mangled coats but growled in sync. I took the literature I had and yelled " Shoo, shoo, get away." I then picked up a branch and held it out towards the menacing three. I then yelled "Yahhh, Yahhh. Get backkkkkkk" As soon as I said get back I slipped on the pavement with my dress shoes and flew a few feet in the air along with my literature. I landed on my stomach as I braced my fall with my hands and elbows. I laid on the ground approximately five feet away from the dogs and I still had my stick stretched out towards them and yelled "Get back, get back." Robin of course was at the car door with tears of laughter streaming from her watery eyes. The three dogs walked away without accosting me; probably because they felt bad for me. While we were able to generate a lot of support from the listed conventional and unconventional methods the parades and Sunday morning campshipping was the most effective.

Chris Jones and Mike Fields, two men I consider as brothers from another mother, were very instrumental in taking the campaign to another level with our parade participation. The parades gave us instant exposure to a group voters that we would be unable to touch due to our limited resources. There were parades in most of the twenty-one wards in the City of Cleveland starting in late spring and concluding in mid fall. Chris or Mike would give me prior notice and the procedures the campaign had to follow to receive a spot in a parade. I would complete the application, get a check from Brenda and deliver it to the organization that was coordinating the parade. We would use campaign funds to purchase water for the volunteers who were walking with us in the parade and candy to distribute along the parade route. Our first parade during the campaign was at the New Day in Hough event in May. I was fortunate to have a significant following with family, friends and volunteers all donning white t-shirts with green lettering that said on the front "Elect Cleveland Municipal Court

Magistrate Michael John RYAN to Judge for Cleveland Municipal Court." The back of the t-shirt read Fairness, Integrity Toughness... RYAN is FIT to Sit on the Bench." I also was blessed to have a female motorcycle group ride with us in this parade. I knew I had some very loyal and dedicated people, especially the women, because everyone walked the entire route despite the fact that it started to rain halfway through the parade. All of the women, including my wife, hair was matted on the ends due to the rain. They all complained, but did so in a loving fashion and said they would do it again to help support me.

Each parade we would gain additional supporters and it required that we purchase even more t-shirts. We, however, also started to show our strength to our opponents who were unable to compete with the number of   walkers that we flooded the parade route with each time. The walkers either had literature, candy or signs that were attached to wooden sticks and allowed them to hoist them in the air for people to see my name. We also had people driving cars that had magnetic signs on them again allowing people to see my name. I was able to gain even more excitement and exposure at one of the most popular and well attended parades and festival- Glenville. Chris was able to convince a group of young people who were playing several different drums to wear our t-shirts in exchange for a spot in the parade. They lacked a spot due to some technicality and we needed something unique to set us apart from the other opponents. The young people began to play their drums as we started to walk down the street. They were the intro for me as I began to walk down the street. I would zigzag from one side of the street to the other shaking hands with as many people as possible, unlike my opponents. Mike, a very stout man with a booming voice, would shout my name via his megaphone as we walked the parade route. I also received a resounding loud shout out from the parade master of ceremonies who would be shocked when we walked past the parade stage. They would literally shout " Wow Magistrate Michael Ryan has his own band ya'll." The momentum of the campaign just grew and grew and came to a crescendo at the Annual 11th Ohio Congressional District Caucus Labor Day Parade.

I asked all of my family, friends, co-workers, volunteers, and anyone willing to wear a Ryan t-shirt and walk in the parade. We had more than 60 people total that day who were either walking, distributing literature, candy or riding in a vehicle. We had four vehicles with signs on each side, both magnetic and yard signs taped to the sides of the car, driven by my Uncle Harry, my Sister-in-law Brenda, my Brother-in-law Ted and Dewayne. My sister, my nieces, my nephews, my cousins Kristee and Nikki, my college classmate Darren Hudson and his family, my barber Steve Williams and his daughter and so many other concerned people. I had two large signs that had the same wording that the front of the t-shirts possessed. The signs were three fourths the length of a coach bus. I was able to convince an individual who had a spot in the parade that was close to the front to allow me to put one of my signs on the front of his massive coach bus and the other one of the side. We were also able to add the words Seniors for Ryan on the sign and they allowed Ms. Rice and some of the members of the Council of Sisters and Brothers, with their Ryan t-shirts, to ride on the bus through the parade route. My nephews, Steven Doaty, Mike and Patrick Wright rode miniature motorized bikes alongside the motorcycle groups. My daughter, Lauren, lead a cheer that was a derivation on a popular hip-hop song. Lauren would start by saying "Where he at?, Where he at?" and the girls would repeat her statement. I would then surface after being engrossed in conversation with the parade crowd and they would then yell in unison "There he go there he go." It also helped those parade watchers that were looking for me because all they saw was the sign. My popularity skyrocketed from my participation at that parade. Many of the women parade goers were more concerned about whether I was single than what office I was seeking. I was very flattered by the compliments about me being sexy, handsome, cute or fine. I was humbled when the women wanted pictures with me and were reluctant to let go of my hand or my neck if I hugged them.

I was even more astonished by the hug I received from the late Congresswoman Stephanie Tubbs Jones, who coordinated the parade, as I passed the parade stage. She whispered in my ear, "I'm proud of you. Keep up the good work." It was confirmation of our first official meeting that took place in her caucus office. She and I spoke for about thirty minutes regarding my candidacy and my personal life in January of 2005. After the conversation concluded she took me through her office and introduced me to all of her staff. She didn't endorse me but she also didn't endorse anyone else in my race notwithstanding the fact that several of my opponents had known her for a very long time. She said, "The person who works the hardest will win this race." I was working harder than any of my opponents. The latter was evidenced by the weight I had loss during the campaign; I looked more like a twenty-three year old as opposed to a thirty-three year old. My suits were falling off of me, my shirt sleeves were so long that I was buttoning the wrist portion by my fingertips. My appearance wasn't the only indication of my hard work, I received the loudest response from the massive crowd that had gathered at Luke Easter Park after the parade ended. The audience of approximately four or five hundred people screamed, hollered, cheered and clapped louder for me than they did for my opponents after Congresswoman Tubbs-Jones introduced me. My campaign was no longer being seen as an underdog but was quickly emerging as force to be reckoned with in this race.

Although I received a lot of adoration from the parade goers throughout the city but especially at the 11th Congressional District parade, it was my camp shipping at the churches that was the catalyst behind my campaign surge. I knew, from days of sitting in church as a kid and hearing different candidates come before our congregation asking for their support and vote, how important the church was for candidates seeking elected office. The church has traditionally been the place where, especially in the case of African Americans, that people socialized outside of their job and obtained information about what was going on in the local community. I knew that my family rarely read the newspaper, which generally contained more information about candidates, and the television was reserved for the few who had the resources to gain access to that medium. Moreover, the church represents a place of comfort, hope, reliability and truthfulness. The congregation can be influenced by their leaders approval or disapproval of an individual. I found it very difficult when I initially began my campaign to get an opportunity to, at a minimum, be introduced let alone be given a chance to address the congregation because I was not a part of the click. I hadn't run a successful campaign, I was not able to lavish the religious leaders with breakfast, lunch or dinner. I had the Council of Sisters, Chris, Mike and my faith.

My opportunities to speak at the different churches changed when I met with the three religious organizations that were made up of local pastors throughout the Greater Cleveland area. I met with each group and their members after being invited by one of the members. I received invitations based on my personal connection with one member, and the assistance of Ms. Rice for another group and Chris and Mike's influence with the third group.

I was given a few minutes to speak and I was consistent with each organization. I introduced myself and declared immediately my love and affection for Jesus Christ. I then talked about my church home, Emmanuel Apostolic Church, and my pastor, District Elder Gregory Pratt, and my wonderful family Robin, Mike, Lauren and Ma. I then informed them about my professional experience. The last thing I spoke about before I took my seat was my testimony. I spoke sincerely about my tumultuous upbringing, God's preservation of me and the accomplishments I achieved notwithstanding the turmoil. My ability to persevere and overcome the horrific challenges I faced and to acknowledge that it was my faith combined with hard work that was the source of my success resonated with them. They all knew, based on their years of study and pastoring, that their congregation is built up on the testimonies of other believers. The majority of them asked me to come to their churches to speak. I wasn't just a candidate to them but instead someone who could inspire their people to overcome their own life challenges that paled in comparison to mine.

Every Sunday I was visiting a different congregation. I would stay the entire time even if the pastor allowed me to speak or introduced me well before the end of service. I didn't want to disrespect the congregation by only visiting for the purpose of being introduced and then leaving. I also didn't want to leave because I was missing my own church service when I campaigned on Sundays. I was blessed to have my wife join me on many occasions but would at times go solo so that we kept some semblance of a connection with our home church.

As I stated earlier many of the pastors allowed me the opportunity to address the congregations. The pastor would openly state that I have no authority to endorse anyone and I'm not doing that in this instance I just want to give this young man a chance to say a few words. My testimony never changed despite what church I attended. I would usually say, " Praise the Lord, " and the congregation would then respond loudly, proudly and in unison" Praise him. He's worthy to be praised." I would continue with "My name is Magistrate Michael John Ryan and I'm asking for your prayers, support and vote to change my name in November to Judge Michael John Ryan." The congregation would laugh with some responses of "Amen." I then said "While I stand before you as a father, husband and an attorney my greatest title is believer. " Different people in the congregation would then erupt with " Hallelujah. Thank you Jesus. Go head son." Next, I said "While you see me standing here with a nice suit, shirt, tie and "Stacey Adams knockoffs, I wasn't born with a silver spoon in my mouth. In fact the spoon was more like wooden or plastic." Next, I would discuss in a very expedited manner a number of the stumbling blocks I incurred as a child and then as the crescendo approached I spoke about how I turned those blocks into stepping stones due to my faith. The congregation would usually be in an uproar by the time I was finished. They would be clapping and shouting "Glory to God. Nobody but God. Favor ain't fair." It was rare when I didn't receive a standing ovation from them because they knew it was God's hands on me throughout my struggles that allowed me to experience the successes. I saw many of the older women grabbing tissues and taking off their glasses to wipe the tears away. I was literally mobbed with hugs, kisses, handshakes and most importantly promises to vote for me and to spread the word to family and friends. They all stated how proud they were of me and wished God's continued blessings on me and my family. I was able to influence believers and I had three other groups to try and win over: the bar associations, the media and lastly the voters.

All five of the candidates, along with the other seven candidates in the other contested race and the uncontested judicial candidates had to appear before the Judge for Yourself panel. Instead of the previous bar assessments where we traveled to different areas to speak to different organizations they collaborated and we faced representatives from each organization at one time in one area. Additionally, we spoke to the group separately as opposed together in an effort to ensure that our responses were original. I walked into the Cleveland Bar Association, where the panel was meeting and faced attorneys that I had attended law school with, some who had trained me, some who I had practiced with, some who I practiced against and some who had appeared before me in my capacity as a Magistrate. The vast majority of them, however, I had no prior contact with and no idea what area they specialized in if any. We were allowed to give a short introduction and then the questions came at lightning speed. I was asked questions about docket efficiency, recognition of a lawyer's finite time to handle matters in court, my opinion on incarceration and my experience. Some of the questions came from my submission of a resume and answers to a questionnaire.

The last question was one that through me for a loop because it was an issue that had never been discussed throughout the campaign~ "If you did win will you be qualified to sit as a judge?" The question had been posed by a member of the group based on the fact that I had only practiced as an attorney for four in a half years before I was appointed as a Magistrate. In order to be a judge a person must have practiced law for a minimum of six years. One of the attorneys gave me a copy of a case that claimed that Magistrate's don't practice law when they work under a judge. It was a very old case that found that conclusion. I was mortified because according to that case I didn't have the nine years of practicing law I had been touting but instead only four in half. I initially thought that my campaign was over and all the hard work I had completed and things I accomplished were for naught. The lead coordinator of the Judge for Yourself panel asked me to draft a memorandum of law to address this controversy.

I took my lunch and went to the law library at the Old County Courthouse located across from my job at the Justice Center. I did what every good lawyer should do when they get a case that is on point with an issue that is supportive or against their position~ I Shepardized it. Shepardizing a case means that you review the history of the case to see if it has been discussed in subsequent cases and/or by higher courts. I found that the case I was given had been essentially overruled by a higher court. I found a higher court case that concluded Magistrates do engage in the practice of law because they are hearing matters that require the legal interpretation of rules and case law. It went on to also find that Magistrates draft opinions on behalf of the jurist they serve and thus actively participate in making the law. I drafted my memorandum with that case as the centerpiece of my discussion. I delivered the memorandum to the group and discovered that the other candidates both Magistrates and Bailiffs, although they had more prior experience as an attorney before becoming a Magistrate and thus were not subject to the rule, were required to complete a memorandum of law as well. I dropped it off to the receptionist and felt vindicated that I not only was safe but that I was able to demonstrate the legal acumen needed to be a good jurist.

I subsequently received some of the highest marks of any of the candidates once the final assessment was made by the Judge 4 Yourself panel of bar associations. I had over a 3.5 on a 4.0 scale regarding my fitness to be a judge on that bench. You received a 4.0 for an excellent rating and a 0 for a Not Recommended. I received several ratings of Excellent and several Good but no Adequate or Not Recommended marks. I was able to use that on my literature and in my stump speeches both at the ward clubs and in the churches as well as the judicial candidate forums too support my cause.

My literature and stump speeches didn't simply change because of the ratings I received from Judge 4 Yourself it was due to some other endorsements. All five us the candidates in our race met in a room with the Plain Dealer editors a few months before the election. They asked each of us the same question regarding our experience, what we felt was the definition of judicial temperament, should the State of Ohio go to merit based appointments for judges as opposed to elections and whether we supported longer terms in exchange for a requirement of additional years of experience practicing law beyond the current six year period. We all took turns answering the questions and we took turns responding first to the questions. I wasn't as nervous as I was more than a year ago when only Peter and I sat before this same group. The latter experienced prepared me for this interview session. We were very cordial to one another and did not attempt to disparage anyone else in our answers. We made eye contact with each other, including the editors, and had a very productive and affable meeting. I didn't have any information nor would I have ever used any information that would sully the reputation of my opponents. I wanted people to compare us but at the end of the day select me based on my qualifications and not simply because you dislike the person I was running against. Moreover, Cleveland has a very small legal community and I was bound to see them again. Additionally, if I was unsuccessful who ever won would instantly become my boss; I knew better than to create tension between me and a potential supervisor.

A month or so after the meeting I purchased a paper, one of many that I had purchased during the last month looking for an announcement on the endorsement. I desperately wanted to receive the endorsement because it was another sign of validation. If I got the endorsement it meant that I was able to convince a group of astute politically conscious editors for Northeast Ohio's largest newspaper to recommend to more than 200,00 registered voters in Cleveland, Ohio and Bratenahl, Ohio that I should be their choice for Municipal Court Judge. I nearly went to the Sports section out of habit but instead went directly to the last page of the Metro Section and lo and behold there was a 4 x 6 picture of me that I had submitted to the Plain Dealer before our interview. The article that appeared below elaborated on the congeniality that existed between the candidates at the meeting but stated how one of us would be called "Your Honor" in a few months. It spoke about the experience the two Court of Common Pleas judges personal bailiffs possessed and said they would make fine judges but the three Magistrates had separated themselves from those two individuals. It went on to stress how it was much more difficult to distinguish the Magistrates because we all did similar work and would bring a wealth of experience and knowledge to the job that the personal bailiffs lacked. The last comment, however, was that Ryan was the better choice. Despite my youthfulness and my lack of experience, they were influenced by my demeanor, conviction, the reputation I had of being even handed as a Magistrate and of course my ability to persevere could be motivational for those who appeared before me. I would also receive the co-endorsement of the local African American newspaper The Call & Post, and the Sun News (I didn't receive any of their endorsements in my first race for judge).

I was armed with endorsements from organizations that people trusted and relied upon as well as from elected officials like County Commissioner Peter Lawson Jones, Councilmen Kenneth Johnson Sr., Roosevelt Coats, and Kevin Conwell and Ward 7 Political Action Committee. Some of the others Councilman stayed neutral or had chosen allegiance with my opponents. I wasn't frustrated or angry that I couldn't get their support because I had adopted the philosophy that the venerable late Ward 7 Councilwoman Fannie Lewis told me when her Ward 7 PAC didn't endorse me in my first race. She said, "In politics, you can have no permanent friends and no permanent enemies. Those who supported you before may be on the other side of an issue in the future and those who were opponents presently could be your staunchest cheerleaders down the road." I was dealing with that reversal of fortune where everything seemed to be closed off to me in 2004 most of those same doors were swinging wide open for me in 2005. When it appeared that I was the least likely to be successful after 2004 here I was a year and six months later on the verge of making history.

The primary election for the mayor and council seats took place in October. The majority of the judicial candidates took that day off because all of the judicial candidates only competed at the General Election. I, however, secured a small group of volunteers, led by me and my wife and we traveled to the most active voting precincts in the City of Cleveland. I wanted another opportunity to introduce myself to voters or a chance to reinforce my name among those who knew me. I directed people to approach voters who were leaving to avoid any confusion that I was on the ballot for the primary. We distributed literature and reminded them to vote again on November 7th for the General Election and I implored them to ask for their vote for me.

WHY NOT MICHAEL JOHN RYAN AS JUDGE?

Monday November 6th, Election Day eve arrived and we were exhausted. Robin, me, Dewayne, Lauren, Mike and Ma (Doris) had worked extremely hard over the last eleven months all for one day. Robin had sacrificed her career in order to support my dream. She resigned from her position at University Suburban Health Center and decided to operate a daycare for three beautiful girls to help supplement the income she lost from leaving her longtime position. She was able to balance the daycare activities with being co-campaign manager with me. She was my greatest cheerleader but also gave me the best constructive criticism about how to approach most of the issues that the campaign faced. She did all of that while also maintaining our home while I was away at different political events. I am forever indebted to her for loving me, protecting me, encouraging me, believing in me and taking care of my babies. I owed my kids because of the time I missed out helping them with homework and school projects, talking about their day, missing school activities, taking them to the doctor and other parental responsibilities because of campaign obligations. I was grateful to my family for enduring so many long nights and exhausting activity field days of parades, community festivals, stuffing envelopes, putting stamps on envelops, making their acting debut in the commercial we shot, allowing me to plaster their faces on literature and billboards that were positioned throughout Cleveland.

I had taken vacation days leading up to the election and so I had the entire Election Eve day to prepare for Election Day. Robin and I had made confirmation calls all day to people who had agreed to distribute literature at each polling place in Cleveland and Bratenahl. Ms. Rice was also able to secure people to pass out my literature on the Westside of the city at a minimal cost. We had volunteers, family, friends and some paid people to represent me at the polling places. Me, Robin and Ma made sandwiches, put potato chips and water in bags for those who stood from 6:30 a.m. to 7:30 p.m. We had an assembly line going. I was responsible for putting the bread on the counter and spreading either mustard or mayonnaise on the wheat slices. Ma would then proceed to place either ham, hard salami, chicken or turkey breast or combination thereof on the covered bread. Robin would add the lettuce, cheese and tomatoes. I would complete the finished product by slicing the sandwich in either triangle or rectangle shapes and placing them in Ziploc sandwich bags.

We also prepared the separate packages of literature that were to be distributed at the polling places. Robin and Ma, me and Dewayne were entrusted to individually deliver my literature that evening, along with three other judicial candidates literature, to those working the polls for us. We did not have a joint piece but we all agreed to combine resources and since they had people throughout the city we used their people and they used ours. It saved us money but gave us more exposure. We also gave some of those individuals instructions to place our respective campaign signs outside the polling place as another reminder to those voters to cast their vote for me.

Robin and I placed some of the signs in the polling places that traditionally had the largest voter turnout. I was not leaving that to chance because people say they will do one thing but their actions are sometimes completely contrary to their verbal claims. We did not have any adventures similar to what we encountered in the Democratic Primary of 2004 and thus we were grateful. We, however, did have some precarious situations involving dogs again. Robin, with Ma riding along with her, went to a dilapidated home on the Eastside of Cleveland that had little to no lighting near the back door. Robin was advised to leave the literature in the back door but due to the other candidates not providing their literature until after 8 p.m. Robin went to the home when it was dark. She approached the back door to drop the literature and saw a massive dog running and growling. She threw the literature, which was banded together with rubber bands, on the back porch and ran towards the car with the dog giving chase and the chain rattling, the dog barking and foaming at the mouth, Robin was screaming and yelling for Ma to open the door, which she did is a feverish manner. As Robin got within five feet of the car, the dog was yanked backwards, his barking turned into a yelp and then a whimper and he stopped and panted as he walked back towards the back porch.

Robin and Ma drove home and I met them both there at approximately 2 or 3 a.m. Election Day. We were all exhausted and closed our eyes for a few hours in order to make sure our batteries were recharged for the rest of the day.

The alarm clock began blaring with the sound similar to that of garbage truck backing at approximately 5:00 a.m. I threw the covers off and leaped out of bed onto the cold wooden bedroom floor and headed to the bathroom to brush my teeth, rinse with mouthwash and take a shower. After I finished I woke Robin and she begrudgingly woke up and repeated my actions. We then woke Ma up and she repeated our actions. The last two to be awaken were Lauren and Mike. I was completely dressed by the time Lauren and Mike were awake. I was on the phone calling to make sure people knew where they were supposed to be stationed throughout the day. I didn't have to go vote, in fact none of my volunteers who lived in Cleveland or Bratenahl had to vote that day because we all took advantage of the absentee ballot process weeks before the official election. Accordingly, friends and family who needed extra instructions came over to our house before the polls opened. I reminded them to be assertive but not aggressive when approaching potential voters. I didn't want them to be passive and simply let people enter the polling place because they look like they don't want to be bothered. I suggested that they let the potential voter dismiss them but don't assume. I reminded them to ask the voter to vote for me and to thank them for exercising their right to vote. I advised them to make sure they stayed 100 feet away from the entrance while they were distributing the literature. Lastly, I asked them to keep the conversations short so that they could reach as many people as possible.

I left the house and went to pick up my brother David Chatmon from his maternal aunt's house. Dave had flown in from Richmond, California to help his little and younger brother. Dave agreed to stand at the polls all day and pass out literature in my old neighborhood-Outhwaite. I dropped Dave off at the Lonnie Burton Center, the place I used to go the get free lunch, when there was no food available in our Longwood project apartment. Dave made a huge difference at Lonnie Burton because he brought a lot of attention to himself. He is 6 feet and 9 inches tall and at that time weighed close to 300 pounds. He was a massive walking billboard when he put on one of my t-shirts and he "made" people take my literature and convinced them to vote for his little brother. I was overwhelmed by my brother's actions because he left the warm confines of the west coast, a job and his own family to stand at the polling place for me. I drove away wiping a few tears from my eyes. I repeated the same crying and wiping action when my Grandma Edna showed up as well. She had come in a few days before the election from Florida. She left her warm, cozy southern home and her job to come help her grandson realize his dream. She told me, "I wouldn't miss this for the world." My Grandma Edna was a model of strength and perseverance. She did not give up hope, she didn't abandon her faith notwithstanding the fact that all of her children predeceased her. Instead she encouraged me and my sister to reach our full potential. She and my sister came over to the house after I left.

After I dropped Dave off I headed to the New Avenues polling place off of Euclid Avenue because it had the greatest volume of voters on Election Day of any single polling place in the City of Cleveland. I arrived shortly after 7:00 a.m. and there was a steady flow of people going in and out of the polling place. I positioned myself approximately one hundred and one inch from the polling place. I used the same strategy to approach people that I suggested my representatives use when they were at their respective polling assignments. I was very assertive and only spoke for approximately ten seconds if there were four or five people at a time. I reached out my hand and introduced myself. They would respond in amazement that I, a judicial candidate, was out there asking for their vote. Many people responded by saying "I just saw your commercial last night. You got my vote." Some would inquire, "Weren't you just here last month for the primary?" I would answer in the affirmative and they would then state, "I got you Ryan." I received that kind of response for a majority of the time I was there for the first two hours. People remembered me from speaking at their churches, or a community event or a graduation. Some people were walking in with my literature that they had received from family or friends. There were a number of people who had a copy of the Cleveland Plain Dealer and they simply indicated they were voting in conjunction with the endorsements the paper made. I, however, had a few people who refused to shake my hand and simply waived me away when I tried to approach or hand them some literature. There were some older seasoned voters who didn't refuse to vote for me because I was just too young and they were not convinced by the bar associations or the Plain Dealer recommendations. I respected their decision and simply went to approach the next voter.

As I was soliciting votes at New Avenue I had representatives at other locations; it was essentially a family affair. My brother-in-law Ted was on 131st at Holy Trinity passing out the literature and enjoyed his experience especially because most of the women would look at my picture and say in a coy manner, "He's your brother-in-law!?" "Damn he's fine! He has my vote!" My daughter, Lauren and niece Cassandra, had the same experience at that polling place earlier in the morning before Ted relieved them. My Grandma Edna, all 5 foot 6 inches of her with her fine, perm-less salt and pepper shoulder length hair and her bifocal glasses initially stood and then eventually sat outside Emile De Sauze elementary school, which also traditionally had a huge Election Day voter turnout. Grandma sat out there and passed out literature, talked to the voters and the other candidates poll workers and didn't leave even when it began to drizzle, when the temperature decreased or when it grew dark. My sister and Robin were responsible for delivering food, making sure people had enough literature and checking to make sure people were actually distributing the literature. I was also responsible for ensuring that people who claimed to be covering a polling place was present; especially those who we were paying that day.

I traveled to polling places on the Westside and met individuals who were distributing my literature. I would work in tandem with them and thereby get more exposure. I was also able to inspire the poll worker to be more diligent in their approach towards voters and they acquiesced. Moreover, I replenished their literature and left after approximately thirty minutes of conversation and campaigning. I visited more than five or six polling places the entire day and trusted Robin and my sister to visit other heavily used polling places and repeat my efforts.

At approximately 3:40 p.m. I had to dispense with campaigning and change into my role as a parent. I picked my son up from Boulevard Elementary School. His bright smile and his beautiful brown eyes that were slightly hidden behind his wire rimmed glasses caused a warm feeling to overtake my heart and mind. I had been talking politics all day and now had a chance to relax and discuss my son's day, which was more important at that moment than any voter. I asked him how his day went and he responded, "Good." He said he was hungry so we stopped at a McDonald's to get him his favorite at that time—a cheeseburger. He devoured it in a matter of seconds while washing it down with an orange pop. I know it wasn't healthy but he needed to get some fuel for the final leg of the campaign that he would finish with good old dad.

We stopped at another polling place and I was able to include Mike in this memorable process. We both stood the required feet away from the entrance and I handed him the literature and he would give it to the voter while I was shaking the other hand. Many of the voters responded in a very wonderful way in fact one said " That is so sweet. You have your little brother helping you campaign." I had to correct them, lovingly, and say, "No this is my son." Some who knew that he was my son thought it was great that I was teaching him not just about campaigning but about exercising your right to vote and thus becoming engaged in the process of how one is governed. Mike was naturally a quiet, reserved young man, like me, and this was allowing him to come out of his shell and be a more confident speaker.

At approximately 6:00 p.m. Robin, Ma, my sister, Grandma Edna and Mrs. Rice began to return to the polling place to pay the poll workers. Each paid poll worker was given approximately $50.00 along with the donut and lunch we had provided. Some of the poll workers opted to come to the Election Results party and retrieve their pay at that time. My sister and Robin had some adventures trying to deliver the funds. Some of the workers had left temporarily to use the restroom and had no cell phones so they waited until they returned. One memorable deliverance of the $50.00 occurred at a high rise apartment building on the

Eastside. Robin and my sister rode together to the building and were given a name. Robin and my sister both walked into the front foyer of the apartment building and saw several people surrounding an elderly woman. The other individuals appeared to be much younger than her and suspicious. My sister called out the woman's name and the elderly woman sitting in the chair responded "That's me!" My sister and Robin looked puzzled at each other because the woman was blind. My sister asked the woman "What did you do today?" The blind volunteer stated with conviction " I passed out literature for the judge." My sister then said " What judge?" The woman said "For the young judge. Ryan. Michael John Ryan." My sister, Sharese, shrugged her shoulders toward Robin and then took the money and counted it out to the woman and then balled it up in the woman's hands. They then left out but kept looking back to make sure the woman was not accosted by the people who were surrounding her.

While they were distributing the funds to the poll workers Mike and I headed towards New Avenues. I wanted to finish my day were I started and knew there would be a huge crowd since many Election Day voters either voted before or after work. When we arrived I saw a steady stream of people entering the polling location. They were driving up the long hill from the main street, trying to find parking spots, letting people who had just voted out so they could take their spot and some were being dropped off right at the door. I parked my car only a few feet from the 100 foot barrier. I instructed Mike to stay inside because it got much colder after the Sun went down. The wind was blowing, which made it feel nearly ten degrees cooler. The cold temperatures, however, hadn't fazed me all day. I had my gloves in my pocket and would only put them on when there was a lull in the foot traffic. I, however, refused to shake hands with voters with my gloves on I thought it was disrespectful. I wasn't offended if they had their gloves on I just wanted to illustrate to them my genuineness and lack of elitism. My eyes began to water as the wind blew and my ears began to tingle but I refused to take a break and go into the car and get some heat. Myself and other poll workers that I had met on the campaign trail kept an eye on Mike for me. He just sat patiently in the car listening to music and watching his dad. At approximately 7:15 p.m. there were a few stragglers arriving but I didn't want to leave anything to chance and waited until I saw my watch strike 7:30 p.m.

While I was waiting for the poll to close I turned my head towards the polling place door to waive to the voters that were exiting and unbeknownst to me I felt this little hand grab mine and say "Daddy, I want to stand out here with you." I said, "You don't have to stand with me man. I don't want you to get cold." He then said in a confident but low voice, "Daddy I'll be okay. We only have a few more minutes." This time as the tears began to flow it wasn't due to the wind. So, my son, stood on my right side as I continued to shake hands and plead for every last vote. Mike standing on my right side was ironic especially since his middle name is Benjamin, which means the right hand of my father. He stood there until I noticed his teeth were chattering as he was saying", I'mmmmm ooookay Daaaddyyyy" I took his hand and we walked towards the car and I looked at my watch and it read 7:25 p.m.

I opened Mike's door and put him inside and I then walked around and opened my door, started the car to get it warmed up, directed Mike to put his seat belt on and then I put mine on as well. I didn't move the vehicle initially but sat there and reflected on the campaign and queried to myself "What if I loss?" I recalled the community events, the judicial forums, the canvassing, the phone banking, the fundraisers, passing up eating at political and community events in order to shake more hands and kiss more babies, attending service at a different church each Sunday, stuffing envelopes, losing sleep, depleting our bank account, losing weight, missing school and after school activities with for my babies, missing time with my wife, and many more things that I sacrificed for this campaign. I felt that even if I loss it was worth it. I was told you can't win if you don't run. I had exhausted everything and felt that I could not do anything else, with what I had at my disposal. I worked extremely hard and did so to be an example to my babies. I showed them that if you have faith, create a plan, demonstrate humility, prepare yourself to take advantage of opportunities when they present themselves, persevere and don't accept mediocrity then you can accomplish whatever your heart desired. I began this process well before Lauren and Mike were born. I worked hard in everything I did because I knew they were coming and I didn't want them to grow up the way my sister and I did. I knew becoming a public servant wouldn't be complete security for them but it would provide opportunities for them that I could only dream of when I was their age.

I knew that this would not be a simple victory. I was facing several obstacles: lack of significant monetary resources, lack of a known political name or surname, all of my opponents were women and 69% of the judges on Cleveland Municipal Court at that time were women (9 out of 13), I was an African American male, one of my opponents was entrenched with the African American political leadership in the county and one was a former judge. I had a huge amount of support and a great following but I was not overconfident and refused to become cocky and believe that it was a guarantee.

Mike and I pulled up to the Harvard Community Center, which was located in the Lee/Harvard area famous for being the highest voting community in the city of Cleveland. My cousins Reverend Mel and Diane McCray had helped Robin secure the center's main room for our Results Watch Party. The room was very spacious and could easily hold three hundred to five hundred people comfortably. I wasn't expecting that many people to come and watch the results but I knew that family, friends, some neighbors, volunteers and the poll workers would be there to eat, pray and watch. My wonderful wife had made sure the center was decorated with my campaign colors mixed in with my fraternity colors as well. There were green, white and royal blue balloons with helium in the ceiling. The napkins that were on the tables also depicted the campaign and fraternity colors. My cousin Diane made one of my favorite dishes~ Hot Tamales. We had other great food as well along with snacks, pop, water and juice. We made sure that people left full and happy. We made sure that they would be full the happy part could only be fulfilled by the voters. I entered the center and was met with hugs, kisses, pats on my back, I reciprocated the hugs, kisses and pats on the back. I located Lauren and walked briskly and wrapped my arms around her and kissed both cheeks. My wife was jealous because Lauren would resist everybody else's kisses and hugs except mine. I got a chance to give my Grandmother a huge hug and kiss and a sincere thank you. I grabbed my brother around his waist and hugged him and told him I was truly appreciative of the sacrifice he made not just to fly here but to stand outside one of the lower voting polling places in the city. He, however, was determined to get every vote, no matter the number, from that polling place. I was elated to see everyone but no one else caused my heart to flutter more than Robin. Robin, however, was in an unrecognizable zone.

I didn't immediately see Robin when I first walked in with Mike because she was busy trying to make sure everything was just right. She wanted to make sure we had enough plates, plastic ware, cups and of course food to feed the approximately fifty people we believed would be attending. When I did get a chance to see Robin face to face she appeared to be in a daze. She was active but her eyes were wide as the sea and she was abnormally quiet. I wasn't the only one who noticed her bizarre behavior. My sister asked me "Is Robin was okay?" I said, "I think she is nervous about the results." I intensely watched her as she moved from one area of the center to another. Her hands were shaking and thus anything she carried shook as well. I saw her constantly wiping her eyes like she was internalizing a deep secret and the guilt was starting to manifest itself in her outward actions. I eventually was able to remove her to a corner of the center and reassured her that we would win. I felt confident even though we didn't spend the amount of money others said we needed to win. She seemed to accept my comments but she was still walking around on egg shells most of the night before the results began to trickle in and were relayed to us by the television.

After most of us had eaten we began to watch the small 25 inch television that was running a ticker under the programming updating certain races. The main race of course was the one for mayor. Mayor Jane Campbell was trying to avoid being a one-term mayor and was fighting a fierce challenge from the then Council President Frank Jackson. Councilman Jackson did not endorse anyone in my race, and I was very thankful because I knew he had known some of my opponents much longer than he knew me. He, however, gave me some very sage advice by stating,", Tell your story every time you speak. You may think that everyone in the room has heard it. I assure you there is at least one person who hasn't and who will benefit from hearing your story of perseverance." I did just as he suggested, even if I had visited the particular Ward Club on previous occasions. He was absolutely right because at least one person would approach me at previously visited places and say "I've never heard of you but I'm voting for you and so is everyone in my family!" The news, rightfully so, was more concerned about the mayoral race. It wasn't until 9:30 p.m. until we received any information regarding the status of judicial election results.

The first piece of information we received relating to the election results was from my frat brother T.J. Dow. He was able to gain access to information that was being generated from the Board of Elections. As the Board was providing preliminary results to the internet and the media he was able to get it before the media could post it. I saw his number appear on my cell phone and answered, "What's going on Tuan? Where are you? I thought you were going to stop by?!" T.J. then said, "I had other things to do but I can help in another way. Do you have any results?" I responded in the negative and he said, "Well, I'm here to tell you that you are in the lead." He then cheerfully laughed and I said, "Are you serious?" I was pleasantly surprised because the absentee votes are the first ones to be tabulated. Our campaign lacked the resources to mail literature to each registered Democrat let alone voter in Cleveland and Bratenahl. I didn't possess nor was I able to raise the $50,000, I was advised by a former judge I would need to win. I, however, knew that all of my opponents were mailing to each registered voter because I received their mail at my home address. I decided to be resourceful and I had literature developed where a blank space was left for an address sticker to be placed amid my campaign information. I then made a trip to the Board of Elections each day and retrieved the list of voters who had requested an absentee ballot. Robin, me, Lauren, Mike and Ma would then place the labels supplied by the Board of Elections that had the absentee voter's name and address, along with a stamp, onto the distinctly created literature and mail take them to the main U.S. mail post office on Orange Avenue before the last pick up. Our strategy had obviously worked to perfection cause we now had an improbable lead. I gathered everyone around and informed them we had the first results. They all looked at me with eyes wide open, ears protruding, with a look of great anticipation. When I told them the initial results the room shook from the thunderous applause and yells. I told them to calm down because it was going to be a long night.

We waited for approximately thirty more minutes when we got a call from my Niece Tavia Clark-Pauling, who was living in North Carolina at the time with her son Evan and Husband Veotis, and she relayed results to my Sister-in-law Wanda. Wanda quickly put Tavia on speaker phone and she said "Uncle Michael is leading by _____many votes (I can't recall the number)" I then said "that can't be right because the television says I'm only leading by a lower amount." Tavia chimed in that "Well, I'm on the internet and I have access to the Cuyahoga County Board of Election's website and they are updating the Election results every five to ten minutes." I said "Wow. You are hundreds of miles away and can get more up-to-date information than us!" Tavia and everyone else in earshot of our call began to laugh. After hearing Tavia hang up my confidence increased exponentially.

One of my supporters advised me on how to evaluate the results. He stated that if I could finish at least second or third after the votes stream in from the Westside of the City and I was able win the majority of the Eastside wards I would have a more than fifty percent chance of prevailing. I, however, held a lead, sizable but not insurmountable, from the Westside wards. I began to walk around the room with more a pep in my step. I was less nervous and more talkative with my guests. Robin, however, was still walking on pins and needles, our conversation did very little to assuage any of concerns about me possibly losing. I saw her biting her nails, scratching her head and being very short and distant with people-completely out of her character because she is normally the life of any gathering.

At approximately 10:00 p.m. Tavia called us back as more results were pouring in from the Eastside wards. My lead had shrunk and the position of the candidates had switched. The individual who was in third place after the votes had been tallied on the Westside was now in second place and trying to move up. This made for a very tension filled remaining hours. I failed to waiver on my belief that we were still in a very comfortable position especially since I had not been reduced to second or third place. Moreover, I was still ahead by more than 4,000 votes. I was still very engaged in conversation with other adults or talking to little Mike about something trivial when my phone rung.

"Hello?" I said with waited anticipation and few seconds later T.J. Dow's voice cracks and says," Your Honor," with a chuckle and then says with a serious tone," You are ahead by more than 6,000 votes and 98% of the precincts have been counted. Congratulations Judge Ryan. I mean Judge-Elect Michael John Ryan. GOMAB" I think I hung the phone up without even saying good-bye. I again gathered everyone around me because our attempts to watch updated results from the television was becoming annoying and frustrating. I asked everyone to quiet down for a second and to actually turn off the television. I grabbed Robin's hand and said, "I just received word from my frat brother T.J. Dow that I was ahead by more than 6,000 votes and 98% of the precincts had been counted." I had a smile on my face but I might as well have been speaking Chinese because I didn't get a reaction from most of the people other than Mrs. Rice. She began to scream

" Yes, Yes, Yes he did it!" I then re-stated what I had just spoke a few seconds ago" Guys. I'm ahead by more than 6,000 votes and only 2% of the precincts haven't been counted. There is no way there are 6,000 votes in the two remaining precincts. I cannot be caught. I won!" Immediately, everyone threw their hands, arms, and voices up in the air in unison. People were hugging me, each other and slapping high five. I, however, grabbed my wife first and said", We did it. We won! Thank you for everything. Thank you for believing in me and supporting me as I ventured after my dream...my calling" Robin was so much more relieved afterward she discovered that I won. She then revealed that she wasn't nervous for herself but more so concerned with my potential mental health status if I would have loss. She knew how hard I had worked, the sacrifices I made, the challenges I endured both physically and emotionally and she didn't want a loss to devastate me and subsequently our family especially since it was only three years removed since we had reunified. I always said that my mom was the wind beneath my wings well Robin represents the wings that keep me flying on the right path.

We eventually dispersed and Robin, the kids and I all went home and tried to get some sleep. I said tried because every ten minutes before midnight I received calls congratulating me on the victory. Eventually, Robin and I were able to get a few hours of sleep before the calls recommenced. I didn't get any real substantial sleep until well after 1 p.m. The next few weeks were filled with me completing my assignments from the magistrate's department and fulfilling all of the election requirements to take the oath of office.

January 3, 2006 is a day that will be forever etched in my mind. It was the day that my family, friends, Cleveland Municipal Court employees, fellow judicial colleagues, Chairman Jimmy Dimora of the Cuyahoga Democratic Party, Congresswoman Stephanie Tubbs-Jones, Clerk of Court Earle Turner, Mayor-Elect Frank Jackson and many other distinguished guests joined me in the Cleveland City Council Chambers for my swearing-in-ceremony. I had envisioned myself, in 1985 when I first visited Cleveland City Council as the president of my student council, as a member of council or mayor of my home town. Although I wasn't either one of those important governmental actors I was entrusted to make sure that I checked the actions of those two offices. Essentially I became a participant in how we are governed just not what I first imagined. I began to prepare myself for that day well before November 2005. Some would say that my attainment of that high honor of being a judge was due to luck. I, however, would respond that I don't believe in the traditional definition of luck. I define luck as the time when opportunity meets preparation.

I prepared by not allowing life circumstances to be a crutch for me and preclude me from walking, without any difficulties, into my destiny. I didn't allow my natural surroundings, my family's dysfunction, my tumultuous childhood, my unstable housing situations, death of loved ones, my lack of resources or my lack of name recognition to deter me from where I knew that my talents, hard work and faith was preparing me to ascend. The opportunity came when Judge Mabel Jasper's age limited her ability to run for office. I took full advantage of that opportunity but could not have if I hadn't laid the proper foundation many, many years ago.

I now stood at the President of City Council's seat with Robin, Lauren and Michael with my right arm and hand raised and my left hand on the Bible taking the Oath of Office. Me, the kid whose mom was only a year and five months removed from just becoming a teenager when she got pregnant with me. Me, the kid whose biological father had no opportunity to assist his mother in performing his natural duty of raising his child. Me, the kid who witnessed Domestic Violence on such a frequent nature that I could have adopted the belief that is how loved ones relate to each other. Me, the kid who watched his parents get high on drugs and subsequently neglect him and his sister. Me, the kid who attended eleven different schools before college. Me, the kid who watched his mom die and then Grandmother Lula the next year. Me, the kid who spent a significant portion of his childhood in the Longwood projects. Pastor of the Word Church, Dr. R.A. Vernon, my friend, former classmate and neighbor when I lived in Longwood said it best when he did the Invocation for me at my swearing-in", Can anything good come out of Nazareth.?" He was referencing a scripture in the Bible when someone was speaking about Jesus from Nazareth. Nazareth was a city that was deemed to be insignificant, poor, filthy and tiny and thus the question was how can anything good come from that city. Longwood was seen as an insignificant, poor, filthy, small and crime ridden neighborhood in Cleveland; the modern day Nazareth. A pastor like Dr. R.A. Vernon, who is the leader of a flock that measures in the thousands maybe tens of thousands, a church that gives back huge amounts to the community both to satisfy the natural man and spiritual man, was something good that came out of "Modern day Nazareth". I too was now able to answer the question can anything good come out of the "Modern Day Nazareth" with a profound Yes! I was doing the unexpected but clearly I am not special and the same things I did to overcome others could accomplish the same things.

I hope that people who read this book will walk away with one of two beliefs for their own lives. One, if you have encountered some of the same difficult challenges I did or worse then my expectation is for you to use this book as a tool to reach your highest potential; you too can become a part of the illustrious group of the least likely. Two, if you have not experienced the same circumstances that I was able to persevere through then you have no excuse not to obtain the success your talents are preparing you to reach. It is your responsibility to unlock them and use them to make your community, your city, your region, your state, your nation and this world a better place. Take it from me the Honorable Judge Michael John Ryan you too can be a member of the group the Least Likely.

21855641R00265

Made in the USA
San Bernardino, CA
09 June 2015